W9-ABE-072

THE CONTAINMENT OF LATIN AMERICA

The containment of Latin America

A history of the myths and realities of
the Good Neighbor Policy

by David Green

Chicago
Quadrangle Books
1971

THE CONTAINMENT OF LATIN AMERICA. Copyright © 1971 by
David Green. All rights reserved, including the right to
reproduce this book or portions thereof in any form. For
information, address: Quadrangle Books, Inc., 12 East
Delaware Place, Chicago 60611. Manufactured in the United
States of America. Published simultaneously in Canada by
Burns and MacEachern Ltd., Toronto.

Library of Congress Catalog Card Number: 76-130384
SBN 8129-0160-6

For Walter LaFeber
with deep respect and admiration

The politics of benevolence

Franklin Roosevelt died on April 12, 1945. The eulogies and tributes that were offered from all over the world attested to the fact that in his twelve years as President of the United States, Roosevelt had built up a personal following unequalled by any political leader in modern times. From no area were the tributes more heartfelt than Latin America. Millions of people scattered throughout twenty republics had come to look upon Franklin Roosevelt as the embodiment of the Good Neighbor, the neighbor who, as the President himself had put it in his first inaugural address, "resolutely respects himself and, because he does so, respects the rights of others—the neighbor who respects his obligations and respects the sanctity of his agreements in and with a world of neighbors."[1]

In view of the almost universal esteem in which Roosevelt was held by Latin Americans at the time of his death, historians have concluded, not surprisingly, that the President's Good Neighbor Policy was a success.[2] By and large, disagreements among historians have centered more on Roosevelt's originality in developing the policy than on his success in implementing it.[3]

There is also general scholarly agreement as to the reasons for Roosevelt's success. Initially the rationale of the Good Neighbor Policy was the doctrine of nonintervention in Latin American internal affairs. This abandonment of the old Big Stick approach was acclaimed throughout the hemisphere. Nonintervention was, however, only a negative policy, and so had limited usefulness. Toward the end of the 1930's, Roosevelt began to supplement nonintervention with other more positive measures designed to help the Latin Americans develop their economies and raise their standards of living. It was this later, more positive Good Neighbor Policy that really enshrined Roosevelt in the hearts of Latin Americans. The eulogies upon the President's death were no more than a climax to the almost unanimous support which Latin Americans had given the United States in building hemispheric solidarity and meeting the Axis challenge during World War II.[4]

After the war, when a slow but steady decline in hemispheric unity set in, it only served to bolster the image of
success associated with Roosevelt's policies. Some observers
attributed the postwar decline to an abandonment of positive economic aid policies that had characterized the late
Roosevelt period. Others stressed the tendency of both the
Truman and Eisenhower administrations to give undue aid
and comfort to military dictators in Latin America.[5] Whatever the causes of the decline, its results were clear. The
hostile reception accorded to Vice-President Nixon on his
1958 tour of Latin America indicated how far inter-American
relations had deteriorated. By the early 1960's, the Kennedy
administration was pushing for renewed and expanded programs of hemispheric cooperation in a manner which clearly
suggested an updated revival of Roosevelt's Good Neighbor
Policy.[6]

To assess the results of President Kennedy's Alliance for
Progress is not the point of this book. What is relevant, however, is that in his call for such an alliance Kennedy suggested that Latin America's basic economic structure was
still badly in need of modernization. Certainly it could be
argued that the Alliance was made necessary by a postwar
lapse in inter-American economic cooperation. But it was
also possible that Roosevelt's program had not been as successful as was generally believed.

During the late 1930's and early 1940's, Latin America
was moving into an age of widespread revolutionary nationalism.[7] The revolutionary nationalist process developed
under different circumstances in different countries. For example, in Mexico, where the social revolution begun decades
earlier was entering a new and more militant phase, leadership was provided by one large and internally diverse political party. The party governed within a civilian-controlled
democratic framework, though up to 1946 the Mexican President was invariably a former general in the Mexican army.
In Brazil, leadership was provided by the civilian dictatorship of President Getulio Vargas. In Bolivia, a series of
military juntas attempted to provide direction in the immediate prewar and late wartime periods, while in Chile a
multi-party civilian "popular front" government attempted
to launch a far-reaching program for the modernization and
industrialization of the Chilean economy. In such countries
as Peru, Venezuela, and Guatemala, nationalist leaders spent

the wartime period in opposition to the governments in power—even, in some cases, in exile or in jail; they did not assume power until the end of the war. Nonetheless, however diverse in political style, organization, and strength, all nationalist groups had one common problem: their programs could proceed only if their nations were able to gain full control of their own economic resources, large sections of which were owned and controlled by foreigners, particularly Americans.

Soon after assuming office, the Roosevelt administration began to develop a strongly negative attitude toward this militant Latin American nationalism. Administration officials were not opposed to development of Latin American resources. Nor were they rigidly committed to a defense of all existing arrangements whereby United States citizens owned Latin American property. Roosevelt's abandonment of Big Stick interventionism demonstrated that point very clearly. Rather, in the main, administration policy-makers felt that they, rather than the revolutionary nationalists, had a more realistic and sensible perception as to how Latin American resource development ought to proceed. Partly through fortuitous wartime circumstances, and partly by design, the Roosevelt administration ultimately strengthened the power and influence of the United States over many Latin American national economies.[8] The long-run result was an intensification of the clash between the interests of Latin American nationalists and those of United States policy-makers.[9]

The postwar deterioration of inter-American relations did not occur, then, entirely because of an abandonment of Roosevelt's policies. On the level of economic policy-making, Roosevelt's successors ran into problems at least in part because they accepted his basic anti-nationalist approach. Portents of this result could be seen even before Roosevelt died: his postwar economic planning had come under strong fire from Latin American delegates at the Mexico City Conference in 1945. Thus the eulogies that followed his death did not necessarily represent unqualified endorsement of all his policies. On the contrary, Roosevelt bequeathed to Harry S. Truman a Latin American policy fraught with contradictions and tensions.[10]

In his perceptive study *The Making of the Good Neighbor Policy*, Bryce Wood has remarked:

When President Roosevelt dedicated his nation to the policy of the Good Neighbor, he set up a huge red, white, and blue target for the barbed shafts of his critics at home and abroad. He made use of a homely and familiar notion that invited the judgment of every man, and he left the way open to other governments to claim, not merely that some future Rooseveltian policy was unjust or immoral in universal terms, but that it was violative of his own principles and aspirations.[11]

The point of my book is not to take aim at any such targets. It is, rather, to look again at what Roosevelt's principles and aspirations really were, and to see why, despite his success in translating his principles into practical policies, Roosevelt was nonetheless unsuccessful in resolving basic inter-American conflicts.

Two final introductory points are in order. First, it has been necessary to carry the narrative well into the Truman era in order to demonstrate how Truman provided both continuities and discontinuities with Roosevelt's Latin American policy. Second, nothing in this study is meant to suggest that either Roosevelt or Truman harbored malevolent intentions toward Latin America. They were not selfish men who gleefully or carelessly sacrificed the best interests of the hemisphere for the greater power and glory of the United States. The Good Neighbor Policy, as developed by Franklin Roosevelt and his associates and continued into the Truman years, really was intended to embody the politics of good neighborhood—indeed, of benevolence. Therein lie the roots of the tragedy of modern inter-American relations.

For generous help in facilitating the research upon which this book is based, I would like to express my appreciation to the staffs of the following libraries and manuscript collections: the National Archives and the Library of Congress, Washington, D.C.; the Cornell, Harvard, Yale, Princeton, and Columbia University Libraries; the Libraries of the Universities of Delaware, Virginia, and Michigan; the Council on Foreign Relations, New York City; the Franklin D. Roosevelt Library, Hyde Park, New York; and the Harry S. Truman Library, Independence, Missouri. Special thanks go to Dr. Arthur Kogan of the Research and Review Division of the Department of State; Drs. Philip Brooks and Philip Lagerquist of the Truman Library; Dr. Edgar Nixon of the Roosevelt Library; Mr. Arthur Wasson of the Council on Foreign Relations; and Mr. Howard Peckham of the William L. Clements Library, Ann Arbor, Michigan.

For financial assistance in connection with preparation of the manuscript, I would like to thank Dr. Carlyle King, director of the Publications Fund, University of Saskatchewan. The Cornell University Latin American Program generously provided me with a travel grant to visit Latin America in the summer of 1967 to conduct research and interviews. I would like particularly to thank Professor Tom E. Davis, formerly director of the Latin American Program, for his kind interest over several years.

A number of colleagues and former teachers read all or part of the manuscript at various stages of preparation, and provided many helpful insights and constructive criticisms. Former teachers, all members of my graduate committee, include Paul W. Gates, Cornell University; John W. Lewis, Stanford University; and Richard Graham, University of Utah. Colleagues include Mary Young, Ohio State University; James Wilkie, now of the University of California at Los Angeles; and J. Michael Hayden, Ivo Lambi, Lawrence Kitzan, and Gary Hanson, all of the University of Saskatchewan. Among the many friends who shared their extensive knowledge of Latin America with me during my student days, I would especially like to express deep appreciation to Sergio Sismondo, Celso Lafer, and Barent F. Landstreet, Jr. My thanks go also to Mrs. Margaret MacVean for the care and patience with which she typed large portions of the manuscript.

The dedication is to one who, as chairman of my graduate committee at Cornell University, and as close adviser and friend over a period which now spans more than ten years, provided aid and encouragement far beyond the call of duty. Both in his teaching and in his own published writings he has set a standard of academic excellence and humane understanding which it will always be my study to emulate. Needless to say, neither he nor any of those persons listed above bear responsibility for errors or other shortcomings contained in this book.

Saskatoon, Saskatchewan   D.G.
March 1970

Preface: The politics of benevolence   *vii*
Acknowledgments   *xi*

I. United States policy and the
challenge of nationalism   *3*
II. The new technique:
Giving Latin America a share   *37*
III. Skeptics north and south   *59*
IV. The impact of war   *85*
V. Planning for peace:
The politics of optimism   *113*
VI. Hedging the bets   *137*
VII. The postwar role of Latin America:
View from the north   *169*
VIII. The postwar role of Latin America:
View from the south   *185*
IX. Building one world   *209*
X. Champion and challenger:
Fly swatter versus flypaper   *237*
XI. Formalizing the system:
A closed hemisphere in an open world   *255*

Epilogue:
The containment of Latin America   *291*

Notes   *299*
A note on sources   *355*
Index   *359*

THE CONTAINMENT OF LATIN AMERICA

I. United States policy and the challenge of nationalism

1. The historical background

The interplay between politics and economics has long been part of the United States' approach to inter-American relations. As early as 1818, while wars for independence still raged in Latin America, Congressman Henry Clay called for United States recognition of *de facto* revolutionary governments there for political and economic reasons. Politically, Clay declared, the United States could not help but identify with "the glorious spectacle of eighteen millions of people, struggling to burst their chains and to be free." On a commercial level, the people of the United States needed only to look ahead to the days when "millions and millions will be added to our population, and when the increased productive industry will furnish [to Latin America] an infinite variety of fabrics for foreign consumption, in order to supply our wants.

> There can not be a doubt [Clay argued] that Spanish America, once independent, whatever may be the form of the governments established in its several parts, these governments will be animated by an American feeling, and guided by an American policy. They will obey the laws of the system of the New World, of which they will compose a part, in contradistinction to that of Europe.[1]

Secretary of State John Quincy Adams did not share Clay's optimistic view of Latin America's political and moral propensities. "As to an American system," he wrote in 1820, "we [the United States] have it; we constitute the whole of it; there is no community of interests or of principles between North and South America."[2] But for reasons both of political security and economic advantage, Adams was soon ready to create such a community of interest where none existed. "In all your consultations with the government to which you will be accredited, bearing upon its political relations with this union," he wrote in 1823 to the first United States minister to Colombia, "your unvarying standard will be the spirit of independence and freedom [from European influence], as equality of rights and favors will be that of its commercial relations." Adams convinced President Monroe that any concession of special economic privileges to Spain in the area formerly under her imperial control would be contrary to United States interests. "We trust to the sense of justice, as well as to the interest of the South Americans," Adams wrote, "the denial of all exclusive privileges to others."[3]

The Monroe Doctrine, announced to the world as official United States policy on December 2, 1823, stated one prerequisite for the effective functioning of an inter-American system. "We owe it . . . to candor," Adams' chief pointedly told the European powers, ". . . to declare that we should consider any attempt on their part to extend their [European] system to any portion of this hemisphere as dangerous to our peace and safety."[4]

During most of the nineteenth century, though United States commerce with Latin America grew steadily, the Monroe Doctrine was honored more in the breach than in the observance. British and French naval forces made forays into both the Caribbean and the Rio de la Plata (at the entrance to Buenos Aires). During the American Civil War, the Union government was powerless to prevent the establishment of a French imperial beachhead in Mexico.

By the end of the 1880's, however, the United States had moved to a new peak of industrial strength, and took up with renewed vigor and confidence the Clay-Adams-Monroe search for an inter-American system based upon a hemispheric community of interest. Significantly, the late nineteenth-century approach, championed by Secretary of State James G. Blaine, contained the same dual emphasis upon politics and economics as had that of Blaine's predecessors. The Pan American Union, established in Washington in 1889 at the time of the first Pan American Conference, functioned both as a political secretariat for inter-American consultations and as a trade information agency.[5] Blaine stressed an aggressive United States effort to bring commercial reciprocity to the Americas in order to stimulate the northward flow of raw materials and the southward flow of manufactured goods. Sensing the potential danger of an aggressive political approach, he preferred to underplay United States political and military strength. He relied in-

stead on conciliation and persuasion to cement the Pan
American alliance. His particularly restrained behavior in
the Chilean-American diplomatic crisis of 1891 was a case in
point.[6]

While Blaine's aggressive search for commercial reciprocity was continued by his successors, his political restraint was not. He was partially overruled in the Chilean
crisis by the more militant President Benjamin Harrison.
Three years after Blaine's death, during the Venezuelan
boundary dispute of 1895, Secretary of State Richard Olney
told England's Lord Salisbury: "The United States is
practically sovereign on this continent, and its fiat is
law upon the subjects to which it confines its interposition."[7]
To those who accepted his assumption of American good intentions, the logical conclusion of Olney's view was that the
United States ought to take steps, when necessary, to intervene in Latin American affairs for the purpose of restoring
order and progress to the "community." This was especially
true when there was a danger that interested European
powers might otherwise intervene.

This conclusion was institutionalized as official policy
in December 1904, when President Theodore Roosevelt enunciated his Roosevelt Corollary to the Monroe Doctrine as a
defense of United States intervention in the Dominican Republic. Said the President:

Chronic wrongdoing, or an impotence which results in a general
loosening of the ties of civilized society, may in America, as elsewhere, ultimately require intervention by some civilized nation,
and in the Western Hemisphere the adherence of the United
States to the Monroe Doctrine may force the United States, however reluctantly, in flagrant cases of such wrongdoing or impotence, to the exercise of an international police power.[8]

Reinforcing the benevolent motive behind his action, T.R.
linked his policy to economic gain for the Latin Americans
themselves: "They have great and natural riches, and if
within their borders the reign of law and justice obtains,
prosperity is sure to come to them." United States marines
were soon withdrawn from the Dominican Republic, but
returned in 1916 for an eight-year occupation. The United
States government continued to administer Dominican customs houses until 1941.[9]

Both before and after the "first Age of Roosevelt," the
idea of an inter-American community of interest remained

at the core of United States policy. Senator Albert J. Beveridge of Indiana, a staunch expansionist, expressed the idea when he talked of building a "soap and water, common school civilization" in Cuba. Woodrow Wilson advocated it when he talked of teaching the Mexicans to "elect good men." The assumption of mutuality of interest, and of the United States' good intentions, even benevolence, was a constant.[10]

At the same time some Latin Americans were developing a more skeptical view of United States policies. In 1900, Uruguay's leading essayist, José Enrique Rodó, published his famous work *Ariel*. Rodó won instant acclaim with his portrayal of the United States as a misbegotten Caliban bent upon the spiritual and cultural destruction of Latin America. He reversed all of the Americans' assumptions about themselves. Where they posited their own grace, he discerned ineptitude. Where they assumed their own benevolence, he detected malevolence. Rodó's work became "sacred writ for generations of youth in Uruguay (and elsewhere in Latin America)."[11]

Without necessarily subscribing to all of Rodó's ideas, many Latin American diplomats did attempt to hobble United States power in the hemisphere through juridical limitations. During three Pan American conferences, at Mexico City in 1901, Rio de Janeiro in 1906, and Buenos Aires in 1910, a number of Latin American nations, led by Argentina, tried without success to get the United States to adhere to a mandatory nonintervention pact.[12]

For the time being, Americans continued to take for granted the Rooseveltian definition of inter-American political relationships. When in 1903 the Colombian government balked at ratifying an Isthmian canal treaty, Roosevelt supported a revolution which detached the strategic territory of Panama and made it an independent republic under United States protection. "While Congress debated," Roosevelt later boasted, "I took the Canal."[13] In the economic field, United States officials continued to stress increased commercial cooperation and interchange. Every President from Roosevelt through Coolidge encouraged an influx of private capital into Latin American railroads and agriculture. Such policies were most successful in the Caribbean area, where United States military power could be deployed to back up or even open up profitable and secure

opportunities for United States businessmen.[14] In the
stronger South American countries, and in Mexico (a special case to be discussed later), United States definitions of
the policy relationships could be resisted with somewhat
greater force. These countries, particularly the South American leaders Argentina, Brazil, and Chile, tended to maintain
strong financial ties with Europe.

In all, the first three decades of the twentieth century
saw an almost constant battle over the terms on which
inter-American relationships were to be conducted. At the
Havana Conference of 1928, hemispheric political relationships became particularly strained as former Secretary of
State Charles Evans Hughes, heading the United States delegation, defended recent United States interventions in Mexico, Haiti, the Dominican Republic, and Nicaragua as legitimate temporary moves in defense of American lives and
property. Not until 1933 did the United States first sign a
nonintervention pledge in regard to Latin America, and not
until the Buenos Aires Conference of 1936 was such a pledge
formalized in a joint inter-American declaration. Meanwhile,
economic relationships also began to receive increasing
notice. Theodore Roosevelt's successor, William Howard
Taft, hoped that a substitution of "dollars for bullets" would
make American diplomacy more acceptable. But Taft soon
found that vigorous dollar diplomacy could lead right back
to military diplomacy. The marines he sent to Nicaragua in
1912 to enforce economic stabilization remained there for
nineteen of the next twenty-one years. Shortly thereafter,
Taft's successor, Woodrow Wilson, also found himself involved in a serious clash of views over control and development of economic resources in Latin America. This new
conflict developed out of the Mexican Revolution, the first
full-scale social upheaval of the twentieth century.

The revolution began in 1910. By 1917 its major principles had been formalized in a strongly progressive, strongly
nationalistic constitution. The 1917 constitution held out not
only to Mexicans, but by example to all Latin Americans, a
promise of better life for the masses. Its new political system gave control of the nation's main economic resources,
much of which had recently been bought up by European
and American capital, to native elements.[15] The seriousness
of the challenge to United States interests was underlined
by the none-too-subtle efforts of Wilson's Secretary of State,

Robert Lansing, to help in the writing of the Mexican constitution. Lansing wanted to prevent Mexican interference with existing foreign property holdings, particularly in oil. The government of President Venustiano Carranza not only insisted upon maintaining the right of expropriation, but wanted to make the nationalization provisions of Article 27 of the constitution retroactive. Lansing opposed the move. The controversy raged unresolved through the balance of the Wilson administration and was not even temporarily settled until the Harding era.[16] Even then, the Mexican government continued to shift position with changes in its own administration, and the oil problem remained unsolved well into the New Deal period.

In the meantime, while the controversy over the Mexican Revolution and constitution raged, the First World War had brought much of Latin America increasingly into the United States' economic orbit. With the closing off of European markets, the Latin Americans turned to the only large-scale industrial market capable of absorbing their commodity exports. While the need for markets on both sides brought Latin America and the United States into closer economic contact, the possibility of further nationalist revolution in Latin America raised serious questions about the kinds of relationships this increased contact would lead to.

The postwar decade raised more questions than it solved, as events brought out conflicting perceptions north and south. For the United States, the 1920's was a decade of general optimism and expansion. Involvement in Latin American economic enterprises increased sharply, particularly in the fields of oil exploitation and banking. Between 1919 and 1929, direct United States investments in Latin American enterprises increased from $1,987,000,000 to $3,519,-000,000, while portfolio investments (bonds and securities) increased from $419,000,000 to $1,725,000,000.[17] "Scattered" political incidents involved the use of United States troops in Haiti, the Dominican Republic, and Nicaragua, as well as a replay of the controversy over the nationalization provisions of the Mexican constitution. But from the American point of view, the financial statistics largely told the story. Venezuelan oil prospects under the Gomez dictatorship were excellent; mining concessions in Bolivia, Chile, and elsewhere became increasingly profitable; and United States

investors rushed to get in on the "dance of the millions" in
Cuba. The military and political "incidents" were merely ripples on the surface of fundamentally calm waters.

To the Latin Americans, the troubling aspects of the 1920's were far more serious. In the first place, the twenties was a time of great intellectual and social ferment for Latin America, including the growth of revolutionary currents as exemplified by the APRA movement in Peru and the powerful anti-clerical movement in Mexico. In the first decade following the 1918 Cordoba reforms on university administration in Argentina, students became increasingly active in the political, intellectual, and economic affairs of many nations. Hundreds of young Latin American student leaders became schooled in Marxist economics and political science. Some went to study briefly in Russia and other European countries. In many nations, organized labor movements began to spring up, not always enjoying stunning victories but often bringing to a focus a great deal of social unrest. An abortive revolution occurred in Brazil in 1922, led by a group of young disaffected military officers and a scattering of intellectuals. In relatively stable Chile, social unrest culminated in the first interruption of Chile's long history of continuous constitutional government in more than thirty years, when General Carlos Ibáñez seized power in a military *coup* in 1927.

From the Latin American point of view, external conflicts with the United States were as serious as internal disorders. Mexican leaders were angered by Secretary of State Kellogg's position in the revived oil controversy—Kellogg having declared that the Mexican government was "on trial before the world." Nor were they pleased when Kellogg accused them of harboring "bolshevik" agents who were interfering with United States intervention in Nicaragua. It was true that the Mexicans were channeling arms to the rebels there, but whether it was the United States or Mexico which was "intervening" depended on one's national point of view. The Americans ultimately were successful in restoring a measure of "order" in Nicaragua, even to the point of supervising an election there. But the Nicaraguan rebel leader Augusto Sandino opened a new chapter in inter-American relations by taking to the hills and successfully eluding his United States pursuers for several years, thus becoming the first in a long line of Latin American revolutionary guerrilla leaders stretching all the way to "Che" Guevara and beyond.[18]

Apart from such direct political and military confrontations, the Latin Americans also experienced economic problems in their relations with the United States. Just as the Americans wanted to sell more manufactures to Latin America, the latter hoped to place more agricultural exports in the American market. But United States responses to such efforts were largely negative. The Fordney-McCumber tariff of 1922 offered no encouragement to Latin American exporters. Nor did the reduction of the Cuban sugar quota in the same year, or the Argentine meat embargo of 1927. At the end of the decade, passage of the towering Hawley-Smoot tariff only increased Latin American suspicions of the United States' approach to commercial interchange.[19]

The United States' financial involvement in Latin America's economy was also a factor in inter-American conflict. In some Latin American nations, politically weak or irresponsible governments declined to adopt strong taxation policies which would channel local surplus capital into productive economic enterprise. Such governments were either allied with or fearful of local financial oligarchs, who preferred to leave their money in unproductive land mortgages or else export it to foreign banks. Many governments therefore preferred the politically safer course of trying to attract foreign capital, particularly from the United States. In their efforts to attract such capital, many governments demonstrated irresponsibility by floating badly secured loans and encouraging unproductive investments. Many of the loans would become political sore points in the following decade, when, due to financial stress, the borrower governments would become unable to meet their payments. On the other hand, American investors were also lax about checking into the soundness of their ventures, the anticipated returns on which were unusually inviting.

In fact, although it was not generally realized at the time, as early as the 1920's there was developing in Latin America a phenomenon which would become a central issue in inter-American controversies in the 1940's and after: "decapitalization." This meant simply that with incomes on investments as high as they were, more money actually flowed out of Latin America in the form of investment income than came in as new investment capital. In other

words, foreign investments were contributing to a net loss
of working capital in Latin America. In the period 1925-1929,
the total investment income paid out by Latin Americans to
foreign investors everywhere was three times as great as
capital inflow in the same period. In the case of United
States investors, the average annual American capital inflow
in these years was roughly $200 million, while the average
outflow in investment income was about $300 million.[20]

Part of the deficit was made up by a trade balance in
favor of Latin America. But the Latin Americans discovered
shortly after 1929 that their export-centered foreign trade in
agricultural and mineral raw materials was at best a tenu-
ous basis of prosperity. World markets for such products
collapsed again in the depression, this time with stunning
economic and social impact in Latin America.

2. The significance of the depression

The depression of the thirties had serious long-range
consequences for Latin American economic development. It
was a turning point both in Latin American history and in
the history of inter-American relations. Its first and most
obvious impact was the collapse of political stability in a
number of countries. The weakness of the Radical party
government in Argentina in the face of economic crisis led
to a military *coup* in 1930, and to the installation of an
authoritarian military government. In Brazil, the depression contributed to the revolution of 1930, which began as an
attack on the entrenched power of the conservative oligarchies of the two dominant states of Minas Gerais and São
Paulo. In Chile, on the other hand, the depression helped
lead to the overthrow of the military government of Carlos
Ibáñez. After a brief interlude of experimental "socialist
radical" administration, Chile returned to constitutional
government with the re-election in 1932 of former President
Arturo Alessandri. The depression contributed to social unrest and, in turn, the imposition of military governments in
other countries, particularly the Central American republics
of Guatemala, Honduras, and the Dominican Republic,
where Civil Guard commander Rafael Trujillo began his
thirty-one-year dictatorship in 1930. In Peru, the APRA was
driven underground after being denied the fruits of what
was almost certainly a substantial election victory in 1931
(though the results were concealed from the public).

In short, in a number of Latin American countries (Chile being the notable exception), the depression signaled a movement away from traditional liberal parliamentary government and toward stronger forms of authoritarian control. This is not to say, of course, that all pre-depression parliamentary regimes in Latin America had been models of open democratic administration. On the contrary, in Brazil the revolution was directed against two exclusivist groups which had used their control of the parliamentary process to perpetuate a not very subtle form of collective "continuismo." The depression-born movement away from parliamentary government was rather a vote of no confidence in the ability of traditional governing groups to handle the problems of modern economic and social stress.

The turn away from traditional governing groups in the depression had striking consequences for inter-American relations. Aside from the specific problems which followed the general economic collapse, problems of tariff arrangements and bond defaults, the depression brought home to many Latin American officials a fuller understanding of the degree to which their entire economic and social systems depended on the actions of foreign individuals and foreign governments. In some countries, only the depression brought to public notice the actual rates of profit and capital outflow connected with the larger foreign investments in their economies. One American banker said later that it was only by collecting information on the operations of foreign firms in Latin America, pursuant to the possibility of general tax reform, that the various governments found out how much money the firms had been taking out of the country. Discoveries like these stimulated nationalist resentment wherever they occurred.[21] The combination of nationalist resentment and anti-parliamentary authoritarianism posed a dual challenge to United States interests in Latin America. It presaged a combination of Latin American motivation and means for undertaking a radical redefinition of inter-American relationships.

As President of the United States in the early depression period, Herbert Hoover clearly recognized the implications of many of these problems. As Coolidge's Secretary of Commerce during the twenties boom, Hoover had struggled courageously, though unsuccessfully, to prevent some of the grosser (and more self-defeating) forms of exploitation of

foreign economies by United States investors. In particular,
he had tried to use moral suasion to put a damper on over-
valued, nonproductive loans.[22] Moral suasion, however, was
as far as Hoover was willing or able to go, and it had little
political effect in the Roaring Twenties.

Having failed to effect a preventative in the boom era,
Hoover was manifestly unable to effect a cure in the depression period, despite his increased authority. In the first
place, domestic crises absorbed most of his energies. In the
second place, his tenure in office was actually relatively
brief, and circumstances during that tenure were frequently
beyond his control. Hoover did manage during his one term
as President to begin the liquidation of direct United States
military intervention in Latin American affairs, most notably
in Nicaragua. But given the internal economic situation in
the United States, he also felt compelled to sign the Hawley-
Smoot tariff, which probably caused as much antagonism as
did the marines. Furthermore, Hoover never did sign a
general nonintervention pledge. The famous "Clark Memorandum" on the Monroe Doctrine, which he endorsed, by no
means repudiated the practice of sending United States
troops south without Latin American consent. It repudiated
the Roosevelt Corollary—but reserved the American right of
pre-emptive intervention under the "doctrine of self-preser-
vation." By accepting the Clark Memorandum as United
States policy, Hoover indicated that there would be no
fundamental change in the United States approach to inter-
American political problems.[23]

By the time Franklin Delano Roosevelt entered the
White House in March 1933, depression nationalism in Latin
America already had a full head of steam. Roosevelt and his
advisers were immediately confronted with an incipient social revolution in Cuba, where the United States exercised
a political protectorate under the Platt Amendment of 1902,
and where the Cuban economy, dominated by the sugar industry, was coming increasingly under the control of American private investors.[24]

Determined to avoid military intervention, President
Roosevelt in May 1933 sent Sumner Welles as Ambassador
to Cuba with instructions to stabilize the situation through
political persuasion. While Welles worked quietly to convince dictator Gerardo Machado of the need to reorient his
government's policy, opposition elements brought the situa-

tion to a head by calling a general strike. Seeing the hand-writing on the wall, Machado fled the country on August 12 and was replaced by a provisional government under the leadership of Carlos Manuel de Céspedes.

Céspedes, a moderate, had Welles's approval. Welles immediately asked Washington to extend Céspedes a loan and to increase United States purchases of Cuban sugar, so as to bolster the regime economically.[25] But Céspedes' government lasted only three weeks. It was overthrown on Sep-tember 5 by the famous "sergeants' revolt," led by Fulgencio Batista. Batista promoted himself to the rank of colonel and assumed the post of army chief of staff. A few days later he appointed Ramón Grau San Martín, a biology professor at the University of Havana, to the post of Provisional Presi-dent of Cuba.

Welles's reaction to the new government was as im-mediately negative as his reaction to Céspedes had been positive. Without waiting to see what the new regime would do, Welles notified Washington that Cuba was now under the control of irresponsible army enlisted men, "extreme radical" students, and professors "whose theories are frankly communistic." The new government was not only a nationalist threat to American property holdings but a revolutionary threat to the entire Cuban social order. Welles recommended diplomatic nonrecognition and the landing of United States troops. He also began to marshal internal opposition to the regime. In a discussion with political lead-ers not involved in the new government, Welles suggested that "through consultation among themselves they deter-mine whether they can devise any plan to prevent the utter break-down of government which in my judgment is inevita-ble under the present regime."[26]

Neither Roosevelt nor Secretary of State Hull was willing to go as far as Welles asked. Roosevelt agreed to send a few ships to Cuban waters to reassure American citizens living in Cuba; but he refused to land troops. Hull, for his part, told Welles in a telephone conversation that he need not be so alarmist about the property situation.

I am telling people who have property there to let it be injured a little, while the Cubans are establishing a government them-selves, because should the Cubans themselves establish a govern-ment, the outbreaks will gradually cease, business will return to normalcy, and the owners will recover their losses.[27]

On the other hand, Roosevelt and Hull accepted Welles's

recommendation on nonrecognition and adhered to that decision for the remainder of Grau's tenure in office. Hull told the press on September 12 that the United States would "welcome any government representing the will of the people of the Republic and capable of maintaining law and order throughout the island.[28] The unmistakable inference was that the Grau regime was not such a government.

The Grau regime, however, did not fall immediately. Batista's troops remained loyal to Grau during an attempted counter-*coup* in early October. Welles now began to woo Batista away from Grau. He told the army chief of staff that he, Batista, was "the only individual in Cuba today who represented authority," while Grau's supporters consisted chiefly of "a small group of young men, who should be studying in the university instead of playing politics, and . . . a few individuals who had joined them from selfish motives." The United States, Welles indicated, could never recognize such a government. The import of Welles's advice was that given the weakness of the regime, Batista should save his own position, and Cuba's, by dissociating himself from Grau and the radicals.[29] During this same period, Welles also notified Washington that several sugar mills in the interior of Cuba had been occupied by groups of laborers who had set up what he called "soviet government" in the mills. Welles telegraphed to Secretary of State Hull that the policy of continued nonrecognition was "one which [would] hasten rather than retard the creation of a constitutional government in Cuba and one which [would] expedite eventual stability." United States "commercial and export interests in Cuba," Welles added, "cannot be revived under this government. Only confidence can accomplish that, and there is no confidence either in the policies nor [sic] stability of this regime, whether it be recognized or not."[30]

Ultimately, United States nonrecognition had its effect. By January 1934, Batista was convinced that the Grau government was doomed. The army chief of staff now threw his support to an opposition leader, Carlos Mendieta. On January 15, Grau resigned, and three days later Mendieta was installed as Provisional President of Cuba in a ceremony before the Cuban Supreme Court. Five days later, the United States government formally recognized the Mendieta regime as the official government of Cuba.

It is possible, and has been suggested, that neither President Roosevelt nor Secretary Hull understood why Welles attached such importance to nonrecognition of the Grau government.[31] In some circumstances, to be sure, diplomatic nonrecognition might not have made any difference. In the Cuban situation, however, it meant in effect an economic strangulation of the island, since the United States would not negotiate a new sugar purchase agreement with a government it did not recognize.

Whether or not Roosevelt and Hull initially understood the situation in these terms, evidence suggests that by January 1934 they could hardly have avoided seeing the true import of nonrecognition. In the first place, by that time the connection between nonrecognition, sugar, and the Cuban economy was a matter of public discussion. Two days after Grau resigned, the *New York Times* reported that January 15 was the date which "Cubans had generally set as the deadline on which the political situation had to be settled if Cuba was to be able to make a sugar crop this winter."[32] Of more importance was the way in which the Roosevelt administration now moved to help stabilize the Mendieta regime. The terms of the rapprochement were revealing.

The United States would give up the Platt Amendment, but would retain its naval base at Guantanamo. The Cuban government would not nationalize any American holdings in Cuba. In return, the United States would reduce its tariff on Cuban sugar and set up a favorable quota system for Cuban sugar exports to the United States, even to the point of limiting competing domestic production. The sugar arrangement was formalized in the Jones-Costigan Act of May 1934 and in a separate tariff reduction the following month. Jones-Costigan set the quotas and production limits, while the June 1934 tariff reduced the Cuban sugar duty from 2¢ a pound to .9¢ a pound. The Cubans could now not only continue to sell their sugar in the United States, but could sell it at a better net income.[33]

The result, however, was not to increase Cuba's freedom of action or economic independence. On the contrary, as one member of the United States Tariff Commission put it, the result was that Cuba became more fully incorporated "within the protective system of the United States," repeal of the Platt Amendment notwithstanding.[34] United States consumers would have to pay the same price for sugar, because of the artificial limitations placed by their government on

the available total supply. The difference between the old [17
tariff rate and the new tariff rate, which normally would
have gone into the United States Treasury, was simply returned to Cuban sugar producers through the mechanism
of the tariff reduction. As one American economist summed
it up: "The results of the arrangement were about equivalent to a draft upon our Treasury for funds that may be said
to have been disbursed in higher prices to Cuban producers
of sugar according to their respective shares in total American imports from Cuba."[35] For a few dollars more, the
United States retained effective control over Cuban affairs
without incurring the public opinion liability connected with
the Platt Amendment. Moreover, the threat of social revolution was blocked; as one writer put it, Cuba's "pre-1930 social and economic class structure was retained, and the important place in Cuban economy held by foreign-owned enterprise was not fundamentally disturbed."[36]

The Roosevelt administration's handling of the Cuban
situation left certain questions unanswered. For example,
how could Roosevelt and Hull be so sure after only five days
that the Mendieta regime was really a "government representing the will of the people of the Republic and capable
of maintaining law and order throughout the island"? The
Grau regime had lasted more than four months without apparently meriting such a description. As regards law and
order, under Grau there had been remarkably little of the
kind of street violence that had characterized the late
Machado era. Welles passed off this appearance of stability
as "the quiet of panic," while State Department adviser
Adolf Berle ingeniously described the situation as "passive
anarchy."[37] Even allowing for the possibility that Welles
and Berle were right, was it then so clear after only five days
that the appearance of stability under Mendieta was based
on something else?

As to which government more adequately represented
the "will of the people," another question remained. At one
point, Welles's replacement, Jefferson Caffery, testified as
to the "inefficiency, ineptitude, and unpopularity with all
the better classes in the country of the de facto [Grau] government. It is supported only by the army and ignorant
masses who have been misled by utopian promises." Two
months later, when the new Mendieta government was having trouble maintaining stability among these very masses,

delegation of congressional power to the Executive. A large Democratic majority nevertheless assured passage of the bill, and it became law on June 12, 1934.[42]

The progression was a logical one. The New Deal's recovery program implied an early drive toward economic internationalism. This in turn provided the rationale for cultivating major foreign market areas both politically and commercially. In the case of Latin America, the program meant adding a crucial economic dimension to the Good Neighbor Policy, a dimension involving bold action to increase inter-American economic interchange.

The State Department soon discovered that obtaining authority from the Congress to pursue this aim was not equivalent to obtaining foreign acquiescence. Because of the special relationship between the United States and Cuba, it had been easy to secure a trade agreement once the Grau regime had been brought down. Cuba was in fact the first country with whom the State Department negotiated under the new reciprocal trade act. But other Latin American nations were skeptical, particularly such industrializing nations as Brazil, where industrialists were reluctant to give up their own tariff protection just when the great industrial powers were maintaining the highest tariff walls in modern history.

The Brazilian response was symbolic of a major change in inter-American relationships in the 1930's. It was one which challenged not only the traditional United States policy of close guidance of Latin American economic activity, but even the usefulness of Hull's "cooperative" policy of commercial reciprocity. Commercial interchange was only one aspect of international economics, and not necessarily the primary aspect. Quite as important was the question of who produced what kinds of goods, and indeed who owned the goods that were being exchanged. For many Latin American nations, whose economies had become dependent on both foreign manufactures and foreign capital, the question was significant.

The Latin American situation spotlighted the whole problem of the New Deal's relationship to American private enterprise abroad. And the fact that the New Dealers wished to set a pattern for the future made the question that much more urgent. First in the Cuban Revolution of 1933, then in the Brazilian reciprocal trade agreement negotiations of

1935, events indicated how intimately connected were the issues of Latin American development and United States private enterprise in Latin America.

Private American investors had put a considerable sum
of money into Brazilian and other Latin American governmental bonds in the twenties. During the depression, most
Latin American governments, including Brazil, defaulted on
interest payments on such bonds. Angry United States investors began to press the State Department to insist upon a
debt settlement as a precondition for economic negotiations
with defaulting countries. The situation in Latin America
was, of course, simply a variation of what the United States
was facing in regard to defaulted European debts.

The New Dealers' main interest, however, was not in
the redemption of old debts so much as in the reopening of
badly needed foreign markets. The State Department therefore attempted to take the debt issue out of intergovernmental trade negotiations by sponsoring the creation of a
private organization to represent the bondholders in negotiations with defaulting countries. The result was the Foreign Bondholders' Protective Council, whose active participants included a number of former United States government functionaries such as former Under Secretary of State
J. Reuben Clark (author of the Clark Memorandum); chief
counsel was the prominent international lawyer John Foster
Dulles. In a memo to President Roosevelt, dated November
9, 1933, Secretary Hull noted that with the creation of the
Bondholders' Council the debt problem was now out of the
State Department's hands. "The problem," Hull said, "is not
inter-governmental."[43]

Ironically, the creation of the Bondholders' Council had
an effect precisely opposite from that anticipated by Hull.
The Council itself became a lobbyist on behalf of the bondholders, and continued to press for the inclusion of debt arrangements as a precondition for economic negotiations.
In the spring of 1934, Congress added its own demand by
passing the Johnson Act, which prohibited government loans
to countries that had defaulted on their obligations to American investors.

By the time Hull sat down to negotiate a reciprocal
trade agreement with Brazil the pressure for a debt settlement was intense. Hull nonetheless decided to stick by his
original decision and to exclude the debts from inter-govern-

mental negotiations; he went ahead with the trade agreement alone. The bondholders were furious. Then, when private industrialists in Brazil began to delay Brazilian ratification of the agreement, Hull himself became upset. In a conversation with the Brazilian counselor of embassy in Washington in August 1935, Hull warned of the "terrific opposition and severe criticism" under which the State Department had been operating since it had decided not to insist first on a debt settlement. Brazil's creditors in the United States, Hull stated, were becoming "more and more vociferous" and threatened to take severe political action against the New Deal administration in the halls of Congress. Hull implied that the bondholders and their congressional allies were considering an attempt to force through a stiff United States import duty on Brazilian coffee, which was at that time coming into the country duty free. Destruction of the trade agreement by São Paulo manufacturing interests in Brazil, Hull warned, would present a condition such that the administration could not much longer defend its policies against attacks by these creditors. "Serious developments" might arise very soon. Moreover, said Hull, the death of this agreement might seriously injure and discredit the New Deal's entire reciprocal trade agreements program.[44]

The Brazilians finally took some of the pressure off Hull by ratifying the trade agreement in November 1935. Ironically, the commercial effect of the agreement was quite inconsequential, at least for the first few years. In the mid-1930's, Brazil found it much more profitable to import cheaper German goods on a barter basis. The Germans outsold the Americans in Brazil in both 1936 and 1937.[45]

Negotiations over the trade agreement had nonetheless indicated that the question of the New Deal's relationship to United States private enterprise abroad would become one of the most serious ongoing problems in United States foreign policy. The State Department would have to tread carefully in attempting to implement a "cooperative" internationalist approach to Latin American development. From the New Dealers' point of view, the main question became: Given the necessity of making some concessions to Latin American nationalism, how far could the United States government go in bypassing or ignoring the immediate interests of specific private investors in designing a foreign pol-

icy to revive and advance the larger long-term interests of
the North American free-enterprise system?

Hull's answer to this dilemma was at first improvised. In the case of the Brazilian debts, he felt the State Department could manage to contain the anger of the bondholders. He assured them that the trade agreement would ultimately benefit them by giving Brazil enough added foreign exchange earnings to permit her to pay off her debts. This of course did not solve the debt problem; it only temporized with it. But at the time that was all Hull needed to do. A somewhat more serious problem arose early in 1937, involving something more than money owed to United States creditors by Latin American nations. It raised the difficult question of American property holdings abroad.

4. Confrontations

On March 13, 1937, the Bolivian government expropriated and nationalized the Bolivian properties of the Standard Oil Company of New Jersey. The nationalization came in the middle of a dispute which had been smoldering for years, and which was in process of being submitted to the Bolivian Supreme Court for adjudication. In addition to the nationalization of the oil properties, the government attached all bank accounts of the Standard Oil Company in Bolivia, and all banks were prohibited from engaging in operations with the company.[46]

The reason given publicly for the expropriation was that Standard Oil had defrauded the Bolivian nation by failing to pay taxes on certain oil properties. The government charged Standard Oil with falsifying production records in order to avoid paying taxes for which the company became liable once its activities advanced from the "exploratory" stage to the "production" stage. It soon became clear, however, that the real reasons for Bolivia's action were as much political as legal.

In the first place, Bolivia was then engaged in protracted diplomatic negotiations in an effort to settle the recent Chaco War with Paraguay. Bolivia had been greatly weakened by the war, and was looking desperately for South American allies. The government hoped in particular to win Argentine support by offering the Argentine government exploitation rights in Bolivia's national oil fields. It was therefore necessary as a first step to seize the oil fields in the name of the nation. In the second place, the Bolivian government was at that time composed mainly of young army officers who had taken power the previous year. By early 1937, with its first year coming to an end, the junta needed some dramatic assertion of sovereignty to bolster its popular support. An attack on a rich and unpopular foreign enterprise was a natural and obvious gesture.

The Bolivians made no particular effort to hide these political motivations from United States officials in Bolivia. On the contrary, immediately after the expropriations occurred, a leading pro-government newspaper hailed the move as "a measure which only a military socialistic government, free of the bourgeois limitations of the preceding governments, could have adopted." In the future, the newspaper noted, exploitation of the Standard Oil properties would take place under the supervision of the new Bolivian oil corporation (initials: YPFB), which, "in representation of the Government, will take charge of all the property which the Standard Oil had." In such a manner, the newspaper commented, "there will be nationalized a great industry and to the credit of the Government there will be noted the realization of one of the most vehement collective aspirations."[47] Bolivian Foreign Minister Finot bluntly told the United States Minister in La Paz: "After all, it is but a natural aspiration for a country to control its petroleum resources and Bolivia must do so—it cannot again be at the mercy of an international company. The Standard should never have signed a [contract] with the power against it such as this." In his report of the conversation, transmitted to the State Department, Minister Norweb commented: "I do not recall any such bald statement from a Foreign Minister of a friendly country. However, it served to clear the air and Sr. Finot continued the discussion in a more open manner." In a separate report to Secretary of State Hull, Norweb remarked on the "ruthless nature" of the Bolivian military government and referred to the government's "socialistic political doctrines."[48]

The State Department soon began to receive letters of protest both from Standard Oil representatives in the United States and from other leading spokesmen for American business interests. In a letter to State Department Political Adviser Laurence Duggan, the general counsel for Standard Oil pointed out that, inasmuch as the military junta in

Bolivia had recently reorganized the entire Bolivian Supreme Court, Standard's attorneys in La Paz were "strongly
of the opinion that we should not take the matter to the
Supreme Court, as we cannot expect an unbiased opinion."
Standard asked for State Department intercession instead.[49]
A representative of General Motors wrote to Secretary of
State Hull, warning of the effect the Bolivian expropriation
might have elsewhere in Latin America. "In the present disturbed state of world affairs," he noted, "indignities perpe-
trated by one nation, if left unchallenged, too often serve as
a precept and precedent for other nations to seize upon in
the furtherance of their apparent ends."[50]

As the State Department accumulated more information
regarding the expropriations, it became clear that the legal
case was arguable on both sides. The Bolivians pointed to
the inclusion in Standard's contract of the well-known Calvo
clause, which pledged the contracting foreign company not
to seek the aid of an outside governmental power in disputes over the nature of the contract. State Department
officials nonetheless tended to take the view that the Bolivian government's action was more a political than a legal
one. In a memo prepared on April 28, 1937, the State Department's Duggan wrote:

Technically, the failure of the company to exhaust its remedies
in the Bolivian courts, and its agreement to the Calvo clause in
its contract, may weaken its case as far as assistance from this
Government is concerned. There apparently has been, however,
a very manifest denial of justice and arbitrary action on the part
of the Bolivian Government.[51]

On May 5, the United States Minister in La Paz reported
that the Bolivian Foreign Minister had reconfirmed the political nature of the government's action. "The Standard Oil
Company," Sr. Finot remarked, "has been driven out of
Bolivia for political reasons, and it is now merely a question of legalizing this move. It was never our intention to
allow it to reenter the country to do business. It is a crooked
company and has been deceiving the Government for twenty
years." The Foreign Minister added: "I do not hesitate to
reaffirm that if providentially the present cause for action
against the Company had not been found, some other
grounds would have been sought."[52]

Under these circumstances, State Department officials
decided that the main question for the United States was a

tactical one. Given the larger long-term goals of the Good Neighbor Policy, and given the intricate relationship between political and legal considerations in this particular case, how far should the State Department go in backing up the Standard Oil Company? Secretary of State Hull sent up a trial balloon early in May, in the form of a telegram setting forth general State Department policy in regard to the foreign activities of American enterprises. Without taking any position on the Standard Oil case itself, Hull assured the Bolivian government that

the Government of the United States, in accordance with its consistent efforts to practice the policy of the good neighbor to the fullest extent, does not at any time or in any instance contemplate support for one of its nationals who seeks to exploit the government of another country or the nationals of such government, or who pursues methods or practices inherently unfair or unwarranted.

Foreign Minister Finot replied, through Minister Norweb, that in the Standard Oil case he would "cooperate fully toward whatever adjustment may be feasible which, without entering into the legality of the measures adopted, would demonstrate that in Bolivia foreign capital is guaranteed and protected." Finot assured Hull that on the Bolivian side there would be "no sparing of efforts and sacrifices to show that foreign capital has security and protection, thus giving the lie to any propaganda interested in maintaining the contrary to the detriment of the credit and good name of the country."[53]

Having thus received assurances that the larger principle of foreign participation in Latin American economic development was not being denied, the State Department decided not to contest the Bolivian government's insistence that Standard Oil take its case through the Bolivian judiciary system. Under Secretary of State Welles informed Standard Oil representatives accordingly. "This Department," Welles wrote, "will continue to extend to the Standard Oil Company of Bolivia all assistance that the Department considers proper and possible, but is not prepared at this time to give consideration to making formal representations to the Bolivian Government." A memo prepared in the State Department's Division of American Republics, not sent to the Standard Oil representatives, gave further reasons for the Department's position. It was important to

know more about Standard's actual behavior in Bolivia. It
was important not to compromise United States influence
in the difficult Chaco peace negotiations which were still
going on in Argentina, particularly inasmuch as Bolivian oil
was "not unrelated to the Chaco controversy." Finally, it
was important not to give the Argentine government any
"opportunity to make capital—in connection with the Chaco
Peace Conference and otherwise—of any controversy between the Governments of the United States and Bolivia
over the Standard Oil Company properties."[54]

At first, Standard Oil representatives in the United
States balked at the State Department's decision, and continued to press for intercession with the Bolivian government. But the Department held to its position that the Good
Neighbor Policy would best be served by having the company go through Bolivian judicial channels.

In February 1938, Standard made one last attempt to
get State Department intercession. An attorney in the Department's Legal Adviser's office did prepare a memo advocating such intercession on the grounds that Standard could
not be expected to receive equitable treatment from the
Bolivian Supreme Court. A separate memo from the same
attorney suggested that the Calvo clause might be circum-
vented because the contract containing the clause had itself
been canceled. But Hull and Welles held firm, and on March
31, 1938, a Standard Oil representative wrote to Welles notifying the Under Secretary that Standard had filed suit in the
Bolivian Supreme Court so as not to have "failed to exhaust
all local remedies."[55]

To all intents and purposes, the Bolivian government
had won its point without a fight. Neither the nature of the
crisis nor the specific circumstances surrounding the operations of Standard Oil seemed to recommend United
States intervention.[56] In the meantime, however, the Bolivian oil crisis had already been overshadowed by a second
and far more significant one.

On March 18, 1938, President Lázaro Cárdenas of Mexico
announced the nationalization of British and American oil
properties in Mexico. The State Department's response was
quite different in this case. First, the properties involved
were much more extensive. Second, because of the much
greater prestige of the Mexican government throughout
Latin America, this expropriation was more likely to stim-

ulate a wave of similar actions (which was, ironically, just what Standard Oil executives had warned Hull about during the Bolivian crisis).[57]

To understand how the Mexican oil crisis developed, one must understand the background against which events occurred. What gave the Mexican government such prestige in Latin America was precisely what also made it so dangerous to United States interests. That is, the Cárdenas administration stood at the head of the most powerful revolutionary nationalist movement in Latin America. And, in contrast to the situations in both Cuba and Bolivia, the government in Mexico was constitutionally elected and represented a revolutionary tradition going back over twenty years.

The revolution had never quite stopped in Mexico; it had merely slowed down in the late twenties and early thirties. Cárdenas, on taking office in December 1934, accelerated it again. He greatly increased the pace of land expropriation and redistribution. He nationalized the Mexican National Railways, which was still a partly foreign-owned company. And he supported, and was supported by, the increasingly militant trade-union movement in Mexico. It was the clash between militant trade unions and the foreign-owned oil companies which ultimately brought on the expropriations.[58]

The oil crisis did not develop all at once. It had first flared up during the Carranza-Wilson period and continued into the presidencies of Alvaro Obregón and Warren Harding. In the late 1920's, United States Ambassador Dwight Morrow had secured a useful compromise for the oil companies: they would recognize Mexican national sovereignty over the oil fields by seeking "confirmatory concessions" from the Mexican government, while the government would undertake to issue the concessions in perpetuity. The agreement was informal, however, and by the time Cárdenas took office in December 1934, some of the major confirmatory concessions still had not been issued. Moreover, the Mexican government had recently set up a government corporation, Petróleos de Mexico (Pemex), to exploit government-owned reserves. American oil companies viewed Pemex as the first step in a government plan to ease them out of Mexico.[59]

Tensions were exacerbated when the new Cárdenas administration began to raise taxes on oil production. The most threatening development from the companies' point of view, however, was the organization of the militant nation-

wide syndicate of Mexican Petroleum Workers in 1936. The
syndicate had the support of both the Cárdenas administration and the CTM, or Confederation of Mexican Workers,
with which it quickly affiliated.

In November 1936, the oil workers' syndicate presented
the various companies with new wage and fringe-benefit demands in the form of an industry-wide collective contract.
The companies, imitating the strategy of the workers,
adopted a common position for the whole industry: they rejected the demands. On May 28, 1937, the oil workers went
on strike across Mexico. The syndicate also appealed for a
decision by the federal Board of Conciliation and Arbitration, a mixed-membership body on which the Mexican government held the balance of power between labor and
management.[60]

From here events moved rapidly. After an investigation
of the financial condition of the companies, which the Board
was empowered to make in such cases, its technical experts
decided that the companies could afford to meet most of
labor's demands, and the Board handed down its decision
accordingly. The companies immediately appealed to the
Mexican Supreme Court for an injunction to block implementation of the Board's decision.

Interim negotiations between a representative of the
oil companies and the government proved futile. On March
1, 1938, the Supreme Court denied the injunction and up-
held the ruling of the Arbitration Board. The companies still
refused to comply. Two weeks later the Arbitration Board
announced that the companies were being guilty of defiance,
thus making them liable for loss of their properties. Last-
minute direct negotiations between the companies and
President Cárdenas collapsed when the companies refused
to accept the President's personal guarantee against further
wage or tax demands. Two days later Cárdenas expropriated
the oil properties of all American and British companies involved in the dispute. The threat to the Good Neighbor Policy had become reality.

It would be a mistake to suppose that it was only at
this point that the Roosevelt administration became actively
involved in the oil dispute. In truth, the State Department
had been an active observer, even a sometime participant,
in the dispute for years. So had the United States Embassy
in Mexico.

The United States' Ambassador to Mexico during the

Cárdenas administration was Josephus Daniels, a long-time North Carolina newspaper editor and former Secretary of the Navy in the Wilson administration (Franklin Roosevelt had been his Assistant Secretary). Daniels was fundamentally sympathetic to the aspirations of the Mexican Revolution. To be sure, this was because he saw the Cárdenas program as being only in part revolutionary nationalist, and in part a kind of Mexican analog of the New Deal. Nevertheless, in his attitude toward the crucial question of foreign private enterprise in a revolutionary setting, he was considerably more sympathetic toward the revolutionaries than were most of his State Department superiors.

During the oil dispute, Daniels, while not wishing to see the companies expropriated, did not generally support their position. He told President Roosevelt in September 1937 that the companies had already "made big money on absurdly low wages," and that Mexico could "never prosper on low wages. . . ." Daniels added:

I need not tell you that as a rule the oil men will be satisfied with nothing less than that the United States Government attempt to direct the Mexican policy for their financial benefit. They are as much against fair wages here as economic royalists at home are against progressive legislation.

Shortly thereafter, Daniels wrote to Secretary Hull that he did not think Cárdenas really wanted to nationalize foreign oil properties. The companies, he noted, were "mistaking an insistence upon better wages with a desire to nationalize the oil industry."[61]

Hull took a different view, not because of any inherent sympathy for the companies but because he saw revolutionary nationalism getting out of hand altogether in Mexico —and, by extension, in all Latin America. Hull was determined to limit such nationalism at its base. For that reason, well before the expropriation took place, Hull was disputing Mexican government policy by questioning the nature of the Mexican constitution (just as Lansing had done before him). Hull opposed the idea of Mexican government royalties on oil production, since a royalty implied ownership of the subsoil rights. Under Article 27 of the constitution, Mexico did claim ownership of such rights; but this was precisely what Hull wished to avoid recognizing. He also took the position that the recommendations of the Mexican Arbitration Board were a matter for international dispute. In a note drafted by

Sumner Welles and other State Department officials, Hull stated: "It is not always easy to draw a sharp line between matters purely of an internal and domestic character and those of an international character." In particular, it was not solely an internal Mexican question as to "whether as a matter of justice the demands of the workers are reasonable or unreasonable."[62]

On his side, Daniels found an ally in Treasury Secretary Henry Morgenthau, Jr. Morgenthau's main concern was to keep Mexico from turning to the fascist nations of Germany, Italy, and Japan for economic assistance. For this reason he tended to side with the Mexican government, so as to prevent a breakdown in Mexican-American official relations. In December 1937, despite the oil situation, Morgenthau decided, over State Department objections, to purchase an extra amount of Mexican silver so as to support the sagging Mexican peso. "I think with any kind of sympathetic treatment, intelligent treatment," he noted, "we may be able to help them pull through and have a friendly neighbor to the south of us."[63]

When the expropriation finally occurred, the split between the Hull-Welles approach and the Daniels-Morgenthau approach became even more pronounced. Daniels was personally both surprised and dismayed by the expropriation, though more because of its likely effect on Mexican-American relations than because of any sympathy for the companies. He privately referred to the decree as "very regrettable." Nevertheless, in his first public statement after the expropriation, Daniels stated only that he was keeping the State Department informed of events and that he hoped agreement could ultimately be reached. A talk with President Cárdenas four days later convinced Daniels that the decree was irreversible. After the talk, he wrote to Hull noting that the State Department had "no course open but to seek to aid the companies in securing compensation," which, in fact, Cárdenas had already offered to provide.[64]

The State Department's attitude was quite different. The day before Daniels saw Cárdenas, Sumner Welles called Mexican Ambassador Francisco Castillo Nájera to his office, where he lectured the Ambassador sternly about the oil policy of his government, terming it "absolutely suicidal." It was in Mexico's own interest, Welles suggested, that Cárdenas "rescind the decree and . . . permit the companies to continue operating." Meanwhile, Hull was telling Daniels to indicate to Cárdenas that his position "would prove disastrous to Mexico and extremely embarrassing to the United States." Two days later, the State Department initiated a successful pressure campaign to get Morgenthau to halt Mexican silver purchases after all.[65]

For a short time it looked as if Mexican-American relations would break down entirely. On March 26, Hull cabled Daniels a long, strongly worded protest note concerning the expropriation. Hull indicated that after delivering the note to the Mexican Foreign Office, Daniels was to return to Washington for consultations. At the same time, the State Department would release the text of the note to the press and announce the Treasury Department's decision to suspend purchases of Mexican silver. It was evidently the State Department's collective judgment that a strong stance would induce Cárdenas to back down. For all the obvious differences between the Cuban situation of 1933 and the Mexican situation of 1938, the Department was going to try to resolve the latter crisis with the same unilateral pressure it had used in the former.

Only quick action by Daniels prevented such a course. First, Daniels convinced Hull over the telephone that the March 26 note should be kept at least temporarily confidential pending developments. Second, because of the harsh language of the note, Daniels on his own authority (and without informing Hull) assented to a request by Mexican Foreign Minister Hay that the note be considered as not formally presented. This move, which relegated the note to a mere unofficial expression of State Department views, probably did more than anything else to prevent a diplomatic rupture. Finally, with negotiations continuing, Daniels decided to ignore instructions to return home. He belatedly received authorization to stay in Mexico City.[66]

After March, the focus shifted from a discussion of the expropriation itself to a discussion of what constituted appropriate compensation. The companies meanwhile appealed the expropriation to the Mexican Supreme Court (and quickly lost). But after April 1, when President Roosevelt publicly approved President Cárdenas' offer to discuss compensation, the United States government ceased its efforts to roll back the expropriation decree. This shift marked the end of one aspect of the crisis; but it by no means ended the threat to the Good Neighbor Policy. For one thing, it soon developed that the oil companies and the Mexican government were far apart in their estimates of the total value of the properties. For another, the State Department was still faced with a basic problem, namely, how best to manage the situation so as not to provoke an epidemic of expropriations in Latin America. In particular, the question was how to prevent future assaults now that the State Department had abandoned its efforts to roll back the Mexican expropriation.[67]

Wall Street pundit Bernard Baruch caught the larger significance of the dilemma in terms of its impact upon the American way of life.

The money involved is important, but it is not important compared with something of deeper significance.

The ownership, control, and direction of the natural resources such as those are important to America because they bring not only these raw materials, but the profits therefrom, increasing the American standards of living.[68]

Baruch caught the threat not only in terms of the direct Mexican-American relationship but also in terms of the growing danger that Mexico—and other Latin American countries as well—might begin to play off rival industrial powers against each other, so as to improve their bargaining position. "If the Mexican government permanently takes these properties over," Baruch noted, "they will be unable to operate them but will turn to others to do so. Those others might readily be Japan, Italy, and Germany who need these raw materials. If this condition spreads to Central and South American countries, America may readily find herself not alone denuded of the investment represented but also shut off from the supply of those materials, except at prices that can be dictated by others." The long-range danger to the United States was manifest: "We might readily find a revolt in Mexico and at our very door a situation similar to that in Spain." In a letter to Daniels, Baruch noted, "I fear some such move starting south of the Rio Grande and going to the tip of Patagonia."[69]

Meanwhile, the oil companies announced a boycott on shipping and distribution of Mexican oil taken from the expropriated wells. The Mexicans now began to talk of turning to the Axis countries for markets—not by choice but in self-defense. This raised yet another question involving the element of rival European competition. Baruch expressed his fears in a second letter to Daniels in June 1938:

> I know you must realize that if Japan, Italy, or Germany had the tankers, they would take that oil and pay for it with goods made by them, displacing American-made goods. I think we ought to help the poor peons in Mexico, but I am sure that the taking away of the American markets by the sweated labor of the Nazi and Fascist countries will destroy the labor standards in this country. . . .
>
> Another thing—we are endeavoring to expand our trade by Hull's policies. If these foreign countries are going to seize American properties, banks are not going to lend money to American exporters. All of this will have a tremendously restricting influence on our economy, and no one will be affected more than our agricultural growers and laborers.[70]

The situation was indeed one to give rise to substantial American fears. Aside from the spectre of aggressive European competition in Latin America (to say nothing of the ideological propensities of the new competitors), the Mexican oil situation suggested that the consequences which the New Dealers had feared ever since the Cuban crisis were coming to pass. A powerful Latin American nation was not only fighting back against foreign economic domination, but was using strong governmental action in the economic arena as a means of increasing its economic sovereignty. Moreover, internal Latin American nationalism might be finding a useful ally in external European anti-American nationalism. Thus a dual threat loomed. Bernard Baruch saw an ideological as well as tactical alliance in the making and took a dim view of such developments. "The dictator idea is growing in these South American countries," he wrote to President Roosevelt in October 1938, "and with it propaganda is being used to create fear and hatred of the only country that can defend them, the United States."

On the other hand, Baruch noted, if the present trend could be reversed, it would not only restore the traditional harmony in inter-American relations, but would also effectively undercut the United States' Axis competitors and ideological rivals. "If we stop her [Germany] in Latin America," he wrote to James F. Byrnes, "we will close the only door by which she might be able to escape the economic collapse which will surely be hers in time." Mayor Fiorello La Guardia of New York City suggested a strong American drive to undersell Germany in Latin American markets. To

La Guardia, Baruch wrote: "Such a drive for trade in the Americas south of the Rio Grande, as you suggest, would be the final blow to Germany's hopes of dominating the world."[71]

But American goals, as Baruch, Hull, Roosevelt, La Guardia, and other policy-makers and commentators knew, required new strategies. In the past there had admittedly been an American tendency to approach hemispheric problems by unilateral fiat. A major Latin American government had now shown that more than one could play the game. Despite the initial progress made in late March 1938, inter-American relationships were still in danger of deteriorating into a dangerous series of unadorned economic and political power plays.

The Mexican oil crisis indicated that Latin Americans were demanding two things of the United States: greater authority in their own economic decision-making, and a greater share of the wealth produced from their own resources. If the United States was to maintain anything like its own preferred measure of both decision-making authority and wealth without scuttling the Good Neighbor image in the process, then a new approach was in order. The United States would have to find some way to maintain its position without either antagonizing or giving too much free rein to Latin American nationalists.

It was a demanding situation, perhaps an impossible one. It was certainly one which would tax the ingenuity of the Americans to the utmost. Nevertheless, given their own assumption that continued United States influence over Latin American development was more in the interest of the hemisphere than a victory for Latin American revolutionary nationalism, no other alternative was possible.

II. The new technique: Giving Latin America a share

1. Defining the approach

"At the beginning of the thirties," wrote State Department Political Adviser Laurence Duggan, in describing United States policy toward Latin American economic development, "the United States Government was doing even less than private organizations; it was doing nothing at all. By the end of the thirties it was white hot with enthusiasm, born of fear of the Nazis. And therein lay the weakness of its new policy."[1] In one respect, Duggan's analysis was correct. United States economic policy toward Latin America was weak insofar as it sprang from motives unrelated to Latin America's own needs. Duggan's analysis was wrong, however, insofar as it suggested that Nazi competition was seen as the only threat, or even the primary threat, to United States interests in Latin America. Even before that threat took shape, the State Department's attitude in the Cuban and Mexican crises had shown that leading government officials saw the internal Latin American revolutionary nationalist threat as being quite important indeed. Leading private business organizations in the United States had taken the same view even in the Bolivian crisis. As we have seen, references to the dangers of "socialism," "extreme radicalism," and "communism" were numerous in the correspondence of both public and private officials during these three confrontations.

The rise of fascist expansionism in Europe nevertheless did increase the threat to the United States' position in Latin America. As Bernard Baruch had pointed out, American exports were certainly in danger of being undercut by cheap German goods produced under controlled labor conditions. Germany was also promoting special barter arrangements in Latin America to give her exports even further advantages. Ironically, the intransigence of the American and British oil companies in the face of Mexican nationalism was helping to increase the Axis threat: Mexico reluctantly turned to Germany, Italy, and Japan to take up the slack in her oil exports caused by the American boycott. Those countries in turn were happy to barter heavy machinery for the oil they so badly needed. Josephus Daniels pointed out a particularly unpleasant aspect of the American dilemma when he told Cordell Hull: "We cannot properly object to such [Mexican] sale because the Standard Oil Company sold to Japan and Germany before the expropriation."[2] All such considerations pointed toward the same policy conclusion for the Roosevelt administration: some kind of rapprochement with Latin American nationalists was necessary to avert serious consequences. The old question remained, however. How far could the United States go in that direction without sacrificing its position in the hemisphere?

President Roosevelt himself best expressed the emerging United States approach in a remark he made to a gathering of newspapermen on January 12, 1940. "That is a new approach that I am talking about to these South American things," the President told his audience. "Give them a share. They think they are just as good as we are, and many of them are."[3] The "share," as the President made clear, was to include both a share of decision-making authority in inter-American economic concerns and a share of the wealth being developed from Latin America's vast resources by private and public capital.

The new approach could be applied to both government policy and the policy of United States private enterprise in Latin America. In light of the developing situation, private firms might well have to give up a share of their foreign wealth to the host country, or else stand to lose everything, and not necessarily through violent revolution. Latin American governments were developing a political need of their own to "give a share" to their peoples. This meant taking control of economic assets which would not otherwise be available for distribution or management in accordance with such sharing principles. Oil was only one such asset. There were many others.

In some countries, the governments were coming increasingly to institutionalize these political needs into broad grants of legislative authority, designed to give them ample leverage to work out the political necessities of economic "sharing." The highly nationalistic Brazilian constitution of 1937 was a case in point. Although this document had been

drawn up, in the main, as an adjunct of President Vargas'
self-perpetuating *coup* of that year, and had included a provision (Article 180) which gave the President power to
suspend the constitution at his discretion, the *potential* economic power vested in the Brazilian government by means
of this document was enormous, particularly in its implications for foreign holders of Brazilian properties and capital assets.[4]

Under this constitution, a strong executive such as
Getulio Vargas could with perfect legality take unprecedented sweeping action to acquire for the Brazilian government and people more than just a "share" of the nation's
wealth. Moreover, the political authority to decide how resources were to be organized and allocated was vested
almost entirely in the government. Any Latin American government which really implemented the powers granted in
this type of document would be making an unequivocal
declaration of economic sovereignty. In any international
economic transactions, it would be *giving* rather than *receiving* a share of its own nation's resources.

All these threats drove New Deal policy-makers toward
the same conclusion: if the old goal was to be preserved, a
new technique was needed. And the old goal *was* to be preserved. Roosevelt had stated as much in his January 1940
press conference.

Once again, circumstances pointed up the interplay between domestic and foreign policy considerations. As early
as May 1938, Bernard Baruch had with characteristic clarity
pointed out a domestic analog of Roosevelt's "give them a
share" principle. Baruch's insight, enunciated in two letters,
one to Ambassador Joe Davies in Moscow and the other to
General Motors board chairman Alfred P. Sloan, Jr., showed
a striking resemblance to the President's Latin American formula of January 1940.

I think the business men [Baruch wrote to Davies] have been
fighting for silly, losing, rearguard actions all the time. Roosevelt
has awakened the consciousness of the people of this country to
the necessity of an attitude of helpfulness towards the under-
privileged or incompetent, or whatever you may call them by,
and it is well for us not to be lulled to sleep again.

In his letter to Sloan, Baruch noted:

American industry has done a great job in production and distribution, but not, apparently, in its relationship with its labor,
and not as regards the general public understanding of its actions

and its needs. It seems to me we could do a better job to retain our workers, and the good opinion of the public.[5]

Such differences as administration officials did have among themselves or with representatives of corporate management—and there were, as will become clear, areas of serious disagreement in regard to Latin American policy— sprang from conflicting perceptions of means, not ends. Sometimes this meant that businessmen and certain government officials did not quite understand some of the long-range implications of New Deal tactics. At other times it meant simply that the businessmen were unwilling to give Latin America quite as large a "share" as were the leading New Dealers. In the main, however, the government-business coalition in the United States was able to proceed along several lines in formulating a Latin American policy. The common tactical assumption was that Latin American consessions would be required along with North American consessions. Reciprocity, though in a different setting, was still the byword.

2. *Interests north and south*

This tack came out very clearly in the United States government's approach to the problem of opening up Latin American markets to American exports. A major problem facing Latin American governments during the depression had been their shortage of foreign exchange due to declining export revenues. A number of countries had had to institute strict controls over the expenditure and transfer abroad of scarce foreign exchange by their importers. Once in operation, however, such controls also proved to be useful tools in the hands of nationalistic governments which preferred, for political reasons, to encourage trade with some countries and restrict trade with others.

Early in 1939, the Department of Commerce went on the offensive to remove such controls in Brazil. When the Brazilian government approached the United States to ask for an emergency loan to meet balance-of-payments problems, the Americans insisted that Brazil lift exchange controls as a condition of such a loan. Reconstruction Finance Corporation chairman Jesse Jones negotiated the loan through the Export-Import Bank. Interestingly, despite further pressure from United States holders of defaulted Brazilian bonds,

Secretary of State Hull still refused to insist upon tying a
debt settlement into the loan arrangement. The State Department wanted to preserve a certain freedom of action
vis-à-vis private interests in the United States.[6]

If the federal government was not yet willing to go the
whole mile in support of holders of defaulted bonds, it was
nonetheless willing to take active steps to encourage new
investment in productive enterprise, even to the point of
rewriting tax laws governing investments by American nationals in Latin America. In a memo to Commerce Department officials, Dr. Julius Klein, a former director of the
Bureau of Foreign and Domestic Commerce, suggested that
relevant provisions of the old China Trade Act of the 1920's
be applied in the case of Latin America. These provisions
would exempt United States–incorporated firms from income tax payments if they did all their business in Latin
America. Klein pointed out that the China Trade Act had
through such provisions "not only assisted American corporations doing business in China in competition particularly with the Germans, but also opened up a new field of
investment for Chinese businessmen who were able to invest their capital jointly with American corporations operating exclusively in China under the provisions of the Act."
John McClintock of the Office of the Coordinator of Inter-
American Affairs assured Dr. Klein that the relevant principles were indeed being applied to Latin America.[7]

All in all, the Commerce Department took extensive action to assure that under the new reciprocity the activities
of private United States enterprises would be both encouraged and protected against unfair treatment. The Department refused to go as far as lobbying for government subsidies to stimulate machinery exports to Latin America. It
did, however, provide extensive trade information to help
stimulate such exports and also sponsored an extensive investigation and report on trade opportunities in Brazil. The
report was prepared by the Business Advisory Council of the
Department, the membership of which read like a small
Who's Who in American Business. Included on the committee which drafted the report were such key corporation
leaders as Juan Trippe of Pan American Airways (chairman
of the Business Advisory Council), Curtis Calder of the
American and Foreign Power Company, Berent Friele of the
American Coffee Corporation, Curt Pfeiffer of the National

Council of American Importers, and Eugene Thomas, president of the National Foreign Trade Council.

The Business Advisory Council adopted a series of resolutions calling for resumption of payment on Brazilian debts to American bondholders, and the repeal or revision of "nationalistic legislation" in Brazil which tended to "hinder the investment of American capital and the employment of American technical and business skill in the development of Brazil's resources." Interestingly, the Council took note of a November 1938 speech by Brazilian President Vargas in which he warned against the depredations of certain types of foreign investors whose capital might become a "passive and sometimes negative influence in the march of national progress." But the Council emphasized that Latin American governments should not be permitted to go too far in unilaterally deciding when foreign capital was becoming a "negative influence." Specifically, the Council stated that "nothing would contribute more to sound economic cooperation between the United States and Brazil than a firm and frank attitude by the American Government which insists upon justice and fair treatment for private business under international law."[8]

While moving on these fronts to assure respect for American rights under the new policy of "giving Latin America a share," the New Dealers also set about building policies designed to pacify Latin American resentment over past United States actions. They attempted to expand the activities of the Export-Import Bank so as to stimulate Latin American trade and economic activity in general. At first Congress was reluctant to grant increased funds for "Eximbank" operations. In June 1939, Congress turned down President Roosevelt's request for an additional $500 million to promote trade with Latin America. The money was quickly appropriated in September 1940, however, when it became clear that only the United States could prevent another early collapse of Latin America's export economy, which had been seriously damaged by the closing of European markets in the Second World War.

The whole problem of the relationship between Latin America's exports and its internal economic development was one to which the State Department began paying more attention in the early wartime period. United States Ambassador to Cuba George Messersmith noted the interrelationship between stable export earnings and the financing of development projects in Latin America. Late in 1940, Messersmith sent a confidential message to Under Secretary of State Sumner Welles urging the speedy conclusion of the new Cuban sugar purchase agreement. Messersmith linked the agreement directly to other efforts toward economic growth in Cuba. "I am convinced," he wrote, "that this sugar arrangement will be the most constructive thing that we could do in the Cuban situation now." Aside from allaying the threat of short-term economic distress, which might well be followed by political disorder, the sugar agreement would be vital on a long-term basis, Messersmith noted, for it would "help to stabilize the economic situation until we can get some constructive action on credits for agricultural diversification and public works."[9]

During the war, American economists would trace this connection in more general terms, pointing out that whereas in the advanced industrial countries domestic savings and investments were the main sources of capital for economic growth, the same role was played in less developed areas (such as Latin America) by the inflow or outflow of foreign exchange.[10] Unsteady or declining export revenues thus had a highly significant—and detrimental—effect upon major capital-consuming activities. Messersmith's reference to the use of credits rather than local earnings as a base for agricultural diversification programs indicated that he himself may not have completely understood this aspect of the problem. But the relation of export revenues to production growth was clear enough, and this was a problem not merely for wartime consideration. United States policy would have to be reoriented to consider both production and marketing on a long-term basis.

The next step in this progression was an important one. The Colombian educator, Dr. Daniel Samper Ortega, told a University of Chicago Round Table discussion group that the United States would have to not only buy Latin American products but also make sure that not all the payments found their way back to United States owners of the export-producing properties (such as oil wells and banana plantations).[11] This added yet another link in the chain which was pulling American policy-makers in the direction of "giving Latin America a share" of its own wealth.

The new policy, however, involved much more than a

reconsideration of inter-American trade relations or the use of American capital to stimulate trade in existing lines of production. By the end of 1940, the Export-Import Bank was making loans to stimulate wholly new lines of production in Latin America. Beginning with a small loan in 1938 to the Haitian government, the Bank became increasingly involved in "development" loans.

A key turning point was the Bank's decision to assist in the financing of a steel mill in Brazil. President Vargas had requested American aid early in 1940. The Roosevelt administration, while sympathetic to Brazilian ambitions, had not planned to use public funds to help finance the project. On the contrary, it hoped that as part of the new reciprocity program private American steel manufacturers would come forward to offer assistance. Besides, a number of important government officials in the United States did not think the Eximbank should go quite this far in participating in the development of Latin America's economy. At a meeting with Under Secretary of State Welles and President Roosevelt in April 1940, Jesse Jones, who as RFC chairman had supervisory authority over the Eximbank, advised against Eximbank financing of the steel project. Jones noted that the Bank "might afford to cooperate with the United States Steel Corporation, Bethlehem Steel, or some of the other companies if they would undertake the construction and operation of the mill as owner and we [the Eximbank] have the mortgage for a share of the cost." But that was as far as Jones was prepared to go on his own initiative.[12]

Under Secretary of the Navy James V. Forrestal disapproved the entire project. "The Brazilians would like to build a steel mill," he wrote to Bernard Baruch. "That seems to me just about as practical as a proposal to grow cotton in Montreal. What we can do is to improve the railway and dock facilities and ship the ore to this country where there is a good market." Baruch wrote back agreeing with Forrestal, and expressing doubt that the United States could maintain proper control of the venture. "After the property is developed," he asked, "will they turn a Mexican stunt on us?"[13]

Nonetheless, when one after another the private steel companies in the United States declined to participate in the venture, the State Department finally prevailed upon Jesse Jones to float the necessary loan through the Export-Import Bank. Baruch immediately warned Jones of the

need to maintain tight control of the project so as not to
strengthen elements in Brazil which might be opposed to
United States influence in the hemisphere.

May I suggest to you`[Baruch wrote] that in lending money to a
South American country like Brazil, for a specific purpose, that
instead of lending all the money at once, you lend it as the project
is built. . . . In case of a change of government that was inimical
to us, the payments could be stopped. In other words, if you gave
all the money now, they would have nothing to look to the future
for and might thumb their nose at us, whereas if you gave them
the money as it was needed, you would have some hold upon the
enterprise.

Jones replied that not only was he keeping a tight rein on
payments, but would "only provide the money necessary to
purchase the machinery in this country. . . . The money will
be paid out by the Bank as the machinery and equipment
are shipped from this country."[14] On that basis the steel
project went forward.

The Roosevelt administration's decision to help finance
the Brazilian steel project was important because it indicated a readiness to move into certain developmental activities in Latin America even without the stimulus of the Axis
threat. There was no chance in 1940 of Brazil's getting German aid for such a project: the whole situation had developed, so to speak, through intrahemispheric stimulus and
response. It underlined the independent importance of the
revolutionary nationalist factor in inter-American relations.

It would of course have been possible to point to parts
of Article 61 of the 1937 Brazilian constitution, which empowered the National Economy Council to "promote the
corporative organization of national economy," or to the
pro-Axis "neutrality" of certain Argentine public figures in
the early days of the war, or even (by stretching one's imagination to the limit) to the Mexican sale of oil to Germany
and Japan as alleged evidence that these so-called "revolutionary nationalist" movements in Latin America did not
spring from authentic indigenous roots at all but from
pernicious foreign influences. Bernard Baruch did go so far
as to suggest to President Roosevelt—shortly after the
Munich Conference in September 1938—that there was "no
question but what the expropriation of properties in these
countries, which is now taking or about to take place, has
been fomented by the representatives of Japan, Italy, and
Germany, particularly the last named."[15]

To be sure, Axis officials were clearly pleased by anti-

American nationalism in Latin America, just as they were infuriated by Baruch's proposals that the United States act to build Latin American military defenses against Axis penetration. But to point to such reactions as justification for treating Latin American nationalism itself as an imported phenomenon would have been, as most State Department policy-makers knew, poor propaganda at best, and at worst a dangerous self-delusion. Later on, Secretary of State Hull and many of his advisers would fall into precisely this trap in trying to deal with the Perón regime in Argentina. In the late 1930's and early 1940's, however, the State Department usually was aware of the fact that revolutionary nationalism in Latin America could be supported or combated on its own merits, but never safely ignored or explained simply within the context of European influences.

3. *Responding to the Axis menace*

Axis activities in Latin America, however, particularly after the war began, could not safely be ignored either. The danger that nationalistic regimes might become allied with or subjugated by Axis powers made the building of Latin American economic strength that much more urgent. Some Washington officials had been thinking along these lines well before the war broke out. Treasury Department monetary expert Harry Dexter White was one such person. As early as October 1938, White sent a memorandum to President Roosevelt asking for a large-scale constructive program of economic aid for China and Latin America ("the two areas," White wrote, in which "we can move most effectively and with the least complication") in order to "use our great financial strength to help safeguard future peace for the United States, and to make your 'Good Neighbor' policy really effective."[16] By March 1939, White was calling for large long-term loans for "productive investment" in Brazil, plus a $50 million currency stabilization loan to the Brazilian government. White also suggested de-emphasizing such prior conditions as Brazilian repayment of debts owed to private North American creditors, fearing that such repayments would "serve to offset in large part any economic assistance we grant her."

White's program for Latin America was actually part of a three-pronged economic defense against fascist advance. The other two parts involved massive aid to Russia and

China, intended to build up local capacity to resist arbitrary and lopsided bilateral economic arrangements with the Axis powers. White castigated the State Department's "do-nothing" approach in Latin America, and warned that unless the United States embarked on a "program of assistance to Latin-American countries on a scale appropriate to the problem with which we are faced . . . Latin America will gradually succumb to the organized economic and ideological campaign now being waged by aggressor nations."[17]

Under Secretary of State Welles also understood these developments, at least in respect to Latin America. In a letter to the President in June 1939, Welles discussed the importance to the United States of cooperating with the increasingly influential Argentine Popular Union, a sort of quasi-official Radical party caucus and shadow cabinet, which had recently strongly endorsed President Roosevelt's pledge of "economic support so that no American nation need surrender any fraction of its sovereign freedom to maintain its economic welfare."[18] By the time of the Panama Conference of September 1939, at which the American nations met to work out a common policy vis-à-vis the war in Europe, the President's pledge was in process of being implemented by State Department officials. The United States–sponsored agenda at the Panama Conference included two basic points under the heading "Consideration of measures to safeguard in the present situation the economic and financial stability of the American republics." One point proposed "measures to preserve commercial and financial interests of the American republics"; the other asked for "continuation and expansion of long-term programs for commercial and economic cooperation among the American republics." Each of these received equal emphasis.[19]

The Panama Conference also created the Inter-American Financial and Economic Advisory Council, which in turn set up the Inter-American Development Commission and the Inter-American Bank, two key instruments for multilateralizing control of Latin American economic development. By the time of the fall of France in the spring of 1940, many Washington observers had come to believe that the best defense in Latin America against the spread of fascist influence lay in the development of balanced and prosperous internal economies. On June 15, 1940, President Roosevelt sent a letter to the Secretaries of State, Treasury, Agriculture, and Commerce, asking their combined judgment on ways and means of strengthening inter-American economic relations under wartime conditions. On June 20, the department chiefs responded with a joint letter advocating not merely arrangements for disposing of war-born commodity surpluses in Latin America, but also some vigorous new action in the "broad field of development in some American Republics of new industries and production," together with new credits and a program for strengthening Latin American monetary systems upon the request of individual governments.[20]

While seeking policy suggestions from government officials, Roosevelt did not ignore the views of private businessmen. What had in fact prompted his request to the Cabinet committee was a memo he had received from a group of New York bankers, lawyers, economists, and oil executives. On June 14, White House assistant Harry Hopkins met with the group's spokesman, Nelson Rockefeller. Rockefeller, though not quite thirty-two at the time, was fast becoming a central figure among businessmen concerned with Latin America. His family, one of the most influential in the American business world, had long held key interests in the Standard Oil Company of New Jersey, the Chase National Bank, and other firms. Rockefeller himself had personal investments in the Creole Petroleum Company, a Venezuelan subsidiary of Jersey Standard. He had also helped set up the Companía de Fomento Venezolano, an investment firm designed to finance local industrial development in Venezuela.[21]

The memo which Rockefeller presented to Hopkins was really a blueprint for the economic defense of the Western Hemisphere, based on cooperation between the public and private sectors in all concerned countries. Not all recommendations included in the memo were developmental in character. But they did include important provisions for governmental as well as private investment, along with measures for refunding external debts. Those debts would be converted into domestic currencies so as to obtain sums for local investment. The plan included the dispatching of numerous United States government technical personnel to Latin America, and provided for the organization of interdepartmental United States government planning committees to work closely with private interests in coordinating economic efforts.[22]

On the basis of the New York group's memo, as modified
by the June 20 letter of the Cabinet committee, Roosevelt
resolved to create a new federal agency to coordinate various aspects of policy planning for hemisphere defense. The
new agency, established in August 1940 by executive order,
was originally named the Office for Coordination of Commercial and Cultural Relations Between the American Republics. It was soon shortened to Office of the Coordinator
of Inter-American Affairs. Rockefeller was appointed Coordinator, with instructions to cooperate with the State
Department in all policy matters. By the late fall of 1940,
Rockefeller's office was hard at work on a pilot "country
study" of Colombian development needs, to be used as a
possible model for similar studies in other Latin American
countries.

Meanwhile, the Axis threat also prompted vigorous
United States actions in support of private American inter-
ests. The still-thorny Bolivian oil question was a case in
point. A Commerce Department memo of January 1939 com-
mented with alarm on recent "serious encroachments" upon
American investments in Bolivia, Mexico, and elsewhere.
Commenting on the memo, Grosvenor Jones, chief of the
Finance Division of the Bureau of Foreign and Domestic
Commerce, noted that he considered the phrase "serious
encroachments" to be "euphemistic."

When one contemplates the contribution which American enterprise has made to the development of the economic resources of
Latin America through the investment of hundreds of millions in
mining, petroleum, railroads, public utility, and plantation under-
takings, one must wonder how most of these countries will fare
if the inflow of foreign private capital is cut off, as it will be if
existing investments are subjected to "serious encroachments" or
worse.

Jones pointed out that foreign investments had been for
generations "the backbone" of economic development in
Latin America, and that it was therefore questionable
whether the United States should tolerate expropriations
even as a matter of protecting Latin America's own interests. "Both in their own interest as well as in ours," wrote
Jones, "this Government should, therefore, in my opinion,
take decisive steps to protect existing American investments
in countries which have dealt unfairly with American enterprises within their borders."[23]

A few months later, in April 1939, Secretary of State Hull

linked such arguments directly to the problem of the Axis threat in Latin America. In a conversation with the Bolivian Ambassador in Washington, Hull talked at length about the seizure of the Standard Oil properties in Bolivia, which was still a matter of dispute. Having previously declined to become seriously involved in the Bolivian case, Hull now gave stern warning to the Ambassador that such controversies could not long remain unresolved, given the increasingly turbulent world situation. Hull told the Ambassador that Latin America was a "ripe plum dangling before the eyes of the lawless nations, hungry as wolves for the rich natural resources of Latin America." In such times, the Secretary noted, it was of vital importance that the American nations pursue "lawful, friendly" courses of action with respect to each other's interests. The dollars and cents of the oil situation, Hull observed, was a small consideration "compared to the great injury that would result to Bolivia, as well as to the United States and other countries, if that sort of an act should go uncorrected and the friendship between the two countries be seriously impaired."[24] The soft line was getting harder as the seriousness of the expropriation question in Latin America grew more pronounced.

In one sense, Hull was following previous State Department policy. In March 1938, the Department had stayed out of the Standard Oil dispute partly on the grounds that the company had not yet exhausted all legal remedies available in Bolivia. The company, for its part, had agreed to appeal the seizure of its properties to the Bolivian Supreme Court. In March 1939, the Court turned down the company's challenge. Since this decision did in fact exhaust the local remedies available to Standard Oil, Hull felt free to take up the question with the Bolivian Ambassador.

Nevertheless, events indicated that it was through economic diplomacy amid changing international political circumstances, rather than through compelling legal arguments, that the State Department finally got the Bolivian government to pay compensation to Standard Oil. The Department soon made it clear to Bolivia that no economic assistance of any kind would be forthcoming until the Standard Oil controversy was settled.[25] Significantly, this carrot-and-stick approach produced no results so long as Bolivia maintained its revolutionary nationalist momentum under the Busch regime. President Busch, however, committed

suicide on August 23, 1939, apparently in despair over his
inability to get around a British stranglehold on Bolivia's
all-important tin-mining industry.[26] Vice-President Carlos
Quintanilla succeeded Busch, and held office until an elected
successor, Enrique Peñaranda, was inaugurated in April
1940.

Both Quintanilla and Peñaranda were less nationalist
than Busch, and more amenable to close Bolivian-American
economic relations. In particular, they were interested in
American financial and technical aid, especially as other
Latin American countries had begun to receive such aid after
the Panama Conference. Even so, they had to move slowly
to avoid antagonizing nationalists in the Bolivian Congress.
In the fall of 1940, the Peñaranda regime asked for congressional authorization to negotiate an agreement with Standard Oil, arguing that Bolivia would receive no American aid
until it did so. The Bolivian Senate granted the authorization; the Chamber of Deputies refused, and adjourned in
April 1941 without acting on the matter.[27]

The Axis threat, however, ultimately gave the State Department and Peñaranda the leverage to overcome the remaining Bolivian nationalists. In July 1941, a plot to overthrow the Peñaranda regime was discovered; both a German
official in Bolivia and a Bolivian official in Berlin were al-
legedly implicated. Washington immediately responded with
a proposal for a comprehensive economic aid program as
well as a military mission to be sent to Bolivia. The military
agreement was signed on September 4, the aid agreement
shortly thereafter; a group of United States economic experts arrived in La Paz on December 17, 1941. Meanwhile,
the Japanese attack on Pearl Harbor brought the two American governments even closer politically. At the inter-American conference in Rio de Janeiro in January 1942, Sumner
Welles and the Bolivian Foreign Minister, Eduardo Anze
Matienzo, arrived at a preliminary agreement on the oil
question. The Bolivian official offered an "indemnity" of
$1 million to be paid to Standard Oil. Ultimately the figure
agreed upon was $1.5 million, plus 3 per cent interest to be
calculated as of the date of the seizure, March 13, 1937.
Standard Oil officials successfully insisted that the transaction be considered a "sale" rather than an "indemnification,"
so as to support their contention that the seizure did not
spring from misconduct by the company. The day after the

agreement was signed, the United States government announced the establishment of a $25 million economic aid program for Bolivia.[28]

This settlement effectively ended the oil controversy as an international incident. There was yet one final act to be played out in Bolivia, however, and it demonstrated the continuing strength of nationalist feeling in that country. In November 1942, a motion of censure of the Peñaranda regime in the Bolivian Chamber of Deputies failed to pass by one vote. Thirteen months later, a nationalist resurgence overthrew the government, which by that time had degenerated into a repressive, anti-nationalist, though pro-American, military dictatorship.[29]

The war also provided the circumstances for the final settlement of the Mexican oil expropriation dispute. As in the Bolivian case, the development of the Axis threat first inclined the State Department to a harder rather than a softer line. Direct negotiations between the oil companies and the Mexican government during most of 1939 came to naught. Both sides remained equally confident of their positions, strategically and ethically. The oil companies were convinced that Britain's wartime blockade of German ports would bring Mexico to its knees by depriving it of its best oil customer; Mexico was equally convinced that either Italy or the Western democracies themselves would soon have need to take up the slack. In addition, in December 1939, the Mexican Supreme Court issued a final rejection of a request by the various oil companies that it set aside the expropriation decree.

The Roosevelt administration's reaction was to increase rather than decrease pressure on Mexico. In November 1939, before the Mexican Supreme Court decision, the State Department concluded an executive agreement providing for the importation of foreign oil from certain countries at reduced tariff rates. Mexico was pointedly omitted from the list of assigned quotas. The following month, after the court decision was announced, Sumner Welles told Mexican Ambassador Castillo Nájera that until the expropriation dispute was settled, Mexico should not try to ship any oil to the United States even under the unassigned quota allotment (which amounted to only 3.8 per cent of the total anyway).[30]

By the beginning of 1940, negotiations between the Mexi-

can government and lawyer Donald Richberg, representing
the oil companies, had broken down completely. Richberg's
report of the negotiations was then published by the Standard Oil Company of New Jersey. The format of the publication was so blatantly anti-Mexican as to offend even Richberg, who resigned in disgust soon after learning that certain representatives of Jersey Standard in Mexico were actually working against his efforts to reach a compromise
solution. At this point, oilman Harry F. Sinclair broke with
the united front of oil companies and authorized attorney
Patrick Hurley to negotiate a separate settlement between
the Sinclair interests and the Mexican government. On
March 1, 1940, Hurley notified Secretary Hull that Sinclair
and the Mexican government were close to a settlement; the
only major question outstanding was whether oil received
by Sinclair as compensation could be brought into the
United States at the preferential tariff rate.

The State Department gave Hurley no encouragement.
Instead, it continued to press the Mexican government to
submit the entire dispute to international arbitration, although President Cárdenas had consistently and publicly
vetoed the idea as an infringement on Mexican constitutional sovereignty. The very day after Hurley notified Hull
of the impending settlement, Hull called in the Mexican
Ambassador and requested him once again to sound out
Cárdenas on the subject of arbitration. Hull remarked
parenthetically that it would be difficult to bring in Mexican
oil at the reduced tariff rate under the plan contemplated
in the Sinclair negotiations.[31]

Again the Mexican response was negative. Hull now escalated the pressure. On April 3, he handed the Ambassador
a note formally demanding that Mexico submit the dispute
to international arbitration, the decision of the arbitrator to
be binding as to the amount and means of payment of the
compensation for the expropriated properties. Hull released
the text of the note to the press at the same time, obviously
not wanting to risk a replay of the earlier episode involving
his note of March 26, 1938. As an added precaution, Hull did
not notify Josephus Daniels in advance of his decision, possibly fearing that Daniels might either try to talk him out of
it or else appeal directly to President Roosevelt to stop the
note.[32]

Predictably, Hull got a very positive reaction from most

oil companies, but an equally negative one from Mexico. The Mexican government, with considerable finesse, timed its latest negative response to the arbitration proposal to coincide with its announcement that a settlement had been reached with the Sinclair interests. This reinforced Mexico's contention that international arbitration was not only improper but also unnecessary when oilmen were inclined to be reasonable. Then, early in June, the Mexican government came forward with a counter proposal, namely that each of the two governments appoint a representative to a two-man commission which would evaluate the remaining oil properties for compensation purposes.

The State Department and the other oil companies were visibly embarrassed by the Sinclair settlement. Instead of following Sinclair's lead, however, the other companies stepped up their propaganda campaign against the Mexican government, concentrating on Mexico's refusal to bow to American demands for international arbitration. The State Department, for its part, first brushed aside the new Mexican proposal, then persuaded the Navy Department to reject a Sinclair bid on a substantial oil contract. The State Department took the view that Sinclair's oil might be considered to have come from "stolen wells" because part of Sinclair's supply was purchased from the Mexican government under the compensation agreement.[33]

Ultimately, the war softened the State Department's approach. The increasingly ominous Axis menace caused American policy-makers to place a higher value on inter-American solidarity, particularly in view of United States strategic defense requirements. In January 1941, President Roosevelt was making overtures concerning the building of naval bases on Mexico's Pacific coastline. By April the two nations had agreed on reciprocal rights to the military use of each other's airfields. The United States also contracted to purchase Mexico's entire output of strategic minerals. In these circumstances, State Department officials soon realized that resolution of the oil dispute, even on terms somewhat more concessionary to the Mexican point of view, was imperative. The Department now stepped up its pressure on the oil companies to accede to the procedure outlined in the Mexican proposal of June 1940. Characteristically, Hull himself was still reluctant. When the companies flatly rejected the Mexican mixed-commission idea, Hull also wavered, reluctant to go ahead without the agreement of the companies. Once again, timely intercession by Daniels brought Hull around. On November 19, 1941, the two governments announced the establishment of the two-man commission despite lack of advance approval by the oilmen. Only after further denunciations of the Mexican government, as well as further delay and hesitation, did the oil companies agree to supply data needed for the evaluation of their former properties.[34]

The evaluation process brought out some interesting facts. For one thing, the oil companies had been consistently claiming that their expropriated properties were worth some $450 million. State Department officials already knew that this was a vastly inflated figure. A study prepared in 1941 at the Department's request by the Interior Department's Geological Survey had concluded that the properties in question, including the Sinclair properties, were worth less than $25 million. Moreover, also at the State Department's request, Treasury Department tax experts had gone over Jersey Standard's domestic tax records and reported that the value of the Mexican properties declared by the company itself for tax purposes closely matched the appraisals offered by the Interior Department. The State Department had kept both these revelations secret, however, possibly in order not to have to admit that for three years the Department had uncritically accepted the companies' own claims about the value of the expropriated properties.[35]

In any case, the investigators for the mixed commission independently turned up some intriguing items—"obsolete equipment twenty-five years old and badly in need of repair, miles of pipeline corroded almost beyond use." The commission also examined Mexican tax records in respect to the companies, and confirmed the fact that their total investment was much less than the companies had claimed. The commission ultimately valued the properties at just under $24 million.[36]

There were many conclusions that could be drawn from the Mexican oil crisis. One, certainly, concerned the gallantry and political intelligence of Josephus Daniels. Another concerned the ultimate willingness of the State Department to break loose from its pro-business point of view in moments of great crisis. A third involved the ability of State Department officials to learn from their own experiences. Learn they eventually did, because the Department soon took the lead in encouraging United States oil companies in Venezuela to give a larger share to the Venezuelan government in order to obviate a trend toward expropriation.[37]

One further conclusion, however, while not contradicting any of the above, nonetheless puts the whole episode in a rather different light. Taken as a whole, considering all the issues and circumstances, the Mexican oil crisis showed that the State Department went into and came out of the entire affair with little sympathy for Latin American revolutionary nationalism. It was determined to concede only enough so as not to disturb the larger position of American private enterprise and economic influence in the face of that revolutionary nationalism. In other words, the Department acted out, in the broadest sense, the meaning of President Roosevelt's dictum: "Give them a share."

The Mexican oil crisis, however, was not the only episode which revealed the State Department's point of view. By 1939, the Department had shown it was prepared to go even further than protecting United States interests in Latin America or interceding to resolve expropriation disputes. The Department was now ready to aid private organizations in the United States in the acquisition of new property and commercial concessions in Latin America, all in the name of security against the Axis threat. The major case in point was that of the airlines. By early 1939 the State Department had become apprehensive over the extent to which Axis-controlled interests dominated the field of commercial aviation in Latin America, either through direct financial control or through the use of key operating personnel.

The Germans had made particularly serious inroads in the Andean countries, where due to the topographical problems involved in constructing railroads, air transport was of even greater significance than elsewhere in Latin America. They had acquired a strategic network of routes which, in the opinion of many United States policy-makers, directly threatened the security of the Panama Canal. Such firms as Scadta, Lati, Condor, and others were seen by American officials as the advance guard of the Luftwaffe.

The State Department, as Assistant Secretary of State Adolf Berle stated, "initiated a campaign to clear these lines out." One technique was to aid the Latin Americans in training technicians so as to halt Latin American dependence upon German and Italian technical experts. Another

was to encourage Latin American legislation which would
restrict key jobs—such as pilots and management officials—
to Latin American citizens. This particular device was a
curious one in that the United States was actually encouraging Latin American nationalism, which it so generally feared
and distrusted. In this case, however, the Americans felt
that nationalism could be controlled and harnessed to promote United States interests, inasmuch as the Americans
still maintained considerable leverage through their control of aviation gasoline, spare parts, machinery, and other
material items basic to the functioning of the aviation
industry.[38]

The main tactic which made this program relevant to
the aviation industry in the United States was the State Department's effort to establish American-controlled routes in
direct competition with Axis-controlled routes. This had the
double advantage of moving Americans in as Germans and
Italians were moved out.

Sometimes American airlines had direct connections
with Axis firms, and this embarrassed the program somewhat. Pan American Airways, for example, held majority
stock in Colombia's Scadta, through Pan American's affiliate, Pan Air. At first Pan American refused to insist upon
the discharge of German pilots from Scadta, because German pilots could be paid less than United States pilots.[39]
The United States Ambassador to Colombia, Spruille
Braden, described the situation as a "headache." Braden
noted that "Pan-Air had not the remotest idea of what was
happening here and steadfastly refused to take our advice."
By 1940, when Pan American realized that in the long run
the State Department's program would greatly benefit the
position of American aviation firms—and that of Pan American in particular—its officials reversed their position and
gave full cooperation in such details. In January 1941, Coordinator of Inter-American Affairs Nelson Rockefeller
launched an all-out campaign to eliminate remaining "anti-
American" personnel from business firms throughout Latin
America. The last Axis influences were removed by mid-
1942.[40]

4. Balance sheet of the theory

Altogether, the approach which the United States developed toward Latin American affairs between late 1938 and
1941 seemed promising at first glance. It took account of

the needs both of American private enterprise and of Latin American societal growth. It seemed to harmonize those needs with the larger policy interests of the United States and the New Deal. It utilized the energies of a wide range of government agencies and private organizations. And it undercut European rivals, while appearing to give to Latin American allies a considerable share of the policy-making responsibility in inter-American affairs.

In short, the new approach appeared to institutionalize President Roosevelt's stated goal of "giving Latin America a share." If the administration could translate these appearances of harmony into permanent realities, it would establish a truly permanent foundation for the Good Neighbor Policy. The only question was: Could this harmonizing of North American and Latin American interests succeed in the long run? More specifically, what would happen once the cohesive force of the Axis threat had been removed?

III. Skeptics north and south

Melhor practica do que gramatica—literally, better practice than theory—runs an old Brazilian proverb. By the end of the 1930's, the Roosevelt administration had worked out the *gramatica* of its new Latin American policy very well. But there was trouble from the start with the all-important *practica.*

Trouble came from within United States policy-making circles. Acceptance of the principles of government participation and cooperation in support of Latin American development, however realistic the motivation behind such acceptance, did not mean that policy-makers agreed on the mechanisms for implementing these principles. State Department officials and those from the Office of the Coordinator for Inter-American Affairs (OCIAA) did not always concur with each other or among themselves. Leading opposition spokesmen in Congress attacked the policies of both these executive agencies. And policy splits developed between the views of some conservative New Dealers and their more daring or innovative colleagues in other governmental agencies as well.

Trouble came also from leading spokesmen of private industry and finance in the United States. Many who accepted the theory of the approach with great enthusiasm found that the practice took matters entirely too far. They foresaw a situation in which government would hinder rather than expedite the successful functioning of United States private enterprise in Latin America. They saw certain New Deal policies in Latin America as designed to give the Latin Americans far too great a "share." They also saw some of these policies as tending to place the Roosevelt administration itself in competition with, rather than in cooperation with, private American banking and industry in the general struggle for power in Latin America.

Trouble came, finally, from the Latin Americans themselves. Neither the representatives of Latin American governments nor the representatives of private enterprise in Latin America were uniformly enthusiastic or encouraging about the specifics of the United States approach. Some

Latin Americans thought the United States commitment to multilateralism and to economic assistance did not go far enough. Others thought it went too far, but in the wrong direction. They feared "assistance" that would increase Latin American dependency upon the United States, and they feared a "multilateralism" that would establish a façade of shared decision-making power behind which all key decisions would in fact be subject to an American veto. The fears and skepticism of Americans and Latin Americans alike appeared very quickly as the State Department moved to set up its first major multilateral instrument for promoting Latin American economic development—the Inter-American Bank.

1. The Inter-American Bank

In September 1939, when the Panama Conference convened, the State Department was not committed to the establishment of an Inter-American Bank. Multilateralism in such fields as trade promotion was one thing; a multilateral approach to banking was quite another. Department officials felt that the Export-Import Bank, which had been making bilateral trade promotion loans since 1934, was a sufficiently "cooperative" mechanism for present purposes. Besides, the influential New York banking community got along well with the Export-Import Bank, whose president, Warren Lee Pierson, took careful account of their interests in all Latin American transactions. There was no telling how the New York bankers might react to an internationally managed and possibly competitive Inter-American Bank.[1]

The American draft resolution on economic cooperation originally submitted to the Panama Conference accordingly contained a fairly narrow financial program which emphasized cooperative action for stabilizing monetary relationships, foreign exchange management, and balance-of-payments problems. The resolution concentrated on policies designed to increase trade.

At the opening session of the conference, Under Secretary of State Sumner Welles, speaking for the United States delegation, sketched out a carefully restricted schema for financing cooperative programs:

Financial assistance and cooperation may be developed to assist individual countries to tide over short emergency periods and to

develop new fields of production to replace those temporarily
depressed.

I am authorized to state that the United States Government wishes to cooperate with all other American Republics in the efforts of each to develop the resources of its country *along sound economic and non-competitive lines* and when desired to assist them through the services and facilities of its privately owned banking system as well as its Government-owned agencies when the latter have funds available for such purposes.

Welles made no mention of any multilateral long-term development financing agency.[2] The State Department was prepared to go only so far as to establish an inter-American "Financial and Economic Advisory Committee" to consider common wartime problems.

In the conference sessions, however, the Latin Americans took a much broader view. They recognized both the economic restrictiveness and the political danger of relying primarily on the bilateral Eximbank approach. The Mexican delegation took the initiative in proposing the "creation of an inter-American financial institution of a permanent character." In reporting this Mexican proposal to the State Department, Welles remarked: "It will be seen that this proposal goes farther than our own draft but seems to us in accord with ideas discussed at previous conferences and at Washington." Welles asked for advice. The State Department replied with a telegram which set forth clearly the disinclination of both State and Treasury officials to sponsor a full-fledged Inter-American Bank. The telegram read in part:

The . . . suggestion has been carefully considered with the Treasury Department, which feels that the Mexican draft carries implications going beyond those discussed in conversations in Washington. The Treasury feels it is not (repeat not) advisable to spell out the details of what is to be considered by the [proposed Financial and Economic] Advisory Committee because of the danger that it might give rise to expectations which subsequent study might indicate were not realizable; it feels especially that the formal resolutions should not specify the agencies or devices by which the objectives contemplated are to be attained. It would have no objection if you find it desirable to amend the American draft resolution by adding in its first paragraph the following subparagraph:

QUOTE. To instruct the Advisory Committee to prepare in time for consideration at the meeting of representatives of the Treasuries at Guatamala a report embodying suggestions for the most practical and satisfactory ways of promoting greater stability of monetary and commercial relationships among the American Republics. END QUOTE[3]

The Latin Americans were nonetheless adamant in supporting the Mexican initiative. They successfully insisted that the final conference resolution on economic cooperation include a clause authorizing the newly created Inter-American Financial and Economic Advisory Committee (IAFEAC) to "study the necessity of creating an inter-American institution which may render feasible and insure permanent financial cooperation between the treasuries, the central banks, and analogous institutions of the American republics." The resolution set no limits on the types of programs permitted.[4]

The Panama Conference appears to have convinced Washington policy-makers of the inevitability of such a bank. They immediately agreed that the United States had better have a substantial say in setting it up. Governmental officials, led by Assistant Secretary of State Adolf Berle, set quickly to work on a draft convention for the Bank, in cooperation with a subcommittee of the IAFEAC. Late in December 1939, IAFEAC sent to the Latin American governments a questionnaire asking for information relevant to the needs and wishes of the various nations in connection with the Bank. It included questions concerning anticipated needs of the various national economies for commercial notes guaranteed by such a bank, needs for short-term trade promotion credits, needs for long-term industrial and public works loans, and possible uses of the Bank in connection with international "clearing-house" arrangements, currency stabilization, and exchange control.[5] The approach was thus a fairly broad one.

The Bank's planners, however, failed to include in their preliminary sketches one commitment of overriding importance. They omitted any American commitment to provide the Latin Americans with the means of paying back the money which the Bank would lend them. Specifically, they failed to commit the United States to buy more of the new products which Latin Americans would want to produce and sell. This omission brought Latin American skepticism quickly to the fore.

2. Latin American responses

In responding to the subcommittee's questionnaire, many Latin American governments, including those of Colombia, Chile, El Salvador, Guatemala, Haiti, Uruguay, and Venezuela, flatly stated that credit facilities were not the main problem in their inter-American trade. The Bolivian government noted specifically that one of its major needs was for the United States to buy more of Bolivia's products. Venezuela pointed out that its trade problems arose not from lack of credits but from a "similarity of products" between so many of the American republics.

In general, Latin American responses to the questionnaire were neither uniformly enthusiastic nor substantially complete in detail. The Latin Americans wanted to be able to borrow, but their enthusiasm for doing so was dampened by a lack of assurance that they would be able to pay back. Some of the smaller countries presented very specific estimates of capital needs for such planned projects as road and railway construction, industrial development, and public health programs. Cement industries, fishing and forest products industries, and mineral processing were among those projects often mentioned. Among the larger countries, Colombia submitted estimated needs of $4 million for agrarian credits, $6.5 million for railroad construction, and $5.5 million for highway construction. Panama, however, sent in its questionnaire with the somewhat dry response: "This country has no need of long-term investments for rehabilitation of industries since it has none, but, undoubtedly, facilities for obtaining long-term loans would notably increase the establishment of such industries." Only a very few countries could estimate recent capital flight from their banks and industries.[6]

Not all the Latin American responses were merely half-hearted or incomplete. There were also some outright attacks on the entire form of the proposed banking arrangement. The Peruvian delegate to the IAFEAC subcommittee on the Bank, Dr. Pedro Larranaga, submitted a memorandum to the subcommittee even before the questionnaire was sent, challenging the idea that the Bank engage in any commercial lending operations at all. In such an arrangement, he observed, there would probably be twenty borrowers and one lender. Under the circumstances, he noted, the same purpose could be accomplished with much less fanfare by going directly through the American banking system. "Why obscure the meaning of this solution," Dr. Larranaga asked, "which instead of giving the Americas a new independent and neutral credit structure is merely going to increase our indebtedness to the United States?" In a later memo, Dr. Larranaga argued that if the Bank was to be able to rediscount the assets of Latin American central banks, it would have to have some independent assets of its own—with which its planners had not provided it—or it would fall into a "vicious circle of absurdity [where] the central banks would be trying to borrow their own previously contributed money from the new Bank to rediscount their assets," while the new Bank itself would thus become a simple parasite.[7]

Despite the incomplete data, occasionally negative replies, and some outright objections to the entire proposed form of the Bank, the drafters continued to work. By mid-February 1940, a preliminary draft of the Bank convention was ready. It met some of the stated objections; it failed to meet others. The Bank was to have broad lending authority for a wide range of projects. It would be able to make short-term (up to one year), intermediate-term (one to five years), and long-term (over five years) loans in any currency to participating governments and their agencies, provided the governments guaranteed repayment of such loans. The Bank would be able to deal in securities of the various governments as well as in the obligations of their nationals, again if such obligations were guaranteed by the governments. On the other hand, the various governments were given virtual veto powers over dealings of the Bank with their constituent nationals and agencies through the somewhat nebulously defined mechanism of the "timely objection." The capital stock of the Bank was to be subscribed by the member governments, according to a ratio based on the foreign trade of each government in the year 1938. All major operating decisions of the Bank were to be made by a four-fifths majority of the total votes of the shareholders.[8]

It soon became clear that the Latin Americans had at least four fairly common objections to the Bank convention. First, they disliked the rather rigid insistence upon government guarantees for loans to Latin American nationals, a procedure which they considered unduly restrictive. But this actually bothered them the least. They objected more strongly to the proposed voting procedure. Under the four-fifths rule, through an expenditure of $100 million over and above its initial outlay of $50 million for its minimum bloc of votes, the United States could acquire more than 20 per cent of the votes and thereby maintain a veto over all the Bank's

essential operations. The Latin Americans were also upset
over the size and timing of the required payments for their
initial stock subscriptions. Finally, they strenuously objected to the lack of an American commitment to buy the
goods which the loans would help produce. Without this
commitment, they argued, the Bank would merely increase
Latin American indebtedness to the United States. The Bank
would become economically useless and politically counterproductive for the Latin Americans.[9]

By early May, the situation looked bleak. Adolf Berle
seemed quite discouraged. He wrote to Welles asking if the
United States should even bother to go ahead with the
formal signing of the convention on May 10, in view of the
fact that only two other countries, Colombia and Nicaragua,
had so far indicated their approval (Nicaragua still having
stipulated that it could not afford to subscribe its shares immediately). Welles indicated that it was best to go ahead
anyway, hoping that in the interim enough signatures could
be assured to give the project some semblance of reality.[10]
Evidently between May 4 and May 10 considerable behind-
the-scenes negotiating was done, for by the latter date Washington had secured the adherence of eight of the Latin
American governments. Plans for the signing ceremony went
forward, though there was no mention of immediate payments for shares.

Curiously, the formal signing of the convention was not
followed by speedy submission of the needed enabling legislation to the United States Congress, whose ratification was
required before American participation in the Bank could
begin. During the summer and fall of 1940, OCIAA and State
Department desks were full of correspondence and memoranda regarding various financial aid projects for Latin
America, but most of them were about bilateral arrangements involving the Export-Import Bank. There were very
few references to the Inter-American Bank until the OCIAA
executive committee met on September 11. At that meeting,
Assistant Coordinator Rovensky summarized the views of
the OCIAA's Commercial and Financial Division:

We do not believe the Inter-American Bank to be absolutely
necessary.

We have doubts that it will become an outstanding success in
(a) promoting normal commercial relations, and (b) that in itself it can accomplish much in the investment and development
field.

At the same time, Rovensky noted, there was evidence to indicate

that apparently a strong desire exists in Central and South America that a bank of this character be created.

That a negative attitude by the United States at this time may be considered unfriendly.

That sufficient reasons and hopes exist that its activities in the long run may be fruitful.

Rovensky concluded that "in the event that the largest states of South America approve and agree to participate and that the substantial majority of the republics of the Americas subscribe, that the United States [join] in its organization and agree to lend its best cooperation" was a sound idea.[11] The OCIAA was evidently beginning to revive old doubts about the wisdom of this kind of multilateral financial institution.

Despite Rovensky's rather halfhearted support of the Bank, nothing else was heard until November 7, when Emilio Collado, special assistant to Sumner Welles, sent a memo to Welles, Berle, and State Department Political Adviser Laurence Duggan, reporting widespread inquiries from members of IAFEAC, the press, and the Latin American diplomatic corps regarding the fate of the Bank. Collado recommended that the convention be sent to the Senate for approval. Duggan's memo of the next day to Welles and Berle was interesting in its tone and implications. In approving Collado's position, Duggan pointed out that submission of the convention would be good for inter-American relations, even if there was little prospect of immediate Senate action. Berle added in a handwritten comment that Jesse Jones of the RFC "[had] the matter in hand," and was only waiting for the American presidential election.[12]

3. North American responses

This last remark only hinted at the existence of what had already become a very serious *internal* American problem regarding the Inter-American Bank. By the fall of 1940, not only were the New Dealers facing clear signs of Latin American skepticism; they were also finding that powerful forces in the United States were opposed not only to the establishment of the Bank but to the whole New Deal approach to Latin American development. The entire Latin American policy, in fact, was merely one focal point of this

opposition, which came from both public and private officials. At bottom, the domestic opposition rested upon a disagreement with the New Dealers' approach to the whole
question of governmental involvement in the economic
growth of society—both at home and abroad.

Bernard Baruch, while essentially sympathetic to Roosevelt's idea of "giving Latin America a share," caught the
essence of the dilemma. Government, he noted, should have
wide latitude to act strongly and promptly in order to protect and foster the growth of private enterprise. But it
should never be allowed to adopt any policy which might
work to supplant the private sector of either the United
States or any other national economy. "I hope," he wrote to
President Roosevelt in June 1940, "our Latin-American efforts will not have too much government action, but rather
more by individuals. The American exporter and importer
must be brought into this undertaking with our government
and all of its diplomatic, consular, and economic resources
behind them." In a later letter to another friend, Baruch
developed his point even more explicitly. "Even our government may have to take action," he conceded, "in granting
subventions for South American trade against the totalitarian powers." But, Baruch added, there was still a crucial
difference between the way the United States and its statist
and totalitarian rivals operated. "There," he noted, "it is all
the state. Here I want the individuals to do the work and
the government to stand back of them if they need protection and aid. That is the reverse of what is being done in the
totalitarian states."[13]

The crux of the matter was simple: even a sympathetic
critic like Baruch did not entirely trust the Roosevelt administration to act with restraint in respect to the prerogatives
of private enterprise. Baruch feared that the developing
world crisis would lead the administration to become involved in international economic adventures which would
inevitably result in the further aggrandizement of the federal government and the weakening of the international political autonomy and economic position of the private sector.

Republican Senator Arthur H. Vandenberg of Michigan
feared not only the growth of governmental power but the
eclipse of congressional autonomy within the government
under the driving blows of the New Dealers in the Executive
branch. Of Hull's reciprocal trade agreements program,

Vandenberg wrote: "This particular delegation of power represents the greatest single concentration of bureaucratic authority which has occurred under the New Deal."[14] Vandenberg became one of the strongest congressional opponents of the Inter-American Bank.

Senator Robert A. Taft of Ohio, also a Republican opponent of the New Deal, was skeptical about the basic validity of the New Deal's impulse to altruism. Taft opposed the federal government's financing of the Volta Redonda steel project in Brazil. "As far as I can see," Taft wrote, "the loan is simply based on the theory that we would thereby be promoting the general prosperity of Brazil, from which we might or might not benefit. I certainly object very strongly to the argument that because we are spending money for defense, we have to make loans to South American countries, or do any one of the other thousand things which the spenders want to do."[15]

Baruch, Vandenberg, and Taft—each in his own way—were raising fundamental questions about the nature of United States policy. Baruch's concern centered upon the problem of the relationship of government to private enterprise. Vandenberg, fearing a power grab by the administration, was primarily worried about the future of constitutional government in the United States, as reflected in his concern over the issues of separation of powers and checks and balances. Taft addressed himself to the nature and significance of foreign aid. When discussions got down to the specific question of whether or not to establish an Inter-American Bank, all of these considerations loomed large. Events soon gave them a very practical importance.

On May 29, 1940, less than three weeks after the signing of the Bank convention, Under Secretary of State Welles received a letter from a New York law firm acting for the National City Bank of New York, the largest American bank operating in South America. The communication enclosed another note written directly to Secretary of the Treasury Henry Morgenthau by National City vice-president W. Randolph Burgess, who stated bluntly:

There is no reason under the statutes why this [Inter-American] bank may not establish a competing branch across the street from each one of this [National City] bank's South American branches. Its privileged position with respect to taxation, exchange controls, etc., would make it a competitor which might damage the business of this and other commercial banks.

Burgess also noted that the Inter-American Bank could compete with the various national central banks, inasmuch as it was not specifically designed to work through them, and would therefore probably arouse opposition, "except to the extent that they might use the new bank as a dumping ground for bad loans." The Bank, Burgess argued, would also be tied much too closely to politics.[16]

Welles replied on June 11, assuring the National City representatives that the new Bank had clearly been designed to complement rather than compete with existing financial institutions, and that United States participation would be managed by an interdepartmental supervisory team which would "give due consideration to all American interests, including those of the commercial banks." National City's apparent acceptance of this position, expressed in a second letter to Welles dated June 16,[17] evidently did not close the issue, however. The Roosevelt administration found it necessary to send OCIAA officials Joseph Rovensky and Nelson Rockefeller, along with Deputy Federal Loan Administrator Will Clayton, for a series of personal meetings with Burgess and a group of New York bankers during January and February of 1941. Noting the general positive effect which the new Bank, as part of the New Deal's overall Latin American development effort, would have upon expansion of the Latin American economies, Rovensky tried to reassure the New York group that the Inter-American Bank would help create new opportunities for them, too. "The beauty of this thing," he told them, "is that it is good business." Nevertheless, the price of their acquiescence was Washington's agreement to insert into the Bank's charter specific provisions restricting the Bank's short-term lending operations to government-guaranteed loans. This move would eliminate from the Bank's sphere of operations a considerable number of projects, which, though possibly worthwhile and based on sound planning, might not for political or other reasons be blessed with the "legitimizing" benediction of a government guarantee. Project planners would then, of course, be forced to turn to the private commercial banks for help.[18]

Even after this concession, however, the matter was not settled. Early in May 1941, Berle, Collado, Rovensky, and Clayton appeared before a subcommittee of the Senate Foreign Relations Committee to testify in favor of the Bank convention. Berle's testimony made it clear that to some degree the Bank actually would move into areas which the New York private banks might tend to regard as their exclusive preserve. Stressing the international "cooperative" nature of the Inter-American Bank's purpose, Berle noted: "There must now be a means of making capital available to these countries on some basis which is less dangerous than the mere somewhat whimsical operations of overseas financial houses." One great advantage of the new system, Berle noted, was that by raising the general level of confidence in Latin America's economy, it could encourage local Latin American investors to put their capital directly into Latin American projects instead of exporting it to the more secure New York money market. This was clearly a feature which would, in some measure, cut into the New York group's volume of capital transfer in regard to Latin America.

"The object," Berle continued, "would seem to be capital movements which are worked out not merely because some concessionaire wishes to make a profit but following the more careful plans of the various governments involved with a view to the steady development of the country." It required little imagination to see this as a warning that intergovernmental financial planning might begin to replace hit-or-miss profit-taking. Rovensky, who was himself a vice-president of Chase National Bank on leave in government service, offered the more comforting opinion that the Inter-American Bank could be "made an instrumentality for improving the defaulted debt situations of the presently outstanding defaulted debts [sic]." But Will Clayton's expressed hope that in time the Bank might "take over the functions of the Export-Import Bank" must have given little comfort to those private bankers who until then had been able to work so satisfactorily in Latin America with the Eximbank, due to Eximbank president Warren Lee Pierson's well-known solicitude for the interests of private United States creditors in Latin America.[19]

The subcommittee of the Senate Foreign Relations Committee, headed by Senator Claude Pepper of Florida, strongly approved the convention and recommended its passage to the whole Committee on May 14, 1941. "No objections to ratification of this convention have been made," the subcommittee report stated, "and the possible fears of unwarranted competition with commercial banking institutions have been satisfactorily resolved."[20] The New York bankers, however,

were evidently still not satisfied, and the fight continued. At
this point, the balance of power began to shift. Sponsors of
the Bank bill now met with a strong tactical alliance between the bankers and a key senatorial opponent of the bill
—Senator Carter Glass of Virginia, the powerful chairman
of the Senate Banking and Currency Committee. Rather than
permit the Foreign Relations Committee to report the bill
directly onto the Senate floor, Glass insisted that his committee also be given a chance to scrutinize it. He then
initiated a correspondence of his own with both George
Harrison of the New York Federal Reserve Bank and Randolph Burgess of National City.

In his first letter to Harrison, dated May 27, 1941, Glass
solicited Harrison's opinion of the Inter-American Bank
convention, and offered by way of encouragement his own
somewhat farfetched feeling that the Bank might possibly
become a drain on the resources of the whole Federal Reserve System. "It seems to me," Glass wrote, "that it ex-
pands the powers of the Federal Reserve System . . . and the
Export and Import Bank, and of the Reconstruction Finance
Corporation, happily run chiefly by Jesse Jones, who may
die at any time [Jones was then sixty-seven; Glass was
eighty-two], leaving it to do foolish things just as the Federal Reserve Board has done in recent years." In a second
letter to Harrison, dated June 17, Glass objected that the
Inter-American Bank was "to be managed largely by South
American Republics; whereas the Ex-Im Bank is now managed exclusively by American citizens."[21]

Glass and Harrison met to discuss the Bank problem
during the last week of June 1941. The following week, on
July 3, Harrison responded in writing to Glass's request for
an opinion. Though he had at first opposed the Bank, Harrison had for political reasons since reversed himself, and now
suggested that the Bank convention be ratified, subject to
more effective limits on its scope of operations and lending
resources. "Considering the fact," he wrote, "that we are
devoting much of our thought and effort in the preparation
for possible war and in solidifying hemisphere relations, it
would, I believe, be a grave error for this country, now that
it has signed the Convention, to withdraw."[22]

But Glass was not satisfied. On July 11, he wrote to
Burgess, asking the leading concerned private New York
banker for *his* opinion. Burgess responded on July 22 with a

seven-page letter which, though extremely restrained in tone, left little doubt as to how he felt about the Inter-American Bank, even after the State Department's concessions restricting the Bank in the field of short-term commercial transactions. He noted that he had objected immediately to the Bank's becoming a competitor with private commercial banks in Latin America. Even the State Department commitment to restrict the Bank's short-term operations was not a firm one, he added, inasmuch as it would be written into the bylaws of the Bank rather than into the charter itself, and might "later be reversed" by the Bank's board of directors.

Burgess also noted that the Bank "would invade the central banking field but would be itself a government bank." In other words, it would take on not only lending but also general supervisory and regulatory functions in the various national economies, yet would be at the same time subject to the influence of those who made the very government policies which had to be regulated. "Long experience," Burgess stated, "has shown the dangers of political control in central banking."

Burgess found other objections. The charter of the Bank appeared to be beyond revocation for the next twenty years, inasmuch as the charter (which established the initial life of the Bank at that figure) could not be amended except by a four-fifths majority of the Bank's board of directors. "Action now," he stated, "is a twenty-year commitment." Moreover, Burgess noted, the board of directors had extensive authority under the charter to extend their own powers, subject to the limitations of the general "purposes" of the Bank. The United States could probably prevent obnoxious developments on this score through its effective veto power (assuming the United States "would presumably always hold more than 20 per cent of the stock, with corresponding voting power") but there was no direct means by which Congress could prevent changes in the Bank's powers unless it went so far as to instruct the United States representative on the board of directors as to how to vote on key issues. Finally, Burgess stated, the broad question of delegation of powers for twenty years was "more a political than a banking question," and one "to which I assume the Congress will wish to give careful study."[23]

With Burgess' letter in hand, Senator Glass took no

further action on the Inter-American Bank convention. The
issue remained quiescent for the remainder of 1941. Early
in January 1942, a small group in the Senate Foreign Rela-
tions Committee made an attempt to work around Glass.
They tried to have the Bank convention reported out to the
Senate directly through the Foreign Relations Committee
simultaneously with the opening of the second wartime
meeting of the inter-American foreign ministers in Rio de
Janeiro. This timely but obvious gesture failed. Sumner
Welles, for the State Department, then attempted to get
President Roosevelt to intervene. Late in March 1942, the
President agreed to ask Glass to come see him about the
convention, and shortly thereafter Glass announced that he
would ask for an "early" meeting of the Banking and Currency Committee to act upon the Inter-American Bank proposal. But Glass never did hold hearings on the bill, despite
another exchange of correspondence, this time between
Glass and Federal Reserve Board chairman Marriner Eccles,
to whom Glass wrote in June 1942 stating that he was in
essential agreement with Federal Reserve's latest proposed
amendments to the enabling legislation, which were "in all
practical sense precisely the same as the amendments proposed by me." After June 1942, neither the State Department
nor the OCIAA made any serious further efforts to dislodge
the Inter-American Bank bill from Glass's committee, where
it remained in limbo until President Truman finally withdrew the convention from the Senate in 1947.[24]

The stillbirth of the Inter-American Bank illustrated
quite clearly how skepticism from both sides—United States
and Latin American—worked to undermine a key aspect of
the New Deal's approach to Latin American development.
It is interesting to speculate upon how the fight over the
Bank might have turned out had the proposed charter been
more acceptable to the Latin Americans. Glass might have
had less excuse to bottle up the enabling legislation; but the
opposition of the New York bankers might have been even
stronger, considering the fear expressed by Burgess that,
once set up, the Bank would almost automatically draw
Latin American customers away from the commercial banks
because of its operational privileges and advantages. In any
event, what did happen was that despite their efforts to
placate everybody, State Department officials and other New
Dealers who worked out the shape of the Inter-American

Bank proposal wound up pleasing nobody. The bill finally
died in committee.[25]

4. *The remainder of the multilateral program*

If the Inter-American Bank was not to function as the
key financial instrument of the new multilateral approach,
the United States would be forced to retreat to the essentially bilateral mechanism of the Export-Import Bank. Both
the Americans and the Latin Americans knew that project
planners would now have to rely for their main financial
support upon a United States government agency that was
demonstrably oriented more toward promotion of United
States exports than toward Latin American development
financing. Perhaps even more serious from a political point
of view were the indications that such a retreat may have
been under consideration even before the Senate hearings
on the Inter-American Bank. Congress had agreed to raise
the capitalization of the Eximbank from $200 million to
$700 million during the summer of 1940. One unsigned memo
written in an OCIAA office in August 1940 pointed out that
the timing of the Eximbank capital increase coincided with
the holding of the emergency wartime Havana Conference,
in order to give the United States delegation increased political leverage vis-à-vis the individual loan applicants it would
meet there.[26]

Nonetheless, the failure of the multilateral banking plan
did not in itself signal the failure of the whole multilateral
approach. There was still the second major arm of the program, the Inter-American Development Commission (IADC).
The Commission was organized and underway fairly quickly,
and by the end of 1941 it had both a complete hemispheric
roster of partcipants and a skeletal collection of specific
projects in the works.

The IADC, like the Inter-American Bank, had been
founded by the Inter-American Financial and Economic
Advisory Committee after the Panama Conference of September 1939. It had been organized largely by a small group
of Latin Americans comprising Subcommittee II of the
IAFEAC; they worked together with OCIAA officials and
representatives of the United States Department of Commerce. The idea behind the IADC was intriguing from the
point of view of hemispheric economic cooperation. The
original IAFEAC resolution authorizing the creation of the

IADC provided for a permanent commission of five members to promote "formation and financing, with mixed United States and Latin-American capital, of such enterprises as will undertake the development of new lines of Latin-American production for which a new or complementary market can be found in the United States or in other Republics of the Western Hemisphere." In other words, on one hand the Commission was to stimulate a certain diversification of Latin American production in the expectation that the Latin Americans would find ready markets in the hemisphere; on the other, such diversification was to be limited to products not competitive with existing lines of production in already established Western Hemisphere markets.[27]

This form of multilateralism could be viewed in a number of ways. On the surface it looked as if the IADC might do what the Inter-American Bank did not do, namely, provide assurance of United States markets for Latin American products. But on what terms? If the notion of noncompetitiveness were strictly adhered to, it might also act to restrain the Latin Americans from certain important developmental activities in areas where they would perforce have to compete with, and attempt to undercut, established United States sellers in their own Latin American markets. At the same time, there was no guarantee that the United States would absorb more of their traditional commodity exports.

This raised complicated questions. The original IAFEAC resolution did refer to the development not only of mineral resources and agricultural products but also of industrial plants. Yet the preliminary report prepared by Carlos Dávila of Chile, with the help of United States Commerce Department assistants, indicated that the development of Latin American industrial exports was by no means necessarily built into the scheme. On the contrary, the Dávila report stressed that "the development of Latin America's capacity for *purchasing more United States manufactures* depends chiefly upon the capacity of the United States for absorbing more Latin American imports [of unspecified type]."[28]

Indeed, the specific projects first undertaken by the IADC were all of a consumer-goods rather than a producer-goods variety, underlining the point that the IADC was not initially prepared to concentrate upon the development of heavy industry export products even in the largest and po-

tentially most industrially powerful Latin American countries.[29] The purpose of IADC was certainly not to cut into
the United States' "share" of exports to Latin America. In
practice, this meant machinery and heavy industry exports
in particular.

Even the Volta Redonda steel project in Brazil, which
ultimately went forward with United States aid after private
American steel companies refused to help finance it, was
carefully designed to promote rather than hinder American
exports. OCIAA economist Simon Hanson pointed out that
Volta Redonda would mean a "shift in the type" of American
steel exports to Brazil, but not necessarily a loss in total
volume or value. Brazil would have to buy plant equipment
in the United States. Once set up, the plant would produce
"semi-manufactured products and the simpler manufactured products." This, in turn, would lead to "increased
undertaking of projects hitherto considered impossible and
[would] require import of more complex materials," plus
requiring a "higher coefficient of technical skill." This, Hanson noted, "is where we come in."[30] Volta Redonda, though
not an IADC project, was considerably more daring than
any IADC project ever was. If export markets for United
States goods were safe under the Volta Redonda scheme,
they would certainly be safe under the less ambitious IADC
programs.

The IADC schema, however, contained even further
safeguards against Latin America's acquiring an undue
"share" of control over her own economic growth. Viewed
in conjunction with the State Department's traditional aver-
sion to high tariff barriers, the schema provided a dual
obstacle to the development of dangerously competitive
products in Latin America, inasmuch as a minimal tariff-
protected breathing space was almost a *sine qua non* for the
initiation of the more ambitious capital-consuming and
initially high-overhead enterprises. As Harry Dexter White
wrote to Vice-President Wallace: "It is hard to see how any
of the Latin-American countries . . . could have any significant expansion of most industries unless they pursue a
policy of protection for those industries."[31] But under the
State Department's definition of economic "cooperation,"
low tariffs were essential. And with OCIAA officials Rockefeller, McClintock, and William Machold serving as chairman, executive secretary, and projects director, respectively,

of IADC, it was clear that IADC would not undertake to establish any Latin American enterprise that required tariff protection in excess of State Department–approved limits.

Despite these problems of conception and execution, the establishment of the IADC was seen in Latin America as a positive step. The two members of the parent commission in Washington who toured Central and South America in 1941 in order to help organize the twenty Latin American national subcommissions of IADC were enthusiastically received. In most countries, men of considerable commercial, financial, and industrial prominence eagerly came forth to participate in the various planning programs. In Argentina, the national subcommission included the president of the Central Bank, the president of the Argentine Rural Society, and the president of the Industrial Union. In Peru it was headed by an ex-Minister of Finance. In Colombia, the membership of the local subcommission was identical to the membership of the board of the Instituto de Fomento Industrial de Bogotá (Industrial Development Institute of Bogotá).[32]

Yet without the aid of a complementary, truly multilateral financial agency, the IADC was forced to take a piecemeal approach from the start. This not only handicapped planning efforts on a hemispheric scale but also put the IADC at the mercy of existing financial institutions, particularly the United States Export-Import Bank and American private investors. The significance of this situation came out very clearly as soon as the IADC began trying to find financial support for specific projects.

One of the first IADC-sponsored projects was a pilot plant in Brazil for the processing of manioca starch. It was supposed to be a cooperative, run by the Brazilian government to assure access for all Brazilian producers so that they might learn its methods. The processed starch was to be sold in the United States. At first plans went smoothly. The Brazilian Ministry of Agriculture offered its cooperation; the São Paulo Federation of Mandioca Cooperatives agreed to build the plant, using mainly Brazilian capital and Brazilian labor, with a proviso that the necessary machinery be imported duty-free.[33] But when it came to negotiating with the Export-Import Bank for even a fairly small ($150,000) loan to provide foreign exchange for the import of the machinery, the Bank balked, insisting that the loan be guaranteed by the Bank of Brazil and made to the Brazilian government or an agency thereof (which the São Paulo Federation was not). The Brazilian Ministry of Agriculture replied that considering the terms of loan and sale, it would perhaps be more advantageous for Brazil to buy German rather than American machinery.[34]

In the end, after the negotiations had become stalemated, the IADC dropped the project in favor of simply sending United States technical advisers to Brazil. By that time, IADC officials noted, there was already more good-quality tapioca starch available for shipment in Brazil than there was shipping space available to transport it to the United States, due to wartime shortages. In the meantime, no arrangements had been made regarding financing of the machinery purchases.[35]

By January 1941, some OCIAA personnel who had been working closely with the IADC were casting about for some large-scale alternative to the Export-Import Bank as chief creditor for developmental enterprises. OCIAA economist Simon Hanson noted in particular the negative political approach which the Eximbank seemed to be taking toward such projects:

The prospective creditor now goes at it in somewhat the following fashion—this is crude but not wholly inexact—
1. Can we get away with it politically if we refuse to lend?
2. Can we get away with less than they ask if we must lend?
3. Had we not better offer a loan of less than we are prepared to make, to leave something for the next time they come knocking at our door?

"Are we today prepared," Hanson asked, "to take the initiative in developmental activity, in selecting test countries or a test country for a broad developmental program, in indicating to that country that we are prepared to go ahead with financial cooperation on a long-term developmental program, possibly involving nine figures instead of seven?" The Export-Import Bank, Hanson noted in a later memo, had, apart from its disinclination to think in terms of large sums, also rejected many Latin American loan applications because the loans would not be government-guaranteed, though in the opinion of the OCIAA Commercial and Financial Division the proposals were sufficiently sound. From the Latin American point of view, the type of loan which the Eximbank was currently making was for activities so irrelevant to Latin America's immediate needs that as of June

1941 only $10 million of the $200 million allocated for Latin {9

American credits by the Bank had actually been drawn on
by the Latin Americans. Clearly a change in approach was
needed.[36]

The OCIAA therefore began experimenting in June 1941
with the idea of an Inter-American Development *Corporation* to act as a financial agent working with the IADC,
though independent of it. A draft bill to charter the Corporation as a United States corporation under federal law was
drawn up in the OCIAA Commercial and Financial Division.
The draft charter vested half the voting power of the six-man
board of directors in United States representatives, and provided for subscription of half the capital stock by the United
States government. It also gave the Corporation the power
to purchase bonds, stocks, and other securities of Latin
American corporations, either directly or through other
agencies or lending institutions. Finally, the draft charter
granted the Corporation authority to "acquire, own, hold,
use, or dispose of such real and personal property, as may be
necessary or convenient for transaction of its business."[37]

The dangers inherent in such a plan were seen immediately by many OCIAA staff members. A departmental memo
pointed out that the United States government or an agency
controlled by it could not possibly, for political reasons, go
into the development of such heavy-risk and high-profit resources as oil or other minerals. "The cry that would arise
in Latin America," the memo stated, "if the United States
Government hit oil in a country would make the current cry
against exploitation by United States companies seem a
friendly baby's wail." Then, too, such a corporation would
be politically barred from going into such projects as transportation and public works; such operations could not
"hope to thrive under the dangerous propagandistic cry of
imperialism which must inevitably attach to a foreign government's ownership of utilities." Finally, for the same
reasons, the corporation obviously could not become a large
landholder.[38]

The Commercial and Financial Division therefore finally
decided to recommend against establishment of such a corporation. It requested instead that existing legislation and
policies be modified so as to permit financing of development projects without prior insistence on government guarantees. This was the prime stumbling block upon which

Export-Import Bank financing had faltered, giving rise to the idea of the proposed Corporation in the first place. In any case, Division officials noted, even if it were ultimately decided that some kind of corporation of this type could be useful, no such action could be considered "until the Inter-American Bank has been disposed of in Congress."[39]

5. *Prewar balance sheet*

By the summer of 1941, the dilemma of development financing was clear. The New Dealers' announced intention —the skepticism of the New York bankers notwithstanding—was to use government aid to strengthen the growth of private enterprise in Latin America's developing economy. But while many private investors in the United States were reluctant to move into new areas of economic activity in Latin America, particularly into those activities such as transportation and electric power development which might require large amounts of long-term capital at low interest rates, they were equally disinclined to have the federal government, which many of them strongly distrusted, move in instead and thereby set itself up as a willing competitor to private American capital in Latin America. Leading administration officials, for their own part, were still reluctant to insist too strongly that United States assistance programs in Latin America be generally predicated upon prior settlement of outstanding Latin American debts to American investors; for this reason they were unable to give the private investors much reason to expect that new private investments in Latin America would be significantly more secure than many of the older ones.[40] And both government officials and private investors continued to fear the spread of the Latin American nationalization impulse—the "Mexican stunt," as Bernard Baruch had called it—to wider areas of economic activity. There was, finally, no easy way for the federal government itself to pour large sums of money into Latin American economic development without jeopardizing public funds in a "giveaway" program unsatisfactory both to many members of the Congress and to certain policy-makers within the Executive branch, or else having to insist upon such a strict measure of control over the funds as to make the programs unpalatable to the Latin Americans.

Last, but certainly not least, there was the problem of dealing with the many government officials—congressmen,

senators, Export-Import Bank officers, and even some State
Department and OCIAA personnel—who agreed with the
private bankers in preferring governmental inaction to the
initiation of policies which would make the United States
government a competitor of private American capital in
Latin America. Paradoxically, some OCIAA staff economists
opposed the Export-Import Bank's insistence upon government guarantees for loans on the grounds that such demands tended to "discourage healthy private investment
and to canalize industry and trade permanently into govern-
ment-dominated enterprises" in Latin America. Such a policy might tend to foster in the long run a greater Latin
American tendency toward state capitalism, or, possibly,
state socialism. For this reason, most OCIAA planners concerned with this problem, including Assistant Coordinator
Joseph Rovensky, favored having the Export-Import Bank
make unguaranteed loans.[41] Beyond this principle, however,
there was still considerable disagreement within the OCIAA
as to how far the United States should go even in the matter
of helping the Latin Americans work out plans for development programs, much less helping finance them.[42]

Publicly, the Roosevelt administration continued to adhere to the optimistic rhetoric of inter-American cooperation. On June 24, 1941, at the fourth Conference on Canadian-
American Affairs in Kingston, Ontario, Assistant Secretary
of State Adolf Berle explained the radically new nature of
the United States' approach to Latin American economic
development. Nineteenth-century economic imperialism, he
stated, was "as dead as the brontosaur, for the good and
sufficient reason that it no longer meets modern conditions."
The idea of "capital export" as a philosophy was equally
outmoded:

Today, when an inter-American development scheme is proposed,
"capital" is really the last thing we think about. There are often
endless problems as to whether the scheme is a good one; whether
there is real need for it; whether it can be done effectively; and
what real need there is for the material.

Once these problems were solved, Berle continued, the question of getting capital reduced itself to one of two methods.
Application could be made either to private bankers, or, if
they were not interested ("and of recent years," Berle remarked, "private capital has not been interested in exporting itself in the old sense"), to some governmental institu-

tion. "In the case of my own country," he stated, "it is either the Reconstruction Finance Corporation or the Export-Import Bank." Berle pointedly refrained from mentioning the Inter-American Bank. "Both of these concerns," he went on, "are vividly interested in whether the development is a good thing in itself. Neither of them feels under any pressure to export capital for fear that a profit might escape them."

In other words [Berle continued] we have shifted our entire point of view. Instead of being anxious to find a place where a group of people who have privately saved money can secure a private stream of profits, we are anxious rather to find opportunities for sound development which may add to the general safety, security, and well-being of the Western Hemisphere. The Marxian pressure to export capital simply does not exist.

Behind this revolutionary change in governmental outlook, Berle explained, was the fact that as economic management had become a governmental concern—indeed, "the chief concern of every state in the world"—governments had come to see economic interests in foreign relations as demanding consideration on their own merits rather than on "old conceptions." It permitted governments, in Berle's own words, "to grapple at long last with social realities." The resulting re-examination had led in the United States to "certain very definite conclusions as to the true economic interests of the United States in the American Hemisphere."

First, we are both morally and economically better off as the American nations strengthen their economic position. Any rise in their standard of living we consider a direct benefit to our economy and to our hemispheric security. Second, the steady and continued development of the other American countries is in the economic interest of the United States as well as of those countries.

Third, in the many areas in which private business initiative obviously offers a better method of fostering development and progress, the Government of the United States has encouraged a partnership of interests between its citizens interested in such development and citizens of the country in which the enterprise is to be located, so that there shall be mutuality of position. . . .

It will thus appear that the economic hemisphere is slowly emerging.

Berle summed up the meaning of the new view in terms of hemispheric economic policies:

Carried to its logical conclusions, all this must require a higher degree of economic planning and, at the same time, a higher degree of open trade between the American nations. We can no longer look at a hemisphere chopped up into economic segments, each of which endeavors to manipulate its interests against the others. In the combination of the new conceptions with the new mechanisms we have already gone a long way towards establishing the foundation of what will be the cooperative international economics of the future.

It is no accident, in my judgment, that this has occurred in the New World. Our great contribution has been the erection of an American system within which different nations and different race groups have found it possible to live without hatred, at peace, and in a smooth working relationship. We are now on the way towards making a second and equally significant contribution: the creation of a system in which economic interests of the various nations are found to be not in conflict, but in cooperation.[43]

On the surface, the "new approach" looked quite promising. Speaking for the United States government, Berle was enunciating clearly and unequivocally a policy of wholehearted and energetic economic cooperation in the Western Hemisphere. But, beneath the surface, what was left of this policy in June 1941? One could talk of cooperative multilateral action; but the Inter-American Bank, chief multilateral financial instrument of the new program, was virtually dead already, thanks to a lethal dose of combined Latin American and United States skepticism. One could talk about government moving into economic development activities on a socially oriented, cooperative basis; but with the Inter-American Development Commission restricted to promoting projects "not competitive" with existing powerful American lines of production, and with the Export-Import Bank the only available financial instrument (the RFC being overwhelmingly preoccupied with domestic financing in the United States), the new policy could not be genuinely multilateral on any serious level. Given the restrictions placed upon the IADC, and given the Eximbank's approach to development financing, particularly its concern for the interests of private American bankers, an American policy based on these two instruments might well turn out to be only a newer and somewhat more subtle effort by the United States to control Latin America's economic and social development by unilateral action beneath a façade of multilateral cooperation.

As he spoke, in fact, Berle's buoyantly optimistic rhetoric was already anachronistic. Skepticism of New Deal intentions was rife. Major programs were totally quiescent or badly stalled. Within another six months, the military entry of the United States into the Second World War would deal still another heavy blow to the new "cooperative" approach by forcing both Americans and Latin Americans to adapt themselves to the exigencies of a war economy. But in June 1941 the Roosevelt administration could not yet blame the failure of its "cooperative" Latin American program on the war. The new program, predicated upon the President's formula of "giving Latin America a share," was already seriously under fire from many agencies, organizations, persons, and governments invited to participate in it.

IV. The impact of war

The paradox of inter-American relations during the Second World War is rarely appreciated even today. The rhetoric of wartime "hemispheric alliance" has obscured the effects of the war upon the inter-American situation. What really happened between 1941 and 1945 was that while the "multilateral" approach of the New Dealers was finally demolished, the war did more than anything else to help the United States maintain and even strengthen its traditional position of influence over the nature and direction of Latin American economic development. Had the war not intervened, both Latin American and American skepticism toward the New Deal approach might have become even more widespread within a short time. But just as the war bailed out the faltering New Deal at home, it bailed out the faltering New Dealers in Latin America.

By the summer of 1941, the Inter-American Bank, financial agent of the new multilateralism, was already a major victim of inter-American skepticism. The Inter-American Development Commission had gone ahead with a number of small development projects and had begun to plan for others. But the transition from a peace economy to a war economy in the United States slowly undercut even these relatively modest activities. The undercutting process began several months before December 1941.

1. Development and defense

On January 22, 1941, Coordinator of Inter-American Affairs Nelson Rockefeller wrote to Secretary of Commerce Jesse Jones, recommending that the Export-Import Bank, in considering loans to Latin America, ask each borrower to "submit an estimate of the volume of various classes of goods (textiles, machinery, vehicles, iron and steel, etc.) that will be required by the country in 1941." The purpose of the request was to help the war priorities board with estimated Latin American requirements in the face of the growing demands of the United States' own incipient transition to a war economy.[1] On May 10, the projects director of the Inter-American Development Commission sent a memorandum to

OCIAA official Joseph Rovensky pointing out that the defense needs of the hemisphere were already coming into conflict with development needs of Latin America. "In some cases," the memo read, "it must be expected that emergency action will not tie in, and may even conflict, with long-term planning."[2]

On June 4, Rockefeller sent to Under Secretary of State Welles the drafts of two circular letters to be sent to the various IADC country commissions concerning development programs. One letter requested suggestions for individual projects, promising IADC help in obtaining financing and technical aid. The other asked the commissions for their essential economic requirements in light of the wartime emergency, and asked that development projects be chosen that would require "only such materials as may fall into the 'essential' category, as the defense program of the United States for the defense of the Americas requires a very large part of the production capacity of the United States." The letter also asked that projects be chosen involving materials "which might require a minimum of shipping space." Welles approved these drafts on June 6, and they were sent.[3]

The emphasis was shifting. As late as March 1941, an OCIAA memo stated: "Initiation of development programs directed at mass consumption IS DISTINCTLY IN THE IMMEDIATE ECONOMIC DEFENSE PICTURE. They can be a steadying factor for uncertain republics to the extent they can be entered into at once. They are a rallying propaganda base." Even in August 1941, Rockefeller was still telling Vice-President Wallace that "economic defense of the Hemisphere requires concrete evidence *now* that this nation is irrevocably committed to a long range, continuing program of Hemisphere economic development and cooperation. Long-range commitments are the best form of emergency economic defense in the Hemisphere." To support this view, Rockefeller cited an OCIAA public opinion survey taken in Brazil, where it appeared that many people were asking if the Good Neighbor Policy would outlast the Nazi threat.[4]

Nonetheless, the June IADC memos indicated that what little development finance the United States was sponsoring would be restricted even further, to include only activities directly related to the war effort. Before the war economy era, the Latin Americans had at least some indication that they could look for help in developing processing and con-

struction industries; once the war economy took hold, they
were told they would have to concentrate primarily upon
extractive industries, particularly those involving materials
regarded as strategic and critical for the United States' war
effort.[5]

The reason for all this was simple enough. The Americans believed that with their increasing involvement in the
European war, they could no longer afford the luxury of
helping Latin American economic development efforts, or
even, in some cases, tolerating such efforts if they hampered
the United States' war economy. Because the American war
machine would be heavily dependent upon Latin America for
a number of critical and strategic raw materials, Latin America's economic activity would have to be redirected toward
fulfillment of the war needs of the United States, "cooperative multilateralism" notwithstanding. An IADC bulletin of
December 1, 1941—released a week *before* Pearl Harbor—
quoted War Production Board director Donald Nelson as
saying: "It is hardly an exaggeration to say that from now
on, this country is going to be just one thing: a gigantic,
one-purpose factory for the production of armaments.
Everything else will be secondary to that." The IADC bulletin commented, with calculated understatement: "So
much for the fact. The result may not be as serious in your
[Latin American] country as in the United States, but it
will be impossible for you to insulate your economy entirely." The bulletin recommended to the Latin Americans a
four-point program of "conservation, simplification, substitution, and salvage."[6]

In reality, Latin America's economy could not be insulated at all. This became apparent even with such problems as finding shipping space for the normal prewar flow
of American exports to Latin America. Shipping facilities
could be found for transporting strategic metals such as
manganese and iron ores from Brazil to the United States,
but the means to send United States machinery to South
America were distinctly at a premium. By late 1941, return
voyages from the United States to Latin America were
often routed through war zone areas, so that cargos consisted of goods bound for the war zones rather than for
Latin America.[7]

The exigencies of the war situation began to cause a
highly intensified reappearance of the old pre–New Deal

pattern under which Latin America supplied raw materials
for manufacture in the United States while remaining
largely dependent upon American industrial supplies. Ironically, while this relationship had proved unacceptable in
peacetime, the war gave the Roosevelt administration an
unassailable justification for re-establishing it.

OCIAA, as a leading agent of United States policy toward
Latin America, sensibly attempted to make a virtue of
necessity by describing the wartime policy shift in the most
positive terms possible. A memorandum by the executive director of OCIAA, dated January 7, 1942, noted that as a result
of United States entry into the war, OCIAA had acquired
"additional objectives" which included the maintenance, so
far as possible, of the economic stability of the other American republics, and the increase of production of strategic
and critical materials needed in the common defense effort.
To these was added the objective of formulating plans for
large-scale development projects for the *postwar* period.[8]

The new situation meant in practice that not only would
most long-range projects have to wait for the end of the
war, but certain IADC projects already underway would
have to be restricted or even discontinued. Indeed, one of
the first casualties was one of IADC's more ambitious
schemes, the promising Merchandising Advisory Service
project. This plan was designed to increase sales in the
United States of Latin American retail and consumer goods
in order both to stimulate diversity in Latin American production and to provide Latin America with needed foreign
exchange resources. The Service, which had been set up in
New York City in February 1941, had to be discontinued in
August 1942 when the "need for giving war materials priorities for cargo space between Latin America and the United
States ports and other wartime restrictions and controls
made it advisable to suspend efforts to increase the volume
of inter-American trade in non-essential commodities."

Thus the Service ended despite the discovery by the
Projects Division of the IADC that there was "an unlimited
potential demand in the United States for many new non-
competitive lines of commodities from Latin America." Indeed, as a summary report from Nelson Rockefeller to Sumner Welles in March 1942 stated, even between the time of
the organization of the first ten country commissions of the
IADC, in May 1941, and the organization of the last ten, in

December of that year, the increasing American involvement in the Allied war effort in Europe demanded a change
in "the focus of the work of the IADC from matters of primarily long-term nature to those relating to the dislocation
of economic conditions caused by war."[9]

It was not the case that United States officials wished to
curtail or work at cross-purposes with Latin American development plans. On the contrary, as late as August 1941,
OCIAA officials were trying to work up a huge cooperative
development project to take in the whole Amazon valley of
Brazil. Economist Simon Hanson considered it a "major
planning project . . . sufficiently big and isolated from the
current war effort to permit a group of technicians to spend
full time with it."

Get together a hell of a big party [Hanson advised the OCIAA
staff] or even organize a corporation jointly with Brazil immediately. In other words, can we not break the whole jam on developmental legislation, on development corporations, on planning
techniques, on technical cooperation, on IADC, etc. by taking this
Amazon job as a real operating job and giving it the works?[10]

But nothing could really be isolated from the war effort.
Not only did this Amazon project come to naught, but once
the United States got into the shooting war Washington
wound up vetoing literally dozens of other projects on the
grounds that the United States could not spare either the
required material or the shipping space.

Virtually every IADC quarterly report from 1942 on
contained numerous references to project difficulties in
the various countries. The IADC report for the fourth
quarter of 1942 reminded the Latin Americans of the "necessity of using this period of *enforced developmental inactivity*
to encourage the making of such studies and surveys and
the formulations of such plans for industrial development
as will best safeguard and expand the economic and industrial life of the American nations in the probably troubled
years that will follow the war" (emphasis added).[11]

Some projects never got as far as the drawing board. In
May 1942, a Carnegie Institute technician wrote to State Department Adviser Laurence Duggan proposing a hydroelectric power project for the Paraná River area of Paraguay
and northern Argentina. Duggan replied that while the idea
had promise for the future, the wartime scarcities of hydroelectric equipment made it inadvisable to discuss the matter

at that time. Similarly, a project for the construction of a zinc smelter in Argentina, the products of which, though of relatively small quantity, would be partially used in connection with the war effort, was turned down on the grounds that the planning alone would take six months and the construction another eighteen months.[12]

In response to an inquiry by the Reynolds Metal Company regarding the possibility of building a large aluminum plant in Brazil, the OCIAA replied that "unless WPB [the War Production Board] decides they have to have more aluminum and that the best place to get it is Brazil, it likely is out for the duration." This decision was made despite the fact that the Board of Economic Warfare's (BEW) Industrial Mission to Brazil, headed by engineer Morris L. Cooke, had specifically recommended aluminum as the key light industrial metal in an integrated long-term development scheme for Brazil.[13]

Not all Latin American requests were rejected for military or economic reasons. In July 1942, an OCIAA Financial Division official wrote to BEW emphasizing the need for extreme care in considering export licenses for shipments to Argentina. "Due to the political situation and the fact that the Argentine has not severed relations with the Axis powers," he noted, "there are indications that BEW has rejected certain applications more from a political angle than an economic angle." He warned that there were a number of firms in Argentina of essentially friendly disposition, including some connected with parent American companies such as Westinghouse, International General Electric, Armco International, Lone Star Cement, and IT&T. These were in danger of being forced out of business by BEW's almost blanket anti-Argentine policy. The Axis powers, moreover, would be pleased to see such firms fail. "While I think we should bring pressure in certain instances by rejecting export applications," this OCIAA staff member concluded, "I strongly feel that we should try to supply the people on our side who control industries."[14]

By the same token, certain applications were *accepted* more for political than for economic reasons. At the April 2, 1942, meeting of BEW's Inter-agency Foreign Research Committee, a Navy Department spokesman announced that the Brazilian Volta Redonda steel project would not be able to count on receiving any turbo-generators (a critical item in steel plant operations) because all turbo-blowers sched-

uled for production in the United States that year had already been assigned for domestic use in plant expansion. At
the April 7 meeting of the committee, after considerable
inter-agency negotiation, a War Production Board spokesman announced that because of State Department concern
over the strong political implications of the Volta Redonda
project, a method had been found to include turbo-generators in the Brazilian export shipments without disturbing
domestic production schedules. The Army-Navy Munitions
Board had agreed to give the project A-1-A priority, a rating
given rarely except to full-scale certified war projects.[15] So
the Volta Redonda project moved ahead.

On balance, however, the vast majority of development
projects received unfavorable treatment at the hands of the
United States government, which simply felt indisposed to
risk misallocating resources that might be needed in the
war effort. Shortly after the Rio Conference of January 1942,
called to give the Foreign Ministers of the American republics a chance to discuss common wartime policies and problems, an OCIAA memo warned that the war situation could
be expected to produce outright negative effects in certain
economic fields in Latin America:

It may dictate the production of raw materials in a manner opposed by economic and technical considerations. It may dictate
health and sanitary programs in strategic areas regardless of
long-time usefulness or local pressures. It may dictate communications of fact and idea without consideration of balance in a
cultural pattern. It will subordinate what can be deferred to what
must be done without delay . . . the consequences will be un-
balance, excess capacity, distortion, all of which must be understood and accepted as deviations from policy—deviations caused
by the necessity of winning the war to preserve the policy.[16]

Not only development, but even principles of sound economy
and particularly of multilateral decision-making would face
rough going in the war era.

There were two sides to this coin. A Commerce Department memo of October 1940 summed up the situation:

(1) Extension of the war would leave Latin America dependent on Great Britain and the United States.
(2) Prompt and comprehensive aid on the part of the United
States would be necessary to prevent social and political disturbances.[17]

By 1941, with the British increasingly unable to lend economic aid to Latin America, the United States became virtually Latin America's sole source of assistance in the transi-

tional period. In the short run, this placed an added burden on the United States economy. In the long run, it increased United States power in the hemisphere.

2. *Obligations and opportunities*

The immediate task of the United States was simple enough. It had to cushion the shock of economic dislocation that would occur in Latin America as a result of the extension of the war economy to the Western Hemisphere. An economically unstable Latin America was potentially a politically unstable Latin America, which was in turn a distinct defensive liability. At the Panama Conference of September 1939, delegates from the American republics had begun to think about ways of insulating the hemisphere from the economic effects of the European war. Between the Panama Conference and the Havana Conference of July 1940, the State Department had set about designing a large-scale purchasing system to handle Latin American agricultural exports and take up the slack in Latin American export earnings lost due to the closing of the European markets.

The program enjoyed the enthusiastic support of a number of leading United States exporting and shipping firms. Obviously, any program that increased Latin American foreign exchange holdings, especially dollars, might reasonably be expected to stimulate Latin American purchases of United States goods.[18] One American trading company wrote to the State Department saying that it had "been literally flooded with inquiries for merchandise that has heretofore come from Europe," and that only the lack of Latin American credit facilities had kept it from doubling or tripling its recent sales. "We fully realize," the firm noted, "that if we are to hold this business after the war is over, we can only do so by the active help of our Government." It asked vigorous governmental action to extend credits to Latin America through the Export-Import Bank "so that American exporters will have the opportunity to accept all the business they are able to develop."[19]

National Foreign Trade Council president Eugene Thomas advocated the use of United States government loans to Latin America to offset the loss of Latin American earnings from reduced exports. Without such aid, Thomas warned, Latin America might be reduced to "depression and despair [which] are the forerunners of revolution, inspired

by Fifth Column activities, and resultant political subordina-
tion to countries which offer to take the goods which will
otherwise deteriorate or be destroyed." On the other hand,
he noted, a wise American policy could "assure the continued availability to the world's markets of essential raw
materials from non-American as well as American sources,
and permit the United States to exert and increase its influence as the principal gold-holding and creditor nation; all of
which would be in the interest of its own living standards
and a means towards assisting in the betterment of the
standards of other peoples."[20]

Thus the emergency situation had both its dangers and
its opportunities for the United States. Defense and ambition indicated that the proper course for the United States
was to ward off German influence in Latin America by tying
the Latin American economies as closely as possible to its
own. Moreover, government and private enterprise in the
United States could work quite harmoniously toward this
end without creating a threat to private enterprise, such as
some private spokesmen had feared in the case of the prewar development programs. "No implication need arise of
governmental regimentation of foreign trade," stated
Eugene Thomas, ". . . if American private corporations, and
the enlistment of experienced expert American talent, will
insure against any encroachment upon our system of free
enterprise in foreign trade."[21] The war situation might actually foster cooperation between public and private officials in the American struggle for supervision and control
of Latin America's economy.

By late 1940, this possibility was becoming evident not
only to Americans but to Latin Americans as well. The State
Department began working on a proposal for a full-scale
inter-American commodity cartel, which would act as a
clearing-house for the purchase and distribution of surpluses. This time the Latin Americans themselves balked,
fearing an arrangement which might leave them permanently restricted and handicapped after normal trade relations had been restored. The Chilean newspaper *La Hora* of
Santiago warned against "excessive cooperation with the
United States" leading to reliance upon "the benevolence
of the financiers of . . . Wall Street." The Brazilian *A Noticia*
of Rio de Janeiro noted that such a plan would "tie Brazil's
exports of raw materials to those of the United States," pre-

venting Brazil from disposing of its own export surpluses in exchange for European manufactured goods that would be just as useful to Brazil as free foreign exchange. This newspaper expressed special concern over giving the United States control over cotton prices, inasmuch as Brazil and the United States were competitors in cotton.[22]

In a conversation with the United States agricultural attaché in Buenos Aires, a representative of the Argentine Congress of Rural Societies of Buenos Aires and La Pampa insisted that Argentina must have complete freedom of action in disposing of her surpluses. The only American aid Argentina wanted, he noted, "was a trade agreement or improved trade relations which would enable the United States to make larger purchases in Argentina." The Mexican Minister of Finance ironically told Ambassador Josephus Daniels that he favored the "proposed Pan-American consortium" if it were given the authority to "take over the American petroleum companies." One Chilean writer favored the idea of an inter-American cartel on the rather pessimistic grounds that most of the Latin American countries had no real economic independence anyway, and might as well cooperate with those "who can aid us."[23]

The United States, however, ultimately decided to abandon the cartel projects for reasons of its own. State Department Far Eastern Adviser Stanley Hornbeck warned that any scheme to channel Latin American trade through the United States would encourage Japanese militarists to demand the same privilege for Japan in regard to Chinese trade.[24] Will Clayton told an OCIAA executive committee meeting that the United States was in a weak position even to be considering the idea of commodity cartels based on Latin American production, inasmuch as the Latin Americans did not enjoy a monopoly on the production of *any* commodity, coffee included. The cartels could thus be undersold in cutthroat competition. "Cartels," Clayton noted, "must be world cartels—not Hemisphere cartels." The negotiating as well as the policing problems connected with world cartels, he added, were enormous. He did not know of a single example of a successful agricultural cartel. OCIAA Assistant Coordinator Joseph Rovensky added that any attempt to set up a preferential hemispheric system would discriminate against friends of the United States outside the hemisphere, would force the creation of a "complicated procedure for handling of many commodities, administering and policing of which will become an economic monstrosity," and invite retaliations, thus "destroying all Free Foreign Trade."[25]

The cartel approach was consequently abandoned in favor of bilateral purchasing programs with each country. Coffee, because of its overwhelming importance in so many Latin American countries, was the one exception which received multilateral treatment. State Department officials toyed for a while with the much more innocuous idea of "announcing" a trade agreement program "to include all Latin American countries" so as to "stimulate more enthusiasm than the mere announcement of single agreements," but this obvious and rather empty gesture was also abandoned. Wartime commodity buying was simply easier to do on a bilateral basis.[26]

The general objective, however, remained the same, regardless of the negotiating technique employed. United States policy-makers wanted to cushion the war's effect on Latin America's economy by substituting a United States market for the temporarily unavailable European market for Latin American raw materials exports. That is, they were willing to substitute dependence upon the United States for dependence upon Europe. A Council on Foreign Relations study of July 1940 pointed out that this could easily be accomplished in the Caribbean, Central America, Colombia, and Venezuela, inasmuch as these areas already had "a high degree of dependence upon the United States as a market for exports and as a source of imports." The policy could also be extended fairly easily to include Ecuador, Peru, and Bolivia, which were normally less dependent on the United States market but could still be integrated into a stable hemispheric arrangement by increased minerals exports to the United States. Argentina, Brazil, Chile, Uruguay, and Paraguay would be the hardest to "integrate" because they were exporters of products "heavily competitive with the agricultural exports of the United States." A special note on Cuba stated: "Given our present sugar quota arrangements . . . complete integration of the Cuban economy with ours does not appear to present serious difficulties because of the obvious fact that integration is already fairly complete."[27]

At the same time, the Council warned in another study against the idea of creating a "self-sufficient," isolated hemispheric "trade bloc" during the war, because hemispheric isolation would cost the United States up to two-thirds of its normal foreign trade revenues. This warning was unnecessary. No State Department official was seriously thinking of limiting United States activity or influence to the Western Hemisphere.[28]

There was another dimension to the problem, however. It involved an unfortunate coincidence in timing. When the European supply sources were first closed off, United States exporters hoped to replace European exporters in Latin American markets, and felt limited only by lack of Latin American purchasing power. By late 1941, however, Latin America was acquiring purchasing power through its raw materials exports to the United States; yet the private American exporters were having growing difficulties getting their goods through to Latin America. In September 1940, President Roosevelt had issued an Executive Order establishing priority treatment for Latin American exports of essential materials to the United States. In April 1941, the President complemented this with an Executive Order recommending priority treatment for the *delivery* of vital goods needed *in* Latin America. But the included escape clause, which provided "that there should be no prejudice to the National defense program of this country," virtually assured the long-run inadequacy of the priorities arrangement, however well meant.[29]

As early as May 28, 1941, Nelson Rockefeller sent a memo to the President pleading for a slowdown in the Maritime Commission's requisitioning of Latin America–bound merchant shipping for use in the war effort. Losses already incurred in Latin America through curtailment in deliveries of needed goods, Rockefeller noted, had created an aggregate effect "more severe in its implications than the loss of our entire foreign trade would be to the United States." He warned of a breakdown in the entire Good Neighbor Policy should the United States, "through the withdrawal of ships (which is in effect a blockade of Latin America) allow economic conditions to become acute and the people to become desperate and unruly." On January 15, 1942, Will Clayton warned Admiral Land of the Maritime Commission that if further cuts had to be made in shipping allotments for Latin America–bound goods, then for the sake of hemispheric stability *"no indication of such cuts should be divulged by any branch of the government."*[30]

Shipments for long-range development projects were
not the only ones curtailed by these wartime exigencies. In
July 1941, the OCIAA received word that already-established
factories in São Paulo and Argentina were shutting down because they could not get machinery replacements from the
United States. A few Latin American governments attempted
to use their National Development Corporation offices in the
United States to insure delivery of machinery for established industries. "If this tendency continues," one OCIAA
official noted, "we shall soon have nothing but governmental
customers all demanding diplomatic passports for their
materials."[31]

Other problems arose in connection with wartime deliveries to Latin America. As early as January 1941, OCIAA
officials noticed that some United States manufacturers preferred not to export to Latin America because they felt it
was safer, and essentially no less profitable, to hold their
goods for domestic sale. The price schedules established by
the federal government's Office of Price Administration
(OPA) did not permit higher prices for exported goods. One
OCIAA official suggested the immediate institution of export price markups of 5 per cent to 15 per cent in order to
give American manufacturers an incentive to sell their goods
abroad. By August 1941, OCIAA was receiving widespread
complaints from American producers and from Latin American buyers, both of which were feeling the squeeze put on
by black-market operators taking advantage of existing
price schedules to sell in Latin America at huge markups for
exorbitant profits. OCIAA appealed to the State Department
to request some sort of realistic realignment in the relationship between domestic and export prices.[32]

By October 1941, the export price schedules problem was
visibly affecting both normal operations of established
American export firms (which dealt through approved official channels) and the political sympathies of Latin American customers who were paying up to four and five times
established official prices for goods "bootlegged" through
New York middlemen. "The impression is getting abroad
in these countries," one high OCIAA official wrote to Nelson
Rockefeller, "that we are not granting export permits at
normal prices in order to make a huge profit through . . .
devious channels." On the other hand, as another OCIAA
staff member pointed out, American producers needed some
sort of profit incentive to get them to sell abroad in wartime,

especially if they would continue to depend on domestic customers after the war. They did not wish to jeopardize their domestic positions by refusing domestic orders in order to sell abroad.[33]

Some government officials blamed the severity of the problem on domestic "fly-by-night" firms which had gained access to clandestine supplies. Others argued that as much profiteering was occurring at the other end of the line—inside Latin America. After some debate, BEW agreed that the only solution was a full-scale switch from the mechanism of priorities, which still left the sales initiative to the American producer, to the mechanism of allocations, which essentially was a recourse to government requisitioning. This was in principle clearly a more equitable solution, both with regard to the interests of American suppliers and with regard to those of Latin American consumers. But it assumed that the Roosevelt administration would not play favorites among the American producers from whom supplies were requisitioned. It also involved a delicate political problem of assigning comparative quotas to the different countries, and led, as might have been expected, to numerous complaints from Latin American governments which claimed not to have received treatment equal to that given their neighbors.[34]

Many firms in the United States were distinctly enthusiastic about export possibilities in Latin America, and initially feared European competition rather than United States government requisitioning. For them, the major problem was that of export restriction posed by the complicated licensing system of the BEW and other agencies. An OCIAA observer commented in July 1941 that there were places in Latin America, such as Colombia, where local people felt that the British were doing better than the Americans in regard to deliveries of machine goods. In some places, moreover, there was still little opposition to the idea of carrying on barter trade with Germany as long as delivery of goods was assured.[35] A BEW inter-office memo of May 1942 warned that although the United States was rigorously screening all shipments of "non-essential" goods to Latin America, the British were consistently shipping nonessentials as well as essentials, and had space to spare. "Retention of markets requires tonnage over and above the minimum figure," the memo warned. "Our policy of shipping only essential mate-

rials is the antithesis of 'Britain delivers the goods.' " The
memo closed with the suggestion that the United States attempt to work out triangular arrangements whereby British
ships would travel to Latin America by way of the United
States to pick up additional American goods en route.[36]

Eventually this aspect of the supply problem worked itself out, as the British were forced by their own war effort
to cut back on deliveries to Latin America. But United States
restrictions remained as an inconvenience to American exporters. By the end of 1942, some firms were beginning to
fear a new form of competition from indigenous Latin American manufacturers. An American chemical exporting firm
wrote to the OCIAA complaining of the injurious effects of
United States export restrictions. "Industrialists in the
Latin-American countries," the firm noted, "are fully aware
of the golden opportunities these conditions have brought
about and they are making the most of them to our disadvantage."[37]

To a United States exporter concerned more with sales
than with long-range Latin American economic development
(particularly if that development threatened to undercut his
own sales), such competition was serious indeed. Apart
from these private business fears, however, the major wartime problem remained one of getting enough essential supplies to Latin America, let alone supplies for significantly
large or long-term development projects. The situation was
summed up by an OCIAA official who, in April 1942, questioned the wisdom of granting further import-promotion
credits to Latin America as long as delivery of American
goods was so difficult.

Except for special and limited purposes, credits granted by the
United States have reality only if the borrower can get possession
of goods here, or if services are rendered to him. . . . Under present conditions credits as credits are meaningless. They are simply
museum pieces until priorities can be obtained, the goods purchased, the export license granted, and the shipping space made
available. . . . There is serious question of the wisdom of our
apparent readiness to grant more and more credits, or at least to
encourage Latin-American countries in the belief that more and
more credits will be forthcoming, when as a matter of fact we
are not prepared to let them spend the money on things that they
want.[38]

This particular coin bore an ironic reverse side. The increasing inability of the United States to supply needed develop-

ment material *to* Latin America coincided with particularly intense American efforts to get better delivery of defense materials *from* Latin America. Purchase of such materials from Latin America was a complex problem. At first, the BEW made a number of preclusive buying contracts, undertaking to purchase entire national outputs of certain materials in order to keep them out of the hands of unfriendly powers. Bernard Baruch had warned President Roosevelt as early as June 1938 that the Latin Americans must be discouraged from selling strategic materials to the Axis powers. By the fall of 1940, the United States had established a program for buying copper and nitrates in Chile, even though neither resource was as yet in short supply in the United States. Within a short time, as the defense economy rolled into high gear in the United States, it became apparent that there *would* be copper shortages. The preclusive buying program now took on the added importance of supplying the United States with much-needed cheap raw materials. By June 1941, the United States had negotiated exclusive purchasing contracts for twelve Brazilian strategic materials, and had secured control of the entire production of Bolivian tungsten for the next three years.[39]

Increased buying of Latin American raw materials did not always mean significant gains in income for the Latin Americans, however. Particularly in the cases of Chilean copper and nitrates, a leading Santiago newspaper pointed out in February 1941 that the United States government was buying from firms controlled largely by American capital, so that the profits from these purchases were largely returned to the United States itself. "It would greatly interest us," the paper editorialized, "if the United States purchases were extended to other products whose prices would return to the Chilean economy more than simple wages and a few dividends."[40]

By 1942 the United States Board of Economic Warfare was negotiating with Latin American governments to get them to increase production of strategically important crops such as sisal, henequen, peanuts, soybeans, quinine, and rotenone. Ironically, while Latin American governments were complaining of United States failures to supply them with machinery for long-range, consumer-oriented agricultural development projects, BEW was sending a representative to discuss Latin American needs for machinery in con-

nection with a variety of export-oriented defense projects.[41]
The BEW strategic-crops program raised the entire question of diversification of agriculture in the various countries.
The Latin Americans had wanted to diversify production for
years. In 1931 the Chilean government had enacted a "law
of overproduction," which provided that new factories for
manufacturing or producing articles "officially declared to
be in a state of overproduction" could not be established
without government authorization. In Cuba, a decree-law of
the Batista government, dated February 4, 1942, required all
farmers with more than 167 acres of land, and all sugar
mills growing their own cane, to devote a specified portion
of their land to food crops other than sugar. In both these
examples—one an attempt at industrial diversification, the
other an attempt at agricultural diversification—the goal
was increased production of goods needed for domestic consumption. But the BEW's wartime approach to diversification in Latin America naturally centered on the increased
production of goods needed for the American war effort,
rather than goods useful only for raising Latin American
living standards. This reinforced the impression expressed
by one Mexican observer even before the BEW policies
crystallized: "The first aspect of continental solidarity," he
told a University of Chicago Round Table audience, "that of
solving the fundamental economic problems of Latin-Amer-
ica—has been completely forgotten, and that is the impression created now through Latin America."[42]

3. Dependence and independence

What was becoming most clear to the Latin Americans
in all these operations was the degree to which the war had
made their economies more than ever dependent upon the
economy of the United States. When a policy question came
down to choosing between development programs and conflicting defense programs, the decision rested not with the
Latin Americans but with the United States. Not only could
Washington veto Latin American economic development
during the war; it also had the power—and, even with the
best of intentions, used it—to cause severe dislocation to
the economies of a number of Latin American countries. In
particular, the strategic materials production programs
were responsible for drastic and sometimes costly rear-
rangements of Latin American economies.

The wartime experience in Bolivia was a case in point. In January 1942, a United States economic mission to Bolivia recommended an increase in the price of tin in order to stimulate production there. The mission attached to its recommendation the condition that the Bolivian government agree not to raise the export tax on tin, as that would cancel out the stimulative effect of the price increases. The Americans ignored the fact that this condition would expressly prevent the flow of any increased profits to the Bolivian public treasury, whence they might be used for public works or other public programs; the increased profits would instead revert to the private treasuries of the tin companies, some of the largest of which were owned by foreign—particularly American—investors. Less than three months later, an OCIAA memo repeated this need to increase Bolivian tin production, again without taking a position designed to assure any diversion of increased tin profits to public projects. The memo simply stated: "There is no question of weighing increased production in Bolivia against increased production in the United States, or in some other Latin American country. If we must have tin, the situation justifies an all-out effort to get it in Bolivia." A BEW report also prepared in April 1942 added tungsten to the tin discussions and stated flatly: "*Any project should be approved which on balance will favor the war effort.* Any such project must necessarily be in the interest of both countries."[43]

The OCIAA memo added an interesting note concerning the effect which a tin promotion project might have on wartime Bolivian economic development as a whole. It stated in regard to the possibility of expansion and diversification of the Bolivian economy:

Any estimate of increased production of individual minerals that deals with each separately on the assumption that adequate labor is available, may give a most misleading result. The total production that can be gotten from Bolivia is not the total in each particular line, assuming that the other lines were making no demand on labor, power, or transport facilities. Those responsible for the larger strategy of Bolivian development will have to make a choice as between different lines of development.

In other words, labor scarcity plus power and transportation scarcity meant that an "all-out" effort on tin might seriously hamper other important areas of economic activity by precluding the availability of adequate labor and other resources in those areas.[44]

The United States did go ahead with a tin and tungsten

procurement program, however, with pretty much the re- sults predicted in the OCIAA memo. Other lines of activity were cut back, while the United States put considerable pressure on Bolivian tin and tungsten producers to increase production. In the case of tungsten, American officials initially quoted wartime prices as high as $26 a ton. By July 1944, when the need for tungsten began to level off, the United States was offering the mine owners prices ranging from $12 to $16 a ton, and was threatening to cut back purchases with alarming rapidity. Only through the timely intervention of State Department Political Adviser Laurence Duggan was the United States Foreign Economic Administration (which by that time had taken over the functions of the Board of Economic Warfare) persuaded to agree to an "orderly withdrawal" from the tungsten purchase program.[45]

With regard to tin, the resulting situation was even more serious, for tin was the largest earner of foreign exchange in Bolivia. The State Department agreed to a Bolivian public statement that proceeds from the price increases were to be used for "working-class benefits," only to see the purchasing agent of the Peñaranda regime turn the additional profits back to the private tin mine owners. When conditions in the tin mines led to labor unrest and an outbreak of strikes late in 1942, the mine owners, in collaboration with the government, replied to the unrest with military force. Hundreds of miners were killed in the "Catavi massacres." The United States made no serious protest over the matter, evidently not wishing to create a situation which might jeopardize the tin supply for the war effort. Yet when a revolutionary junta led by members of the nationalistic, anti-oligarchic, pro-labor MNR (National Revolutionary Movement) deposed the Peñaranda regime and seized power in December 1943, promising to end mine-owner exploitation of Bolivian workers, the State Department immediately denounced the new regime as "pro-fascist," and refused to recognize it until MNR elements had been removed from the government by pressure from the military members of the revolutionary junta. All in all, the wartime minerals situation in Bolivia brought far greater benefits to Americans than to Bolivians. To Bolivian workers, the metals procurement programs brought little besides longer hours, tougher working conditions, and a repressive response to their protests.[46]

The story of wartime dislocation in connection with the United States' strategic-goods procurement program was repeated in a different form in the case of the rubber development program in Haiti. In 1941, the United States Rubber Reserve Corporation, a subsidiary of the RFC, signed an agreement with the newly formed Haitian Development Corporation (French initials: SHADA) for a project to inaugurate the planting of cryptostegia rubber trees. ("What is 'cryptostegia'?" asked President Roosevelt of Vice-President Wallace. "It sounds like a horrid disease. All I know is that the President of Haiti thinks well of it!") All rubber produced under the program was to be purchased by the United States. Washington officials sent technicians to help manage the SHADA operation, and ultimately the United States invested $6,200,000 in the project. But in May 1944, the project was suddenly canceled, with President Roosevelt's approval, on the grounds that it could not be expected to produce significant quantities of rubber in the foreseeable wartime period.[47] One OPA economist ,writing shortly before the SHADA contract was terminated, inquired:

Suppose the investment in cryptostegia does not pay out. What will be the *cost* to the United States? The real labor cost, of course, is borne by the Haitian peasants, who work harder than before. The investment has involved no diversion of labor and production on our part. Our loss will be whatever transfer problem is created by the impairment of the capital of the Rubber Development Corporation.

Shortly after the contract was terminated the same writer concluded: "The shift from hired employment back to self-employment will be a relatively easy one. Nevertheless, the monetary deflation will impede real productive activity and hamper the nation's economic progress." To get the full significance of what Haiti was being "shifted" back to, however, this statement had to be juxtaposed against an earlier statement in the same article, in which the writer noted: "Haiti is an agricultural economy literally without a plow. Consequently, the peasants live at the Malthusian level."[48]

Another striking example of wartime dislocation arising out of the strategic-materials procurement program—this time involving a major Latin American power—was the case of the rubber development program in Brazil. Months before Pearl Harbor, the United States Rubber Reserve Corporation had negotiated exclusive purchase contracts for both Bolivian and Brazilian rubber, to keep these products out

of the hands of unfriendly nations. The prices agreed upon
were in both cases substantially lower than the prices being
offered at the time by other competitors—Axis interests in
the case of Brazil, Argentina in the case of Bolivia. At the
same time, the Roosevelt administration directed the RFC
to stockpile rubber in the United States and to develop a
domestic synthetic rubber program in order to offset decreasing supplies from Far Eastern sources, which were
rapidly falling under Japanese sway.

Until well after Pearl Harbor, however, the RFC neither
made any purchases of Brazilian rubber nor moved ahead
vigorously on the stockpiling and synthetics programs. After
Rubber Reserve's neglectful policy had caused the price of
rubber to fall four cents a pound lower than the Brazilian-
American contract price, the United States Embassy in Rio
de Janeiro had to agree not to object to Brazilian sales of
rubber to other American republics provided there were adequate safeguards against the rubber's falling into Axis hands.
Under this arrangement, substantial quantities of Brazilian
rubber were exported to Argentina. After the United States
entered the war as a combatant, the Brazilian government
voluntarily cut off these exports, reserving all shipments for
the United States, despite efforts by Argentina, Uruguay,
and Mexico to obtain what one OCIAA official described as
"large supplies." All this was done despite the fact that Rubber Reserve still had made no purchase of Brazilian rubber.[49]

The situation became more complicated by RFC's evident failure to move on the stockpiling and synthetics programs. Secretary of the Interior Harold Ickes wrote to
Bernard Baruch:

One of the worst results of Pearl Harbor was the discovery that
Jesse Jones [Secretary of Commerce and overall supervisor of
RFC] had been betting with himself that the war would be over
shortly and that we might not even be involved, particularly in
the Far Pacific. He hadn't built up a stockpile of rubber that he
had been instructed to build up, and for which he had been given
plenty of money. He had even slept peacefully on the synthetic
rubber program. So we were hit in a vital spot.[50]

The Roosevelt administration immediately moved to rectify
this error by setting up a special rubber development program and arranging with Brazil to establish a crash program
of rubber procurement in the Amazon basin, which had been
a leading supplier of rubber until it was undercut by cheaper
rubber from the Far East. Brazilian Economic Mobilization

Coordinator João Alberto Lins de Barros agreed to a program involving resettlement of "several hundred thousand" laborers from other parts of Brazil. João Alberto immediately undertook to establish a recruitment program which would move fifty thousand able-bodied laborers from the State of Ceará and other neighboring states to the Amazon basin by the end of May 1943. Thus to the exclusive purchase contract on which the United States had not yet made good was added a program involving resettlement of large numbers of Brazilian laborers.[51]

Rubber Reserve finally did make good on its agreed purchases once the United States was seriously involved in the shooting war. The exclusive purchase agreement and the rubber development program in Brazil were both "vindicated." But from the Brazilian point of view, there was still one problem. In March 1942, Price Administrator Leon Henderson visited Brazil and told the Brazilians that he did not believe that even with the new circumstances of United States involvement in the shooting war, an increase in the low contract price for Brazilian rubber was warranted or would be useful in bringing about any substantial increase in production. By early 1944, Foreign Economic Administrator Leo Crowley had agreed to raise Brazilian rubber prices by 33⅓ per cent over 1942 prices, both in order to "offset the increase in production costs that [had] taken place in Brazil since the spring of 1942 and to provide an incentive for maximum production." In May 1945, Assistant Secretary of State Nelson Rockefeller told a House Ways and Means Committee hearing that the United States had obtained Latin American rubber, all things considered, at "about a fifth of what they could have obtained." This evidently was done despite the intense labor relocation which the Brazilians undertook; it was also achieved despite Brazil's having carried on the rubber negotiations through a governmental monopoly purchasing agency, a procedure to which the North American Board of Economic Warfare had attempted to take exception on the grounds that it would "increase the ability and inclination of our Brazilian friends to bargain." Brazil, having little leverage with the United States, had to agree to conduct these programs on a basis of both high dislocation and low price.[52]

Other countries in Latin America also suffered economic dislocations from the strategic-materials procurement programs. In the case of Mexico, a United States–sponsored oil-

seed production program resulted in food production cut-
backs. This time, because the United States *did* offer high
prices for the desired product, so many Mexican peasant
landowners shifted their land from corn to oilseed production that the Mexican government finally had to intervene to
restrict areas in oilseed, and to turn back certain areas to
corn production in order to prevent a famine. In the case
of Peru, the United States–sponsored rubber development
program shifted needed laborers out of food production into
rubber production. The OCIAA sent a Food Supply Mission
to Peru, but it did not fully solve the food shortage problem.
After the war, State Department Political Adviser Laurence
Duggan summarized the effect of these war-induced trans-
fers of labor power upon the food situation by noting that,
particularly in the case of the poorer nations, the resulting
food shortages were "not of [the American] type . . . where
no one went hungry, but *shortages of the few staples which
comprise the diet of these low-income countries*" (italics in
original).[53]

4. Inflation and distress

Food scarcities, imported goods scarcities, machinery
replacement shortages, and the influx of United States
money into Latin America as payment for the strategic-
materials procurement programs—all added up to a classic
inflationary situation in wartime Latin America. With much
more money than usual chasing much fewer goods than
usual, virtually every country in Latin America suffered a
serious inflationary spiral. In many countries it more than
offset wage increases for the great masses of the laboring
population. At first glance, it might seem paradoxical that
the United States, which had in many instances performed
so poorly from the Latin American point of view with
respect to the delivery of goods, should have been so valuable in helping Latin Americans control prices and combat
inflation. On closer inspection, this is no paradox at all; such
technical assistance was, apart from dollars, virtually the
only commodity of which the United States had sufficient
reserves to spread around. This is not to say that American
assistance was effective in halting the spread of inflation in
Latin America during the war. On the contrary, by the end
of the war almost every country was in the grasp of increasingly severe inflation, which continued well into the postwar
period.

Unable to increase the supply of consumer goods available in Latin America, the United States government concentrated on price control as its chief anti-inflationary tool. OPA Export Price Control director Seymour Harris and other officials toured Latin America trying to work out price-control programs with various governments. The Americans soon discovered that the task was exceedingly difficult.

Effective price control depended upon effective political pressure from local Latin American consumers and laborers whose real income was most seriously hurt by inflation. Yet importers and other businessmen who tended to profit from price increases had more effective political influence than did laboring groups or consumers in general. Moreover, Latin American governments could always point out—and many did—that without supply shortages created by the war economy needs of the United States, upward pressures on prices would not have been nearly so severe. What the price-control situation in Latin America showed more than anything else was that even with the best of intentions, United States price-control experts were essentially powerless to aid Latin America because of the overall supply structure of the war economy.[54]

OCIAA did set up an emergency Food Supply Division under its Institute of Inter-American Affairs; the Division in turn set up a $2 million program in Brazil, a $1 million program in Venezuela, and various smaller programs in seven other countries. The Coordinator's office also sent a field party to Peru late in 1942. After months of work, and some rather sharp exchanges with the State Department, which feared that OCIAA's apparent excess of enthusiasm might result in charges of United States interventionism, the field party succeeded in setting up a bilateral cooperative food production service.[55]

All these programs, however, were small compared with the task involved. Moreover, such programs could not compensate for the great shortages created by breakdowns in existing transportation systems and the unavailability of replacement parts or machinery for new ones. As for shipping from the United States, officials in Washington did attempt to adhere to the State Department's announced policy of taking whatever steps were possible to compensate for losses resulting from lack of southbound tonnage.[56] But the most serious problems, particularly those of internal transportation systems within the various countries, were much

more difficult to solve, especially in countries where railroad
equipment was hard to obtain and automotive transport arrangements were almost fledgling in nature due to bad roads and few vehicles.

As expected, Latin American transportation systems whose proper functioning was essential to the conduct of the war effort did receive prompt and careful consideration. In November 1942, President Roosevelt allocated $2.5 million from his special emergency fund ($4 million more was added in May 1943) for rehabilitation of the Mexican railroads, in order to facilitate transportation of strategic materials to the United States. The President declared this refurbishing to be an "emergency affecting the national security and defense" of the United States.[57] In May 1942, the Export-Import Bank agreed to advance $14 million to the Brazilian government under an agreement by which Brazil was to acquire ownership of the Vitoria-Minas railway, extend it to the Itabira mining properties, rehabilitate it, and agree to transport at least 1.5 million tons of iron ore annually for sale to the British government and the United States Metals Reserve Corporation. A noteworthy Good Neighbor Policy fringe benefit of this transaction was a supplementary arrangement by which the British government agreed to acquire from certain of its nationals—and transfer gratuitously to the Brazilian government—title to the Itabira mining properties. The properties were to be operated, as long as the Eximbank loan was still outstanding, by a nominally Brazilian company managed by citizens of both Brazil and the United States, chosen jointly by the two governments.[58]

Areas not specializing in needed war materials did not do so well. In Peru, as labor shifted from farms into mines and public works projects, there resulted, as one United States Embassy official noted, an "increased buying power simultaneously with a reduction in food production." Although some labor was also diverted into highway and railroad repair and construction, Ambassador Henry Norweb reported in September 1943 that these were still areas, along with the farming areas, where labor shortages existed. As for other areas in such countries as Brazil, as early as May 1942 the national subcommission of IADC warned that a recent United States order prohibiting export of road-building machinery and equipment was going to affect greatly Brazil's road-building program. A survey of motor equipment in

Brazil, compiled for the Foreign Economic Administration in the period July–October 1944, revealed that of 98,000 vehicles studied, almost 33,000, or over one-third, had been built before 1935, while only 27,000 had been built since 1940. A more general survey of automotive transportation in Latin America, done by the OCIAA in 1944, linked rising food prices directly to the breakdown in automotive transport, and pointed to a United States bottleneck in supplying spare parts as a key factor. In this particular case, the responsibility was again mutual; the survey pointed out that while there appeared to be adequate supplies of parts available in the United States, there had been no coordinated effort by Latin American auto manufacturers to secure release of more parts. The Latin American dealers evidently hoped that a lessening of available auto transport in Latin America would increase the vacuum to be filled by postwar new car sales.[59]

For a time, OCIAA had entertained hopes of being able to set up some kind of coordinated program for the shipment of idle machinery to Latin America. In September 1942, the Coordinator's office sent out a preliminary circular to United States Embassies in Latin America announcing the possibility of such a program. But it soon became clear that there simply was not that much machinery available. In February 1943, Nelson Rockefeller wrote to the president of the Studebaker Corporation rejecting the idea of a wartime inter-American trade fair; transportation shortages, he noted, would make it impossible to deliver the goods. Such a fair would only result in a situation similar to the one surrounding the "idle machinery" program, where "thousands of requests were made for the machinery and much bad feeling resulted when they all had to be turned down for lack of shipping space." The situation was aptly summarized by the head of the OCIAA Commercial and Financial Division's transportation section, who wrote to Assistant Coordinator Joseph Rovensky in January 1943 pointing out that for Brazil and Colombia, the transportation available was "so extremely inadequate that the BEW [was] about helpless." It was "almost a hopeless job," he noted, "to try to select the particular goods that are the most essential and get them through the needle's eye."[60] In general, it appeared by the middle of the war that the United States simply was not managing to offset the damage done to Latin American economies by the forced integration of those economies into the general war effort of the United States and the other Allied powers.

To the Latin Americans, the most salient characteristic of the war economy was its tendency to accent Latin American economic dependence upon the United States. If the immediate prewar years had heralded new Latin American efforts toward national economic independence from the northern neighbor, the war years had essentially undercut such efforts. If the Latin Americans had replied to the Roosevelt administration's prewar "new approach" with a certain measure of healthy skepticism, the war had brought Latin America to a sort of forced agreement with United States policies: there was nowhere else to turn for needed goods and markets.

As United States observers themselves knew, the wartime program of inter-American economic "cooperation" had not resulted in equal and reciprocal benefits for both Americans and Latin Americans. Price-control expert Seymour Harris observed:

In short, in exchange for vitally necessary war materials we have provided these countries with paper credit, with dollars that are manufactured by our banking system, and with gold for which we have no use. In the postwar period it is hoped that they will obtain adequate compensation for their natural resources, for their additional work, and for the reduced standard of living which they have encountered during the present war. . . . It does seem that on the whole the United States has had the better of the bargain.

Laurence Duggan described the dollar balances built up by the Latin Americans through their raw materials exports to the United States as a "three billion dollar non-interest-bearing 'war loan.'" This "war loan," Duggan added, had also led to inflationary problems through the inability of the United States to deliver goods to soak up this expanded Latin American purchasing power.[61]

A Latin American confirmation of Harris' and Duggan's assessment of the wartime experience was given in an article written by Peruvian educator Luis Alberto Sanchez early in 1945. Sanchez' article, entitled "What's Left of Inter-Americanism?", bitterly indicted the wartime system which had been forced on Latin America:

In Latin America, the war has further inpoverished the poor and enriched the wealthy. It has increased the army's power, both politically and militarily. At most, salaries have doubled, while at the very least, the cost of living has tripled. . . . The large exporting concerns of Latin America, generally financed with United

States and British capital, are making fat profits. Meanwhile, the people, enthusiastically democratic, are doing without essentials. . . . Our average man has yet to see material or moral benefits from this war on which he staked his hopes long before his government took a stand. . . . For us, the outcome of the war has been settled. Although "democracy" is clearly the winner, we fail to see any benefits.[62]

In all of this lay one essential irony, easily visible to all who dared look in Latin America. Of all the Latin American countries, only one had maintained throughout the war period a fair semblance of prosperity unencumbered by serious economic dislocations. Argentina, the malevolently "pro-Axis" neutral, the Bad Neighbor to the South, was a maverick nation which had continued to sell meat and grain to the British in order to preserve the basis of her prosperity, but had at the same time refused to go along with the United States in a common anti-Axis hemispheric front, much to the chagrin and indignation of Washington policy-makers. The Argentines were emerging from the holocaust indisputably stronger than any of their Latin American neighbors.

Noncooperation had not created Argentine prosperity. On the contrary, because she was prosperous, Argentina could afford not to cooperate to the extent demanded by the United States. Secretary of State Cordell Hull, knowing this to be the case, tried consistently and unsuccessfully throughout late 1943 and all of 1944 to undercut this prosperity at its source, by halting British purchases of Argentine beef. But the British refused to go along, and Argentina continued to prosper.[63]

As the war drew to a close in Europe and Asia, amid mounting economic distress in the rest of Latin America, the Good Neighbors south of the Rio Grande might well have begun to wonder who had had the best of the bargain. Was it they, having of necessity fitted their economies to the war machine of the northern metropolis? Or was it the Bad Neighbor to the deep south, who, having an independent base of national prosperity, could afford to thumb her nose at the United States and leave the fight for freedom and democracy to others? It would soon become clear that the rest of Latin America was developing grave doubts about "multilateral economic cooperation," North American style, as a more productive approach for Latin America than the militant economic nationalism of Argentina.

V. Planning for peace: The politics of optimism

1. The [North] American Century

"The twentieth century," wrote Henry Luce in March 1941, "is the American Century."[1] Writing even before the United States became involved in the shooting war, when the United States had carefully limited its role to that of an "arsenal of democracy" in the fight against Axis imperial expansion, the influential publisher of *Time, Life,* and *Fortune* magazines had already formulated a bold and striking blueprint for a postwar world organized in consonance with United States national interests. Isolationism, Luce noted, was dead for the United States, and there was no use "distract[ing] ourselves with lifeless arguments" about it. The postwar world—the world of the American Century—was to be built upon the forward-looking principles of American internationalism, upon "a sharing with all peoples of our Bill of Rights, our Declaration of Independence, our Constitution, our magnificent industrial products, our technical skills." Paraphrasing Abraham Lincoln, Luce declared that an American internationalism would have to be "an internationalism of the people, by the people and for the people."

Emphatically our only alternative to isolationism is not to undertake to police the whole world nor to impose democratic institutions on all mankind including the Dalai Lama and the good shepherds of Tibet.

America cannot be responsible for the good behavior of the entire world. But America is responsible, to herself as well as to history, for the world-environment in which she lives. Nothing can so vitally affect America's environment as America's own influence upon it, and therefore if America's environment is unfavorable to the growth of American life, then America has nobody to blame so deeply as she must blame herself.

In its failure to grasp this relationship between America and America's environment lies the moral and practical bankruptcy of any and all forms of isolationism.

Luce sketched out four main areas of "life and thought" in which the United States should seek to realize his vision of

national political responsibilities and greater economic opportunities in the postwar world was an assumption common to a great many public officials and private men of
influence. Old Wilsonians like Cordell Hull, Bernard Baruch,
and Josephus Daniels agreed with New Dealers like Dean
Acheson, Adolf Berle, and Nelson Rockefeller on the need to
accept such responsibilities and opportunities. The common
denominator in the thinking of all these men was that the
United States, as a matter both of national self-interest and
of world betterment, should use its power to help develop
the resources, standards of living, and levels of prosperity of
peace-loving countries the world over. Indeed, despite the
fact that Luce distrusted the New Dealers themselves, and
expressed in his essay a sharply exaggerated fear of the
Democratic party's sympathy for "all manner of socialist
doctrines and collectivist trends,"[4] the American Century
proposal was in many respects a kind of globalized postwar
New Deal. The images of the United States as protector and
promoter of the free-enterprise system, as exporter of technology to the world, as international Good Samaritan, and
as powerhouse of ideals were, by 1941, all good New Deal
images.

2. One world, open world

The scope of the American vision for the postwar world
was summed up in Wendell Willkie's famous phrase, "One
World." Peace, like prosperity—as Will Clayton told a Senate
committee—could no longer be achieved on a local basis, but
had to be based on world-wide cooperation. Luce himself
pointed out that the world of 1941 was "for the first time in
history one world, fundamentally indivisible." The purview
of the Atlantic Charter likewise included "all the men in all
the lands."

If the vision was to be realized in a One World context,
however, it required one further refinement of the One
World concept. In the American view, One World had also
to be an Open World—a world in which no significant geo-
graphic area could be closed off by fiat of some rival power
for exclusive exploitation and dominance. Closed blocs led
not only to *intra*bloc exploitation by the strongest nation in
the bloc, but also—as Cordell Hull had been warning for
years—to *inter*bloc rivalry with international war as the
ultimate result. Such had certainly been the general world

experience in the 1930's, as one imperialistic power after another had attempted to extend its sway over one region after another. Moreover, closed economic spheres of influence would undercut the basis for an American Century, which assumed a huge postwar outpouring of United States capital, technology, and goods into all parts of the world.[5]

Secretary of State Hull expressed with great directness the Open World approach of the United States. On November 18, 1943, Hull delivered an address before a joint session of Congress. He had just returned from Moscow, where the Foreign Ministers of the leading powers of the United Nations alliance had met in conference, and had issued a joint declaration pledging to continue their wartime cooperation into the postwar period. Hull described the plans of the four major powers for setting up a general international organization to safeguard the peace. "As the provisions of the four-nation declaration are carried into effect," he noted, "there will no longer be need for spheres of influence, for alliances, for balance of power, or any other of the special arrangements through which, in the unhappy past, the nations strove to safeguard their security or to promote their interests."[6]

The Moscow Declaration was a major step forward in the struggle for a One World approach to the peace. Both the British and the Russians had been reluctant to accept it. Churchill had co-sponsored the Atlantic Charter with President Roosevelt; but the man who had "not become His Majesty's First Minister to preside over the dissolution of His Majesty's Empire" had been extremely reluctant all through the early phase of the war to accept any plan which might undermine Britain's exclusive control of her Empire. In regard to the Atlantic Charter itself, Churchill insisted that the clause pledging the United States and Britain to "endeavor . . . to further the enjoyment by all states . . . of access, on equal terms, to the trade and to the raw materials of the world" be qualified by a reference to the "due respect" of the two countries "for their existing obligations." This meant in essence an exemption for the British Empire system from any arrangement aimed at establishing world free trade.[7]

Stalin likewise preferred the security of knowing that Russia's nearest geographical neighbors, who formed a collective buffer zone between Russia and the Central European powers, would be subject to direct Russian influence after the war. For this reason, Stalin tried to insist upon arranging postwar territorial settlements in the areas closest to the Russian homeland virtually as a precondition of a three-power military alliance. The United States, however, successfully postponed the territorial settlements until the military situation was somewhat better in hand.[8] The Roosevelt administration did not care to tie its hands in such a way as to weaken its ultimate chances of building a world truly open at all points to United States influence.

Indeed, the main reason why Hull pressed so hard for a strong world peacekeeping organization with centralized authority was precisely that such an organization was the best way to undercut Russian and British closed regional security blocs. Centralized authority would prevent big-power autonomy in regional areas. Churchill, realizing this, attempted to substitute the principle of regionalism for the concept of a world organization. In the spring of 1943, he publicly proposed the establishment of a series of regional "councils"—one for Europe, one for Asia, one for the Americas, and so on—each to be responsible for keeping the peace within its own area. Council on Foreign Relations director Hamilton Fish Armstrong immediately warned Hull that Churchill's proposal, "presented as wanting to make it easy for Americans to cooperate," would in reality "make it easy for the wrong Americans to cooperate on an inadequate scale." Armstrong feared that the regional councils proposal would give isolationist senators a chance to restrict United States participation to a Council for the Americas, leaving the other regions to "fend for themselves" and probably drag the United States into war again, despite lack of American decision-making power in other regional areas.

A memorandum prepared in June 1943 by a Council on Foreign Relations study group likewise warned that the United States "could not acquiesce with safety in an arrangement which would make it impossible for this country to intervene" in a European dispute. "Experience has shown," the memo stated, "that the security of the United States is closely dependent on the existence of peace in Europe."[9]

The Roosevelt administration soon made it quite clear that it did not intend to be frozen out of *any* region. In the summer of 1943, the Big Three invited China into the council

of the major allies as a Big Fourth. President Roosevelt announced the "four-sheriffs" plan as a transitional step to a
larger world organization.[10] But the four-sheriffs plan was to
precede the central organization, not replace it. Hull made
this clear at the Moscow Conference. While the conference
did not entirely solve the problem of regional groupings,
Hull did come home with pledges from the other powers
that they would direct their best efforts toward the creation
of a strong world peace system in which the central organization was paramount.

Just as the projected world security organization was to
be the political expression of the One World ideal, the United
States began moving as early as 1942 to give the ideal an
economic expression through two complementary international economic agencies. Assistant Secretary of the Treasury Harry Dexter White was the principal author of a plan
which envisioned the creation of both an International
Monetary Fund and an International Bank for Reconstruction and Development. The IMF was intended to stabilize
world currency and commodity transactions. The IBRD
would assist the war-torn industrial areas to recoup their
economic health quickly, and would also help underdeveloped areas to modernize and strengthen their economic
structures. Treasury Secretary Morgenthau called the White
Plan a "New Deal in international economics."[11]

The idea was to do on an international level what the
New Deal had tried to do on a national level—to use the
power of government to revive and stimulate a prosperous
system of free enterprise in which ever-increasing numbers
of hitherto economically disfranchised people were, to use
President Roosevelt's words, "given a share." With United
States government capital playing a major role in the financing of both the IMF and the IBRD, public capital would
be enlisted in the world-wide expansion of the free-enterprise system, in line with Luce's dictum that a free-enterprise system could not prevail in the United States if it prevailed nowhere else. As in the case of the domestic New Deal,
the projected global New Deal was designed to help American private enterprise, not replace it.

Like the proposed world political security system, the
projected world economic program was based upon a combination of ambition and necessity. In October 1941, Vice-
President Wallace underlined the need to keep world chan-

nels open for the free flow of United States capital and goods.

It is to be hoped [Wallace wrote to Jesse Jones] that the world peace situation will be such after the war comes to an end that *private* capital will flow in larger quantities than it has been able to do during the decade of the thirties. But, in any event, excessive unemployment and disastrously low farm prices cannot again be allowed to develop. The figures indicate that our financial strength (governmental and private) is such that we can prevent such a disaster.

Jones himself, in an April 1943 speech to the influential businessmen's Committee for Economic Development, outlined the necessity and the advantage of postwar government-business collaboration. Describing the tremendous wartime increase in the United States government's financial and manufacturing activities—undertaken in connection with the war effort—Jones declared:

If business and industry seek to cooperate wholeheartedly with government . . . much of the war expansion can be put to work usefully for the United States and for many parts of the world. . . . Many parts of the world will have to be rehabilitated both physically and materially. This will greatly increase our foreign trade. There will be markets enough. The problems will be to fill, and of course to finance, orders, not to get them.[12]

In a February 1944 memo, Harry Dexter White showed how the IBRD fit into this scheme of using governmental economic power to bolster the position of United States private enterprise on an international scale. The Bank would make loans only where private funds were not available. White justified the Bank's stepping in where private investors feared to tread: "Private investors are not always right in their evaluation of foreign loans," he noted tersely. "Just as they have at times made bad loans, so at other times they have refused to make sound loans." The IBRD would be used to compensate for such shortsightedness, and in so doing would further the long-range interests of the investors themselves by building up underdeveloped areas to the point where private capital would be willing to take over.[13]

Henry Wallace stressed the role of the IMF as a means to "clear the channels of foreign trade of discriminatory restrictions and controls so that there can be a genuine expansion of world trade." With the help of the IBRD, Wallace added, "American capital can play a great constructive role —and a profitable role—in the development of the economies of other countries. It will provide us with enormous

postwar foreign markets. For our greatest markets are in
prosperous, industrialized countries." Interestingly, the IMF
was also designed to eliminate currency restrictions which
could be used to keep American goods out of certain foreign
markets. The sterling area restrictions imposed by the
British in order to protect their own position in Empire
markets were an obvious target. As State Department official
Emilio Collado remarked: "The IMF was intimately linked
to free trade; no use to have free trade if you have exchange
controls, and vice versa."[14] The White Plan was thus an economic analog of the political Open World proposal embodied
in the projected United States security organization. The
Bretton Woods and Dumbarton Oaks conferences of 1944
laid the respective groundwork for international acceptance
of each of these plans.

3. Organizing Latin America

For United States policy-makers working on postwar relationships with Latin America, the principal features of the
American Century and the Open World approaches—embodied in the United Nations organization and the White
Plan—raised striking questions. The American Century approach contained a fundamental tension between the desire
to avoid "policing the whole world" on the one hand, and
the desire on the other hand to be "responsible for the world-
environment" in which the United States as a nation lived.
The Open World, anti-regionalist approach contained a similar tension: United States policy-makers did not wish to
give up the inter-American "system" through which the
United States supervised and guided Latin American development. But neither did they want to do anything in the
Western Hemisphere to give either the Russians or the
British an excuse for parallel action in their own spheres of
influence.

This tension became apparent as soon as United States
officials and policy analysts began working on the problem
of the postwar role of the inter-American "system." In 1941,
international relations expert Quincy Wright of the University of Chicago warned that too rigid an approach to the
building of "hemispheric solidarity" could have unfortunate
repercussions upon other United States policy goals.

If you organize a region politically, far from leading to cooperation with the rest of the world, it is likely to set up oppositions
with the rest of the world. . . . That is one reason why I think the

defense aspect of inter-American solidarity ought not to be emphasized except in times of such great emergency as we now have. Political security in our shrinking world is fundamentally a universal problem. In this respect regional institutions should be subordinate to world institutions.[15]

Secretary of State Hull agreed with this line of reasoning. He carefully refrained all during the war from making any commitment to an autonomous inter-American security system. When in August 1943 the Colombian government suggested that the seven remaining nonbelligerent nations of Latin America unite in a bloc of "associated powers" to assist the war effort, Hull vetoed even this relatively modest proposal on the grounds that it would be dangerous to the principle of One World organization to establish a precedent of any sort of "united bloc action" in advance of the peace arrangements. At the Dumbarton Oaks Conference in 1944, the United States initially took the position that even if regional organizations were to be set up as adjuncts to the central peacekeeping organization, such regional agencies should not have the authority to undertake any enforcement action on their own without the express consent of the central organization.[16]

Latin American reaction caused the United States to retreat somewhat from this position, but the primacy of the central organization emerged as a clear principle of the Dumbarton approach to world security. A November 1944 memo prepared for the Council on Foreign Relations by political scientist Grayson Kirk of Columbia University emphasized that too much peacekeeping autonomy for an inter-American security system would probably encourage the Russians to close off Eastern Europe under the claim of a similar regional prerogative.

If it is considered desirable to bring Russia to accept the principle that there shall be no action taken in this region [Eastern Europe] except upon the authorization of the world organization, then there should be a gain in this resolution by applying the same procedure to disputes arising in this hemisphere. On balance, this would seem to be a more compelling reason than any which can be adduced in favor of hemispheric security organization.[17]

In general, the United States' approach during the war was to lean in the direction of subordinating an inter-American security system to a world peacekeeping organization—pre-

cisely in order not to set a dangerous example for the other
major powers.

In no way, however, did this imply an abandonment of the traditional United States goal of guiding and supervising Latin American development. On the contrary, what made it both possible and sensible for the United States to soft-pedal the political security aspects of the inter-American system was the fact that, as the war itself was clearly demonstrating, the United States could dominate the hemisphere through economic power instead. It would emerge from the war not only much wealthier in absolute terms, but also in terms relative to the wealth of the other industrial powers. While the war was damaging British industrial capacity and devastating Soviet industry, it was giving the geographically protected American industrial system an uprecedented incentive to expand. President Roosevelt himself jokingly remarked that "Dr. Win-the-War" had replaced "Dr. New Deal" as resident physician to an ailing economy. Given this greatly strengthened and vastly wealthier industrial system, the United States would be able to outproduce, outsell, and outinvest any other power which attempted to make inroads upon its position as supply house for Latin American industrial development.

Thus the traditional goal of dominating Latin American development needed no artificial insulation of the hemisphere from outside competition. On the contrary, the most probable result of any attempt to establish a closed hemispheric economic bloc would be to limit the foreign expansion of the American industrial system elsewhere, by encouraging the creation of closed economic blocs in other areas. A closed hemispheric economic system would set as dangerous a precedent as a closed hemispheric political security system.

Within this context, then, United States policy-makers began to work out the details of their postwar approach to Latin American economic development. On April 9, 1943, President Roosevelt asked Secretary of State Hull for a quick policy memorandum based on a survey of a number of problems, including (1) the beneficial and/or detrimental effects of past American efforts to help raise living standards and productivity in other countries; (2) the probable size of the job to be done in a selected group of underindustrialized countries, including the magnitude of financial and material aid that the United States, in cooperation with the other leading United Nations, could usefully render in these areas for a reconstruction-and-development period of five or ten years; (3) the probable broad effect of helping underindustrialized countries on the overall pattern of world trade and on the trade of the United States; and (4) the minimum safeguards required to secure the greatest common benefit with the least ill effect on the United States and the aided countries.

In response to this request, the State Department set up an interdepartmental committee, consisting of members of the Board of Economic Warfare, the OCIAA, the Department of Commerce, the Tariff Commission, and the Federal Trade Commission, in addition, of course, to State Department personnel.[18] The committee included Assistant Secretary of State Dean Acheson (the chairman), Emilio Collado (special assistant to Under Secretary of State Welles), Nelson Rockefeller, and Assistant Secretary of Commerce Will Clayton, among others. On November 22, 1943, Secretary of State Hull sent to the President the completed report of the committee, along with a seven-page covering letter by Hull himself, a general summary statement by the committee, and three appendices. The third appendix was a forty-six-page paper prepared by the Resources Division of the OCIAA and entitled "Industrial and Other Economic Development in the Western Hemisphere." These documents represented the thinking of an important group of high-ranking United States policy-making officials on postwar Latin American economic development.[19]

The general summary statement included some candid assessments of past American mistakes in handling investment in underdeveloped countries. These mistakes, both American and Latin American, were summarized as follows:

(1) Protective tariffs by the government [of the country] in which investments have been made;

(2) Lack of United States foreign banking experience led to the loss of funds without benefit to the United States;

(3) High interest rates attracted inexperienced investors; and onerous terms did not permit self-liquidating debts;

(4) Investments fixed in terms of United States currency placed heavy burdens on borrowers in periods of depreciating currencies;

(5) Investments disappeared in the downward cycle of business;

(6) Difficulties—avoidable—arose by improper conduct of

investing, thus raising a protest of exploitation; nationalistic
movements impeded United States investments.[20]

In particular, the comment on "improper conduct" by investors provided a needed warning to government policymakers. They could no longer assert that United States capital had to be "protected" regardless of its effect or behavior in Latin America. This warning was in essence a reaffirmation of the need to "give Latin America a share," on pain of losing everything.

The OCIAA view on tariff protection was questionable. Certainly there was much to be said for the belief that a Latin American industry which could survive *in the long run* only behind a high protective tariff wall was probably inefficient and costly both to the consumer and to the nation as a whole. Treasury Department economist Harry Dexter White had pointed out, however, with particular reference to Latin America, that "any attempt to expand the industrial element in the economies of the least industrialized countries would be very difficult without the aid of a tariff schedule which would protect such industries *during their infancy*" (emphasis added). The OCIAA report conceded that if after the war there developed a tendency for "large foreign firms to dump their products at less than cost in Latin America," then "protective tariffs [might] be necessary to protect *newly developed* industries against this type of competition."[21]

The key question, however, was what kinds of industries the United States would most like to see the Latin Americans either develop or not develop for themselves *in the long run*. OCIAA operated on the old IADC assumption that in the long run, Latin America's major industries should be complementary to, not competitive with, the major export industries of the United States. Potentially competitive Latin American industries were therefore to be discouraged. A key means of achieving this end was to discourage high tariffs in Latin America.[22]

The summary report's section on anticipated capital needs in Latin America was equally important. It began with the assertion: "In the immediate postwar period, the U.S. will probably be the only important exporter of capital. . . . Preliminary study points to the conclusion that [needed] exports in the form of capital and consumers' goods might be smaller than the U.S. would reasonably be in a position to invest." If these predictions were correct, the United States would indeed have both the ability and the opportunity to "go it alone" in regard to capital exports to Latin America. The report then presented estimates taken from the OCIAA appendix to indicate that the United States should be prepared to invest up to $3.5 billion in Latin America over the next ten years, of which "about 75% . . . might have to be under government auspices."[23]

This was a key point. At long last policy-makers agreed that, as one OCIAA economist had asserted back in January 1941, it was time to start thinking of Latin American development in long-run terms and in terms of nine or ten figures rather than seven. It also recognized that in the absence of adequate private initiative, the United States government would have to be prepared to furnish the major share of key investments on a long-term, low-interest basis. As for the private capital which did venture forth, the United States government "must assume increased vigilance over U.S. investors and enterprises abroad."

Finally, in regard to the "probable broad effect" of these policies, the summary statement concluded:

(a) It will provide immediate markets for capital and consumers goods during development of foreign economies.
(b) The shock of reconversion in the United States will be moderated and spread over a longer period.
(c) (1) Exports of certain U.S. commodities may be affected adversely; but with the rise in living standards abroad, other United States exports will increase, so that there should be a net gain. There is little likelihood of injury to United States domestic markets, since foreign goods would have to overcome transportation, tariff, and other competitive disadvantages. (2) There is always idle capital available in the United States. Using it would tend to absorb otherwise unemployed labor; it would also affect the rise of wages by reducing the cost of living due to lowered cost of imports. The amount of exported capital would be so relatively small as compared to domestic capital that the effect on capital and labor proportion would be negligible.[24]

Thus the whole program was looked upon as a high-yield, low-risk proposition.

The report of the OCIAA Resources Division detailed the types of projects most needed in Latin America, including such large general projects as power plants, highways, railroads, and cargo planes. The development of these projects, the report noted, would lead naturally to the creation of others dependent on cheap power and efficient transporta-

tion. The cumulative effects of investment in Latin America
("greater production, higher national income, and increased
per capita purchasing power") would in turn increase the
"capacity of these countries to absorb capital," thus leading
to a self-sustaining increase in the rate of investment. "It is
suggested, therefore," the report stated, "that the annual
rate of investment [of United States capital, both public and
private] should be approximately 250 million dollars in the
first 3 years, 350 million dollars in the next 4 years, and 450
million dollars in the last 3 years." Quick returns at high interest rates, however, would not be a feasible part of such a
program. "To insist upon high speculative rates and quick
repayment," the report warned, "would be unsound because
maximum benefits from invested capital could be realized
only over a long period of time."

As to which sources could best be expected to supply
capital, the report noted that "investment in transportation
and power development is likely to need support from public sources as well as private because the returns are limited
and frequently delayed, and the amounts required are generally too great for private financing." This was also true
with respect to health and sanitation programs, "which must
be undertaken in some parts of Latin America as a prerequisite of further industrial development." Other fields
such as manufacturing and mining could be left to private
United States capital, "a large part of which," it was hoped,
"will be invested in conjunction with local capital." Finally,
this section of the report stated:

It would seem desirable that private and government investments
should be integrated to insure proper timing and an orderly flow
of capital to the various countries. It might be advisable, therefore, to establish a quasi-public agency to assist in the development of such a program.[25]

After a rapid survey of the general wartime economic
situation, the report continued with a most overoptimistic
section dealing with agricultural and mineral commodities.
A comprehensive consideration of the leading export commodities of the various countries, including coffee, bananas,
wheat, corn, meat, sugar, and the leading minerals (copper,
mercury, tin, lead, zinc, and manganese) was followed by a
survey of probable postwar markets for these goods and a
conclusion that apart from certain serious dislocations to be
expected in mining, "Latin America should be economically

stable at the end of the war."[26] Though this view was proven
to rest upon a peculiarly generous definition of the term
"stable," it did not, nonetheless, appear to detract from a
genuine concern for industrial development and diversification of agriculture.

The report closed with a section on "Possible Obstacles
to Development." These included "inability to obtain essential materials—a current obstacle," as well as such problems as market limitations; selective lacks of raw materials,
power, and labor; trade barriers; currency instability; restrictions on foreign investment and personnel; and, finally,
"competition—external and internal." In this last category,
the report stated that protective tariffs might in some cases
be necessary as a defense against "dumping." Also mentioned was the possibility that industrial competition between the various countries might become a problem if
governments tried to sustain many small competing firms by
means of subsidies. But there was no mention of one of the
more obvious ways of circumventing competition, namely,
by establishing hemispheric production and marketing arrangements to apportion markets and production on some
multilaterally agreed-upon basis.[27]

The reason for this omission lay in the fear that hemispheric marketing agreements could lead to the exclusion of
outside competition and the establishment of a closed regional economic system. Since the entire report had been
written in conformity with the principle of hemispheric cooperation within an Open World framework, it could not
culminate in any suggestion which might lead to such a
closed system. The requirements of wider world multilateralism placed limits on the extent to which hemispheric
multilateral arrangements were acceptable.

The report was actually a synthesis of two separate
policy requirements. The global requirement of building
One World, an Open World, could be fulfilled only through
the avoidance of self-contained regional blocs; the hemispheric requirement of "giving Latin America a share" demanded both an aggressive American government-business
partnership and even some measure of direct United States
government supervision of private American interests in
Latin America. The report was significant in that it represented a high-level official attempt to weld these two requirements into a single consistent policy. It also reinforced the

increasingly popular idea among United States policy-makers that American prosperity and Latin American development were mutually beneficial and perhaps even interdependent.

The report fit in well with President Roosevelt's own thinking on Latin American development. All during the war, the President had been stressing the idea that Latin American economic development would benefit the United States. As early as January 1941, he had asked Nelson Rockefeller to explore the possibility of increasing the distribution of basic low-cost consumer goods in Latin America through the use of ten-cent stores. Roosevelt's idea was that any increase in the size of the consumer market in Latin America would be of direct benefit to the United States. In June 1943, he asked Nelson Rockefeller for a public relations campaign based on the annual report of the OCIAA's Basic Economy Department: "I do want to get across the idea," the President wrote, "that the economy and social welfare of Jesus Fernandez in Brazil does affect the economy and social welfare of Johnny Jones in Terre Haute, Indiana." On January 14, 1944, Roosevelt acknowledged receipt of the interdepartmental committee report on postwar development in a letter to Secretary Hull. "The conclusions of your survey," the President wrote, "seem to bear out what I have long believed and what I included in my Annual Message of January eleventh, namely that helping the standard of living in neighboring countries generally has a reciprocal beneficial effect."[28]

4. Pros and cons within a consensus

Many key figures in private industry and finance supported the general thesis of the OCIAA Resources Division report. United States Chamber of Commerce president Eric Johnston, who was also chairman of the United States national subcommission of the IADC, told an American Forum of the Air radio audience in May 1944:

I am convinced that Brazil's increase in steel production will be a great benefit eventually to our workers. . . . During past years, Brazil has been importing many elementary steel products from abroad which she could better make herself. The increase in Brazil's productive capacity in steel will result in an increased earning power which the steel plants in the United States can enjoy by selling steel in Brazil in fabricated forms. In other words, Brazil will be able to buy more automobiles, refrigerators, railroad equipment and other things. . . . I believe that you can

increase the purchasing power of a people better through industrialization than through any other means.

Shifting from the particular to the general, Johnston noted:
"We will be amazed as time goes on to discover how many
finished products of those nations we will need, and the
more we buy, the greater will become our markets and the
greater our volume of sales, the greater amount of employment in all nations involved."[29]

Joseph Rovensky, who left the OCIAA in 1943 to return
to the Chase National Bank, told a Boston audience that although only a few Latin American countries, such as Mexico
and Brazil, had the capacity to become heavy-industry nations, all the others in varying degrees could become fabri-
cators and light manufacturers. "I see no reason," Rovensky
commented, "why this should be viewed with alarm, or why
we should attempt to forestall it. To me it is a logical se-
quence, and if we do not cooperate someone else will. The
more the development, the greater the increase in living
standards; the more trade and business for all."[30]

A number of independent scholars also agreed that
large-scale, long-term development projects in Latin America would benefit the United States. "To put the matter in its
lowest terms only," stated a National Planning Association
study,

the demands of these impoverished millions for food products,
building materials, clothing, household equipment and hundreds
of other items essential to a decent standard of life would, if
made effective, provide a stimulus to the world's production such
as has seldom been felt. Their own productivity would of course
be greatly increased in the process, and it is an axiom of economic experience that the most productive areas also provide
the most active markets.[31]

A Council on Foreign Relations study provided the inverse
reason for doing the same thing. "If we are content," it
warned, "to become merely an industrial machine into which
these countries feed their raw materials, then we must expect that their social systems will remain static, that the
economic factors which hinder these republics in their struggle to achieve democracy will persist, and that both political
and economic instability will continue to menace the security of our investments." Liberal journalist Duncan Aikman
thought that "in Latin America, in the development of its
wealth and purchasing power, its fuller settlement, lies per-

haps the last frontier that may keep at least a modified form
of capitalism afloat for the next several generations or even
centuries." University of Chicago economist Jacob Viner
recommended that the United States government encourage
sound investment in Latin America as an "alternative to
non-American foreign capital investments and their political
implications re the Monroe Doctrine."[32]

In regard to the problem of sources of material, there
was also considerable support for the OCIAA position. Reliance mainly upon the "stimulus of private profit," the
National Planning Association study noted, would not necessarily result in a high rate of reinvestment or development.
"Neither the Latin American nations nor the United States,"
it said, "can rely on the automatic action of private enterprise to play the leading role in the kind of development here
envisaged"; the study suggested the writing of reinvestment
provisions into all new loans to Latin American industry or
Latin American agriculture. OPA economist Seymour Harris
took the position that governments should first agree on loan
terms; then perhaps private capital might be forthcoming
"under a full or partial guarantee by the United States government." If, Harris noted, "despite these safeguards, losses
are incurred, they should be paid by the American people,
since the main economic and political gains are shared by
them."[33]

The National Planning Association study supported
OCIAA's contention that governmental, possibly even inter-
governmental, enterprise was necessary and proper for large
projects such as transportation development. It also con-
curred in the recommendation that there be much closer
international supervision of all investments, including private investment. The study advocated the creation of an
International Planning Board for this purpose.[34]

Some people both inside and outside the United States
government were opposed to aspects of the OCIAA position.
They did not, in the main, object to the overall idea that the
United States would tend to profit politically and economically from Latin American development. On that fundamental point most observers agreed. Opposition to the
OCIAA position involved mainly the degree to which the
United States government could be trusted to participate
actively in Latin American development without becoming
a burden to the private American businessmen operating

there. The National Foreign Trade Council, possibly fearing the same type of government competition which the New York bankers had feared in 1941, included in the Final Declaration of the Council's 1943 convention two resolutions specifically reaffirming the primacy of private enterprise in Latin American economic life. Resolution No. 5 on Inter-American Affairs asked for government protection without government competition:

The large and mutually beneficial trade and economic relationship existing between the United States and other countries of this hemisphere was built up through private enterprise. The maintenance of close and friendly economic and political relations among these nations should continue to be a cardinal principle of national policy. It can best be implemented by a continuance of the principle of individual liberty and free enterprise. . . .

Resolution No. 16 on Protection of American Foreign Properties recommended "recognition of the inviolability of private property against confiscation." The Council termed such recognition the "sole assurance of a supply of international capital and credit, which has been the cornerstone of the economic development of the world," and asked that it be made an explicit condition of all United States cooperation with developing nations.[35]

Some of the corresponding resolutions of the Council's 1944 convention went even further. Resolution No. 3 on Direct Private Foreign Investments stated in part: "The participation of local capital should never be made compulsory by law." Resolution No. 5 urged the government to negotiate "treaties of friendship and commerce, giving adequate protection to American foreign traders as to their property and business abroad, providing for the elimination of discriminatory practices by foreign governments and affording assurance of the continuation of the traditional 'open door' policy of the United States, as reiterated in the Atlantic Charter."[36]

There were other expressions of apprehension, both over the new attitude toward private investments and over certain specific instrumentalities of the Roosevelt administration's new approach. Banker Joseph Rovensky agreed that Americans going south to invest "should be willing to join up in a partnership with those whose land it is, and whose resources are theirs." United States investors, Rovensky stated, "will have plenty to contribute," and, he added, "I have no fears that we will not be treated properly. We are

all sufficiently enlightened to keep in mind the old admoni-
tion 'muzzle not the ox that treadeth out the corn.'" But, he
warned, "if and when shortsighted policies should be
adopted by any of our neighbors and it becomes obvious
that we, as the foreign partner, are not being treated properly, we should stand up for our rights, and our government should back us up."[37] Clearly, the question of who was
to judge what constituted "improper" treatment was crucial.
If the private bankers themselves were to be permitted to
make that decision and then call in the United States government for support, they could essentially negate the OCIAA
idea that government would do the supervising.

Events had already indicated, however, that OCIAA and
the banking community were not so far apart in actuality as
they were in theory. OCIAA still leaned to the view that government participation was to supplement and not replace
private capital in Latin America; private capital was entitled
to a "fair," though not exorbitant, return. The continued
ability of government and business to work together was
convincingly demonstrated in a meeting which took place
in May 1944. The Inter-American Development Commission
had called upon its twenty-one national subcommissions to
meet in New York City for a conference on postwar policy
planning. Prior to the conference, OCIAA Coordinator and
IADC chairman Nelson Rockefeller called a meeting of government and business leaders to discuss the agenda.

While the members of the IADC national subcommissions were primarily private businessmen, the conference
heard from a number of government officials, and there
was considerable give and take between the two groups during the course of the meetings. President Roosevelt's message of welcome, sent from Washington to be read to the
delegates at the first session, praised both the IADC and the
conference as providing "a particularly effective channel for
the direct participation by private business in hemispheric
economic progress." Secretary Hull's message stressed the
role of private business in helping formulate plans for postwar economic development in Latin America. "In the formulation of such plans," Hull noted, "it is highly desirable that
representatives of private business and financial interests in
the American republics consult together on important issues
and make known their views to the governments and to the
public generally." IADC chairman Rockefeller's opening ad-

dress to the conference stated the theme directly: "We need to make recommendations," he urged, "which will be of assistance to our individual countries in the creation of an inter-American framework, within which every businessman can operate with stability, assurance, and confidence."[38]

In a post-conference circular sent to OCIAA representatives in Latin America, Rockefeller's office described the resolutions of the conference as representing "not only the thinking of the representatives of private enterprise of the 21 American Republics, but also the consensus of American business organizations such as the National Foreign Trade Council, the United States Chamber of Commerce, the National Association of Manufacturers, and the Committee for Economic Development, all of whom reviewed the resolutions in draft form prior to the Conference." These resolutions, the circular also stated, represented "the closest approach to unanimity between representatives of private enterprise and of government in the field of economic policy." In November 1944, OCIAA Acting Coordinator John McClintock wrote to the vice-president of the National Foreign Trade Council, congratulating him on the "excellence" of the final declaration of the Council's annual convention and noting the "similarity" between the positions of the NFTC and IADC conference of the previous May.[39] The new consensus would leave plenty of room in the Latin American development picture for independent action by private American entrepreneurs in search of a good return on a secure investment. The only major fear of the private businessmen was that they might be forced to become junior partners, rather than senior partners, in the postwar government-business coalition working to develop Latin America in accordance with United States national interests.

Interestingly, at least one important State Department official anticipated some sort of an eventual rapprochement between the United States government and private businessmen along lines which largely favored the private business point of view. Laurence Duggan, seeing the danger of an arrangement which would undermine the federal government's ability to supervise private American entrepreneurs in Latin America, moved to head it off. In December 1942, Duggan wrote to Under Secretary of State Sumner Welles, warning that OCIAA's Latin American Coordinating Committees, which were groups of United States businessmen in

Latin America responsible for the administration of certain
wartime OCIAA cultural and informational programs,
should be dissolved as government agencies as soon as possible after the war. "Another type of relationship, diplomatic mission to business community," wrote Duggan, "is
desirable. I am in favor of rallying the business community
to support our foreign policy, but the danger is that once the
cohesive force of war is gone, these Coordinating Committees, being semi-official, might serve to balk progressive
foreign policy or to help put across a reactionary foreign
policy. They are, after all, composed of the biggest businessmen—Standard Oil, Guggenheim, General Electric, United
Fruit Company. They have very definite ideas as to what
our general policy should be, and in general their ideas have
been most reactionary." Noting the link between the American business community at home and its agencies abroad,
Duggan added, "The community is responsible to the 'head
office,' and this 'head office' is not the Government of the
United States." Duggan evidently helped to convince Welles,
for in February 1943 the Under Secretary wrote to Rockefeller notifying him that after the war much of the work of
the Coordinating Committees would be unnecessary. In any
case, Welles noted, contacts would be maintained chiefly
through governmental agencies and not through private individuals acting for the United States government.[40]

The issue came down to this: the government and business spokesmen agreed on the fundamental point, namely,
that United States supervision of Latin American economic
development was necessary; they disagreed as to the degree
and type of government involvement required by the development process. Basically, the businessmen wanted to have
their cake and eat it, too. They wanted government protection without government interference or competition—
hardly surprising, considering the government's own position in regard to the larger question of the United States'
postwar role in the world at large. The New Dealers also
wanted to have their cake and eat it, too. They hoped to be
able to supervise events in Latin America in accordance
with an American Century approach, yet not give either of
the United States' two major allies any excuse for parallel
action which might tend to restrict United States involvement in other regions. As the war drew to a close, the major
question confronting United States policy-makers was this:

Assuming that the tactical disagreements between American government and business leaders could be ironed out, and that government and business could then cooperate effectively in bringing the American Century to Latin America, would the rest of the world, including the British, the Russians, and indeed the Latin Americans themselves, go along with the United States' definition of the "best of all possible" postwar worlds?

VI. Hedging the bets

1. Allies and competitors

The vision of an Open World, espoused by United States policy-makers as they planned their approach to the postwar era, was based on a fundamental sense of optimism. This optimism was born of the feeling that the tremendous increase in economic and military strength which the United States had acquired in the course of the war would be sufficient to overcome virtually any obstacle which fate or an enemy might place in the United States' path. There was, indeed, a widespread feeling that most of the peoples of the world would *want* to see the kind of world envisioned in the Atlantic Charter, the Moscow Declaration, the White Plan, and so on. "There is the belief," wrote Henry Luce, "shared let us remember by most men living—that the 20th Century must be to a significant degree an American Century. This knowledge calls us to action now."[1]

It was also clear, nevertheless, that there might yet arise situations or incidents which could hamper the implementation of such an American policy in the postwar world. No one could guarantee, to be sure, that all the other nations would greet the American Century and Open World approaches with enthusiasm. Indeed, early wartime negotiations had already demonstrated that both the British and the Soviet governments would be more than reluctant to open up their respective spheres of influence to "outsiders." It was quite possible, moreover, that the national ambitions of the Big Three would come into conflict as the Allies moved to re-establish stability in post-Nazi Central Europe. Assistant Secretary of State Adolf Berle later remarked that in the opinion of a number of United States observers, the Russians had "made it a three-cornered war" as early as the summer of 1944 with their sweeping westward military advance into areas being vacated by retreating Axis forces.[2]

It was likewise possible that a postwar resurgence of militant Latin American nationalism might threaten the inter-American cooperation needed for the successful functioning of an American Century approach in the Western Hemisphere. Latin American nationalists might even seek tactical alliances or special economic arrangements with other non-American industrial powers, as they had in the 1930's, in order to offset United States power and influence. Under such circumstances, either the Russians or the British (or both) might come to play a role in Latin America similar in economic terms to the role played by the Germans in the prewar period.[3] For all these reasons, despite the fundamental optimism of the United States' approach, it behooved government policy planners to take certain precautionary measures—to hedge their bets, so to speak—in order to eliminate in advance as many of these obstacles as possible.

The problem of extrahemispheric influences in Latin America was actually a relatively minor one compared with other anticipated difficulties; nonetheless, it required attention. As early as July 1943, the British Ambassador in Washington, Lord Lothian, presented Secretary of State Hull with an *aide-memoire* noting the rise of an "impression in some quarters" that the United States desired to supplant the British in their "established and traditional markets." The British Foreign Office wished to serve notice of its intention to help British firms in keeping alive their interests and connections in Latin America; the message suggested that a similar communication should be passed on to United States diplomatic missions in Latin America, laying down the principle that in all economic matters the underlying policy of both governments was "to endeavor to insure that no advantage in overseas markets shall be accounted to either country at the expense of the other" by the respective governments or by their nationals.[4]

All during the war, the British government's Department of Overseas Trade continued to send out questionnaires to British diplomatic officials in Latin America inquiring about the status of British goods in the various market areas. By late 1944, the British were sending one official after another to tour Latin America for the purpose of promoting British exports. Among those who toured Latin America during the winter of 1944–1945 were the chief of the Latin American Department of the Foreign Office, an Assistant Secretary of the Board of Trade, and an official of the Latin American Division of the British Information Ministry. Some of these officials worked directly with British Chambers of Commerce in Latin America, much in the same fashion that OCIAA had linked up with local United States businessmen in Latin America to promote United States policy objectives.[5]

Private British interests also showed considerable aggressiveness in planning for a resurgence of postwar British activity in Latin America. The *South American Journal,* a leading organ of British financial interests, continually editorialized in favor of British commercial expansion into Latin America. One of its editorials attacked wartime Lend-Lease arrangements under which, as a condition of United States aid, Britain had had to cut back on her exports to Latin America and use exportable goods herself so as to lessen the amount she would need from the United States. The journal described these arrangements as a United States attempt to force the British out of their Latin American markets entirely. Another editorial took particular note of a speech by United States Chamber of Commerce president Eric Johnston, in which Johnston had stated his conviction that "just as the last century in Latin America was a 'British Century' the next would be an American Century."[6]

When a leading British businessman gave a ringingly militant speech to the British and Latin American Chamber of Commerce in London, stressing the need for British postwar export expansion, the *South American Journal* first reprinted a large section of it in an article entitled "Dislocation of British Trade: Rising Dominance of the United States," and then reprinted it again in the following week's editorial with strongly approving comments.

I think we ought to talk with the United States in plain language [stated Sir Patrick Hannon]. We have had cases, as you all know, where our export trade was crippled because we had to refer to Washington [under Lend-Lease arrangements] for permission to export to our own Empire. That is the situation in which the great industrial community of this country has been placed.[7]

Indeed, the British had cause to be apprehensive, for the United States certainly appeared to be working to undermine Britain's economic position in Latin America. In October 1940, OCIAA Assistant Coordinator Joseph Rovensky had proposed to British Embassy officials in Washington a complicated three-way deal for financing Britain's war effort. Britain needed to buy Argentine meat and grain to feed both the British population and the British army. The British government was short on cash, but British investors had large holdings of valuable Argentine securities—railroad and industrial stocks and state and municipal bonds in

particular. Rovensky's proposal was that the British government buy from its nationals a large bloc of these securities, then deposit them with the Central Bank of Argentina
as collateral until the British government could raise the
cash to pay for its purchases. The Argentine Central Bank
would in turn pledge the securities to the United States as
collateral for a pending American loan to Argentina. In
other words, the idea was to force the British to give up to
the United States temporary control of some of Britain's
most valuable holdings in Argentina as a condition of
Britain's receiving food supplies for the war effort and for
civilian consumption. The British refused the proposition.[8]

A month later, in November 1940, United States officials
approached the British with a more direct proposal to transfer British-held Argentine securities directly into American
hands as collateral for a United States loan made directly
to Britain for British purchases in Latin America. This proposal was also turned down. The British might not have been
aware of an OCIAA memo, prepared in connection with this
deal, which stated: "There are some good properties in the
British portfolio and we might well pick them up now.
There is also a lot of trash which Britain should be allowed
to keep." Nor were the British perhaps aware of a memo
which reached President Roosevelt's files early in April 1944,
proposing the acquisition by the United States of $1 billion
in British-held Argentine securities in exchange for the
equivalent sum in Lend-Lease credits for Britain. But they
certainly understood that even during the war, certain
United States policy-makers were ready and willing to move
into British preserves.[9]

By late 1943, the British were also becoming apprehensive about investment holdings elsewhere than in Argentina. On January 1, 1944, OCIAA Assistant Coordinator John
McClintock brought to the attention of Nelson Rockefeller a
copy of a cable from Ambassador Winant in London. Winant
enclosed a report from the London *Economist* stating of a
recent Brazilian debt settlement: "The British holder of Brazilian obligations has been made a sacrifice to Pan Ameri-
canism." In July of that year, McClintock brought to
Rockefeller's attention a call by the president of the British
Chamber of Commerce in São Paulo for more British capital
inflow into Brazil in order to help British capital abroad
"not to allow itself to be conquered by American capital-

ism."[10] Incidents such as these served to heighten the awareness on both sides that, the American Century approach
notwithstanding, the United States would still face a vigorous if not immediately powerful British drive to maintain a
British presence in Latin America.

In addition to British competition, there was always the
possibility that after the destruction of Nazi Germany,
Soviet Russia might attempt to move into the vacuum created by the collapse of German influence in Latin America.
United States policy-makers knew that the Russians had
suffered tremendous damage to their industrial system in
the war, and it was therefore not likely that they would pose
much of an immediate threat in terms of export competition. Yet the possibility of Russian expansion into Latin
America still bothered the Americans, who believed that
the Russians would probably attempt to export an equally
dangerous product: social revolution. The United States
could probably handle British competition; the British exported only goods and capital, and despite their enthusiasm
they would probably not have large surpluses of either at the
end of the war. But Soviet efforts to export a competitive
ideology might not be so easy to combat, particularly in an
area where the war had done a great deal to increase already serious social and economic tensions.[11]

In December 1943, the State Department sent a circular
to United States diplomatic missions in Latin America,
warning of the possibility of Soviet activity. The circular instructed United States representatives not to "pass over in
silence any Soviet activities in the hemisphere which we
consider inimical to the security of the hemisphere, to its
political or economic stability, or to our own interests."
From Mexico, Ambassador George Messersmith replied to
this circular by pointing out that the United States had
"such a tremendous advantage in many respects over Russia
that in many lines we need not be concerned respecting developments and competition." Messersmith also wrote to
Secretary Hull, enclosing a copy of his first letter, and adding that he was led to make these remarks because there
seemed to be much "hysterical talk" circulating about Russian designs in the Western Hemisphere. The United States,
Messersmith reiterated, would have to recognize Russia as a
postwar industrial competitor, but that did not necessarily
mean injury to the United States.[12]

By January 1945, Messersmith was writing to Secretary of State Stettinius, reassuring him that the Latin Americans already were on their guard against the Russians. "They see Russia," Messersmith wrote, "definitely bent on establishing spheres of influence within which her political and economic principles and practices will apply and control." Nonetheless, said Messersmith, it was still important for the United States to stay on its guard as well. "If we don't have this hemisphere behind us and Russia struggling for position in the other American Republics," he wrote, "both in the political and economic field, our position will be tremendously weakened." Stettinius himself decided to reject an offer of diplomatic immunity for United States government agencies operating in Latin America, so that the Russians could not claim immunity either. In the Russian as in the British case, the Secretary of State still considered it best that the United States take no unnecessary chances with possible challenges to its postwar position in Latin America.[13]

All things considered, however, State Department officials still felt that in the postwar period, as in the prewar period, European challenges to the United States' position in Latin America would be secondary to the challenges posed by the Latin Americans themselves. Many observers feared a general Latin American return to the same type of militant, revolutionary nationalism which had caused so much inconvenience both to American private enterprise and to the State Department in the 1930's. Latin America's growing anti-American nationalism had been temporarily submerged in the political and economic hemispheric unity of the war years; United States policy-makers were afraid, however, that once the cohesive influence of the war effort faded, the old nationalism would revive and ruin the chances of a postwar American Century. In this context, two crucial developments during the war seemed to herald just such a turn of events; the response of the United States government to both these developments was most significant.

2. Challenge from the inside: Bolivia

The first such development was the Bolivian revolution of December 1943. During the war, the government of General Enrique Peñaranda had generally cooperated with the United States in supplying tin and tungsten for the war effort. But the Peñaranda regime's domestic policy was not

so satisfactory. Labor disturbances in the tin mines at the
end of 1942 had resulted in mass bloodshed in the "Catavi
massacres." During 1943, despite the memory of these events,
labor unrest continued. Labor organizers accused the Peñaranda regime of sweating extra labor out of the miners for
the benefit of the private tin mining companies, many of
which had direct financial connections in the United States.
By mid-December 1943, the situation had come to a head.
Peñaranda "adjourned" the national chamber of deputies
and, on December 13, issued a "security of the State" decree
which stated in part:

Crimes against the Security of the State shall be incurred by . . .
Those who through agitation or extremist propaganda, provoke
labor conflicts, stoppages of work and strikes in the mines of
industries. . . . Those agitators who, infiltrating themselves in
the farms and communities, perturb the agricultural labor in in-
citing or contributing to the abandonment of labor or to passive
resistance.

The regime also postponed municipal elections from December 1943 to July 1944 and arrested persons who distrib-
uted handbills protesting the postponement. Finally, the
government suppressed the newspapers of the opposition
parties, the MNR (National Revolutionary Movement) and
the PIR (Party of the Revolutionary Left). United States Ambassador Pierre Boal reported from La Paz that "with this
step the administration has virtually liquidated the mouth-
pieces of its opposition."[14]

On December 20, 1943, a group of young army officers
together with leaders of the MNR deposed the Peñaranda
regime and seized power. Major Gualberto Villarroel became Provisional President of Bolivia, while MNR chief
spokesmen Victor Paz Estenssoro, a nationally known economist, became Minister of Finance. Paz Estenssoro immediately went on the radio and, according to Ambassador Boal,
"emphasized that the seizure of the Government is a revolution of the people and that the Revolutionary Government
will adhere strictly to all of Bolivia's international commitments including adherence to the principles of the Atlantic Charter." In a later telegraphic dispatch sent to
Washington the same day, Boal noted that in response to a
newspaper reporter's inquiry as to whether the revolutionary junta was affiliated with the right-wing nationalist military government of Argentina, Paz Estenssoro "emphasized

that the revolution was entirely independent." Paz Estens-soro also gave an exclusive interview to a correspondent for the *Baltimore Sun,* in which he reiterated his radio stand that the junta would respect all international commitments and continue to stand "at the side of the United Nations." The new Minister of Labor of the junta, Victor Andrade, sent a message to all miners "admonishing them to continue dili-gently to produce minerals for the war effort and to continue Bolivian economy."[15]

This seemingly auspicious beginning quickly was clouded over with doubts. In a still later telegram on the first day of the revolution, Ambassador Boal reported that he had talked with the Mexican and Brazilian Ambassadors in La Paz; both thought that "regardless of assurances of intention which have been or may be given by the revolu-tionary junta it is desirable that we all proceed with extreme caution and in close consultation" with each other. "I doubt," Boal added, "if any of them will at present recom-mend immediate recognition of the Junta as a government." Boal noted that the Mexican Ambassador in particular ex-pressed a fear that "unsecured recognition" might lead the junta to emulate the Argentine government in assuming a neutral or even pro-Axis stand on the war. Meanwhile, Am-bassador Norman Armour reported from Buenos Aires that Argentina's leading pro-Axis newspaper had "hailed" the Bolivian Revolution as a move to "emancipate the state from the pernicious influence of foreign capital." United States Ambassador Claude Bowers reported from Chile that the Bolivian Ambassador had denounced the new military gov-ernment in his homeland as "purely Nazi and Fascist, the leaders having had their training in Germany and Italy." The Bolivian Ambassador told Bowers that the revolution indi-cated "progress made toward the creation of a pro-Nazi bloc in South America aimed in part at the United States." Bowers later reported that Chilean Foreign Minister Fernan-dez y Fernandez agreed, ridiculing the junta's declaration in support of the United Nations.[16]

Reactions from other Latin American capitals were mixed. Guatemalan dictator Jorge Ubico condemned the revolution in Bolivia and warned that "too prompt recogni-tion of revolutionary governments might encourage dissi-dent groups in other countries to attempt to overthrow existing regimes to the detriment of the common war efforts." Ubico's fear for his own position was obvious (he was finally overthrown the following year). The Trujillo dictatorship in the Dominican Republic also attacked the new regime, defending the Peñaranda government because of its "strong solidarity with the cause of the United Nations." The United States Minister in Lima reported that officials of the Peruvian Foreign Office feared the Bolivian revolution "might have a leftist character."

In Montevideo, Uruguay, the prominent newspaper *El Pais* was uncertain about the "extreme radicalism" of the new government, but also noted that it had never had much confidence in the professed democracy of the Peñaranda regime. Fortunately, *El Pais* added, the new junta contained such "outstanding figures" as the "brilliant economist Victor Paz Estenssoro." *Diario Ilustrado*, a leading daily of Santiago, Chile, expressed a belief that the change of regime in Bolivia was "due to political and economic difficulties especially that of the question of Bolivian minerals."[17]

On December 23, the third day after the *coup*, Ambassador Boal reported from La Paz that both Paz Estenssoro and the new Minister of Government of the junta had made "unsuccessful efforts" to see him. Boal also noted that a member of the United States military mission in Bolivia, who knew army members of the junta "very well" and had had occasion to talk with them, reported an "intense anxiety over early recognition" on the part of the Bolivian military. "They indicated," stated Boal, "a desire to make almost any kind of a commitment and presumably to take previous actions [sic] to secure this."

Ambassador Arthur Bliss Lane reported from Colombia that in the opinion of the Colombian Foreign Minister, "the [Bolivian] regime will not be anti-American as Bolivia cannot afford to offend the United States because of [the] tin market in the United States." Lane quoted the Minister as saying:

The underlying reason for the revolt against Peñaranda was from extremely Left elements who considered that Patino [a leading tin mine owner] had been exploiting the country for his own profit and . . . the profits were not reinvested in the country. In view of the connection of United States companies with Patino these companies are bound to be affected by any action taken against Patino. This might presumably create difficulties with the United States.[18]

Meanwhile, the Bolivian Ambassador in the United States had gone to see State Department Political Adviser

Laurence Duggan. In a memo, Duggan summarized the Ambassador's remarks:

In all sincerity he did not think that the leaders of the present revolution derived their inspiration or support from either Germany or Argentina. He knew many of the people in the Government. They were men of conscience. They felt strongly about certain conditions in Bolivia that needed change. The political forms to which they might resort might be of a dictatorial character, but such forms were characteristic of Bolivian political life.

He was certain that they would give greater cooperation than the predecessor government to the United Nations' war effort.

He thought that internally they would attempt to introduce changes and reforms that undoubtedly would create difficulties with large investments, particularly the mines.

He believed that they would make mistakes from inexperience. It should be remembered that the present [government] really represented a shift of power.[19]

In La Paz, Paz Estenssoro, asked by a newspaper reporter if the new government was "of Nazi tendencies," replied:

That's one way of clouding the issue like so many others when there is no valid argument at hand. It would be like calling the Government of Getulio Vargas in Brazil a Nazi Government. We have of course certain practices of party discipline and order, but the difference between them and the goosestep is as great as from La Paz to New Orleans.

This is a government of essentially nationalist tendencies—and let us say it clearly an eminently democratic government.[20]

Ambassador Boal telegraphed to the State Department a translation of a signed interview with the former president of the adjourned chamber of deputies of Bolivia. Dr. Enrique Baldivieso, a former leader of Bolivia's Unified Socialist party, had not been involved in the *coup,* but was clearly sympathetic to it. The interview read in part:

Question. . . . As a Socialist, do you believe that the new Government is Leftist? Answer: From its program and its composition it is Leftist. Only eight days have passed and it is impossible to expect immediate action but soon this leftist tendency will be clear and unquestionable. Furthermore, all the civilian members of the new Government founded with me the Bolivian Socialist Party around the year 1935.

Question. . . . Is the new Government democratic? Answer: Undoubtedly. And it is proved by the fact that the revolution has tended to reestablish the constitutional regime internally [the junta had proclaimed the constitution of 1938 to be in force] and has shown its full adherence without reserve to the pacts signed in the cause of the United Nations—not as a gesture to secure

recognition but as the sincere expression of the entire Bolivian
Nation which has and will support the principles which ennoble
human dignity and the nations who are fighting for those
principles. . . .

Question. . . . Is it Nazi? Answer: You know well, my friend,
the power of certain words. When we caused the revolution of
1926, it was stated that Bolivia was joining the Communist terror,
and Communism was the word used to bring the revolution into
disrepute. Much care must be taken with the value of words. . . .
I am sure that events will show that the new Government has
democratic elements and principles.[21]

The evidence thus indicated widespread disagreement as
to whether the Bolivian revolution was right or left. Two
things were clear, however. First, the revolutionary junta
was universally believed to be strongly nationalist, and to
be dissatisfied with the behavior of the foreign-owned private tin companies in Bolivia. Second, junta leaders had
shown clearly their desire to reach an accommodation with
the United States and to secure its approval of their social
revolution. ·

Secretary of State Hull quickly made up his mind as to
the American course of action. On December 23, three days
after the revolution began, Hull met with the Mexican Ambassador in Washington.

I discussed [Hull noted in a memo of the conversation] the
dangers from subversive activities and said that the circumstances and facts, as I gathered them, undoubtedly support the
conclusion that the cause of the revolution was to be found in
the use of German money combined with Argentine influences.
I said that subversive activities are rife in the Argentine area, extending to Bolivia, Paraguay, Uruguay, and maybe to Chile and
Peru. I then emphasized that if there should be a procession of
revolutions in the American republics during the war, it would
have a bad effect on the prosecution of the war and largely discredit the good neighbor policy. I emphasized two or three times
that the burden for leadership is on the Latin American countries
as well as ours.[22]

The next-to-last sentence indicated the crux of the matter. A succession of nationalist, "subversive" revolutions in
Latin America—whether of the right or the left—would in
Hull's view be a clear rejection of the Good Neighbor Policy,
insofar as the United States had by its wartime policies
clearly identified itself as the power most responsible for
the continued economic stability of Latin America. For the
future, such nationalist revolutions would permanently
jeopardize the United States' position in Latin America if

they resulted in widespread attacks on American-owned or American-affiliated private enterprises. "Circumstances and facts" did not really "undoubtedly support" Hull's conclusion that the cause of the Bolivian revolution "was to be found in the use of German money combined with Argentine influences." That was of small moment, however. Nationalistic social revolution in Latin America had to be discouraged.

Once again, as in the Cuban crisis of 1933, nonrecognition became the United States' tactic of the moment. And once again, behind nonrecognition stood the threat of economic coercion. By 1944, as State Department official Avra Warren pointed out, the United States did not "need Bolivia economically." The tungsten supply in the United States was adequate; there was a two-year stockpile of tin on hand; "synthetics," noted Warren, "will do the job for quinine"; and Bolivia's output of rubber was "so small in quantity as to be negligible."[23] Unless the Bolivians tooks steps to eliminate from the junta those nationalistic elements obnoxious to the United States, Bolivia might face difficulty in securing new commodity purchase commitments. Bolivia could be crippled economically.

Nonetheless, the new Bolivian regime could not be publicly attacked on the basis of its revolutionary nationalist philosophy. Such an attack might backfire. Hull and his advisers realized that the safest line of attack lay in capitalizing on Latin American fears that the junta was Axis-oriented. By January 1, 1944, less than two weeks after the Bolivian *coup*, the Division of American Republics of the State Department was ready with a seventeen-page report which, rather than publicly expounding Hull's anti-revolutionary philosophy, simply attacked the "Fascist Connections of the new Bolivian Regime."

The sparseness of evidence of "fascist connections" adduced in the report was striking. The report referred to the MNR's 1942 platform manifesto as containing criticisms of "pseudo-democracy" and bankrupt "capitalist democracy." The report noted that "to the MNR the war is only a conflict of rival imperialisms and democracy in Bolivia or in other countries is never mentioned without cynicism." The MNR manifesto proclaimed its faith in the people of Bolivia "of Indian and mixed blood." "Nevertheless," the State Department report noted, "it fails to condemn the Nazi doctrine of racial superiority and lays itself open to the accusa- tion that it favors an American racial exclusivism." In this connection the Department mentioned an MNR reference to the "manoeuvres of Judaism" in Bolivia, this being a complaint against Peñaranda's policy of arbitrarily placing refugee European Jews in preferred economic positions, a gesture designed to win continued support from the United States. "Above all," the State Department charged, "the MNR manifesto and political tracts fail absolutely to take Nazi aggression into account. A party pamphlet states that 'Bolivians have lost their liberty under the rod of foreign masters' and it is constantly repeated that the ills of Bolivia stem from 'Anglo-Yankee imperialism.' " Paz Estenssoro was quoted as once saying that he was "the enemy of the great international financiers."

Aside from these personal and party statements of position, however—statements which illustrated nothing more than the MNR's strong preoccupation with domestic Bolivian affairs—the report contained no evidence linking the MNR to Germany, Italy, Japan, or Argentina. There was no evidence relating to alleged financial support for the revolution from outside the country. There was no evidence concerning organizational ties between the MNR and any foreign Axis-oriented group. The report mentioned a visit by Paz Estenssoro to Argentina but failed to give any evidence of conspiracy between Paz and Argentine personnel. All told, the report was based on little evidence and flimsy argumentation.[24]

Nevertheless, it served a purpose. After it was released to the other American Republics on January 8, it committed the United States not to recognize the Bolivian junta until an important change had been made, namely, that MNR personnel had been eliminated from it. The real reason for this position was clear: the MNR represented the main focus of revolutionary nationalism in Bolivia. As such, it represented not only a long-range threat to hemispheric stability but also an immediate threat to private enterprise in Bolivia. A State Department memo of March 1944 made this clear, in describing the antagonism of Bolivia's three leading tin producers toward the junta. "They are afraid," the memo stated, of the junta's "announced intention to interest itself in the betterment of the workers, fearing this can only be done at the expense of the mining interests."[25] While State

Department officials were not generally sympathetic to the mine owners, they did consider the principle of the security of private enterprise to be a vital one, and one to be preserved for the future.

The State Department felt it could work toward presentation of this principle much more easily with an all-military junta than with a junta containing MNR leaders. Whatever nationalism the military did express could probably be neutralized through a judicious program of wooing army leaders with military aid. Moreover, these military men appeared to pose no ideological or political threat to foreign private enterprise in Latin America. The MNR did pose such a threat. It had to go.

The State Department therefore resolved not to recognize the Bolivian junta until the MNR had clearly been eliminated from all positions of power. The Department did not have long to wait. As early as December 22, two days after the *coup*, the new Bolivian Minister of War, an army man, had told a member of the United States Embassy staff in La Paz that "as a result of an extensive disagreement between the military and civilian forces in the revolutionary junta, he was considering taking steps to remove Estenssoro . . . [and others] from the junta, and forming a wholly military government that could cooperate with the United States more fully." He inquired, Ambassador Boal noted, "as to whether such a step would be helpful in the consideration of recognition," and he "emphasized the importance attached by himself and other military leaders to the attitude of the United States." At this point the Embassy could make no commitments on behalf of the State Department. But this was an early indication that a United States policy of freezing out the MNR might not encounter much resistance from the Bolivian military.[26]

By mid-March 1944, the military leaders of the junta had evidently decided to remove the MNR members. On March 16, the Bolivian Foreign Minister–designate told the United States Minister in La Paz that the military element in the junta was "convinced that recognition [by the United States] is indispensable." To facilitate such recognition, the government had arranged for the three remaining MNR members of the junta to leave office "probably two or three days after the issuance of the decree convoking elections . . . on the pretext that the MNR wishes to be completely free to campaign for the elections." Ironically, when the military decision was effected the first week in April 1944, the MNR Minister of Agriculture, Rafael Otazo, refused to resign. Otazo, actually believing that the MNR resignations from the junta were to enable MNR ministers to run for office, refused to offer his resignation, since he did not expect to be a candidate for anything. Major Villarroel, the Provisional President, finally had to "insist" on his resignation.

Even at this point, because some MNR members remained in lesser government posts, the United States continued to procrastinate on recognition. Finally, after a long talk with the Foreign Minister on April 27, Minister Woodward telegraphed the State Department advising that continued nonrecognition was only undermining the stability of the now all-military junta, and was in fact increasing the possibility of another revolutionary attempt against the government. Woodward recommended recognition in order to "discourage would-be revolutionists for several months at least" and to make it more certain that elections would be held. Recognition, he added, would give the government enough political strength to "seek support among political parties other than the MNR and . . . sever relations with the more extreme element in the MNR." This, Woodward noted, "combined with the branding of the MNR by recognition after the resignation of the [remaining MNR] prefects would inevitably encourage the incipient schism in the MNR which became apparent early in April and might even result in the disintegration of the party." Interestingly, in a little note at the bottom of this dispatch Woodward added: "No convincing evidence have as yet come to the attention of this Embassy to indicate that any elements outside of Bolivia instigated or noteworthily influenced the revolution of December 20, 1943." Meanwhile, Victor Paz Estenssoro told reporters in Cochabamba that the MNR was "maintaining its revolutionary condition" and was "seeking the economic emancipation of Bolivia vis-à-vis the oligarchies which have been running the country for the benefit of big financial interests."[27]

The State Department finally decided to send veteran diplomat Avra Warren to Bolivia in order to get a firsthand picture of the situation. Warren arrived in La Paz on May 7 and held a thirteen-day series of conversations with Bolivian and American officials and with representatives of private enterprise from both countries. He made the Department's position clear in his first meeting with American Embassy officials:

Regardless of the right or wrong of the matter, the State Department, supported by a considerable segment of the American press, has the opinion, which amounts to a conviction, that the MNR, which supported the Villarroel group in bringing about the revolution, is tainted with Nazism and that the recognition of any Government of which the MNR is a constituent part would be characterized in the United States as appeasement.

Warren pointed out the "practical impossibility" of including Paz Estenssoro in a new government "because of his reputation in the United States and elsewhere as an authoritarian to the Right."[28]

Later, Warren met with leading Bolivian officials, including Villarroel and the new Foreign Minister, Enrique Baldivieso, and asked Baldivieso to prepare a memorandum stating the reasons for or against United States recognition of the junta before or after the forthcoming elections, "with explanations of the advantages and disadvantages of each." Baldivieso promised to do so, and delivered the memo shortly thereafter, urging immediate recognition. While in La Paz, Warren also talked with the chairman of OCIAA's Coordinating Committee for Bolivia, who was also head of the local Light and Power Company. This American businessman told Warren bluntly that "in view of his commercial holdings in the country," he was not in favor of the present government even if it were purged of its MNR members. He told Warren quite straightforwardly: "I am a reactionary."

Just before Warren left La Paz, he spoke with Baldivieso again. The Foreign Minister assured Warren that the MNR would elect no more than "twelve to eighteen deputies and a few Senators." With United States recognition undercutting MNR support, "there was no risk of the party's receiving a majority or combining to get one."[29]

Fortified by Warren's visit and report, the State Department moved quickly and recognized the junta early in June. The expected result occurred. The Villarroel military regime was sustained, while the MNR lost considerable strength. State Department strategy had paid off; revolutionary nationalism had been thwarted, and a possible threat to postwar United States leadership in the hemisphere was averted.

3. Challenge from the inside: Argentina

The State Department's approach was not so successful, however, in the case of the second threat, the Argentine Revolution of 1943–1944. Both the circumstances surrounding this event and the behavior of the revolutionaries were quite different from what Washington had had to face in the Bolivian experience.

In the first place, Argentina was a larger and more powerful country than Bolivia. During the war, while most of the rest of Latin America suffered from shortages of all kinds of goods, including food, and became ever more dependent upon the United States for whatever few industrial supplies were forthcoming, Argentina had maintained a strong and independent base of national prosperity by selling much-needed meat to the British. Argentina was also a principal supplier of beef to several South American countries, including Brazil, Peru, Paraguay, and Bolivia. Therefore Argentina had something which Bolivia lacked—an economic base on which to build a strong independent *political* position on the war.

In the second place, whereas Bolivia had generally cooperated with the United Nations in the war effort, Argentina had in fact taken advantage of her economic independence and had refused to do so. A number of factors contributed to Argentine aloofness from the United Nations. Traditional Argentine–United States rivalry, a residue of anti-British resentment based on depression-era concessions which the British had extracted from Argentina in exchange for a guaranteed market for Argentine beef, and ethnic ties with Italy were the leading factors. During the war, Argentina had continued to sell beef and wheat to England in order to maintain prosperity. But the Argentine government also maintained diplomatic relations with the Axis powers, and permitted them an important entry point for their propaganda and subversive activity in South America. This was a particular sore point with Secretary of State Hull, who had been battling the Argentines at inter-American conferences ever since 1936 in his effort to build a solid hemispheric "front" under United States leadership.

The Argentine revolution that was ushered in with a military *coup* in June 1943 was not *primarily* aimed at changing Argentine foreign policy. It grew rather out of a deep domestic struggle for power between the old Conservative party leadership, whose influence rested upon the power of agricultural landlords, and a variety of challenging groups including industrialists, laborers, and their respective military allies. This was no mere barracks *coup,* but a far-reaching and complex social revolution which involved the future direction of an entire society. Foreign policy became involved as an adjunct to the domestic social revolution, but was not in itself the key issue until the United States slowly but steadily made it so.[30]

At first the State Department did not press to extract commitments from the revolutionary government in return for diplomatic recognition. Under Secretary of State Sumner Welles gave the reason in a letter to Ambassador George Messersmith in Mexico: "It would have been . . . extraordinarily unwise," Welles wrote, "for us to have endeavored to trade recognition for certain specific action in the political field by the Argentine Government, particularly if, as in this case, that action were one which the predecessor Government with which we had maintained relations had not taken." A prolonged failure or reluctance to recognize the new government, Welles warned, "would merely . . . have strengthened the extremist elements and have given the Nazi and Fascist representatives a clear field for their activities." Moreover, the new Argentine military government had assured United States Ambassador Norman Armour that all ties with the Axis nations would be severed as soon as the Argentine political situation permitted.[31]

Throughout the rest of 1943, however, Argentina failed to break relations with any of the Axis powers. Relations between Argentina and the United States became increasingly strained as the more outspokenly nationalist leaders among the Argentine military publicly defended Argentina's policy of independent neutrality. By early January 1944, Hull was convinced that the Argentine government was for all practical purposes controlled by Axis forces. On January 5, he told the British Ambassador in Washington, Lord Halifax, that Argentine influence was "behind" the recent Bolivian revolution, and that it threatened the rest of Latin America if it were not checked. Hull asked for a solid anti-Argentine Anglo-American front, warning that if the British did not go along with the United States on Argentina, "propaganda in Argentina [would] say that the British are secretly pleased to see the United States in trouble" in Argentina, inasmuch as an Argentine-American rift might redound to

the benefit of British postwar trade with Argentina. Halifax
immediately asked what arrangements could be made to
supply the British army with needed foodstuffs in the event
of an Argentine-British breach. Hull promised such information from the State Department.[32]

This meeting signaled the beginning of one of Hull's
biggest and most frustrating problems during his last year
in office. Because the United States did not have the economic leverage with Argentina that it had with Bolivia, it
could not bend the Argentine government to its will very
easily. Hull therefore had to try to line up the British against
the Argentines, on the theory that Britain had the economic
leverage and could therefore ultimately dictate Argentina's
policy toward the Axis. But the British soon gave Hull to
understand that it was Argentina who had the leverage
rather than the British. On January 10, the British Minister
in Washington, Sir Ronald Campbell, presented Hull with
a message from Foreign Minister Anthony Eden warning
against "drastic steps which could impede the prosecution
of the war." Nine days later, Halifax called upon Hull again
and made it quite clear that because of the beef situation,
Britain could not, in Hull's words, "do anything in the way of
cooperation." Then, on January 23, the Ambassador presented Hull with a copy of a dispatch from Prime Minister
Churchill direct to President Roosevelt. If the Argentine beef
supply were cut off, Churchill asked,

how are we to feed ourselves plus the American Army for OVERLORD
[the Normandy invasion, planned for that spring]? The joint ex-
amination by the Combined Boards in Washington of the supply
aspects will show you how much these people have us in their
hands. An immediate cessation of Argentine supplies, our Chiefs
of Staff consider, will disrupt military operations on the scale
planned for this year. . . . Before we leap, we really must look.
We can always pay them back when our hands are clear. I must
inject my solemn warning of the gravity of the situation which
will follow if the Argentine supplies are interrupted.[33]

Given his objective, Hull had no choice at this point but
to increase the already intense diplomatic pressure which he
was applying to the Argentine government itself. On January
26, the Argentines broke diplomatic relations with the Axis.
Still Hull did not let up the pressure. He wanted more than
a break in diplomatic relations. To the new Argentine Ambassador who came to present his credentials on February
3, Hull referred to the need for a "thorough housecleaning"

in Argentina; he added that he hoped "any expressions of skepticism" on the part of people in the United States "would not discourage the Argentine Government from carrying out its housecleaning program."[34]

Hull evidently pressed too hard. On February 15, 1944, the government of General Pedro Ramirez was overthrown by another military group, who considered that Ramirez had already gone too far in compromising Argentine independence under United States pressure. At first only two major cabinet officers of Ramirez' government, Minister of Foreign Affairs General Gilbert and presidential secretary Colonel Gonzalez, were actually removed from office. Ramirez was given a "temporary" leave of absence. On February 25, it was announced that Ramirez had formally resigned the presidency and had been succeeded by the Vice-President, General Edelmiro Farrell. In the meantime, other cabinet changes were also made.[35]

Now Hull acted immediately, and let it be known that the United States would not enter into normal diplomatic relations with the new regime until it had demonstrated by concrete actions its commitment to United Nations forces. Hull immediately put pressure on the other American republics to follow the United States' lead. It soon became clear that the emerging political power behind Farrell was Colonel Juan Domingo Perón, whom Farrell at once appointed Acting Minister of War. Perón, still only a colonel, now outranked all the generals of the Argentine army by virtue of his "civilian" authority over them. But it likewise became clear that Perón was by no means fully in control of the government. On the contrary, he faced strong opposition from a powerful group of generals who stood considerably closer to the "extreme nationalist" end of the political spectrum than did Perón himself. On March 2, Perón sent an emissary to try to arrange a meeting between himself and Ambassador Armour. Perón, according to the emissary, realized the "necessity for good relations with the United States and Britain particularly" and was "willing to do everything he reasonably [could] to accomplish this." In reporting to Hull the substance of his conversation with Perón's emissary, Armour stated his own impression that while Perón "might like to carry out" such a program, "well-informed persons doubt his ability to do so at present in view of strong Nationalist opposition in the Army." Armour declined to meet with Perón.[36]

Meanwhile, Hull was having trouble keeping the rest of
Latin America lined up on the side of the United States.
On March 3, the Chilean government acknowledged receipt
of an Argentine note advising of General Farrell's assumption of the presidency. This was tantamount to Chilean
recognition of the new Argentine regime, and it made Hull
furious. The Chilean Ambassador in Washington came in to
see Hull shortly thereafter, and commented that he felt
there was a certain "ill feeling" in the United States over
Chile's position on the Argentine issue. Hull replied that any
government "may make a small mistake now and then," but
there was "no cause for hard feelings between the United
States Government and that of Chile however regretful their
action might have been." The Ambassador then brought
up the subject of Chilean President Rios' long-postponed
visit to the United States, during which Rios was expected
to ask for postwar economic aid. Hull replied that the "first
logical step" in clearing the way for the visit would be for
Chile to "engage in a number of acts negativing her recent
attitude in re Argentina."[37]

On March 6, the United States Minister in La Paz telegraphed to Hull that the Bolivian government, which the
United States had not yet recognized, also felt it could not
afford to break relations with Argentina. Major Villarroel,
the Provisional President of Bolivia, had told a United States
Embassy staff member that "if Argentine retaliation were
aroused, Argentina could totally starve Bolivia out in thirty
days" due to Bolivian dependence on Argentine food supplies. On March 9 came news of a third impending defection. Under Secretary of State Stettinius told Hull that the
Paraguayan Ambassador in Washington had warned that
"his country was completely under the domination of Argentina economically and that his Government had no choice
on the question of recognition." The united front was
cracking.[38]

In the interim, Perón continued his attempts to make
contact with Ambassador Armour. On March 8, he sent his
emissary to see Armour again. The emissary inquired as to
what concrete steps Argentina might take to satisfy the
United States. Armour indicated that he "was sure that General Farrell and Colonel Perón must themselves know steps
to be taken that would convince us and the other Republics."
Perón's position, Armour remarked in his telegram to Hull
describing the meeting, was "clearly a bargaining one."

Perón wished to know, Armour added, "before taking action that will constitute [an] open break with [the] Nationalists that Farrell's regime can count on recognition by us. He would also like to know what they might hope for in the way of war and other material once relations have been established."[39]

The anti-Peronist "Nationalists" to whom Armour referred were now grouping around the Minister of the Interior, Colonel Perlinger. On March 15, Armour told the Brazilian Ambassador in Buenos Aires that "if Farrell and Perón get rid of Perlinger and his henchmen, this would be some evidence they have decided to stand up against [the] Nationalists." Two days later, Perón's emissary called on Armour for a third time. He reported that Perón and Farrell were working on getting Perlinger out, but "the latter and [the] extreme Nationalists have quite a following in [the] Army." Armour summed up the situation in a dispatch to Hull: "It all seems to boil down to this: They apparently at last realize that Cabinet changes and action to implement promises are essential before there will be any chance to secure recognition. This however means a showdown with Nationalists and they are not sure which side controls [the] Army." In a longer separate dispatch, Armour described his impression of Perón's personal position: "Personal ambition may under the circumstances be tempting Perón to evolve toward a 'Vargas' dictatorship—i.e. authoritarian government internally and a pro-democratic foreign policy." The current lack of sympathy for the Argentine government on the part of the United States, Britain, Brazil, and other countries, Armour noted, "may logically be assumed to have impressed Perón with the desirability of such an evolution as promising the greatest security for his own position."[40]

By this time, however, the State Department was caught in its own trap. From March through May, the internal struggle within the Argentine government continued. United States Embassy officials in Buenos Aires clearly hoped Perón would win; but they dared not take, or recommend that the State Department take, any public action on the question of recognition, lest it be construed as pressure of some kind and therefore backfire against Perón. Toward the end of April, Armour reported that Perón was losing ground to Perlinger. "The situation we must face," Armour noted, "is that we are engaged in a test of endurance [against] a

regime which seems confident it can hold out longer than
the united front of the nations refusing to maintain normal
relations with it."[41]

On June 6, Armour suggested that the State Department
prepare two lists—one of preconditions for recognition, the
other of events the Department hoped would follow recognition; the Department might also hint that the United
States would make available to Argentina certain scarce
materials on the same basis as they were now being made
available to the rest of Latin America. If Argentina then
refused to "act favorably," Armour concluded, "then I feel
there is no course open but to order me home 'for consultation' or to announce that I am returning on 'leave of
absence.' "[42]

During the week of June 23, Hull called in a number of
Latin American ambassadors in Washington, a few at a time,
to explain to them the reasons for continued United States
nonrecognition of Argentina. One June 23, he spoke to the
Mexican and Brazilian Ambassadors. The United States' position, he said, rested on the "single consideration" that
Argentina's behavior in regard to the war was contrary to
previous agreements made by the American republics for
joint action at the Rio Conference. In fact, the Rio Conference had produced only a resolution "recommending" the
breaking of diplomatic relations with the Axis powers, but
by this time Hull had long since escalated the import of that
resolution in his own mind. He told the two ambassadors
that Argentine policy was "destroying the whole doctrine of
unity and solidarity" in the Americas, and that any recognition of Argentina by an American republic would encourage
Argentina in its "pro-Axis" stance and would be "equivalent
to ratifying the acts of Argentina."

On June 26, Hull repeated essentially the same arguments to the ambassadors of the six Central American republics. On June 27, he called in the Haitian and Dominican
Republic Ambassadors, along with the chargé d'affaires of
Cuba, to express the State Department's position to them.
When Hull met with the Uruguayan Ambassador on June 26,
the Ambassador suggested that Uruguay faced a particular
danger, situated as it was so close to Argentina. Hull replied
that "the Argentine military group in charge of the government knew far better than to attack one of our allies in this
hemisphere and that this would be the last thing they would

attempt." In other words, Hull assumed that direct Argentine aggression was not a possibility; he was rather taking the line that Argentina's behavior was dangerous because it might set a bad example. Argentina could also serve as a base for indirect or, as Hull called it, "subversive" aggression by Axis sympathizers.[43]

The most important conversation of that week relating to Argentina was Hull's conversation with the British Ambassador, Lord Halifax. On June 26, Hull informed Halifax that Ambassador Armour was being recalled by the State Department for consultation. Hull requested that the British government likewise recall its Ambassador to Argentina, Sir David Kelly. Halifax again pointed out Britain's difficulties in regard to the Argentine situation, noting that the meat purchase contract would be up for renewal again in two months. Hull replied that the Argentines "would be after the British Government on that matter and it had nothing to worry about in that regard." According to Hull's record of the conversation, the Ambassador "abandoned his arguments when I stated our contention, or at least he became silent." A few days later, after another conversation between Halifax and Hull on June 29, the British announced they were withdrawing Sir David Kelly from Buenos Aires.[44]

Within two weeks, Hull had pressed for and obtained the recall of most of the Latin American ambassadors from Buenos Aires. An interesting interchange occurred over the question of Bolivia's stance in this situation. On July 7, Hull received a telegram from the United States Embassy in La Paz, indicating that while Embassy officials believed that the United States could expect "complete cooperation" from Bolivia, the Bolivian government would in turn "request the assistance of the United States in defending herself against economic sanctions which Argentina will in turn apply against Bolivia." The United States Minister in La Paz warned that "we cannot in decency request this [Bolivian] Government to expose itself to Argentine sanctions and risk a wave of public resentment if as a result essential foodstuffs are not available. We cannot risk a situation here in which these necessities are not available and at reasonable prices. Otherwise, there is a very great possibility that the Government itself would fall." But when the Bolivian government hesitated for a few days, Hull called in the Bolivian chargé d'affaires in Washington, and told him that "if Bolivia should continue in an uncertain position for very long, this Government [of the United States] would soon have access to tin. in the Far East, and would naturally make its arrangements, which would be permanent." According to Hull's notes of the conversation, the chargé "fully understood this phase and [said] he would keep this before his Government." Shortly afterward, Bolivia recalled its Ambassador in Argentina.[45]

Still Argentina refused to make the appropriate gestures. Throughout the summer of 1944 the struggle stalemated, while various persons and groups continued to criticize Hull's policy as both self-defeating and ultimately as dangerous to hemispheric unity as Argentina's own behavior. One of Hull's most vocal critics in the United States was former Under Secretary of State Sumner Welles, whom Hull had forced out of the State Department during the summer.of 1943. By 1944 Welles was writing frequent newspaper columns on world affairs and had published a widely read book, *The Time for Decision.* He took the view that Hull was reviving "Big Stick" tactics in Latin America, creating resentment and weakening the United States' position of leadership in the hemisphere. Welles also made Hull furious by inviting Latin American diplomats in Washington to his home where, according to Hull, Welles conducted a sort of "second State Department" of his own. On a number of occasions, Hull took the opportunity to tell Latin American diplomats that, despite the attempts of "snipers" and "pure troublemakers" to interfere, Hull and President Roosevelt were fully in control of United States foreign policy. Nevertheless, Welles's actions continued, and his newspaper articles were widely quoted throughout Latin America, much to Hull's chagrin.[46]

As the State Department persisted in its Argentine policy, more and more frequently United States observers began to hear Latin Americans talking about the "Argentine-American" dispute. This was just what Hull was afraid of. If the other American republics came to think of the Argentine issue as the United States' problem, then Washington would soon be left standing alone as the other Latin American governments abandoned what Hull called their "position of joint leadership" in the crisis.[47]

As summer wore on into fall, the British also became increasingly disaffected. They were still not inclined to risk the military difficulties which might follow from a strict adherence to Hull's position on the Argentine question. By the end of July, the American Embassy in Buenos Aires was sending home frequent dispatches citing and quoting anti–United States articles written in the British press and avidly reproduced in the Argentine press. A particularly strong article in London's *Daily Mail* was reproduced by one newspaper in Buenos Aires under the heading: "London Describes the Methods Used by the United States Against Argentina as Gangsters' Tactics." A pro-American English-language newspaper in Buenos Aires suggested that London's *New Statesman* be prosecuted under the British Defence of the Realm Act for an article so critical of United States policy in Argentina that pro-Axis Buenos Aires newspapers were fairly dancing about it.[48]

By this time Hull was becoming aware of the skepticism of both the British government and the British business community over possible adverse effects of a hard-line policy on Britain's postwar trade position in Argentina. Hull told another State Department official that while the Department was preparing a program for applying economic sanctions to Argentina, it should "be giving attention to that phase relating to our giving assurances to the British that we would not allow our own nationals to make any post-war trade arrangements with the Argentines." In other words, Hull wanted to make sure the British did not think the State Department would be quietly moving United States products into Argentine markets while demanding that Britain refrain from economic interchange with Argentina.[49]

Hull continued to pressure the British all through the autumn of 1944 on the subject of Argentine meat purchases. On October 18, Halifax called at his own request, and spoke to Under Secretary of State Stettinius. Halifax again took up the meat question. He noted that the State Department was essentially proposing that instead of buying Argentine beef, the British accept increased amounts of American beef as a substitute. United States beef, Halifax remarked, was clearly inferior to Argentine beef. The substitution would cause "much resentment in England." Stettinius remarked that the Roosevelt administration had a national election to face soon, in which it would be held accountable, among other things, for the results of its Argentine policy. Halifax replied, with pointed reference to the question of American beef, that Prime Minister Churchill's government would soon be facing an election, too. Once again the talks stalemated.[50]

By the time Hull resigned from the State Department in November 1944—exhausted and in ill health after eleven and a half years of continuous service—the Argentine problem, and the Anglo-American frictions arising out of it, still had not been settled. On the contrary, the controversy was greater than ever. Already tied up not only with the question of the war effort but with the entire prospect of the United States' wartime and postwar relations with the rest of Latin America, the Argentine question now became wedded to a whole complex of other questions concerning the future of the United Nations alliance and the organization and governing of the postwar world. The challenge of nationalism in Latin America, of which the Argentine case was a leading example, became directly linked with the problem of great-power unity in Europe. The connection was a striking one.

4. Impending crisis

The postwar American Century approach worked out by United States policy-planners—an approach embodying both Open World politics and a large-scale effort to support and supervise Latin American economic development —depended in large measure upon the maintenance of great-power cooperation. If events supported Secretary Hull's hopeful prediction that Big Four cooperation would continue into the postwar period, American planners could look forward to an era of relative calm in which large-scale economic projects could go forward without much political interference or distraction. But if the future seemed to portend a collapse of the wartime alliance, followed by efforts by competing powers to refashion their old spheres of influence and other "special arrangements," then a crucial question arose as to how to allocate limited United States economic resources in winning basic immediate political objectives. The United States would indeed be the strongest power both militarily and economically, but it could not reconstruct and develop the entire world at once. In particular, if, as Adolf Berle suggested, the Russians were by their advance into Eastern Europe turning the war into a "three-cornered" war, then the elimination of Nazi Germany would only mean the start of another struggle between East and West over the carcass of the late German empire in Europe.

To policy-makers concerned about the postwar situation in Latin America, the possibility of great-power disunity and strife raised a serious problem. All during the war, Latin America had suffered both consumer shortages and curtailment of its development programs because it was a "low priority" area in comparison with the "high priority" areas where actual fighting was taking place. If the "hot war" were to give way not to an era of cooperative efforts for peace but to some kind of protracted "cold war," then economic priorities might remain virtually the same. Latin America, once again a comparatively low-priority area, would emerge from her wartime status little better off than before, and probably even more resentful than before. United States hopes for a strong program of support and supervision of Latin American economic development would have to be set aside, and Washington would have to find some other way of containing Latin American resentment.

Ambassador George Messersmith had foreseen this danger as early as December 1943. Writing from Mexico City, Messersmith warned a State Department colleague that the United States must not "try hysterically to build up the economies of our enemies [Germany, and possibly Japan]" after the war, but must "do what we can to build up the economies of our friends, including the Republics of this hemisphere."[51] But Messersmith's warning went unheeded. By mid-1944, with the United States and Russia beginning to have serious doubts about each other's intentions, the United States was already planning to channel a massive portion of its economic resources into Western Europe for anti-Russian defenses.

At first the Latin Americans could take a wry amusement in the fact that they of all people were being asked to contribute a standard 1 per cent of their national budgets to European reconstruction, and were being warmly congratulated for their generosity in doing so.[52] But when they began to see that European reconstruction involved a mammoth economic commitment by the United States—one which would, as they had feared, keep them in the back seat in the economic scheme of things—they saw no humor in the situation. Ex-President Eduardo Santos of Colombia, an influential and strongly pro–United States figure, agreed to undertake the job of Deputy Director of the United Nations Relief and Rehabilitation Administration (UNRRA) and to make a promotional tour of Latin America in that capacity. Even before his tour began, however, Santos was having second thoughts about the entire arrangement. In a message sent to President Roosevelt in October 1944, Under Secretary of State Stettinius warned that by means of an "intercept of a telephone conversation between Dr. Santos, in Washington, and President Lopez in Colombia," the State Department had learned that Dr. Santos had indicated that "the situation in this [United States] Government with reference to its inter-American policy was 'much less wholesome' than he had thought it would be."

By the time Santos was due to return to Washington to confer with President Roosevelt in January 1945, the State Department was openly apprehensive about the Latin American view of the European situation. Stettinius sent another message to the President, saying that Santos, as well as "other South American leaders, have felt that the growing interest on the part of the United States in European affairs has caused a certain shift in emphasis away from our relations with the other American republics." Stettinius added: "It would therefore be particularly timely if you could impress upon Dr. Santos that our policy of the good neighbor remains unchanged and as vital as ever."[53]

There was a certain irony in the situation. At the same time the collapse of the One World ideal was causing the United States to move its focus away from Latin American economic development and toward European reconstruction, it was also causing a stepping-up of United States efforts to achieve inter-American political unity. There were two vitally important reasons for this. First, the United States wanted to be able to count on a solid bloc of support at the forthcoming United Nations Conference on world organization. Second, the Roosevelt administration also needed some kind of solidarity program to keep Latin American nationalists in line until such time as the multilateral economic development programs could get moving again. This escalation of efforts toward political solidarity was intimately connected to the State Department's Argentine policy. It accounted for a significant shift in tactics in the Department's policy after Hull resigned in November 1944.

All during the war, Hull had refused to agree to the calling of an inter-American conference on the Argentine issue. The Argentines, he felt, would use such a conference to incite hemispheric disunity and thus weaken the war effort. He had also refused during the summer of 1944 to invite the Latin Americans to the four-power Dumbarton Oaks conversations on the forthcoming international peace organization. None of the other United Nations aside from the Big Four had been invited; and Hull, with his strong preference for centralism rather than regionalism as the organizing principle of the world organization, did not wish to do anything that might be interpreted as giving special treatment to a regional group.

Moreover, the position of the United States government at the conference had been strongly anti-regionalist. The initial American position was that no regional group or organization should undertake peacekeeping action on its own initiative. Under pressure from the Latin Americans, who were kept outside the doors of the conference and briefed daily after the proceedings were over, the United States subsequently retreated to the position that the regional agencies need only "keep the [Security] Council informed of their security activities." When the meetings adjourned, however, the question of the degree of regional autonomy to be allowed was very much up in the air. The principle of centralized overall authority, moreover, was still a part of the world organization idea.[54]

By mid-November 1944, with Hull out of office and the Latin Americans becoming increasingly resentful of their exclusion from the Dumbarton Oaks talks, the new State Department leaders—particularly Secretary of State Stettinius and his newly promoted Assistant Secretary for Latin American Affairs, Nelson Rockefeller—decided that they had no alternative but to agree to an inter-American conference. Russian-American relations, and inter-American relations as well, were becoming too strained. The United States could not risk jeopardizing Western Hemisphere unity, particularly in view of the impending United Nations Conference.

The formal terms for an inter-American conference had been proposed as early as June 1944 by Mexican Foreign Secretary Ezequiel Padilla. It was to be a meeting of American governments cooperating in the war effort, "to discuss common problems of war and peacetime relations."[55] This formula would be an excuse to exclude Argentina, but the

understanding was clear that the Argentine question would
be taken up in order to achieve a unified hemispheric policy
on the matter. Not all State Department officials were initially in favor of the conference. In particular, Assistant
Secretary Breckinridge Long, who had been one of Hull's
key advisers, and who resigned from the Department shortly
after Hull resigned, did not want a conference on any terms.
Long was chairman of a Department policy subcommittee
on Argentina. He did not want to tie American hands by
spelling out a set of conditions upon which Argentina could
rejoin the American family of nations. He wanted, as he
noted in his diary, a complete "change of attitude" by Argentina.[56] But in early November, Padilla essentially forced the
Department's hand by sending out another conference proposal to the other American republics without first consult-
ing the Department. Ambassador Messersmith cabled from
Mexico City warning that the United States would seriously
jeopardize Padilla's position in Mexico, and probably undercut one of its own strongest Latin American supporters, if
it turned down his initiative. At that point, Washington
agreed to go ahead with the meeting, and so notified Padilla
on November 15.[57]

The State Department's agreeing to the convening of a
full-scale inter-American conference (to be held in Mexico
City the following February) signified an important change
in political tactics. But it did not mean that the effort for
political unity was to be accompanied, or even soon to be
followed, by a move toward economic cooperation for Latin
American development. The conference was to be a holding
action by the United States in order to contain Latin American nationalist resentment and perhaps revolutionary nationalism as well.

Certainly the Latin Americans were strongly in favor of
political unity, though their motives were not entirely flat-
tering to the United States. Many of them saw the conference
as a chance to constrain United States power and interventionism by building a series of inter-American legal and
political safeguards. They were therefore pleased by the
prospect of the meeting. Yet there was in Latin America a
growing uneasiness, born of the fear that political solidarity
was being sought by the United States not even as a precondition of economic aid but rather for purposes from which
the Latin Americans would benefit at best indirectly and at

worst not at all. Such uneasiness required more than verbal assurances. As the Mexico City Conference approached, the Latin American governments therefore began working on concrete proposals to present to the United States. American answers to these proposals would indicate clearly whether Latin America's best hope for future development lay in a continuation of the multilateral approach championed by the United States, or in a new independent *Latin* American (as distinct from *inter*-American) multilateralism. Depending on how Washington met their demands, they might choose either an exclusively *Latin* American multilateralism, or even a rejection of multilateralism altogether. They might substitute the kind of militant, revolutionary economic nationalism toward which some Latin American governments had already been tending before the United States push for hemispheric cooperation and the outbreak of war had made nationalism The Enemy and multilateralism under United States leadership the wave of the future.

VII. The postwar role of Latin America: View from the north

1. The regional question

As long as Cordell Hull had been at the helm of the State Department, there could be no wartime inter-American conference on the Argentine issue. President Roosevelt, preoccupied with the war effort, generally left the details of Latin American policy to the State Department, and Hull was firmly opposed to such a conference, fearing that it would disrupt an already precarious hemispheric unity. Assistant Secretary Breckinridge Long, who supported Hull on the Argentine question, summed up the situation. It was one "which only Argentina [could] change and that by her own actions. It needs no conference and we can't deal with her until she does."[1] But now, at the end of 1944, Hull was out, Long was out, and the conference was going ahead. Not to be merely a meeting on the Argentine situation, it was also to discuss in broadest terms the future of inter-American cooperation.

By January 1945, the United States was in a diplomatically difficult position with the Latin Americans over far more than the Argentine question. First there was the problem of the Dumbarton Oaks conversations, from which the Latin Americans had been excluded, along with all other nations except the Big Four, as a matter of principle. President Roosevelt had attempted to allay Latin American fears regarding the status of the inter-American security system within the proposed United Nations Organization. At a Blair House reception in October 1944, the President told an assembled group of Latin American diplomats that "within the framework of the world organization of the United Nations the inter-American system can and must play a strong and vital role."[2] But the Latin Americans wanted a chance for general inter-American discussion of the Dumbarton Oaks proposals and of the inter-American system before the general United Nations conference scheduled for April 1945 in

San Francisco. By January 1945, it was clear to State Department officials that the forthcoming Mexico City Conference would have to include some discussion of the relationship between the Dumbarton Oaks proposals for a strong central organization and Latin American demands for an inter-American security system not subject to a great-power veto in the Security Council of the world organization.

There was also the gnawing problem of inter-American economic cooperation in the postwar world. Seeing a growing United States economic commitment to European reconstruction, some Latin Americans feared that all the prewar and wartime plans for postwar development projects in Latin America would once again be relegated to oblivion. Somehow United States officials would have to relieve this fear, given the requirement that European reconstruction *did* come first and *would* in fact involve massive economic commitments. Other Latin Americans were questioning the very possibility of inter-American economic cooperation, having seen the wartime results of such cooperation in Latin America. With the end of the Axis threat in sight, these Latin Americans were thinking of giving up inter-American cooperation altogether in favor of a return to economic nationalism.

While the United States was thus in a position of temporary diplomatic adversity, it was nonetheless emerging from the war stronger than ever in terms of its world-wide economic power and political prestige. The chief question facing Washington policy-makers as they prepared their conference proposals was this: Could the United States use its economic and political strength in such a way as to overcome Latin American resentment against its leadership in the hemisphere? The answer would depend on the nature of United States proposals, and Latin American reactions to those proposals, at the conference itself.

The political problem was the easier one. President Roosevelt had committed the United States at the Big Three Yalta Conference of January–February 1945 to support the Dumbarton Oaks proposals on regional organization—proposals which clearly subordinated regional peacekeeping bodies to a central world authority. As a matter of keeping faith with its major allies, the United States could not retreat from those proposals in advance of the San Francisco Conference. At the Yalta Conference, as at Dumbarton Oaks,

the United States had continued to underplay the issue of
regionalism. President Roosevelt did not push for strong
regional groups. He reacted negatively to what he thought
were Latin American demands that the United States take
premature action to "rehabilitate" the Argentine government and pave the way for its early entrance into the United
Nations Organization in the name of "hemispheric solidarity." Secretary of State Stettinius did send a "Top Secret,
Operational Priority" message from Yalta to Washington
urging the State Department to get the few remaining nonbelligerent American republics to declare war on the Axis,
so as to have them all qualify for admission to the United
Nations Conference in San Francisco. But the point of this
arrangement (which President Roosevelt referred to as one
which "would save my life") was only that it gave the
United States a face-saving way to exclude Argentina. Washington was counting on the fact that the Argentine government was not about to give in to Yanqui pressure and submit
the required declaration of war.[3]

The Mexico City Conference convened at Chapultepec
Castle outside Mexico City on February 21, 1945. The question of regional organization quickly came up. The Latin
Americans showed clearly that they did not trust any of the
great powers, the United States included, to exercise the
essentially arbitrary power of a Security Council veto in
a manner responsive to Latin American interests. They
wanted, instead, a wholly autonomous inter-American security system. Moreover, they wanted to establish some
mechanism whereby the power of the United States in the
inter-American system would at least be limited juridically
under a majority-rule formula. They therefore attempted to
pressure the United States to agree to a draft resolution
which would bind all signatories to "defend by all means,
including by arms, the territorial integrity and the political
independence of all and each of them, once it had been decided by the absolute majority of all the American states."[4]

Acceptance of such a proposal by the United States
would have had disastrous consequences for the American
approach to world security, for it would have meant a complete surrender to the regionalist point of view. Moreover,
the proposal as written would have put the United States in
a position where, at least theoretically, it might some day
not only have to agree to deploy troops without specific con-

sent of Congress, but might even have to acquiesce in the use of "internationalized" United States contingents against other United States forces. Finally, such a proposal would have created precisely the kind of precedent which the Russians could seize upon as an excuse for similar preemptive behavior in Eastern Europe. Bearing these points in mind, the United States delegation insisted upon watering down the proposal until it became the relatively innocuous "declaration of solidarity" contained in Resolution VIII of the Final Act (called the "Act of Chapultepec").[5]

The continued reluctance of the United States to take a "regionalist" approach came up again in discussions of proposed revisions of the Dumbarton Oaks proposals. The Latin Americans insisted upon including in the Final Act of the conference a list of specific suggestions for such revisions. One suggestion asked for permanent seating for a Latin American representative on the United Nations Security Council. This was an idea first proposed by Ambassador Carlos Martins of Brazil at a Washington meeting of State Department and Latin American representatives at the end of January. The United States evaded an endorsement of the list by having the text ascribe it only to "the Republics here represented which did not take part in the Dumbarton Oaks conversations."[6]

Altogether, the United States delegation managed to temporize effectively with the question of regional security at the Chapultepec Conference. Secretary of State Stettinius did make a public statement supporting the basic compatibility of an inter-American system and a world-wide collective security system. He told a plenary session of the conference on February 22, 1945: "The United States Government believes that the stronger we can make the inter-American system in its own sphere of activity, the stronger the world organization will be." But Stettinius purposely left that "sphere of activity" undefined, and when it came down to specific proposals the United States managed to avoid any commitments that would conflict with the position President Roosevelt had taken at Yalta in preparation for the San Francisco Conference.[7]

2. The nature of postwar economic assistance

The economic problem was not so easy to deal with. The United States was hard-pressed to present any concrete pro-

posals for economic aid to Latin America. Europe was the
current focus of attention for American economic policy-
planners; they felt unable to make firm commitments in
more than one large geographical area at a time. Under these
circumstances, there was little the United States could offer
Latin America by way of immediate aid. In a speech to the
joint economic committees of the conference, Assistant Secretary of State for Economic Affairs Will Clayton explained
immediate American policy intentions in regard to Latin
America's economic needs. Clayton promised "orderly"—
in other words, gradual—termination of wartime commodity
procurement contracts for strategic and critical materials,
so as not to cause instability in Latin American economies.
He also gave assurances that the United States would do
what it could to supply needed capital goods in the postwar
period, so that Latin America would not end up squander-
ing its war-born dollar balances on useless luxury imports.
Finally, Clayton mentioned that the Export-Import Bank
would again be making loans for sound development projects. He urged Latin Americans to take advantage of its
facilities.

When it got down to the actual prospects for supplying
needed goods to Latin America after the war, however, Clayton was not optimistic. "With reference to the availability in
the United States of the capital goods, tools, machinery, and
equipment which you require in implementing your post-war
policy of economic development," he told the Latin Americans, "it must be admitted right off that we face here an
extremely difficult problem." Defending the United States'
wartime record on this score, Clayton noted that while the
American performance had "fallen far short of meeting your
needs," United States industries had also had to do without
needed replacements. Latin America had not been discrimi-
nated against in this respect. But the essence of the problem,
as Clayton stated it, was not past inadequacies; it was rather
the prospect that while postwar demands for capital goods
were certain to be extremely heavy all over the world, productive facilities for such goods had been substantially
destroyed except in "two or three" countries. "In conse-
quence," Clayton noted, "the load which will be placed on
these two or three countries [including the United States]
will be a very heavy one." So long as existing American wartime controls continued, he promised, the United States had

the "means at hand for an equitable allocation of our production," and it was "the intention to continue to make use
of such means to see that you obtain a fair share of such
production." Meanwhile, Clayton added, the United States
government would "carefully investigate other methods of
assuring you of a fair proportion of our capital goods when
our present governmental controls expire."

The implication was clear that because of reconstruction priorities, Europe would be a chief competitor for the
products of the American industrial plant. Clayton made the
point explicit when he remarked that Latin America should
think of itself as gaining rather than losing from rapid European reconstruction. The Latin Americans, Clayton noted,
were particularly worried about a possible decline in the
postwar American demand for their export products. Clayton reassured them that increased European demand would
take up the slack. Therefore, he suggested, the Latin Americans should think of Europe not as a competitor for United
States economic aid, but rather as an area whose speedy rehabilitation would be of direct benefit to Latin America.
Such rehabilitation would restore former markets and perhaps open up newer and greater ones as reconstruction ultimately gave way to new and higher levels of economic
growth, including growth in European purchasing power.
Clayton also noted that the International Bank for Reconstruction and Development and UNRRA would help to promote this mutually beneficial European recovery. "There is,
then," he summed up, "no cause for pessimism regarding
the urgent and, in many cases, desperate postwar need for
useful goods of all kinds, or of the ability to provide the
means of payment. Indeed, it is the expectation that within
a few years after the end of the war the volume of international trade will expand to considerably higher than pre-war
levels."[8]

Clayton, of course, was still talking about the Latin
Americans' selling, while they wanted particularly to hear
about their chances of buying. On the latter point he could
offer them little concrete assurance. It soon became clear
that the United States' approach at Chapultepec was to
stress advice rather than assistance and recommendations
rather than commitments. Some of the advice and some
recommendations were intended to mollify Latin American
resentment over past problems by *implying* future American

commitments. But much of the advice indicated an American attempt to lay down the law, particularly regarding certain Latin American economic practices considered by the
United States to be contrary to the requirements of the inter-
American community. Aside from Clayton's speech, the basic
American approach both to immediate problems of readjust-
ment to peacetime conditions and to future problems growing out of more deep-seated, traditional Latin American
economic difficulties could be found in two documents.
These were Draft Resolutions No. 97 and No. 98 presented
to the conference by the United States delegation.

Draft Resolution No. 97, originally entitled "Maintenance
and Development of the Internal Economies of the American Republics," listed nine principles. The first four dealt
with common commitments to assure a continued flow of
needed goods north and south for the duration of the war
and after. These four also mentioned the problem of needed
improvements in commercial transportation facilities. The
last three points dealt with removing barriers to the movement of technicians and technical information in inter-American enterprises. The fifth and sixth points were the most
revealing as indicators of the United States attitude. They
proposed, respectively, that no industries be built up which
could not survive in the long run without government "subsidies," including high protective tariffs, and that no government go into competition with private interests in development schemes unless public interest clearly demanded such
a move.[9] The strong emphasis on private initiative, and on
curbing "unnecessary" government involvement, was unmistakable.

Draft Resolution No. 98 was the broader and more inclusive of the two statements. It was entitled, somewhat
grandiosely, "An Economic Charter of the Americas." Its
preamble advanced the thesis that the "two pillars on which
a positive economic program can be built to satisfy the basic
desires of the peoples of the Americas are rising levels of
living and economic liberty that will encourage full production and employment." Thereupon followed a "Declaration
of Principles," ten in number, calling for, in order: rising
levels of living, through an expanding economy; equality of
access to materials, raw and manufactured; reduction of
trade barriers; no private agreements to restrict trade; the
elimination of economic nationalism "in all its forms";

equal and just treatment for foreign capital and enterprises; endorsement of the Bretton Woods proposals and the Food and Agricultural Organization of the proposed United Nations Organization; encouragement of private enterprise and a commitment to refrain from setting up state trading enterprises; agreements on marketing basic primary commodities; and respect for the rights of labor as defined by the International Labor Organization.[10]

The draft of the Economic Charter provided striking confirmation that the postwar economic approach of the Roosevelt administration was to be global rather than merely hemispheric. This point came out clearly in regard to the United States position on development financing in Latin America. Up to the middle of 1942, the State Department had still been making sporadic efforts to free the old Inter-American Bank convention from the powerful grip of Senator Carter Glass, who had pigeonholed it in the files of the Senate Banking and Currency Committee.[11] But by early 1945, the United States government had long since discarded the idea of an Inter-American Bank. The whole point of the White Plan, which formed the basis of the Bretton Woods proposals, was to keep the entire world open for an influx of United States capital investments and loans. Special regional economic arrangements could be fully as dangerous as special regional political and military arrangements. The United States government did not wish to set precedents in either case.

The International Bank for Reconstruction and Development and the International Monetary Fund were therefore supposed to substitute for, and not complement, regional banking arrangements such as the Inter-American Bank. The United States–sponsored draft of the Economic Charter presented to the Chapultepec Conference accordingly contained an endorsement of the world-wide financial organizations, but no mention of a hemispheric banking institution. Timing was also of some importance in this respect. United States officials expected that at least in the initial postwar period, the administration would be concentrating financially on European reconstruction anyway, while the Latin Americans would be liquidating large accumulated wartime dollar exchange balances and not be in need of *immediate* loan assistance. But the prime consideration was still the broad principle to be established for the

future, namely that the Open World policy of the United
States dictated an avoidance of anything that could set a
dangerous example leading to closed regional spheres of
influence around the world.

United States views on tariff levels in the Western Hemisphere also indicated a preoccupation with the Open
World approach, though in this case the American aim was
not so much to prevent special *regional* tariff arrangements
as to prevent the emergence of closed economies even on
the *national* level in Latin America and around the world.
Roosevelt administration officials, as well as leading private
businessmen in the United States, were firmly committed to
the thesis that expanding foreign trade was necessary for
full employment and economic prosperity in the postwar
United States. Clayton had himself stressed this point all
through the late wartime period. At a November 1944 joint
meeting of the Research Committee and Research Advisory
Board of the Committee for Economic Development, Clayton had emphasized the impact which loss of foreign markets had made upon employment levels in the United States
during the depression. University of Chicago economist
Jacob Viner agreed with Clayton, noting that "in the long
run the quality of employment in this country depends on
foreign trade." Clayton, Nelson Rockefeller, and others
would soon testify before Congress as to the absolute necessity of extending the Trade Agreements Act once again, so
as to keep employment levels high. Under these circumstances, United States negotiators at Chapultepec could
hardly encourage the use of protective tariffs in Latin
America.[12]

Perhaps it was ironic that by the time of the Chapultepec Conference, the last inter-American meeting held during President Roosevelt's lifetime, the United States had
precisely reversed the position it had taken at the Roosevelt administration's first inter-American conference in Montevideo in 1933. Just before the Montevideo Conference,
Brain Truster Louis Howe had prepared for Secretary of
State Hull a list of subjects "to be avoided like the plague" at
the conference table. Among those subjects was tariff reduction. Because of domestic political considerations, Howe
advised Hull to "touch with regret" upon the economic situation which made tariff negotiation impossible for the
United States at that point.[13] But almost immediately after

1933, the State Department had begun to move forward the reciprocal trade agreements program, and by 1945 the maintenance of low tariffs in other countries was a cardinal prop of the State Department's position.

All told, the United States' position at Chapultepec was exactly what the proposed draft of the Economic Charter said it was—an assault on economic nationalism "in all its forms." From its low-tariff position to its attempted ban on state-run trading enterprises, the United States' position was an effort to make sure that the power of government would not be used in the postwar period to close off any bloc area, regional or national, to United States economic expansion. In this connection, the proposals on "just and equal treatment" for foreign capital in Latin America were crucial.

The Roosevelt administration had been working on this maneuver for years. In going over proposed recommendations for the May 1944 conference of national subcommissions of the IADC, Commerce Department officials had stressed over and over again the importance of preventing unnecessary restrictions on the use of foreign capital in Latin America. "Discrimination against foreign capital and foreign investors," stated one Department memo, "serves only to discourage the entry of foreign capital, and thereby retards economic development and advances in levels of living." In regard to government intervention in general, the same memo stated:

It is generally recognized . . . that in most fields economic development can be carried on most effectively by private enterprise, and the contribution of private enterprise to general economic advancement has been most successful and effective when government participation has been restricted to those fields in which it has not been feasible for private enterprise to operate, and where government regulation has been exercised to the minimum extent consistent with protection of the public welfare.[14]

Nationalism and statism went hand in hand, and both were to be discouraged.

The IADC conference of May 1944 had been generally considered by United States officials to be a triumph for the anti-statist, anti-nationalist point of view. Commenting on the success of the conference, one official of the Bureau of Foreign and Domestic Commerce noted:

Above all, it is unmistakable that the Latin American countries are capital-hungry and will not consciously do anything which

will seriously impede the investment of foreign capital. This obviously does not mean that foreign capital will be acceptable on
any terms, but it does mean that foreign capital is wanted in large
amounts and that concessions will be made to attract it. In making this observation, I am not unmindful of the fact that the
representatives at the Conference were businessmen who are
not likely to express the more extreme nationalistic sentiments of
other elements in their countries. I do believe, however, that what
might be called the business point of view will come to prevail
for the simple reason that the rapid industrialization which the
Latin American countries so ardently desire cannot be achieved
without a strong infusion of foreign capital, and they all know it.[15]

The 1944 approach of the IADC became the 1945 approach of
the State Department, as the best hope for what Eric Johnston, president of the United States national subcommission
of the IADC, had called an American Century in Latin
America.

3. The nature of postwar military assistance

For all the talk about the primacy of European reconstruction and the need to avoid unhealthy government involvement in the economic process, the United States was
becoming increasingly willing to supply one type of aid to
Latin America, even at the time of the Chapultepec Conference. This was military aid, and the style in which it was to
be offered indicated clearly that it fit very nicely into the
larger pattern of postwar policy planning.

During the war, the United States had extended military
aid to Latin America under the Lend-Lease program. Over
$150 million of the total outlay of $262 million had gone to
Brazil in connection with the use of Brazilian bases and military supplies in the preparation and launching of the North
African landing from the eastern Brazilian coast.[16] No Lend-
Lease aid had gone to Panama because the Canal Zone was
administered and defended directly by the United States,
and none had gone to Argentina because of her unsatisfactory political stance toward the Axis powers.

Not all American observers had agreed that the Lend-
Lease program in Latin America was well conceived. One
OCIAA memo warned that the net result of much of the aid
might be to encourage military dictatorships and weaken
the cause for civilian democracy in Latin America. The
memo suggested channeling Lend-Lease funds into productive civilian enterprises such as hospitals, sanitary projects,

and so forth.[17] Another OCIAA memo, written while military aid was being contemplated even before the Lend-Lease program got under way, pointed out that in such nations as Colombia, the army could not possibly defend its frontiers against well-trained and modernly equipped troops anyway. Military aid (as distinct from naval aid) would thus be useful only for helping to "maintain internal order against revolutionary disturbance," which the Colombian army was already capable of doing, provided the disturbance was local in character.[18] During the war, moreover, the State Department also received some serious complaints from the Latin Americans themselves, usually from those who felt they were being slighted in favor of their neighbors and traditional rivals.[19]

The Lend-Lease program nevertheless went forward, and was deemed so successful in Washington in spite of these drawbacks that before the end of the war, military planners were working on a permanent, coordinated military supply system for the Americas. The essence of the system was simple. Staff discussions were to be nominally multi-lateral and to take place under the aegis of the Inter-American Defense Board. Arms and equipment were to be standardized through a system of exclusive supply by the United States. So as not to conflict with the State Department's wish to avoid precedent-setting postwar regional military blocs, the plan centered on the supply aspect rather than on military strategy. Occasionally the planning became bogged down in jurisdictional disputes between the State, War, and Navy departments as to which agency would coordinate and supervise weapons sales. But by the time of the Chapultepec Conference, the policy was firm enough so that a War Department aide reported to Secretary Stimson that progress among inter-American planners was "very good." Shortly thereafter, the Department sent General George Brett to Latin America to discuss terms for building up military establishments there.[20]

There were a number of ways in which the military supply program fit into the larger United States policy framework. In the first place, it was good business for one of the United States' booming industries. In November 1944, Air Force General "Hap" Arnold had told Secretary Stimson of a program which army air corps officials were working out for the use of surplus aviation equipment in South American

training programs. "It was a program," Stimson commented,
"which seemed wise and helpful and it would tend to cultivate good relations with the South Americans which might
prove very profitable to our aviation industry in the future."[21] In the second place, even if there were to be no
closed regional military blocs in the postwar world, by acquiring a supply monopoly on military goods the United
States could hold a significant degree of economic and indeed political leverage over Latin America's military establishments. This was a key point in preventing the emergence
of an unacceptable degree of anti-American nationalism
among Latin America's top military officials, who in many
countries also had considerable political influence.

Third, the program provided insurance against internal
Latin American "subversive" movements sponsored either
by indigenous elements or by external powers. The cultivating of the Latin American military by the United States had
already proved its value as a counter to indigenous "subversion" in the case of the Bolivian Revolution of 1943–1944.
The possibility of externally directed subversion in the postwar period added a new dimension to the problem.

By the beginning of 1945, the State Department was receiving warnings that Russia was trying to use her embassy
in Mexico City as a headquarters for spreading subversive
activity throughout the Western Hemisphere.[22] When in
early January 1945 the Russian Ambassador to Mexico, Constantine Oumansky, was killed in a plane crash en route to
Costa Rica, Mexican officials recovered his briefcase and
reported that it contained between $150,000 and $200,000 in
United States $1000 bills. American Ambassador George
Messersmith sent a secret note to Assistant Secretary of
State Nelson Rockefeller warning that if the report were
confirmed, "we must take it for about as definite proof as
we have yet had that Oumansky was using large sums of
money for various, what we would call, improper purposes.
The only way in which the money could have been used,"
Messersmith added, "would be to suborn Government officials or labor leaders in Costa Rica or some of these other
Central American countries."[23] The report was never confirmed, but by January 1945 the general mood in Washington
required no confirmation. The subversion threat was seen as
quite real. Ironically, General Brett's military mission was
opposed, as Secretary Stimson noted in his diary, by "a num-

ber of American ambassadors [in Latin America] who feel there is danger of feeding military supplies into the hands of potential South American revolutionists." At a State-War-Navy meeting on the program, Stimson waved this objection aside, suggesting that "a good deal of the trouble may have come from unnecessary arrogance on the part of the military missions on the one side and absence of anything important to do on the part of the diplomats on the other side."[24] All told, the military supply program added something of an anti-revolutionary or at least anti-subversive tone to the anti-statist and anti-nationalist approach taken by the United States at Chapultepec.

Yet, as United States officials emerged from the Chapultepec Conference, they did not have the impression, for all the "anti" aspects of their program, that they had presented a negative approach to postwar hemispheric relations. The Economic Charter of the Americas was couched in very positive terms for the most part. Will Clayton's address had concentrated on the positive benefits to be gained by Latin America from European reconstruction. The United States had even agreed to a formula whereby Argentina would be invited to rejoin the inter-American community of nations, and to sign the Final Act of the Conference, as soon as she had demonstrated compliance with her anti-Axis "obligations" by rooting out remaining Axis influences inside her borders.[25] It really looked to some United States observers as if the United States delegation had indeed turned adversity into advantage at the conference, getting Latin America to agree to inter-American guidelines in tune with United States efforts to create an Open World for United States influence and economic growth in all areas, including Latin America itself. Senator Warren Austin returned from the conference to tell his Senate colleagues that the conference had signaled the end of Latin American distrust of the United States. War Department aide General Embick returned to Washington to confer with Secretary Stimson, and told the Secretary that "from his viewpoint . . . it was very good." One historian of inter-American relations described the conference as taking place in an atmosphere of "sweetness and light."[26]

Such reactions as those of Senator Austin and General Embick were encouraging, no doubt, to United States policymakers, and they provided the groundwork for many later

historical accounts. Yet they were also more arbitrary and
less accurate than they might have been. A good deal of
Latin American discontent appeared at the conference sessions, both as to the details of the United States' proposals
and as to some of the underlying assumptions behind the
United States' approach to postwar Latin American economic and social development. A number of Latin American
participants questioned the nature of the role assigned to
Latin America by United States policy-planners who were
intent on building an Open World. The nature and background of these Latin American discontents is the subject
of the next chapter.

VIII. The postwar role of Latin America: View from the south

1. North American perceptions, Latin American realities

"It is my considered opinion," wrote Ambassador George Messersmith to President Roosevelt the week after the Chapultepec Conference ended,

that the reason we had this atmosphere at this meeting, from the very outset, is due to the fact that every one of the Latin Republics came here with a deep fear of Soviet Russia in their hearts, from both the political and economic point of view. They came with a great deal of distrust of England from the economic point of view. They came with the feeling that the United States was the only country attached to the principles of fair treatment for small States, in both the political and economic field.[1]

There was some truth in this statement. A few of the long-term Latin American dictators represented at the conference had for many years been accustomed to "saving" their countries from communists, both internal and external, as a political stock-in-trade. One or two countries, such as Honduras, also had long-standing grievances against the British; and insofar as Britain represented to them the political influence of large, foreign-controlled enterprises in their midst, some of them were indeed anti-British, though their feelings stemmed more from a general economic anti-"colonialism" than from specific Anglophobia. Ironically, Argentina, the Latin American nation most heavily dependent on Britain, and thus potentially the most strongly anti-British, was not represented at the conference.

As a general statement of Latin American perspectives at the time, however, Messersmith's assertion was open to serious question. It was by no means clear that all or even most of the major nations of Latin America came to the conference with a "deep fear" of Soviet Russia. Late in 1943, President Avila Camacho of Mexico had expressed "uncertainty" over postwar Russian attitudes; he did not express deep fear.[2] Ambassador Messersmith offered no evidence to indicate that the President's views had changed since that time. Moreover, Mexico had taken the lead in Latin America in establishing strong diplomatic ties with Russia during the war.

In Brazil, the dominant perception of Soviet Russia, and of communism in general, was by no means a panic-stricken one. On March 14, 1945, two days after Messersmith wrote to President Roosevelt, Brazil established diplomatic relations with the Soviet Union. Under Secretary of State Joseph Grew offered his own home in Washington as a meeting place for the diplomatic representatives of the two countries. Within Brazil, President Getulio Vargas was already in the process of establishing a tactical alliance with the Brazilian communists in order to consolidate his own political position. Shortly after the establishment of Soviet-Brazilian diplomatic relations, Vargas released Brazilian communist leader Luis Carlos Prestes from jail after a nine-year imprisonment.[3] In Buenos Aires, military strongman Juan Perón of the uninvited Argentine regime told newsmen even during the Chapultepec Conference that he favored establishing diplomatic ties with the Soviet government, since the Argentines "as a nation" could not "ignore Russia as a great factor in the world."[4]

Some Latin American politicians openly acknowledged that they were using the communists in their countries for their own political purposes, secure in the knowledge that they could keep them under control as long as necessary. The government-backed candidate for the presidency of Cuba told United States Ambassador Spruille Braden late in 1943 that while he now had communist support for his candidacy, the communists feared him rather than the other way around, because they felt he might turn against them once he was elected. He also indicated explicitly that their fears were justified.[5]

Messersmith's analysis notwithstanding, fear of communism in Latin America was neither universal nor particularly serious. This was true even though the 1945–1946 period marked the height of communistic influence in Latin America, owing largely to the prestige which the Russians had gained by successfully overcoming the Nazi invaders. The rise in Russian prestige was more than offset in many cases by the concurrent rise of popularly based noncom-

munist nationalist movements, such as the *Autentico* move-
ment in Cuba, *Acción Democratica* in Venezuela, the *Gaita-nista* Liberals in Colombia, and the *Apristas* in Peru and *Peronistas* in Argentina.

If there was distrust or a tendency to xenophobia rife in Latin America at this time, it was not directed exclusively or even primarily at the Soviet Union. It vented itself more generally at all the great powers, including the United States. We have already seen how the Latin Americans reacted to the idea of a great-power veto in the Security Council. We have also seen how they wanted an autonomous inter-American system which could be used, among other things, to restrain the United States, not to give it *carte blanche* in the Western Hemisphere. It was for this reason that at Chapultepec the Colombian delegation introduced a draft resolution, in Spanish only (a rather pointed departure from protocol), asking for a general inter-American commitment to preserve territorial integrity against invasion or intervention, using armed force if necessary, upon a majority vote of the American republics. This was the resolution to which the United States had objected on the grounds that, as written, it might force a commitment of United States troops without the express consent of Congress and for purposes inimical to American national interests.[6]

On the whole, the economic aspects of Latin American distrust of the great powers at the time of the Chapultepec Conference were quite as serious as the political aspects. In this respect, moreover, certain Latin American governments, though not all, viewed the communist ideology of the Soviet Union as far less of an actual threat to Latin America than the anti-nationalist policy of the United States. Latin America's economy was only marginally connected with, and in no sense dependent upon, the economy of the Soviet Union; more than ever, as a result of the war, it had become dependent upon that of the United States. Moreover, five years of American-dominated "multilateral" economic cooperation, aimed at undercutting economic nationalism in Latin America, had not seemed to liberate Latin America from the myriad problems of underdevelopment. By March 1945, the Latin Americans were coming to believe that if they could not have a multilateral approach geared more directly to their own developmental needs, the only alternative was a recourse to economic nationalism.

2. A Latin American approach to development

"Economic nationalism," wrote State Department Political Adviser Laurence Duggan in reference to postwar Latin America, "is the common denominator of the new aspiration for industrialization. Latin Americans are convinced that the first beneficiaries of the development of a country's resources should be the people of that country." The demand was even broader than Duggan implied. "The philosophy of the New Nationalism," a former State Department liaison officer with the OCIAA pointed out, "embraces policies designed to bring about a broader distribution of wealth and to raise the standard of living of the masses. The internal market is emphasized, and attention is being given to the development of rail, road, water, and air transportation, which will make for more economic and political unity."[7] Development of domestic markets and a raising of the general standard of living—both were indispensable ingredients in the nationalist drive to make Latin Americans themselves the "first beneficiaries" of the development of their own economic resources. Both were results which had *not* been realized by inter-American "collaboration" under United States leadership. By the time of the Chapultepec Conference, the list of Latin American grievances against wartime United States policies was a long one, and extended over a wide range of economic activities.

One major problem was that of tariff policy. A number of Latin American observers began to fear that the postwar United States assault on high tariffs in Latin America might also include a campaign against existing industrial structures in some Latin American countries. In Brazil, as early as December 1943, the São Paulo office of the OCIAA sent a memo to the head office in Washington, warning that many Brazilian firms, fearing postwar "dumping" by competitive Allied firms, favored high tariffs for protective purposes.[8]

American officials sometimes refused to take such protests at face value. Early in June 1944, the OCIAA Coordinating Committee for Argentina sent to Washington a clipping from the Buenos Aires newspaper *La Nación*. The influential Argentine daily expressed fear of a repetition of the situation after World War I, when the industrial countries racing for markets in Latin America had undersold local manufacturers so as to undercut domestic industrial structures. The OCIAA Washington office replied that in many

Latin American countries, the term "dumping" was being
freely misused as an excuse for the establishment of additional trade barriers, in order to protect uneconomic "hot-
house" industries which had sprung up during the war. Not
all dumping fears were imaginary, however. Will Clayton,
himself a leading cotton exporter until he severed his business connections to move into government service, agreed
that something ought to be done in the United States to
eliminate the need for the government's cotton export subsidy, which was understandably angering the Brazilians.[9]

Both before and during the war, the Latin Americans
had often demonstrated that their high tariff demands were
selective rather than indiscriminate. In the prewar period,
such a prominent economist as Argentina's Finance Minister
Federico Pinedo had even suggested the possibility of general tariff abolition through a customs union among all the
American republics, including the United States. An early
IADC memo of June 1940 noted that the plan for hemispheric
development submitted to the Inter-American Financial and
Economic Advisory Committee (IAFEAC) by Chilean representative Carlos Dávila might eventually call for a customs
union. In 1941, a group of South American nations met to
discuss the idea of avoiding competition in new industries
by agreeing not to extend tariff protection to a local industry in one country once another country in the group had
started manufacturing the same product. Argentina and
Brazil signed a bilateral ten-year agreement of this nature.[10]

As to the question of discriminating against United
States products in the rest of the hemisphere, Brazilian Foreign Minister Oswaldo Aranha observed that the most-
favored-nation principle was still the key to economic peace
in the world. The United States, he noted, would continue
to receive, at least in Brazil, all commercial privileges
granted to other nations by the Brazilian government. In
April 1944, the Cuban government established by decree a
three-year exemption from import duties for all United
States machinery needed to build new industries in Cuba.[11]

The text of a draft resolution on tariff protection presented at the Chapultepec Conference by the Colombian
delegation summarized the legitimate aspects of the Latin
American drive toward protectionism: "The common desire
to abolish unnecessary trade barriers and to increase the
volume of international interchange," the resolution stated,

"can and must be brought into harmony with the diversification of production in those American countries which are not sufficiently developed, and with their attainment of a higher degree of industrialization." Occasionally, the Latin Americans went so far by way of demonstrating the selectivity of their protectionism as to make unilateral tariff concessions to the United States, in anticipation of reciprocal action on Latin American exports. In the summer of 1945, Chile did this, hoping to secure favorable action by the United States on Chilean copper exports. On the other hand, during this same period Brazil enacted legislation to prevent the importation of "obsolete" machinery except in "special cases" where the immediate need was so great that the Brazilians could not afford to hold out for modern goods. These instances demonstrated that tariff policy was becoming as much an integrated part of Latin American development strategy as it had historically been a part of United States strategy after the American Civil War. To the Latin Americans, this policy made as much sense in the 1940's as it had to Americans in the 1860's.[12]

The role of investment capital in Latin America was another key issue which had caused difficulty during the war and which was of concern to Latin American policy planners. The cry against "exploitation" by foreign investors was an old one in Latin America. Some countries had tried to take an optimistic, encouraging position on the problem during the war. Colombia's Industrial Development Institute, for example, set up a program for minority participation by foreign capital in new manufacturing enterprises. The program was designed to encourage not only capital inflow but also the establishment of new types of industries. Other countries such as Brazil tended to take an extremely nationalistic position, putting so many restrictions on foreign participation and ownership as to discourage new foreign capital inflows.[13] At one point in the war, the Brazilians did approach the United States with an idea for a Brazilian development bank backed by Brazilian and American capital. The American capital suppliers would act only as creditors and not as shareholders in the firms financed by the bank. One New York banker wrote to Morris L. Cooke, who headed the United States Industrial Mission to Brazil, expressing agreement with the Brazilian idea that self-liquidating loans were desirable and that American invest-

ments be made in such a way that the recipient firms could
come "entirely under the ownership and control of local interests" within a moderate length of time "if it were desired."[14] Nothing ever came of this Brazilian proposal, however, and Brazilian investment policy generally remained highly nationalistic under the Vargas administration.

Latin Americans had many reasons to fear the power of private foreign capital. In a memorandum prepared for the OCIAA Commercial and Financial Division in March 1942, OCIAA banking authority James H. Drumm, on leave from the National City Bank of New York, reviewed some of these reasons. In the early 1930's, Drumm noted, a number of Latin American governments had set up exchange controls in order to counteract outflows of foreign exchange which had resulted from the impact of the world-wide depression. For purposes of evaluating requests by foreign firms for exchange allotments, these governments had decided to examine the books of the foreign firms. "This," Drumm remarked, "gave the local authorities a much closer insight to the profit side of the picture and eventually resulted in increased taxation as well as jealousy and resentment." Along with these resentments, he noted, there grew up others. Some were based on the shortsightedness of the foreign companies in not training or employing local technical or executive personnel, and some on the feeling that foreign firms were taking all the profits and leaving nothing to the Latin Americans themselves; this latter view was particularly widespread in the cases of firms where all the common stock was held abroad. The time was now opportune, Drumm stated, for devising formulas permitting Latin Americans to participate in ownership and management of some of these firms. In particular, he recommended that ownership and management of all public utilities and natural resources should eventually revert to local groups or citizens.[15]

Considering its date of March 1942, this memorandum was striking. American policy-makers and investors had recently taken a severe setback in the Mexican and Bolivian oil expropriations, partially because of differences in evaluation of the expected compensatory payments, but especially because the American companies had had no intention of selling out in the first place. Now, with the oil companies still maneuvering to get back into Mexico, a prominent New

York banker in government service was suggesting that reversion of natural resources to local ownership was a natural and laudable progression. There were still a great many valuable American holdings of public utilities and natural resources in Latin America; they were not being run as self-liquidating investments. If one counted industries like air transport as potential "public utilities" (not unreasonable considering the growing importance of air cargo flight), then American control was on the increase rather than on the decline. A special assistant for aviation in the United States Department of Commerce estimated that as a result of the wartime program to clear out Axis participation in Latin American airlines and replace it with "acceptable" participants, United States airlines in Latin America would probably have more competition from each other after the war than from either local Latin American or European competitive lines.[16] Drumm's policy suggestion ran directly counter to this trend.

The Drumm memorandum was not made public, however, and did not become the basis for any United States policy statement. In the meantime, American private capital continued either to avoid Latin America altogether or to take an aggressive approach, disdaining the idea of junior partnership or any partnership at all under self-liquidating terms.[17] American aggressiveness was well demonstrated in an incident involving Mexican oil.

While he was Ambassador to Mexico, George Messersmith found out that Ed Pauley, then treasurer of the Democratic National Committee, was trying to pressure the Mexican government into giving him a contract for oil development. Pauley was evidently being supported by Petroleum Coordinator for War Harold Ickes, and opposed by Secretary of State Hull. Messersmith got hold of a copy of the proposed contract, read it, and, according to his own notes on the subject, "found it to be the most one-sided contract that I had ever seen." It provided, he noted, "such special advantages for Pauley that it was quite an improper contract and under no circumstances could our government have supported it." No less a person than President Avila Camacho told Messersmith that he was greatly worried about the matter because he, the President, "understood that Mr. Pauley had made it clear that if the Mexican Government did not agree to this contract and sign it, then he

[Pauley] would be in a position to make difficulties for Mexico in securing the manufactured articles and raw materials and food stuffs which she needed to keep her economy going." Ambassador Messersmith told the President not to worry about the contract, expressing his opinion that it was an "iniquitous" one. He assured Camacho that the United States government would not support it. Shortly after this, Pauley came to see Messersmith, argued the matter with him, and threatened to get him replaced if he did not support the contract. Messersmith was unmoved. Pauley left and went back to Washington.[18]

In Washington, Pauley tried to gain support for his contract from Secretary of Commerce Jesse Jones. Pauley described his plan to build and operate plant facilities for the manufacture of high octane gasoline and other materials, and asked Jones to arrange an Export-Import Bank or RFC loan to the Mexican government to cover the cost of construction. Jones summed up his own reaction to the proposition in a memo to President Roosevelt:

He [Pauley] told me that his compensation was to be 10% of the gross sales. He stated that the plant would convert 20,000 barrels of crude oil a day into these materials. This will give Mr. Pauley a very large management fee, probably in excess of $1,500,000 a year.

I told Mr. Pauley that his management fee was entirely too high. He stated that the Mexican Government would pay it and not the United States, but if we thought it too high, it could be reduced. I told him that we could not make a loan in which any such fees would be permitted.

It does not occur to me that it is in line with your policy that the Secretary [sic] of the Democratic National Committee should use his position to make money out of the Mexican Government.

A note on a later Commerce Department memo concerning the Pauley contract stated tersely: "Mr. Clay Johnson [a Commerce Department aide] said this could be filed," in other words, disposed of—which it was.[19]

An interesting sequel to the Pauley story occurred some time later when Ambassador Messersmith, back in Washington on a visit, went to see Harold Ickes. Messersmith discovered that Ickes had never read the Pauley contract, but had given his support to it, sight unseen, purely as a domestic political move. Messersmith got Ickes to read the contract, whereupon Ickes immediately withdrew his support.[20]

Not all United States Ambassadors in Latin America, however, were as ready as Messersmith to undercut private

American entrepreneurs in order to preserve the larger structure of the Good Neighbor Policy. For many Latin American countries, moreover, the economic activities of official United States agencies and United States public capital were barely less disturbing than the behavior of certain private interests in respect to their tendency to dominate local Latin American economic life. For the stronger countries—Mexico, Brazil, Chile, Colombia, and Argentina—this was not so great a problem. In general, United States public capital was at this time fairly safe for them to work with. But for the weaker countries, even public American money posed a threat. This was particularly true in regard to the operation of many of the Nation Development Corporations (Fomentos). The Chilean and Colombian corporations were partly financed by borrowed Export-Import Bank funds, but were operationally independent. In Haiti, however, the Eximbank held the total voting stock of the Haitian Development Corporation (SHADA) as security for the Eximbank's $5 million credit to the Haitian government. In Cuba, the national development corporation administered the $25 million Eximbank loan of 1941 in collaboration with the United States government. The same arrangement held for the Peruvian Amazon Development Corporation. The Eximbank also held 50 per cent of the voting stock of the Ecuadorean and Bolivian development corporations as security against its loans to them.[21]

Such foreign control over their national development corporations was hardly reassuring to many of the smaller countries. In Bolivia, by 1940, United States economic aid had become conditional upon a settlement of the oil expropriation question. State Department officials wanted concrete reassurance about Bolivia's future treatment of private, foreign-owned property.[22] In this context, United States veto power over Bolivia's own development corporation was even more challenging. Nationalist leader Victor Paz Estenssoro of the Movimiento Nacional Revolucionario (MNR) spoke out in October 1942 against the Bolivian Development Corporation precisely because of its dependence upon the Export-Import Bank. He deplored "placing . . . the Bolivian economy entirely in United States hands." As we have seen, after the Bolivian revolution of December 1943, the State Department responded by refusing to recognize Bolivia's new government until all MNR personnel (Paz Estenssoro in particular) had been removed from it.

In Haiti, the effects of United States control over the Haitian Development Corporation had been demonstrated in an equally graphic way. The United States had unilaterally cancelled SHADA's rubber development program in midstream, forcing a relocation of thousands of Haitian agricultural workers.[23]

As for the dominance of United States agencies over Latin American economic life, Panama offered a unique but striking case in point. There United States commissaries in the Canal Zone consistently undersold local merchants, crippling retailers in many lines of trade. A group of Panamanian merchants told one American reporter that virtually the only things they could profit on consistently were beer, whiskey, cabarets, and prostitution, for these were almost the only commodities which the Canal Zone commissaries did not stock on their shelves.[24]

Against this general background of American control and competition, it was easier to understand such Latin American responses as the Mexican government's decree of August 1944 exempting from income tax all operations by which Mexican nationals acquired foreign-owned properties or enterprises. "The current," one United States observer noted, "is running strong in the direction of Mexicanization of industry." By 1945, a Mexican industrial faction known as the New Group had gained prestige on the basis of its anti-Americanism at Chapultepec, while simultaneously former President Lázaro Cárdenas was frightening Ambassador Messersmith by calling for Latin American rather than inter-American economic collaboration.[25]

Apart from these problems of capital participation and commercial competition, Latin American nationalism was growing stronger in such sectors of economic life as labor policy and land policy. The behavior of foreign enterprises toward labor legislation in Latin America had long been a sticking point with Latin American nationalists. "Labor legislation," a Council on Foreign Relations study had noted in 1941, "regulation of wages, hours, and services, seems to offer an opportunity to retain within the country a larger proportion of the annual income of foreign corporations." The Mexican oil expropriations of 1938 had been set in motion by a labor dispute with the foreign oil companies operating in Mexico. At about the same time the Council on Foreign Relations study was published, a highly placed Mexican official was telling a United States audience essen-

tially the same thing, but he put it in somewhat more foreboding terms. "Foreign investment," stated Dr. Eduardo
Villasenor, director general of the Bank of Mexico, "should
make a firm stand for a certain measure of social reform in
the country. . . . Perhaps the paradise in which all the protection is given to the capitalist and no protection to labor
will one day be discovered to be a fool's paradise when labor,
organized or not organized, will break out in violence to get
by force and violence what law has not provided for them."[26]

On one level, there had been direct confrontation on this
question between United States employers and Latin American workers during the war. OCIAA and Board of Economic
Warfare officials had faced the problem of working out labor
policies in respect to wartime programs in Latin America
for the production of strategic raw materials. An OCIAA
memo of January 1942 noted that the United States needed
to develop programs concerned not only with working conditions but also with living conditions and social objectives.
One problem, the memo stated, was to strike a balance between exploitatively low wages and wages so inordinately
high that they would dislocate the entire wage structure of
the region and incite official opposition. Both local labor
and local management (the latter being in some cases politically equivalent to, and sometimes identical to, the local
government) had to be pleased. Another problem was to
work out social welfare programs of education, literacy, and
such without increasing the dependency relationship of
worker to employer. The goal was to set up programs which
could eventually be taken over by the beneficiaries rather
than by potentially hostile classes.[27]

American policy-makers were not always successful in
solving these problems. In January 1943, Ambassador Messersmith told Vice-President Wallace that he had had to intervene in Mexico to prevent the signing of a Board of
Economic Warfare procurement contract with a certain
Mexican mining company. Under this contract, the company
would have been obliged to enter into a labor contract with
a syndicate of workers in the mine. Messersmith told Wallace that under the Mexican constitution every man was
guaranteed the right to work, and employers were not permitted to exclude workers because they were not syndicate
members. Messersmith finally convinced the BEW, after
considerable discussion, that the Mexican government might
find the proposed contract obnoxious to Mexican law; the

contract might even endanger the procurement program.
Messersmith secured the substitution of a general labor
clause in the various BEW procurement contracts in Mexico;
the clause stated that both buyer and seller would agree to
abide by all pertinent provisions of Mexican labor and social
law. Messersmith added that this was as much as the United
States government could reasonably do.[28]

On another level, United States policy-makers inter-
acted directly with Latin American labor by hiring Mexican
contract laborers to come north to work on specified wartime manual labor projects. Again, not all the arrangements
were uniformly successful. After the war, the Mexican Ministry of Labor blacklisted eight North American states for
alleged abuses of these wartime labor contracts.[29]

Indirect policy contacts also occurred during the war,
between United States labor union representatives and their
Latin American counterparts. The Latin Americans were in
many cases still in the early stages of searching for effective
labor programs and organizational techniques, while the
Americans could tell them what they could expect to accomplish under existing local systems. Such contacts also gave
the Latin Americans an idea of the kind of help they could
expect from their American colleagues.

One such confrontation occurred during a trip to Peru
by a group of leading AFL and CIO officials during the summer of 1943. What was interesting about this meeting was
the Americans' reply to Peruvian questions about how organized labor had made such great advances in the United
States. David McDonald of the United Steelworkers (CIO)
told the Peruvians that American labor "had advanced
through its own struggles, and then had been able to employ lawyers and enforce the legal rights of the working
man and gradually to enlarge such rights." Irving Brown
of the AFL counseled "patience," and pointed out that the
"present status of American labor was the achievement of
many decades, so that it was probable that similar results
would be obtained in Peru only by the children of the men
now active in the cause of labor." The Americans also
stated their opinion that because of the low level of education among Peruvian laborers, agitation for a shorter working day "would be bad because the majority of workers were
not sufficiently educated to use their spare time either in
developing their bodies or their minds."

In reporting highlights of these meetings to the State

Department, Embassy officials noted that to the best of their
knowledge, at no time had the Americans met any *Aprista*
leaders, possibly due to clandestine intervention by the
Ministry of Government and Policy, which had "manifested
considerable interest in the desire and purposes of the delegation." However, the Embassy noted, the Americans had
"indicated their dislike of communism and even of socialism, while expressing a belief in individual initiative, although apparently one of the conditions being some
restraint on unadulterated capitalistic enterprise." On regis-
tering at their hotel, the union leaders had asked to be described in the hotel register as "executives."[30]

An interesting postscript to this visit occurred when a
group of local Peruvian communist members of the Construction Workers' Syndicate referred to the American labor
leaders as "delegates of oppression" sent from a capitalistic
country to learn what South American workers were doing.
The local unionists urged the people to ignore these "moderate Americans who thought [Mexican labor leader Vicente]
Lombardo Toledano too revolutionary." In reporting this
incident, a United States Embassy official noted that David
McDonald had advised Peruvian laborers not to found syndi-
cates of workers, but rather to set up small "religious societies" to which there would be less governmental opposition. The communists, on the other hand, refused to mix
religion with their workers' movement. The Embassy official
also reported that Lombardo Toledano had evidently "made
a considerable impression on local labor groups" during his
visit to Peru in October 1942.[31]

After the war, competition among communists, nationalists, and others for the allegiance of labor groups in Latin
America was to intensify greatly. But this early incident in
Peru showed that even during the war era the rivalry was
underway. To many Peruvian workers, the extremely grad-
ualist approach of the American labor leaders, plus the disinclination of the Americans to make any contact with either
Peruvian communist unions or nationalist *Aprista* leaders,
was convincing proof that Peruvian labor could expect little
help from American labor should the Peruvians embark on
more militant courses of action.

By May 1945, Lombardo Toledano, then president of the
influential Latin American Workers' Confederation (CTAL),
denounced the Mexican government's position at Chapul-

tepec as "subordinating the Latin American bloc to the aims of the United States State Department." He attacked the principle of regional autonomy in its American-sponsored form as "the final adoption of the Monroe Doctrine, which would leave the Latin American republics at the mercy of the United States." Some American observers, such as Ambassador Messersmith, dismissed such attacks by noting the wide base of communist support that Lombardo Toledano enjoyed. But Lombardo Toledano also had considerable noncommunist support in 1945, and his position could not be so easily written off by those who were concerned about the potential effects of Latin American working-class nationalism upon inter-American economic cooperation. The communists by this time had no monopoly on working-class nationalist support. Indeed, by early 1945, many of the popular noncommunist movements such as APRA in Peru and Peronism in Argentina were rapidly gaining power, and were moving so fast to gain labor support that, at least in Argentina, leading communists were either in exile or in clandestine opposition to the nationalists in the regime.[32]

A nationalist challenge to existing patterns of land tenure also loomed in Latin America at the end of the war. A Venezuelan sociologist, M. A. Saignes, summed up the situation in his country:

The economic progress of the country cannot be achieved so long as the semi-feudal forms of production and labor are not obliterated. A dispossessed peasantry, a rudimentary agricultural technique, vast extensions of land insufficiently exploited, landowners' capital stagnating in the national and foreign banks, all these factors inhibit the development of our national economy and place it at a disadvantage in relation to foreign capital in search of propitious ground.

A group of American writers citing Saignes' work declared his statement applicable to Latin America in general.[33]

American observers were aware of the strong relationship between patterns of land tenure and foreign influence in national economic life. A National Planning Association study noted that "monopolization of land has been and still is both the source and the technique of political power in Latin America." The study pointed out that in many countries, particularly in Central America, "the distribution as well as the production of agricultural commodities is largely controlled by a handful of monopolistic grain, livestock, fruit, and railroad corporations, whose headquarters in many cases are in Europe or in the United States." Frequently these companies had an international character through interlocking directorates, while "many of the big landlords and cattle barons in Latin America function merely as their intermediaries."[34]

Land usage was an equally serious problem. "Landholders," the Association's study pointed out, "have depended on peonage and low wages rather than on increased productivity to yield the desired profits. Machinery, fertilizers, and other modern tools and organizational techniques are little used." Under existing patterns, not all or even most of the available land was being cultivated in every country. In Chile, it was estimated that about 37 per cent of the cultivable soil of the large *estancias* of between two and three thousand hectares was actually under cultivation. The estimated figure for those *estancias* over five thousand hectares was 17 per cent. In Cuba, only a "minor part" of the land held by United States–owned and other foreign-owned sugar companies was actually used for growing cane. The study estimated that the Cuban mills could operate using about two-fifths of the land which the companies actually controlled.[35]

An interesting aspect of this problem came out in an analysis made by the Anglo-American Caribbean Commission during the war. Commission co-chairman Charles Taussig pointed out that in a number of Caribbean island countries under British or American rule, the "metropolitan governments," that is, the British or the Americans, agreed on the "desirability of crop diversification permanently," but the richer landowners on the islands preferred to live "by sugar alone." The "upper classes," Taussig noted, "feel that subsidization of sugar is legitimate but the subsidization of industry or other agricultural crops is immoral. Unless the return per acre for sugar can be equalized, there will be no diversification."[36] The case showed that the Americans, and the British, were sometimes ahead of local oligarchs in regard to economic thinking. But unless the metropolitan governments were prepared to intervene actively *against* local oligarchs in order to alter existing patterns of land tenure, economic progress was hopeless. Moreover, if the British and Americans continued to preside over such a status quo, then in some measure they might be politically liable should a day of reckoning ever come between planters and agricultural workers.

The State Department's Laurence Duggan saw this clearly. By 1949 Duggan would be publicly advocating loans to Latin American governments for land purchase and redistribution programs. The loans were to be made preferably by an international organization such as the IBRD. Duggan warned that in cases of "blind resistance of the landowners, revolution may prove the only way to bring about land distribution."[37] Here was the crux of the problem; should none of these relatively peaceful and nonviolent nationalistic programs for economic development be successful, then hitherto nonviolent nationalism could easily become revolutionary *and* violent nationalism, with consequences even more foreboding for foreign interests in Latin America.

3. The Latin Americans at Chapultepec

Even in February 1945, it was becoming clear that Latin America was rife with economic discontent and with distrust of the economic policies of the United States in Latin America. Far from signaling the "end of Latin American distrust of the United States" (in Senator Austin's classic phrase), the Chapultepec Conference showed clearly the distance between Americans and Latin Americans on economic questions. The split emerged clearly on such subjects as tariff protection, foreign capital participation in Latin American enterprises, government intervention in economic affairs, and the problem of multilateral finance mechanisms. In addition to these issues, there was evidence of a strong difference in emphasis on the crucial subject of planning, both in terms of production and distribution arrangements. The splits could be seen quite starkly by noting the nature of a number of draft resolutions introduced by the Latin Americans but never acted upon because of a lack of United States support or encouragement.

Draft Resolution No. 135, submitted by Cuba, indicated that "the investment of capital and of economic resources should be made, under the supervision of the State, under terms and conditions most favorable to the development of the countries benefited." The accent on state supervision here was directly counter to American inclinations. The resolution was never acted upon, though it drew widespread Latin American support. Draft Resolution No. 138, submitted by Brazil, recommended that "the American nations, especially those with ample financial resources, recognize it as a duty to promote investments of capital in countries whose economies are underdeveloped, for financing the purchase by these countries of equipment and essential materials, as well as technical assistance." The resolution also stated, however, that "endeavors shall be made to avoid making loans for financing the purchase of articles of consumption." These resolutions again underlined the principle that foreign participation should be encouraged only on a controlled and planned basis, so as to avoid wasteful or counterproductive efforts. This resolution was likewise tabled.[38]

Some resolutions went much further than the United States was really prepared to go. Draft Resolution No. 53, submitted by Chile and entitled "An American Industrialization Plan," was a case in point. The "whereas" clauses of the resolution read in part:

[Whereas] 2. The majority of the American nations have not yet reached a sufficient degree of industrialization, hence it is feasible that that process be developed within the Continent in a coordinated manner and with due consideration for the principles of a strong solidarity and cooperation in the economic order;

[Whereas] 3. It is desirable that programs of industrialization or mechanization be carried out according to an American plan that will give due thought to the requirements of each country, the utility of promoting a greater commercial interchange among the nations of the Hemisphere, and the advantage of obtaining proper utilization of raw materials, fuels, electric power, and other available resources;

[Whereas] 4. It is necessary to promote special facilities for the development of the indicated program through the cooperation and aid of the American nations, using the means and resources already available and avoiding as much as possible the establishment of parallel industries that will interfere with each other or make free trade difficult.

The resolution went on to recommend that the Inter-American Development Commission, in cooperation with the Inter-American Financial and Economic Advisory Committee (soon to be superseded by the more permanent Inter-American Economic and Social Council), be "charged with the coordination and development of the program of continental industrialization."[39] Nothing concrete developed out of this draft resolution, however, and the matter was dropped.

One major Latin American planning concern was acted

upon at the conference. Resolution No. 46 of the Final Act of
the conference, entitled "Sale and Distribution of Primary
Products," stated that "in exceptional cases of important
primary products in which burdensome surpluses have developed, or threaten to develop," agreements could be made,
"open to participation by all interested countries in the
world," establishing mechanisms to dispose of these surpluses by orderly marketing and eventually by more coordinated production. Such coordination might even include
assigning quotas on exports and imports for the participating nations. It is debatable to what degree the United States
really felt itself committed to specific action when it signed
this resolution, however, particularly when the only international agreement then in force, the Coffee Agreement of
1940, was about to be allowed to lapse on the initiative of
the Latin Americans themselves, who were anticipating
short-term shortages and consequent price increases.[40] Moreover, the United States was already a party to certain
bilateral agreements, such as the Cuban sugar purchase
agreement. Under this agreement, in return for the stability
of a guaranteed market, the Cubans had agreed to sell sugar
to the United States for considerably less than they might
have received had they held out for higher prices on the
free market.[41]

The point, however, was not what kinds of mechanisms
for international cooperation the United States was willing
to commit itself to in the Western Hemisphere, but rather
what kinds it was *not* willing to help launch. During the war,
the United States had taken considerable initiative in making data surveys of needed and potential industrial development in Latin America. The OCIAA had worked closely with
the IADC in setting up many such surveys, and continued in
some cases to do so even after the war.[42] Economists both
inside and outside the United States had recommended international cooperative action in launching large multi-
national efforts such as power and sanitation projects.
OCIAA records even contained policy memoranda on the development of "complementary projects in Latin America," as
well as on the promotion of "greater independence from the
necessity for imports" and on "closer integration of the
various currencies of Latin America."[43] But when it came to
setting up mechanisms for facilitating these programs,
United States policy-makers balked, fearing overextension

of resources and the establishment of dangerous precedents regarding governmental involvement in the economic development process.

The problem, from the American point of view, was not whether or not to cooperate, but rather how and to what degree to cooperate. The United States' position on hemispheric economic cooperation had been spelled out in Draft Resolutions No. 97 and No. 98, presented by the United States delegation to the conference. The Latin Americans clearly preferred different emphases, but simply did not have the leverage to force the United States to alter its position. The outcome of the conference was therefore that the American draft proposals were generally adopted intact, with only those changes that the Latin Americans could obtain through suasion or persistence.

Draft Resolution No. 97 was adopted almost as written, appearing in the Final Act of the conference as Resolution No. 50 on Industrial Development. The Latin Americans were able to effect one important addition to it. Remembering that American private capital had sometimes undermined or displaced local capital, they inserted into Resolution No. 50 a clause stating that foreign capital and foreign enterprises in Latin America should "assure to national capital a just and adequate participation, not only in establishment of such enterprises, but also in their management," and should not attempt to displace national capital.[44] The implication was clear. If the Latin Americans could not look forward to large-scale programs developed multilaterally under comparative safety, they wanted to be very sure that those projects undertaken in the interim did not have politically or economically harmful effects.

Draft Resolution No. 98 was also adopted almost intact. It became Resolution No. 51 of the Final Act, still entitled "An Economic Charter of the Americas," but with significant changes. Countering Latin American hopes for a period of tariff protection for their infant industries, the United States had sought a reduction of trade barriers. The Latin Americans forced the inclusion of a clause recognizing that in certain cases such protection might be temporarily necessary in order to help their new enterprises get started. The United States had sought the elimination of economic nationalism "in all its forms." The Latin Americans retaliated by inserting a clause pledging the American republics to refrain from the "dumping of surpluses of national production in world markets." This addendum was clearly aimed at the United States, and particularly at United States government subsidization of cotton exports.

To the United States suggestion on equal treatment for foreign capital, the Latin Americans added the phrase, "except when the investment of the latter would be contrary to the fundamental principles of public interest." Finally, the Latin Americans insisted on striking out the United States proposal pledging the American republics to refrain from setting up state-controlled trading enterprises.[45]

The Latin Americans also managed at Chapultepec to avoid committing themselves to immediate abolition of exchange controls. Exchange control, like import control, was a vital tool for Latin American governments interested in promoting local development of new industries, particularly consumer goods industries. A number of countries had adopted exchange controls during the war, in order to conserve vital foreign exchange; this was done for the purpose of using such exchange in the postwar period to buy needed industrial equipment. Exchange controls could also be used, however, to protect existing local industries. A report issued in 1943 by the Bank of Mexico warned that when wartime restrictions on United States exports ended, the "indiscriminate import of goods" into Latin America could very well increase so rapidly and widely as to threaten existing national industries with ruinous underselling. The Bank noted that "this possibility would justify the application of measures to select imports with the end not only of maintaining the development of the industrial processes but of preserving a satisfactory situation with respect to employment in the country." In commenting upon this statement, an American economist agreed that in order to avoid both underselling and gradual erosion of scarce foreign exchange resources, Mexico might "have to wrestle with the problem of husbanding its resources if it is best to serve its national purposes."[46]

Beyond these considerations, many observers in Latin America and in the United States believed that exchange control actually affected rates of economic expansion. Foreign exchange played a role in Latin America similar to that played by domestic investment and savings in the United States and other highly developed countries. "For these

[Latin American] countries," wrote OPA economist Seymour Harris, "the amount of investments is in no small part dependent on foreign contributions; and these in turn are dependent on the state of foreign exchange." Another United States government economist added the thought that losses of foreign exchange, due to expenditures for necessary imports not produced locally, slowed expansion rates by decreasing the amount of exchange available for conversion into investments (through government control mechanisms). "It is evident, then," he noted, "that although large-scale government spending will not remain ineffective, its ability to produce an expansion of real income nevertheless is limited by the size of foreign exchange reserves and the capacity of the domestic industries."[47]

Some Latin Americans were almost as anxious as the Americans to get rid of exchange controls, precisely because they wanted to avoid giving the more developed areas and more economically powerful nations an excuse to use such controls against Latin American exports. Liberal Colombian economist (later President of Colombia) Carlos Lleras Restrepo agreed that in the long run, exchange controls were nothing less than an instrument of "economic warfare." In an article published shortly after the Chapultepec Conference, Lleras Restrepo said he looked forward to the elimination of such controls as soon as possible, under international supervision through the mechanisms to be set up pursuant to the Bretton Woods agreements. But elimination of exchange controls did not mean elimination of economic controls *per se,* and Lleras Restrepo took great pains to point out that most Latin American nations drew a "clear distinction between exchange controls and import controls." He defended the latter as part of the right of the Latin Americans to take defensive action to restrict imports "in certain circumstances and for specific purposes."[48] Meanwhile, the Chapultepec agreements contained no specific clause pledging immediate elimination of exchange controls.

Finally, the Latin Americans showed "pronounced misgivings" over the failure of the United States to revive the Inter-American Bank project.[49] Occasionally, United States officials tried to soft-pedal the significance of this disagreement. Under Secretary of Commerce Wayne Taylor told a congressional committee that the Latin Americans did not really have as much interest in obtaining United States government loans in 1945 as they had had in 1940, and so there was no great call for an Inter-American Bank. But Taylor contradicted his own statement when he also pointed out that it had been the Latin Americans who, fearing a dearth of available foreign public investment capital in the postwar period, had insisted on adding the word "development" to the name of the International Bank for Reconstruction and Development. Up to that point, the IBRD had been thought of as almost entirely an international Reconstruction Finance Corporation, at least in the initial stage of its operations.[50]

4. Balance sheet of the conference

All in all, the Chapultepec Conference was no meeting of minds between Americans and Latin Americans in regard to strategies for economic development in Latin America. Insofar as the conference represented a "victory" for United States policy-makers, it was a victory imposed by unanswerable economic power rather than by conversion of the Latin American dissenters. Disagreements were sharp and frequent, and the language of the Final Act of the conference showed plainly that several remained unresolved. Latin American economic nationalism had not been downed; it had merely been temporarily frustrated.

As for the claims, public and private, made by American observers to the effect that fear of communism had bound the Americas together, this was either a delusion or a decoy, depending on whether the claims were made privately or publicly. Informed American observers in Latin America knew perfectly well that indigenous nationalism, not international communism, was the real threat to United States interests in Latin America. As Ambassador Frank Corrigan had reported to Secretary of State Hull from Caracas in March 1944, the Venezuelan communists were so well behaved that even in the labor unions which they controlled, they cooperated with the government's wartime request for a no-strike pledge—which was more than some noncommunist unions did. This was not simply because it was to the advantage of "international communism" to win the war against the Axis powers, though that was certainly a part of the motivation. It was also, as Corrigan noted, because the Venezuelan communists believed that "further capitalistic development in Venezuela" was a necessary prerequisite to a revolutionary situation. Corrigan described the Venezuelan communists simply as "non-revolutionary."[51]

When the war ended, the United States Ambassador in Brazil, Adolf Berle, wrote to President Truman describing in graphic terms the political weakness, indeed irrelevance, of the Brazilian communists. "Their economic program," Berle told the President, "is about that of Theodore Roosevelt in 1904. . . . Unless the Soviet Union and the United States clash, there will not be trouble." Years later, Berle summed up the relevance of the "communist menace" to the entire Chapultepec Conference situation. The conference would have taken place, and would have turned out approximately as it did, Berle noted, "even if the Russians had never been invented." President Roosevelt and his advisers had all wanted a strong "hemispheric alliance," for reasons which essentially had nothing to do with the Russians.[52]

The Chapultepec Conference, however, had temporized with many problems. Before the United States could be fully free to implement the anti-nationalist, anti-statist approach to Latin America which it had staked out at Chapultepec, it had to attend to the larger problem of world organization at the San Francisco Conference. There the United States would face the acid test of its postwar strength and maneuverability, discovering whether it would be able to build an Open World with Russian cooperation or alone. This was the great task to the preparation of which the Roosevelt administration now turned its attention.

IX. Building one world

1. Old era out, new era in

"You can see," wrote Secretary of War Stimson in his diary,

that the State Department has got itself into a mess. Contrary to what I thought was the wise course, they have not settled the problems that lie between the United States and Russia and Great Britain and France, the main powers, by wise negotiations before this public meeting in San Francisco, but they have gone ahead and called this great public meeting of all the United Nations, and they have got public opinion all churned up over it and now they feel compelled to bull the thing through. Why to me it seems that they might make trouble between us and Russia in comparison with which the whole possibilities of the San Francisco meeting amount to nothing.[1]

Stimson, writing the week before the conference opened, had cause to be worried. The Grand Alliance was indeed beginning to crack. The explosive Polish issue was no closer to solution; there were obviously going to be serious problems with the administration of the postwar German occupation; the question of political influence of the great powers in oil-rich Iran was emerging; the old Balkan problem was taking on a new complexion with communists and anti-communists competing for power in Greece, Rumania, Bulgaria, and Yugoslavia; and in France, a combination of communist and other left-wing anti-Americanism along with Gaullist nationalism was starting to threaten the unity of the Western allies. Within three weeks of this diary entry, Stimson was writing to President Truman: "All agree as to the probability of pestilence and famine in central Europe next winter. This is likely to be followed by political revolution and Communistic infiltration. Our defenses against this situation are the western governments of France, Luxembourg, Belgium, Holland, Denmark, Norway, and Italy."[2]

Of course, as Stimson himself had noted, frantic United States efforts to set up an international organization without prior big-power agreement on fundamental objectives would necessarily increase the long-run danger of serious Russian-American antagonism. Yet, as one looked at the world in late April 1945, world organization *without* great-power unity was precisely the direction in which United States policy was heading, and with ever-increasing intensity. One could not yet say that a full-scale Cold War mentality was in control in Washington; but distrust was growing, and the political and economic implications of that distrust were becoming increasingly manifest in the nature of United States planning for the San Francisco Conference.

The main question confronting United States policy-planners in the last two weeks before the conference opened was this: Could the United States still hope to work with the Russians in building One World, a peaceful world open at all points for the type of American growth and expansion envisoned in Henry Luce's American Century proposal? By early April 1945, President Roosevelt was beginning to doubt that such Russian-American cooperation was still possible. He and Stalin had been having some brusque exchanges in regard to the reorganization of the Polish government. But the United States and Russia were still in agreement on certain other very important points. Indeed, there were ways in which the United States and Russian points of view were closer to each other than either one was to the British, or French, points of view. Roosevelt's Open World approach implied a strong attack on Britain's and France's pre-eminent positions in a number of underdeveloped areas. The President wanted to free those areas politically for an influx of United States capital, industry, and technology. Stalin, for his part, was always ready to acquiesce in a weakening of the sway of the Western European colonialist powers in Asia and elsewhere. He had clearly rather enjoyed watching Roosevelt bait Churchill on this issue at wartime Big Three conferences.[3]

One of Roosevelt's last major actions indicated strongly that in regard to foreign markets, the President was as concerned about British competition for postwar influence as he was about Russian competition. Roosevelt knew, as United States policy-makers generally knew, how economically weak the Russians would be at the end of the war. The Russians themselves, in applying for American aid after the war, indicated something of the extent to which German armies had destroyed Russia's productive capacity. A partial list of Russian losses included 31,850 industrial enterprises, 65,000 kilometers of railroad track, 10,000 power stations, 1,135 coal mines, and 3,000 oil wells. Under the circumstances, the Russians, whatever their intentions in matters

of international trade, would hardly be in a position to compete effectively in distant foreign markets.[4]

On the other hand, Roosevelt also knew how energetically the British, who had suffered much less than the Russians, would be attempting to build up their industrial export economy so as to keep from being undermined by the United States in traditionally British export markets. Early in April 1945, the President sent financier Bernard Baruch on a special mission to London to explain to Prime Minister Churchill and other British officials just what the United States expected the postwar international economic situation to look like. The British had indicated that they would be using their Imperial Preference System and sterling bloc arrangements to maintain an advantage in traditional markets while they were reconstructing their industrial facilities at home. Baruch pointed out to the British that in order to undertake reconstruction of export industries, the British would have to import producer goods from the United States, and would be subject to American export priorities arrangements. "Their attitude on Empire preferences and the sterling bloc underwent a sharp shift," Baruch noted, "when I showed them how through the use of our priority power we could override any trade barriers, if necessary. I feel certain," he added, "we can gain a considerable relaxation of these restrictions whenever we stand ready to make a proposal to them either in the form of a 'cylinder head' loan or through the promise of priorities on our production."[5] In regard to the crucial issue of international economic competition in the postwar world, the nation which posed the largest immediate threat to the United States was Great Britain, not Soviet Russia.

This would be offset, of course, in areas on the periphery of Russia itself, such as Eastern Europe, where Russia's political and military power might offset her economic weakness. There Russian military power posed a considerable challenge to United States interests. It was the President's feeling, nonetheless, that while the Russians had to be watched, they could be made manageable if they were not pushed too far in relation to matters affecting their security. Properly handled, the Russians could be held in check in Eastern Europe. They could even be brought to acquiesce in the desire of the United States to build an Open World for American economic expansion.

A number of policy advisers looked forward to including

the economy of the Soviet Union itself in the Open World scheme. "It might be well," noted Bernard Baruch on his return from London, "to point out to the Russians that before the war, business interests [in the United States] acquired great respect for the manner in which Russia kept all contracts and observed all credit arrangements. This has been increased by her incomparable military accomplishments during the war. It would be tragic for the Russians at this point to permit doubts of their motives to mar this splendid record—tragic for both them and us since it would react against all who want peace." It would be just as tragic, Baruch also pointed out, if the United States, for its own part, failed to do what was necessary to permit an "easing of Russian suspicions of the Western powers so lasting Allied unity can be achieved."

War Production Board director Donald Nelson and Chamber of Commerce president Eric Johnston talked with Stalin very frankly about the "wish of American industry to do business with the Soviet Union." Foreign Economic Administrator Leo Crowley agreed that "industrial development and reconstruction in China, Russia, and in other countries will open up vast new markets." Treasury Secretary Morgenthau suggested to President Roosevelt that a $10 billion reconstruction credit to Russia would be "a major step in your program to provide 60 million jobs in the postwar period."[6]

The death of President Roosevelt on April 12, 1945, brought a change in the policy style (though not in the policy aims) of the United States. Roosevelt's successor was a man who not only knew virtually nothing of international affairs but whose assumptions about dealing with adversaries were crude in the extreme. Harry Truman had nicely summed up his feelings about dealing with the Soviet Union in a statement he had made the day after the Nazis had invaded Russia in June 1941. The Senator from Missouri had put the matter very succinctly:

If we see that Germany is winning the war we ought to help Russia, and if Russia is winning we ought to help Germany and that way let them kill as many as possible.[7]

Early in the afternoon of April 23, just before Truman was to meet with Soviet Foreign Minister Molotov, he held a meeting with his leading advisers on the subject of the impending San Francisco Conference and great-power affairs.

Even before listening to the views of his advisers, the President announced his own position with characteristic bluntness. If the Russians did not want to cooperate, he said, "they could go to hell." That afternoon, Truman immediately attempted to face down Molotov on the explosive Polish issue. The President told the Soviet Foreign Minister that the Yalta agreement on Poland was neither vague nor negotiable but was clear and unambiguous; the Russians were violating it and the violation had to stop. "I have never been talked to like that in my life," said Molotov. "Carry out your agreements," Truman snapped back, "and you won't get talked to like that."[8]

It was not that Truman disagreed with Roosevelt's assumptions about the basic goals of United States foreign policy in the postwar period. Truman quite understood the principle of the Open World, and indeed understood the American Century approach as well. They were relatively simple principles to understand. Truman, however, did not feel that it was necessary for the United States to conciliate the Russians at all. If the Soviets were not ready to help build an Open World without prior concessions on the part of the United States, then the United States would proceed to build an Open World alone, while the Russians could "go to hell." Roosevelt's style had been one of firm though flexible negotiation; Truman preferred confrontation.

Ironically, Truman may have been strengthened in this conviction by Bernard Baruch's report of his London mission. Baruch had undertaken the mission at the request of President Roosevelt, and had concentrated in his report on his discussions of postwar economic policy with the British. But Roosevelt had died in the interim, and Baruch had returned to present his report to Truman. Truman appears to have been impressed with Baruch's views, but may have applied Baruch's comments on the postwar strength of the United States more to Soviet-American relations than to Anglo-American relations. In this connection, Baruch's summary statement was particularly striking:

Because of the accomplishments of our arms, waging simultaneous offensives in both Europe and the Pacific, and because of our astonishing productive capacity and because he asks for ourselves only what we will give to the others— namely peace—the President of the United States can dominate the settlement, bringing peace, work and contentment to the world.

Such a statement made heady reading to a man who only
ten years ago had been nothing more than a distinguished
recent alumnus of the Pendergast machine school of Kansas
City politics. It might also have reinforced in him a feeling
that negotiation was unnecessary.[9]

The change in strategy began to appear clearly in the
deliberations of United States officials as the San Francisco
Conference approached. Among the members and advisers
of the United States delegation to the conference, hard-
liners like Senator Arthur Vandenberg and John Foster
Dulles began to speak with increasing authority after Roosevelt's death. Vandenberg was already at San Francisco when
he heard of Truman's showdown with Molotov. He described the news as "thrilling."

This is the best news in months [Vandenberg wrote in his diary].
F.D.R.'s appeasement of Russia is over. We will "play-ball" gladly
with the Russians and "give and take" because we must have
unity for the sake of peace *but* it is no longer going to be all
"give" and no "take" so far as we are concerned. Stettinius
turned to me . . . and said—"*If you* had been talking about Poland
to Molotov not even *you* could have made a stronger statement
than Truman did." Stettinius does not know what the result will
be. Molotov had to report to Stalin and so, pending a reply, they
all moved out to join us here. He said that subsequent meetings
with Eden, Molotov and Soong [the Chinese Foreign Minister]
were very cordial and that the Russians seemed to be more cooperative. But the crisis will come when Stalin's answer arrives.
Russia may withdraw. If it does, the conference *will proceed
without Russia.* Now we are getting somewhere![10]

The change in strategy also became apparent in regard
to inter-American relations. As Adolf Berle had pointed out,
United States policy at the Chapultepec Conference would
have been largely the same even if the Russians "had never
been invented"; the major goal of the United States at
Chapultepec was to set forth the economic basis of the postwar hemispheric "alliance," and this had little to do with the
Russians. But it soon became clear to those engaged in the
pre-conference deliberations of the United States delegation
to the San Francisco meeting that inter-American *political*
relations *would* in fact be intimately connected with the
problem of great-power relationships at *this* conference. The
key specific issue was still the regional security issue. The
larger general question was whether or not the inter-American "system" would slowly be turned into a full-fledged anti-
Soviet bloc.

2. Conflict north-south

The starting point for United States policy-planners was the lingering Latin American discontent which had been building up for months over the issue of defensive regional autonomy for the Western Hemisphere. The Latin Americans were continuing to show distrust of the great powers in general, and to give evidence that they were not content to rest their political security upon a United States veto in the Security Council. At Chapultepec, the Latin Americans had tried a number of ploys to obtain a guarantee of regional autonomy in the postwar world. They had suggested permanent representation for Latin America on the Security Council (the equivalent of a Security Council veto for Latin America), to prevent United Nations action not in accord with their wishes. They had attempted to bind the United States to a mutual guarantee of borders, through united military action against nations intervening in other nations' affairs. After the Chapultepec Conference was over, the Latin Americans had continued to bombard Washington with suggestions designed to win the hemispheric autonomy to which the United States, for reasons of its own, had not committed itself at the Mexico meeting.

For one thing, the Latin Americans attempted to win United States support of compulsory World Court jurisdiction in all cases involving international political disputes over boundaries, interventions, and so forth. The United States delegation to the San Francisco Conference, in its preliminary pre-conference meeting of April 12, agreed to follow the lead of the British and the Russians in *not* supporting such a demand. At a later pre-conference meeting between State Department adviser Leo Pasvolsky and members of the Mexican delegation, the Mexican officials proposed giving the General Assembly review power over important actions of the Security Council. This was yet another manifestation of Latin American discontent and distrust regarding the proposed arrangements. As the date of the conference opening drew nearer, it was becoming increasingly clear to United States observers and strategists that unless some concessions were made to the Latin American point of view, it might be difficult to keep the Latin Americans "in line," as Senator Vandenberg put it.[11]

Once again, it was the Argentine question which brought matters to a head. At Chapultepec, the United States delegation had agreed for the sake of hemispheric solidarity to an arrangement whereby Argentina would be invited to rejoin the "community" of the American republics if she rooted out remaining Axis influences within her borders and declared war on the Axis powers. The military regime in Buenos Aires shrewdly seized the opportunity, declaring war on Japan and Germany and *announcing* a program of anti-Axis housecleaning. On April 4, the United States and the other American republics resumed normal diplomatic relations with the Argentine government. But this did not mean that Argentina was to be invited to the San Francisco Conference, or to sign the wartime "Declaration by United Nations" (a prerequisite for membership). Before the United States delegation left Washington for San Francisco, President Truman, mindful of anti-Argentine public opinion in the United States, explicitly instructed the delegates not to support Argentine admission to the United Nations until concrete evidence showed that the Argentines had fulfilled satisfactorily all their anti-Axis commitments under the Declaration of Chapultepec.[12]

Now, however, a problem arose. President Roosevelt had agreed at the Yalta Conference to support Russia's claim for two additional seats in the General Assembly. The President had not agreed, however, to have two additional delegations, to represent the White Russian and the Ukrainian Soviet Socialist Republics, invited to the San Francisco Conference. After some negotiation, Stalin had specifically withdrawn his request that the two republics be invited to the conference. But in late March, Moscow had announced that a thirty-member delegation would be sent to San Francisco to represent the two republics; the Russians were pressuring the United States to support admission of the republics to the conference. The question facing the United States delegation was this: Should the United States commit itself to support such an invitation, and did United States support imply an American effort to line up Latin American support as well? Moreover, what would happen if, as a condition of support for the Russian republics invitation, the Latin Americans demanded United States support for the immediate admission of Argentina?

Theoretically, the two issues were separate and distinct. The American position on the two extra votes for the Russians had been worked out at the Yalta Conference in Febru-

ary 1945. The Russian republics had been promised eventual
United Nations membership and voting rights. The position
on Argentina had been arrived at separately, after the
Chapultepec Conference. In neither case was the party or
parties concerned supposed to be invited to participate in
the San Francisco Conference. But the Russians had decided
to try to get their two additional seats in the conference, and
had approached the United States to make the necessary
request.

Instead of continuing to treat the Argentine and Russian republics issues separately, the United States delegation decided to link them. At first, the tie extended only as
far as asking the Latin Americans to vote for admission of
the Russian republics. Secretary Stettinius went to the Latin
Americans to make the indicated request. When the Latin
Americans tried to link the Russian republics invitation to a
similar invitation to Argentina, Stettinus refused to do so.[13]
But by the time the issue came to a vote in a United States
delegation meeting on April 25, all but one of the delegates
nonetheless agreed to link the two invitations and to invite
all three governments to participate in the conference some
"two or three weeks" after the conference opening. The lone
dissenter, Senator Vandenberg, voted "no," not because of
his position on Argentina but because of his feelings about
Russia and her claim to two extra votes.[14]

Why did the United States delegation so quickly accept
a connection between these two separate issues? The answer
lay in the increasing disposition among the delegates to regard Western Hemisphere solidarity and the Soviet-American split as two sides of the same coin. Most of the delegates were coming to see hemispheric solidarity as a tool to
be used against Russia in the conference. On matters of
Soviet-American disputation, a solid bloc of twenty Latin
American votes for the United States' position would come
in very handy. Moreover, the Argentine question appeared
to be a natural one on which to make some necessary concession to the rebellious Latin American delegations in the
name of continued hemispheric solidarity.

Much of the initial lobbying for the tie between the inter-
American and Soviet-American issues came from one person
in particular, whose chief official concern was more with
the inter-American than with the Soviet-American aspect of
the situation. This was Assistant Secretary of State Nelson

Rockefeller. The comparative ease with which he succeeded is striking. Rockefeller's progressively persuasive influence came out clearly as the United States delegates and advisers reviewed their position during the crucial pre-conference meetings of April 25.

At the morning meeting that day, Rockefeller initially met with considerable hostility to his position. The Latin Americans, he argued, would not vote "as a bloc" in favor of the admission of the Russian republics unless Argentina was also admitted. If the United States wanted the Latin American votes for the Russian proposal, "there would have to be a settlement of the Argentinian question." Most of those present agreed with Assistant Secretary of State James Dunn, who "did not think we could make a deal of this sort." After some discussion, Rockefeller responded by saying that if Russia insisted on an invitation for her two constituent republics, he "could not be held responsible for delivering the [Latin American] vote if nothing was done on the Argentinian question."[15]

Discussions went on all day. By the time the delegation met again that evening, Secretary Stettinius was himself convinced that the Russian republics issue and the Argentine issue were inseparably linked. Delegate Harold Stassen proposed admitting all three delegations in the third week of the conference. With Stettinius offering no further personal objection, Rockefeller beat down remaining opposition. Referring to Latin American resentment over the whole regional security schema, and to the need for the United States to pacify this resentment, he noted that a failure to invite Argentina "would be giving away our bargaining position with the Latin American countries." Stettinius finally polled the delegation. All agreed with Stassen's proposal but Senator Vandenberg. The next morning, Stettinius reported to the delegation that President Truman had agreed that Argentina be invited in three weeks, provided she was not invited to sign the United Nations Declaration. The Russian republics would also come in at the later date. Stettinius asked for a vote on this position. Again all agreed except Vandenberg, who "reserved his position."[16]

The confrontations began on April 28. At a preliminary evening meeting including United States, Soviet, and Latin American representatives, Mexican Foreign Minister Ezequiel Padilla proposed immediate admission of Argentina.

Instead of simply turning down the proposal, Soviet Foreign Minister Molotov countered by saying that it was impossible to invite Argentina without inviting Poland. Argentina had, he said, "in effect, helped the enemy" during the war, while Poland had suffered greatly as a result of her resistance to the Nazis. This raised still another problem. The reorganization of the Polish government had been a matter of concern and dispute among the great powers ever since the Yalta Conference. A Soviet-dominated provisional government was temporarily in control in Poland, pending further negotiation to admit an undecided number of officials from the pro-Western "government in exile" in London. To admit Poland to the United Nations at this point would have been in effect to ratify the permanence of the Soviet-dominated provisional regime. Molotov knew full well that the Polish question would have to be decided by the Big Three, and that in the interim neither the United States nor Great Britain would accept admission into the United Nations of a government that was entirely Soviet-dominated. He was clearly playing for propaganda points, aware of the unpopularity of the Argentine regime among so many United Nations members.

Brazilian Acting Foreign Minister Velloso told Molotov directly that if Argentina were not invited, the Latin Americans would vote against admission of the Russian republics. Molotov reiterated his own position, and suggested that the matter be put over until the official conference meetings on April 30.[17]

On that date, the matter came to a head. On the morning of the 30th, the executive committee of the conference took up the issue. Then the steering committee did likewise. Finally, that afternoon the plenary session of the conference, which included all the invited governments, voted on the various proposals. Each time the scenario was the same. The Soviets requested immediate admission of the two Russian republics. The request was granted unanimously. Then the Latin Americans proposed admission of Argentina, and Molotov countered with his Polish proposal. Each time the result was the same: Argentina was voted in, and Poland was not. At the plenary meeting, Molotov delivered a long verbal blast against the Argentine regime, citing its record of "collaboration" with the Axis and stressing the damage to be done to the United Nations Organization by admission of a government which stood for everything to which the United Nations had been opposed for the last four years. The next day, the *New York Times* gave extensive coverage to the events and to Molotov's speech in particular. Many American observers, the *Times* noted, feared that as a result of pressing the Argentine issue the United States delegation had seriously "detracted from the ability" of its government to "argue for moral issues" during the remainder of the conference. The *Washington Post* blasted Secretary Stettinius for his "inept handling" of the Argentine situation.[18]

Senator Vandenberg, however, had a different assessment of the situation. Despite his minority-of-one position on the invitations question—a position which stemmed not from anti-Argentine feeling but rather from a strong antipathy toward Soviet Russia—Vandenberg was coming to occupy an increasingly important position in the United States delegation. The mood of the delegation was becoming more and more anti-Soviet, and this added to Vandenberg's stature. Moreover, Vandenberg was the United States representative on the all-important regional arrangements subcommittee of the conference. In this capacity he would have considerable leverage for moving the United States toward a strong anti-Soviet position on regionalism.

Vandenberg had followed the fight on the invitations question very closely. He had seen clearly, and had so noted in his diary, exactly where the United States' pre-conference commitments left off and where the bargaining points on the issues began. After the morning meeting of the United States delegation on April 25, Vandenberg immediately took note of the situation regarding the Russian republics invitations. "We have no freedom of action," he wrote, "regarding our vote on *finally* permitting White Russia and the Ukraine to join the ultimate League [Vandenberg always referred to the United Nations as the "Peace League"]. But we clearly have freedom of action on seating them in this Conference." After the delegation meeting that evening, Vandenberg again took stock of the situation: "It is apparent," he noted, "that Molotoff will demand at tomorrow's meeting of the Steering Committee that they be admitted not only to the ultimate League but also to this Conference. F.D.R. committed us to the former but not to the latter." It was because of this insight that Vandenberg had steadfastly refused to vote for admission to the conference of the two Russian republics.[19]

Once the conference got under way, however, Vandenberg suddenly lost his insight in the general confusion of the developing anti-Sovietism of the United States delegation. When Vandenberg summed up in his diary the events of April 30, the day on which the votes were finally taken and both Argentina and the Russian republics voted in, he seemed to have entirely forgotten the limit of President Roosevelt's original Yalta commitment. Molotov, Vandenberg wrote, "got White Russia and the Ukraine seated unanimously—but *solely* because America and Britain insisted upon the good old Anglo-Saxon habit of living up to international commitments (Yalta)."[20] Only five days before, Vandenberg had been quite clear on the fact that Roosevelt had *not* committed the United States at Yalta to support anything more than eventual admission of the two republics to the United Nations. Now he had forgotten that fact.

The reason for his forgetfulness was clear. Vandenberg was much more concerned with the outcome of the confrontation than with its cause. As a result of the Argentine–Russian republics fight, Vandenberg exulted, Molotov had "done more in four days to solidify Pan America against Russia than anything that ever happened." Then, in a passage which Vandenberg's son omitted from the published portion of the diary, the Senator summed up the true immediate significance of the victory: "He [Molotov] has done more to put the two Americas into a solid bloc than anything that ever happened heretofore. We shall see the results in subsequent events in this Conference."[21]

Publicly, even Vandenberg felt it necessary to make some gesture of concern over the Argentine invitation. On the day after the vote, the United States delegation faced the press. Vandenberg recorded the scene in his diary:

The American Delegation had a full press conference today with about 600 newspaper men. I presided. There were many critical questions asked about the Argentine decision etc. I made the following statement which I wish to make a matter of record. "Some things have been happening here which I do not like. Some decisions have been made which are repugnant to me. But these events cannot be segregated into air-tight compartments and judged exclusively on their own merits. They must be weighed in connection with the *total* situation. It has been necessary to clear away a lot of under-brush to get this Conference under way. We could not permit these situations to jeopardize the larger objective for which we are here gathered. Whether I like all of these situations or not, I intend to await the *final* product of this Conference to determine whether it is worthwhile. I do *not* intend to snipe at it en route."

Yet in a telegram which he sent that day to President Truman, Vandenberg assured the President of his agreement with the actions of the delegation. He was "shocked" at the *Washington Post*'s critical editorial of that morning, he said, adding that he considered it to be "totally without justification." Vandenberg told the President: "I consider that Secretary Stettinius has confronted superlatively difficult situations in thoroughly splendid fashion and I sustain him in every decision he has made." The key point, as Vandenberg had already noted in his diary, was that the "two Americas" had been put into a "solid bloc" which would stand together against the Russians for the balance of the conference.[22]

3. Conflict east-west

The Argentine–Russian republics issue had actually brought to the surface a fundamental conflict within the United States delegation. A real struggle was in process between those who favored a moderate, conciliatory approach to the Russians and those who favored a hard-line policy of confrontation. Ancillary to this struggle were the views of the two groups on how to treat Latin America in the context of Soviet-American relations. The moderates or conciliationists were unwilling to make too many concessions to the Latin Americans for fear that some of these concessions— like the original concession on the Argentine invitation— might become sore points between the United States and Russia. The confrontationists took the opposite approach, preferring a strong stand on "hemispheric solidarity" precisely in order to gain Latin America voting support for the anticipated Soviet-American conference fights.[23]

The problem arose almost immediately as the conference took up the subject of regional defense arrangements. Once more, the focus was on both inter-American and Soviet-American relationships. On the morning of May 4, the United States delegation took up the question of regional arrangements, with War Department military advisers present. At first the primary concern of the delegation members was the effect of the Dumbarton Oaks proposal and the Soviet Security Council veto on inter-American regional self-defense. Senator Vandenberg immediately remarked on the fact that the Dumbarton Oaks proposals subordinated regional defense arrangements to the authoritative control of the Security Council; since the Russians would be able to use their veto against all Western Hemisphere action, the arrangement, said Vandenberg, "spelled the end of the Monroe Doctrine." Assistant Secretary of War John McCloy noted in this connection that it was "extremely important to protect our concept of preclusive rights in this hemisphere." General Stanley Embick put the matter more bluntly: it would be essential for the United States "to maintain our isolation and our preclusive *control over* this hemisphere" (emphasis added).[24]

This view was not precisely what the Latin Americans had had in mind when *they* advocated regional autonomy in defense arrangements. Nevertheless, the views of Vandenberg and the War Department advisers were important for two reasons. In the first place, starting from McCloy's and Embick's assumption that the United States *would* in fact *control* an autonomous Western Hemisphere defense system, regardless of what the Latin Americans preferred, the United States could then publicly ally itself with the Latin Americans on the regional autonomy issue, while simply de-emphasizing the question of who would actually run the hemisphere. In the second place, the United States could use this identification with the Latin American position as a further lever in insuring Latin American bloc support for other United States proposals which the Russians might not like. Indeed, on May 1, the day after the vote on the invitations issue, Soviet Foreign Minister Molotov had made a pointed comment in a Big Four meeting to the effect that the bloc voting strength of the Latin Americans was giving them an influence in the conference somewhat out of proportion with their actual "power and resources." Molotov also noted that he was "concern[ed] at the possible control of the Conference by a bloc . . . opposed to his own conception of having the Conference controlled by the four Major Powers under an agreement to maintain unanimity with respect to all major questions which came before the Conference."[25]

In respect of the regional arrangements question, however, the old problem remained. An overly firm American stand in favor of regional autonomy might encourage the Russians to close off Eastern Europe under cover of the same principle. The United States delegation therefore continued to balk on full support for the Latin American position. At the four-power consultative meeting held on the evening of Friday, May 4, the delegation submitted for the consideration of its Russian, British, and Chinese colleagues a draft of an amendment to the Dumbarton Oaks proposal on regional security. The draft provided that

no enforcement action should be taken under regional arrangements or by regional agencies without the authorization of the Security Council with the exception of measures against enemy states in this war . . . or, to the extent not inconsistent therewith, in regional arrangements directed against renewal of aggressive policy on the part of such states, until such time as the World Organization may, by agreement between the Security Council and the Government concerned, be charged with the responsibility for preventing further aggression by a State now at war with the United Nations.

The idea of this draft was that it clearly maintained the primacy of the central world organization. The only exception permitted in regard to regional initiative was that temporarily given the special anti-Axis bilateral defensive treaties planned by those European nations (including Russia) who needed some "secure guarantee" against Axis resurgence until such time as the United Nations had demonstrated its ability to keep the peace in Europe.

In the four-power discussions, Soviet Foreign Minister Molotov at first objected to the language of the draft. He proposed that everything beginning with the phrase "until such time as, etc." be dropped. This clearly indicated that Russia did not favor putting any time limit on her special bilateral treaties in Europe.[26] Over the weekend, however, Molotov notified Stettinius of his consent to the language of the United States' proposal. This cleared the way for action which would at least preserve one key United States goal. By putting a time limit on the freedom of action given the Russians in respect of their security treaties, the amendment would prevent the legitimizing of a closed, Soviet-dominated treaty system in Eastern Europe which might arise under cover of "anti-Axis defensive" arrangements. But the amendment still did not solve the problem of inter-American regional defense arrangements on a basis acceptable to the Latin Americans or to a number of the United States' own delegates and advisers.

Two of those most concerned about the inter-American problem were Senator Vandenberg and Nelson Rockefeller. Rockefeller had been out of town during the initial four-power discussions of the proposed amendment. He had gone to Washington on OCIAA business, and also to discuss phases of the Argentine invitation fight with Acting Secretary of State Grew and President Truman. He returned to San Francisco on May 5, and was upset to find that in his absence the delegation had approved an amendment which would in effect undercut inter-American regional autonomy. Rockefeller tried to make an appointment to see Secretary of State Stettinius, but the Secretary, evidently somewhat annoyed at Rockefeller's increasing aggressiveness on behalf of the "regionalist" cause, declined to see him. Rockefeller immediately arranged to have dinner with Senator Vandenberg and to work through the Michigan Senator instead.

Vandenberg, for his part, was also upset about the inter-American aspects of the amendment, much as he approved the idea of hobbling the Soviet Union in Eastern Europe. He was particularly upset that under the proposed formula "little [was] left of the Monroe Doctrine." By a "significant coincidence," Vandenberg noted later that night in his diary, "Nelson Rockefeller . . . asked me to join him at dinner where he disclosed these same fears and said the South American Republics are up in arms and cannot much longer be held in line."[27] Rockefeller and Vandenberg worked all evening on a formula to *hold* them "in line" for the duration of the conference. The formula which the two men finally came up with was one which clearly put the cards on the table. It was one by which the United States, if it maneuvered carefully, might ultimately have its cake and eat it, too. Vandenberg immediately put the proposal in the shape of a letter to Stettinius, which he delivered the next morning at 9:30.

"I have been greatly dissatisfied," Vandenberg's letter began,

with one phase of our proposal regarding "Regional Agreements" and I am putting my viewpoint before you before it is too late. I am greatly disturbed lest we shall be charged with a desertion (1) of our Pan American obligations at Chapultepec and (2) of the Monroe Doctrine. The former is a threat to the Pan American solidarity which becomes increasingly indispensable to our own safety. The latter is a threat to confirmation of the entire San Francisco charter by the Senate of the United States.

Vandenberg had no objection, he said, to letting special defense treaties in Europe remain temporarily independent of the Security Council. "I do not object to this exemption," he wrote, "and I am quite willing to continue it for the very good reason that we can't expect our allies to depend upon an untried Peace League for their defense against a resurgent Axis until it has demonstrated its adequate capacity to serve this defense function." But why, he asked, was there no such exemption permitted in the case of the inter-American defensive system?

We have all been troubled about this phase of the matter. We have all wanted an answer to it. But we have been deterred by our fear that an exemption for our inter-American "Regional Agreements" might be an invitation to the rest of the world to divide itself up into similarly immunized blocs and regional balance-of-power groups. There is no such invitation and no such precedent when we recognize only an existing implement which is the expression of a continuous inter-American policy for more than a century and which is without possibility of current parallel anywhere on earth.

Vandenberg now proposed that precisely such an exemption be granted:

. . . Why should we not add to our pending proposal that Paragraph 2 of Section C should be further amended by adding at the end thereof the following: "and with the exception of measures which may be taken under Resolution VIII, known as the Act of Chapultepec of the Inter-American Conference on Problems of War and Peace, signed at Mexico City on March eighth, 1945, until such time as the Organization may, by consent of the Governing Board of the Pan American Union, be charged with this function"?

In this manner, Vandenberg noted, the United States would achieve "three indispensable objectives." First, it would preserve the Act of Chapultepec until the American republics were "prepared to relinquish its functions to the new Organization." Second, it would preserve the Monroe Doctrine "until such time as it is no longer necessary for our security and we are prepared to voluntarily relinquish it." Third, Vandenberg asserted,

we have prevented a veto in the Security Council upon any Western Hemisphere self-defense at all. On the other hand we have not set a precedent for encouraging other regional blocs and therefore we have not endangered the ideology of the new Organization. Furthermore we have not done anything which prejudices the legitimate rights and interests of any of our other United Nations.

The idea was simple enough. From Rockefeller's and Vandenberg's point of view, the antiquity of the inter-

American alliance was justification enough for its receiving
special treatment commensurate with that afforded to the
anti-Axis treaties of the Europeans. Vandenberg referred
to the arrangement as one which would not endanger "the
ideology of the new Organization." In reality, this was short-
hand for not giving the Russians an excuse for parallel action in Eastern Europe. Vandenberg concluded with a warning as to the importance of a satisfactory arrangement in
order to maintain inter-American solidarity, or, as he and
Rockefeller had put it, to hold the Latin Americans "in line":

Suppose [Vandenberg wrote] the united Latin American countries should present the foregoing proposition in behalf of
Chapultepec and the Monroe Doctrine, is it conceivable that the
United States could vote no? Such being the irresistible fact, is it
not infinitely preferable that we should take the initiative?[28]

As Vandenberg noted in his diary, shortly after he delivered his letter to Stettinius, " 'Hell' broke loose" in the
United States delegation. Vandenberg had thrown the regional question wide open again, despite the fact that his
letter had reached Stettinius shortly *after* Molotov had
called to express Russian agreement with the previously
submitted United States draft on the subject. Stettinius
was furious with Rockefeller for his part in reopening the
question, and gave him what Vandenberg described as a
"trimming." But now that Vandenberg, an influential Senate
leader, had been brought into the picture, the Secretary
could no longer ignore the opposition view, and he immediately circulated copies of Vandenberg's letter to all delegation members and a number of key advisers. When the
delegation convened again the following Monday morning,
it was split down the middle over the entire regional question.[29]

Most of the State Department advisers, including International Division advisers Harley Notter and Leo Posvolsky,
opposed the exemptions plan as a dangerous weakening of
the entire United Nations structure. At the Monday morning
meeting, Assistant Secretary of War John McCloy proposed
eliminating the Security Council veto altogether, inasmuch
as it had already been wiped out in Europe, and was now to
be wiped out in the case of the Western Hemisphere. "Having our armies in Europe," McCloy stated, "would . . . keep
us in the picture" there, while the elimination of a Soviet
veto power over inter-American security policy would assure

the position of the United States in the Western Hemisphere. John Foster Dulles warned against any action which might tend to "trade off" the United States' position in Western Europe in return for a guarantee of Western Hemisphere solidarity. Nelson Rockefeller remarked that the Latin Americans felt that the United States was letting them down on the regional security question, and they (the Latin Americans) were now "contemplating the disintegration of the Western Hemisphere system." Assistant Secretary of State James Dunn argued against Rockefeller's position, claiming that the Latin Americans would "see the point" of the exception in Europe. The United States veto in the Security Council, he noted, amply protected the Monroe Doctrine, while the Act of Chapultepec did not itself call for the use of force anyway. Rockefeller replied that this was a "legal interpretation," and that the United States had already pledged itself to work for a full-fledged inter-American defense treaty. "If we wished to continue good relations with the Latin Americans," Rockefeller noted, "we would have to continue to work on the basis of good faith."[30]

Nothing was resolved at this May 7 meeting, and the subject was put over to a later session. Meanwhile, McCloy telephoned Secretary of War Stimson to get his point of view. Stimson, himself a former Secretary of State, had been following the progress of the regional question with interest. At first he had been fairly optimistic, both as to the question of hemisphere security and as to the probability of Soviet-American cooperation. A week before the conference began, Stimson noted in his diary: "Our respective orbits [those of the United States and Russia] do not clash geographically and I think that on the whole we can probably keep out of clashes in the future." On April 26, shortly after the conference opened, Stimson went over the Western Hemisphere problem with McCloy by telephone. "Some Americans," Stimson remarked, were "anxious to hang on to exaggerated views of the Monroe Doctrine and at the same time butt into every question that comes up in Central Europe." The "real Monroe Doctrine," the Secretary stated, "isn't quite as bumptious as those people think it is, and . . . probably an adjustment can be made between the two . . . regional sittings. Our position in the western hemisphere and Russia's in the eastern hemisphere," he concluded, "could be adjusted without too much friction."[31]

As the conference negotiations unfolded, however, Stimson became progressively more worried that "the young men in the State Department [are] trying to push Stettinius into the view that the procedure to be established in the Dumbarton Oaks project will eventually overrule and supplant the Monroe Doctrine." By May 2, Stimson was writing in his diary that he was now seriously apprehensive about the possibility of an arrangement which "places our use of the Monroe Doctrine, in case of enforcement by arms, at the mercy of getting the assent of the Security Council." Stimson noted, "I am very much disturbed at what I find has been the course of the various conferences with South American republics under the Roosevelt Administration during the past twelve years. I am afraid that the Good Neighbor Policy has put serious obstacles in the path of the exercise of the Monroe Doctrine."[32]

On May 8, McCloy and Stimson talked the matter over at some length. McCloy described the situation regarding the problem of regional exemptions from the Security Council veto:

. . . The South Americans are very much concerned. They came here determined to wipe out that veto power which is in Chapter 8. . . . They said that the Act of Chapultepec and the Monroe Doctrine required that that go out . . . and they're pressing to have us take the position that it should go out. But we have agreed with the Russians . . . on this reservation against enemy states. . . . [T]he argument is that if you extend that to the regional arrangement against non-enemy states, Russia will want to have the same thing in Europe and Asia and you will build up these big regional systems which may provoke even greater wars and you've cut out the heart of the world organization.

McCloy told Stimson that the Latin Americans were worried that some non-American power might stir up trouble in the Western Hemisphere and "maybe that same nation that had done the underhanded stirring up might veto any action by the regional arrangement to stop it." On the one hand, McCloy noted, it was a "real fear . . . and they are a real military asset to us." On the other hand, he continued, "we have a very strong interest in being able to intervene promptly in Europe where . . . twice now within a generation we've been forced to send our sons over. . . ."

I've been taking the position [McCloy told Stimson] that we ought to have our cake and eat it too; that we ought to be free to operate under this regional arrangement in South America, at the same time intervene promptly in Europe; that we oughtn't to give away either asset, we oughtn't be forced to take a Hopkins [sic] choice on this matter.

Stimson agreed. "I think it's not asking too much," the Secretary observed, "to have our little region over here which never has bothered anybody . . . outside it, and retain [the] large . . . less easily called upon right to intervene abroad. . . . I mean we don't go abroad unless there's a world war."

McCloy described the tendency of the State Department personnel in San Francisco to deprecate the need for inter-American regional autonomy. "They were standing by Dumbarton Oaks," he noted, "because they've come this far with it." "Well," the Secretary of War replied,

and then of course I suppose that these little South American peoples are likely to throw a monkey wrench into the thing by saying that they are quite willing to let us abandon our unilateral rights, as long as we continue Chapultepec. . . .

"Yes," McCloy answered, "so long as we continue Chapultepec. That's what Chapultepec really did . . . was to sort of make the Monroe Doctrine multilateral instead of unilateral. . . . They think that was a great achievement."

At this point McCloy asked Stimson if he favored Vandenberg's proposal that the Chapultepec agreement be specifically exempted from the Security Council veto. "Well," said the Secretary, "the first part, the thing that we are asking for is first a freer hand as a policeman in this hemisphere; and second, a little freer hand in defending the hemisphere against any outside power other even than the Axis." McCloy asked what would happen if Russia claimed parallel rights in Eastern Europe. Stimson's answer was quick and to the point:

I think you ought to be able to prevent Russia from using that thing in her parallel, alleged parallel position. It isn't parallel to it. She's not such an overwhelmingly gigantic power from the ones which she's probably going to make a row about as we are here and on the other hand our fussing around among those little fellows there doesn't upset any balance in Europe at all. That's the main answer. . . .

"That's all I need," McCloy replied. A few moments later the conversation ended.[33]

The War Department's position was now clear. It was virtually identical to that of Senator Vandenberg, except

that the tone of the War Department position was not so
directly anti-Russian. But the substance was the same. The
United States would press for regional autonomy for the
inter-American system, which it was assumed the United
States would control. At the same time, the amendment
formula would insure that the Russian bilateral "defense"
treaties in Europe did not take on permanent character under United Nations approval. That afternoon, McCloy reported back to the United States delegation on his conversation with Stimson. The Secretary of War, McCloy stated,
was in favor of a frank exception for the inter-American alliance, even at "the expense of the immediate non-concur-
rence of the Soviet Union." Stimson hoped, however, McCloy
added, that there would be no further requests for such
exceptions.[34]

Two days later, Harold Stassen proposed a formula
which combined the War Department's, Vandenberg's, and
the Latin Americans' positions. In a memo which he presented to the United States delegation at its evening meeting on May 10, Stassen outlined his proposal on national and
regional "self-defense":

1. Nothing in this Charter shall be construed as abrogating
the inherent right of self-defense against a violator of this
Charter.
2. In the application of this provision the principles of the
Act of Chapultepec and of the Monroe Doctrine are specifically
recognized.[35]

With minor alterations, this was the essence of the amendment which the United States presented to the other major
powers at a meeting on Saturday, May 12.

Now, however, the British balked. Foreign Secretary
Anthony Eden heard the new United States proposal and
immediately remarked on its obvious "Latin American origin." It would lead, Eden noted, to "regionalism of the
worst kind." Senator Vandenberg described in his diary the
scene that followed:

Thereupon, we and the British huddled. The result was an agreement upon substitute language covering the general point but
omitting any direct reference to Chapultepec. I warned Eden
that if any such language is adopted, the Senate (with my approval) will attach an interpretative reservation saying that we
construe the language to specifically include Chapultepec. He
said he would have no objection. We quit at that point late last
night. I have about come to the conclusion that this is the best

course—to use general language in the Charter (so as not to invite
a lot of other regional identifications some of which would be
obnoxious); then to pass a Delegation Resolution notifying the
Senate of our interpretation. I shall suggest this tomorrow. It is
no good unless it is acceptable to the Pan Americans.[36]

This was the breakthrough. Vandenberg now had a
formula which would: (1) satisfy the Latin Americans, provided the United States gave firm notice of intent to honor
the Act of Chapultepec; and (2) avoid the legitimizing of
other "obnoxious" regional arrangements, such as a Russian regional defense bloc in Eastern Europe. In other
words, the formula would precisely, as McCloy had said,
allow the United States to "have its cake and eat it too."
It would satisfy the British by de-emphasizing the Act of
Chapultepec, and it would mollify the Russians by continuing to recognize the temporary exception of their European
bilateral defense pacts. At the same time, however, it would
tend to bind the American republics together in a "bloc"
which could be used against Soviet Russia in the future.

"After two more days of wrangling and re-writing," Vandenberg noted in his diary the following Tuesday, "we *finished* the troublesome Regional problem, so far as we are
concerned, today." The modified language guaranteeing the
right of self-defense became the cornerstone of Articles 51
and 52 of the Charter and were approved as such on June 9,
1945. Meanwhile, the United States gave notice to the Latin
Americans that it would agree to an early inter-American
conference for the purpose of constructing a hemispheric defense treaty around the principles of the Act of Chapultepec.
The regional problem was over.[37]

4. Assessing the conference results

It was probably not surprising that the successful outcome of the regional arrangements battle—which was carried on mostly within the United States delegation—did not
materially alter Senator Vandenberg's hostile view of the
Russians. Vandenberg had arrived at the conference skeptical of the Russians, and he remained skeptical of the Russians. Even before the first steering committee meeting, he
noted in his diary that he was concerned to "find out *now*
whether Russia intends to work in decent cooperation with
this Peace League or whether we are just launching a per-
petual row."[38] On Saturday, May 19, after the regional prob-

lem had been resolved and the conferees were awaiting final
confirmation of Russian approval from Moscow, Vandenberg had a conversation with Dulles, State Department adviser Isaiah Bowman, and *Foreign Affairs* editor Hamilton
Fish Armstrong. The four men discussed the advisability of
a clause in the Charter allowing for withdrawal from the
United Nations of disgruntled or disillusioned nations.

Armstrong [Vandenberg noted in his diary] said that no matter
how bad the League might prove to be, it is better than nothing;
that *if* we are headed for trouble with Russia, it is better to have
a mechanism that can mobilize the world against her. (I also
share *that* idea.) He made the interesting suggestion that when
we are through with our Frisco labors, we might withhold our
final signature until Truman can have a frank show-down with
Stalin and demand adequate assurances that he will live up to
these new pledges—the assurances to take the form of a belated
performance of some of the broken pledges of the past.

Vandenberg gave vent to his feelings on the basic question
of the conference:

The whole Frisco adventure is shadowed by this Russian question. The basic trouble is that we are trying to unite two incompatible ideologies. In the matter of good faith, the Western World
believes in the integrity of national obligations while Communism
boasts that "the end always justifies the means." In the matter of
economics (covered by the proposed "Social and Economic Council"), Capitalism collides with Communism. Which one will the
new Council promote? So the supreme question here really is
whether two such antipathetic systems can reside together in a
peaceful world (and in a League partnership). AT LEAST WE MUST
WATCH OUR STEP AND TAKE NOTHING FOR GRANTED.[39]

It was ironic that Vandenberg should still have felt so
obviously on the defensive about the "Russian question." His
approach as the backstop of the United States delegation,
and particularly as the United States representative on the
regional arrangements committee of the conference, had
been anything but defensive. Moreover, largely as a result
of Vandenberg's aggressive diplomacy, the United States had
won important tactical victories at San Francisco. It had
secured the ratification of an autonomous regional self-
defense system in the Western Hemisphere, which it intended to dominate regardless of Latin American hopes or
expectations. At the same time, the United States had
avoided compromising its general Open World principle in
other regions by preventing what Vandenberg had called "a
lot of other regional identifications some of which would be

obnoxious." Within a short time, the Truman administration would be moving ahead to implement the Open World policy in these other regions, using economic leverage in such situations as the British loan negotiations of late 1945 and the international monetary conference in Georgia in early 1946.

Thanks largely to the work of Vandenberg and Nelson Rockefeller, the United States had also begun to build a strong inter-American anti-Soviet bloc within the United Nations, to bolster the United States' position as the Grand Alliance continued to crack. Meanwhile, at the same time that Vandenberg was worrying about ultimate Soviet aggressive intentions, President Truman was himself already working out a strategy of future confrontation with the Russians, postponing the Potsdam Conference in order to be able to negotiate from the strong political advantage of having sole possession of a fully tested, working atomic bomb.[40]

Within the Western Hemisphere, only one problem now remained. That was the unfinished business of the long-standing Argentine crisis. If the United States could somehow overcome the dangerously disruptive and challenging force of Peronist nationalism, and check the possibility of a trend toward nationalism and statism in Latin America, thus assuring a totally Open Hemisphere for American private enterprise, the United States would be on the high road to the construction of an American Century in Latin America—and perhaps elsewhere as well. Indeed, as Nelson Rockefeller had remarked at the San Francisco Conference, unless the United States "operated with a solid group in this hemisphere," it "could not do what we wanted to do on the world front."[41] With a "solid group," the world-wide task would much more easily fall into place. Creation of a "solid group," however, demanded neutralization of the threat of revolutionary nationalism in Latin America. The chief embodiment of revolutionary nationalism was the Peronist movement in Argentina. Therefore the policy-making logic of the Truman administration demanded an all-out effort to deal effectively with the Peronist threat. To this problem United States policy-makers concerned with Latin America now turned their full attention.*

---

* There also appear to have been elements of a planned negative response to nationalism in the State Department's treatment of the Vargas

regime in Brazil in 1945. Note Ambassador Berle's strenuous efforts to undercut Brazilian industrial protectionism by pressuring the Vargas government for a new, low-tariff trade agreement. Note especially the wave of anti-nationalist banking, commercial, and industrial legislation enacted by the Dutra government, which was elected in the wake of the anti-Vargas coup of October 1945.[42]

For a time, late in the war, some policy-makers seemed to be thinking of bolstering Vargas as a defense against a militant Argentine-Brazilian nationalist bloc. At one point, Secretary Hull wrote to President Roosevelt asking for aid to the Brazilian transport system to avert a "major breakdown . . . which would have most serious repercussions not only in Brazil but throughout Latin America as well." As late as June 1945, Berle was asking for better treatment for Brazil in respect to fuel and shipping supplies, for much the same reason.[43]

But when Vargas seemed to be turning away from the American orbit and toward nationalism, the United States attitude changed markedly. Years later, Vargas' daughter recalled that Berle's attitude toward her father's government became particularly antagonistic after a late September conference between Berle and Ambassador Spruille Braden, who stopped off in Rio de Janeiro en route from Argentina to Washington to take up his duties as the new Assistant Secretary of State for Latin American Affairs. Braden, she stated, was known to fear Argentina's militant nationalism, and evidently now feared that Vargas would join in, rather than work against, an Argentine-Brazilian nationalist bloc. On the other hand, it was evidently not Dutra himself to whom the Americans turned. I have been unable to discover any evidence linking Berle with Dutra. Indeed, among all the contenders for the succession, Dutra was closest to Vargas personally. The Americans appear to have been closer to those supporting Dutra's rival, Air Force Brigadier Eduardo Gomes.[44]

Late in September 1945, Berle made a widely publicized speech to a group of newspapermen in Petropolis. Without making any direct personal references, Berle made it clear that the United States would be pleased to see Brazil return to constitutional government at an early date. The Petropolis speech became the focal point of a controversy which continued for many years. Berle maintained years later that the speech had been very popular in Brazil, and had in no way constituted intervention into domestic Brazilian politics. On the other hand, the London-based *South American Journal* reported, shortly after Vargas' ouster the following month, that "a speech made by Mr. Berle on September 29th . . . was held by some diplomatic observers to be partially responsible for the enforced resignation of the former President, Sr. Getulio Vargas."[45]

Nevertheless, Argentina is chosen here rather than Brazil as a case study in a United States response to Latin American nationalism, both (a) because the evidence seems clearer, and (b) because, at the time, Argentina was a much more dynamic, militant, and pace-setting nation in Latin America. Failure to grapple effectively with Argentine revolutionary nationalism would have had extremely serious consequences for United States policy all through Latin America.

X. Champion and challenger: Fly swatter versus flypaper

1. Nature of the challenge

Former Secretary of State Hull was hopping mad. Secretary of State Stettinius was deeply worried. Under Secretary of State Grew, caught in the middle, was perplexed. It was May 26, 1945, and Grew, in Washington, had just received a telephone call from Stettinius, who was presiding over the United States delegation to the United Nations Conference in San Francisco. Stettinius told Grew that Hull had just indicated, through a private source, that he was totally disgusted with the way the United States delegation was handling the Argentine situation, and would probably have to make a public statement on the subject as soon as the conference was over.

Stettinius, having finally realized that the State Department's hasty and somewhat inept sponsorship of Argentine admission to the conference was creating serious public opinion problems within the United States, was now working on a radio statement of his own, hoping desperately to keep the situation under control. Hence Stettinius had just called Grew, read him a draft of the proposed statement, and told Grew to take it out to Hull at Bethesda Naval Hospital. Stettinius hoped that if Hull could see the language he was going to use in the broadcast, "it might satisfy him [Hull] and dispose of the whole incident." Grew was understandably reluctant to tangle with Hull on such an explosive issue. Argentina had been a *cause célèbre* with Hull for years.

Grew tried to back out, and asked Stettinius if he might at least send a subordinate to see Hull instead. Stettinius, feeling that the issue was too dangerous to risk Hull's further wrath by dispatching anyone less than his highest-ranking available emissary, insisted that Grew go himself. In an attempt to reassure Grew, Stettinius pointed out that he had a cable from Ambassador Braden in Buenos Aires stating that the proposed statement was "fine," although admittedly Braden would "even make it a little stronger" if it were up to him. "At any rate," Grew noted in his memo of the conversation, "Mr. Stettinius said that the main thing to was get Mr. Hull to be satisfied with what Mr. Stettinius was going to say about the Argentine situation so that he won't feel he has to make a statement."[1]

Grew went out to Bethesda and convinced Hull not to make a separate statement.[2] Stettinius, however, still had reason to be apprehensive. By May 1945, it was clear that United States policy toward the complex and enigmatic pro-Axis, anti-American, and militantly nationalist Farrell-Perón regime in Argentina held the key to the entire problem of inter-American regional security in the postwar world. Just as clearly, any United States policy-maker who was unable to read wisely the signs emanating from Buenos Aires and Washington, as well as other American capitals, ran the risk of seriously undermining his own political position.

A primary aspect of the problem was Argentina's position in the growing East-West conflict which threatened to undermine chances for lasting peace in the postwar world. In the spring of 1945, with the wartime Big Three alliance showing signs of breakdown, Western Hemisphere unity seemed more important than ever. This was certainly no time to permit it to founder on the rocks of traditional Argentine-American rivalry. As long as great-power cooperation remained intact, the Argentine-American conflict could be treated within the context of Western Hemisphere relations. United States policy-makers could concentrate upon the threat to hemispheric security posed by what State Department Political Adviser Laurence Duggan called "the totalitarian character of the Argentine Government itself."[3] But a breakdown in great-power unity put Argentine-American rivalry into a new context. If Soviet Russia were really determined to employ all available means to weaken the United States, it could seize upon such a rivalry and exploit it for Soviet purposes. Argentine anti-Americanism might become more important than Argentine "totalitarianism." The policy significance of such a situation was clear. All during the war, the Roosevelt administration had been calling attention not merely to the Argentine government's pro-Axis foreign policy, but also to its anti-democratic internal structure. Hull in particular had done much to convince the

American public that Argentine "fascism" had to go. Yet if continued United States opposition to Argentine policies tended to increase Argentine anti-Americanism, the United States could no longer afford to take such a militant stand. This was one reason for the State Department's dilemma.

The other reason concerned Argentina's role in Western Hemisphere economic relations. By any standard, Argentina was at the close of the war among the richest and most powerful of all the Latin American nations. In terms of financial independence, Argentina was the only Latin American republic (with the one exception of Panama, described by an IADC official as a "boom town living off the Canal Zone payroll") which had emerged from the war with no outstanding indebtedness to the Export-Import Bank of Washington; Brazil and Mexico, her closest rivals for Latin American leadership, were in debt to the Bank to the extent of $84.9 million and $60.3 million, respectively.[4] In terms of such basics as food consumption, Argentina, alone of all the Latin American nations, stood with the United States and Europe in the "standard" index category of the National Planning Association's statistical summary, while the other Latin American republics had "indices of deficiency" ranging as high as 92 per cent for butter consumption, 86.6 per cent for eggs, 78.4 per cent for vegetables, and 57 per cent for milk.[5]

Argentina was the only country in the hemisphere, apart from the United States and Colombia, where inflation was reasonably well under control; and by 1945 the Colombians were having serious problems. Argentina was also a leader in the wartime accumulation of gold and foreign exchange, adding $200 million to her reserves in 1944 alone and amassing a total reserve by March 1945 of $1.25 billion, or almost one-third of the entire foreign exchange holdings of Latin America.[6]

Though Argentine business representatives did voice some fears of postwar United States wheat export subsidies and anti-Argentine wool tariffs, Argentina's principal export connection, the British market, had remained intact even through Cordell Hull's aggressive onslaught, thus assuring a continued firm underpinning for the Argentine economy. International Monetary Fund economist Harry Dexter White, assessing the relative postwar economic positions of the various countries, placed Argentina in that exclusive category of "neutrals who profited from the war," along with

Switzerland, Sweden, and Portugal, even above the only slightly less exclusive category (which included the United States, Canada, Australia, New Zealand, South Africa, and Cuba) of "participants who had by the end of the war regained their losses or even advanced during the war." Measured in terms of wealth and comparative position within the hemisphere, Argentina at the end of the war was better prepared than any other Latin American nation to challenge the United States for leadership of the hemisphere.[7]

The most important reason why Argentina was a pivotal country in inter-American relations, however, was neither a function of extrahemispheric politics nor merely a question of short-term comparative prosperity. Argentina was of crucial importance because of its emergence into the ranks of the industrialized "mass-participation societies" of the postwar era. The social revolution taking place in Argentina in 1945 was a clear portent of the dawning of a new day in Latin American political economy and socio-economic relationships.

To be sure, Argentina was not the most advanced of the Latin American nations in general industrial terms or in terms of every major specific industry. Mexico and Brazil were far ahead in development of heavy industry. During the early war era, the conservative Argentine landed oligarchy, still in control of the Argentine government, had stifled serious study of mineral deposits for fear that the discovery of coal and iron in quantity would make heavy industry inevitable and thus end the political predominance of the Argentine landowning class. For essentially the same reasons, the landowner government had scuttled the wartime Pinedo Plan for planned industrialization, fearing that it would result in a lessened dependence on agriculture and foreign trade.[8]

But the military revolution of June 1943 overthrew the old Conservative party landowning oligarchy, and signaled the beginning of a shift in political power toward the industrial bourgeoisie and the industrial and urban working classes. All through 1944, a jockeying for position continued among the various socio-economic factions and within the ruling military junta itself. By the end of 1944, the shrewdly opportunistic Colonel Juan Domingo Perón had emerged as the leading figure both in the junta and in the national competition for political dominance among the various economic

groups. Perón, having maneuvered himself into the position
of holding the Cabinet portfolios of both War and Labor
(he was also Vice-President of the Republic), was building a
personal following upon a new and powerful coalition of
military and working-class support. The resulting phenomenon of *peronismo* (in English, Peronism) posed the most
serious challenge yet to the predominance of the old pre-
revolutionary governing groups.

By mid-1945, the land-based political groups were fighting a rear-guard action for the survival of their political influence. As of 1945, agricultural exports were still by far the
largest foreign exchange earner, and the meat-packing
plants still constituted the largest single industry in Argentina; but the next five largest industries, namely, the
building industry, the electric companies, the petroleum
refineries, the flour mills, and the textile mills, all represented groups politically competitive with landowners. The
industrial middle class and laboring class, particularly organized labor, were rapidly gaining power.[9] Even the meat-
packers, who were in economic terms the natural allies of
the landowners, at least over such issues as tariffs, were to a
considerable degree the potential political enemies of the
landowners, for the meat-packers were an urban-based
group employing large numbers of well-organized and economically aggressive laborers. In the rough-and-tumble of
the late 1945 election campaign, Juan Perón was to find some
of his strongest supporters and most useful allies among the
workers of the meat-packing plants.

Politically, this complex and kaleidoscopic pattern created certain paradoxes for Argentine-American relations.
During the war, the industrial and commercial groups, the
former needing machine replacements, the latter depending upon imports, had in general favored good relations
with the United States; they had supported the 1943 revolution in the hope that it signaled the end of the antagonistic,
anti-American foreign policy of the old Conservative government.[10] Many American businessmen, for their own part,
supported Argentine industrialization as the basic means by
which United States investors and exporters of technology
could move into the Argentine economy, replacing British
agricultural investors as the dominant foreign influence in
Argentina. The landowners, on the other hand, had supported the pre-revolutionary Castillo regime precisely be-

cause it leaned more to the British than to the United States. The Castillo regime had refused to cooperate with the United States in an all-American anti-Axis political front; but the regime had continued to sell foodstuffs to the British government. Apart from being good business, this arrangement gave the Argentines more freedom of action inasmuch as a weak British ally was safer to deal with than a strong and overbearing American ally. But when the war was ending, and the threat of domestic upheaval outweighed the threat of foreign reprisals, the tables turned. The landed oligarchy eagerly sought United States support in their fight against the revolutionary nationalism of the military regime and its industrial labor support.

In strict economic terms, the Argentine landowning class had very little to gain from cooperation with the United States, inasmuch as the Argentine and American economies were particularly competitive in agricultural products. The United States had steadfastly refused to buy Argentine beef because of the objections of American cattle producers. But when political influence was at stake, virtually any ally against the military-labor coalition was welcome. One could find such Conservative oligarchic stalwarts as former Foreign Ministers Saavedra Lamas and Cantilo, both ardent Hull-baiters in their time, supporting United States Ambassador Spruille Braden in his opposition to the demagogic appeal of Perón.[11]

Paradoxes notwithstanding, by the end of the war Argentina was in the midst of a revolutionary and potentially violent period of transition. This was a period in which, as one Argentine economist noted at the time, "many of the traditional economic and social concepts [would] have to be discarded to make room for values that conform more readily to economic realities. The carrier of these new values in Argentina today is industry," he added, "and upon it falls the burden of leading the country through the period of storm and stress toward new economic frontiers."[12]

There was no foreordained arrangement, alliance, or antagonism within the groups dependent upon industry in Argentina. It was by no means clear that in the heat of battle the industrialist owners and managers would line up with their own workers against the *estancieros,* or landholders. At first, the military regime had gotten along quite well with the industrial entrepreneurs. The regime's Director

General of Industries, Colonel Mariano Abarca, explained
why in a 1944 speech to Argentina's *Union Industrial*. Industry, he said, was at the base of the economy of every world power, and industrial development would put Argentina on the high road to such international status. "Everyone now knows," the Colonel remarked, "that a country has either the economy of a colony or that of a world power."[13] Thus the interests of the industrialists and the ambitions of the Argentine military seemed to coincide quite nicely.

In 1945, however, Perón, in his capacity as Secretary of Labor, began arbitrarily decreeing pay raises for industrial workers, as a means of winning political support for himself; many industry owners and managers now became violently anti-government and anti-Perón. Until this development, the struggle between landowners and industrialists had dominated Argentine politics. Peronism now emerged as an independent force, benefiting greatly from the peculiar situation of Argentine party politics. Whereas the landowners still rallied to their old Conservative party standard, there was, apart from the Peronist military-labor mélange, essentially no organized political party which could claim to speak for the industrial groups, whether employers or workers.[14] In the struggle to fill this political vacuum and to control the governmental machinery at stake, there hung in the balance a choice which might condition a whole future series of hemispheric relationships.

Peronism, by 1945 the leading political and economic force in Argentine life, was a complex phenomenon; it seemed to contain elements of both fascism and communism in its bases of support and political techniques. How the United States would respond to it depended on how American foreign policy architects perceived this fascist-communist dualism, particularly in the context of hemispheric relationships and the developing East-West conflict. To those who still saw fascism as the major postwar threat to the Americas, Peronism would have to be divested of its fascist overtones to make it acceptable in the hemisphere. But if communism seemed to be the major threat, then the prime task was to make sure that Peronism did not become allied with Soviet communism, or travel too far to the left in its domestic programs. The main question, then, was not *whether* Peronism was a potential danger to the United States; it was rather *what kind* of danger Peronism was, and how best to meet it. This was the operational dilemma that faced United States policy-planners in the spring of 1945.

2. Meeting the challenge: San Francisco . . .

On August 25, 1945, Nelson Rockefeller was fired as Assistant Secretary of State for Latin American Affairs. State Department official Carl Spaeth privately told a member of the United States Embassy staff in Buenos Aires that Rockefeller had been "blown through the roof" of the State Department by the public attacks of two major newspapers, the *New York Times* and the *Washington Post*. The *Times* and the *Post*, Spaeth said, felt that Rockefeller had aided the forces of Argentine fascism by his overenthusiastic support of the Farrell-Perón regime at the San Francisco Conference of the United Nations. The two newspapers had continually attacked both Perón and Rockefeller, and had finally succeeded in forcing Rockefeller's dismissal from the State Department.[15] The *Times* particularly had noted that as a result of United States sponsorship of Argentine admission to the conference, for which it held Rockefeller directly responsible, the United States had "detracted from its ability to argue for moral principles in the forthcoming negotiations with the Russians on the Dumbarton Oaks amendments."[16] The *Times* feared that by backing Argentine fascism the United States would only strengthen the prestige of Russian communism. Therefore, the *Times*, in alliance with the like-minded *Washington Post*, had put pressure on the State Department and had forced Rockefeller's removal.

The logic of these newspapers was a curious one. In the first place, they assumed that Peronism was primarily a fascist movement. But they also argued that indirectly Peronism held a communist danger, in that United States support for a fascist regime would inevitably cause a public reaction in favor of the Russian position and thus strengthen the Soviet Union's standing vis-à-vis the United States. In a curious way, the *Times*'s position synthesized two forms of anti-Peronism; but its root assumption, namely that Peronism itself was mainly a right-wing threat, was still only one way of looking at the problem.

The other side of the coin was seen by Ambassador Spruille Braden, the State Department's representative in

Argentina. Braden arrived in Buenos Aires in May 1945, just
as Perón was beginning his flirtation with the Argentine
communists, who up to that time had vigorously opposed
him. Braden was impressed (though in a negative way) by
Perón's militantly nationalist, pro-labor policies. Perón had
already stopped issuing new charters to foreign banks.
He had not yet nationalized the Argentine banking system,
but the threat was in the air.[17] Perón was already playing off
the industrial countries against each other as they bid for
the Argentine markets. In late February, he had invited the
British to quote prices on buses, locomotives, passenger
coaches, freight cars, and rails for the Argentine State Railways. He was negotiating an agreement with the Swedes for
purchase of agricultural machinery, in direct violation of
the United States–Argentine oilseed agreement, which contained exclusive machinery supply provisions scheduled to
run through 1946.[18]

Most important, Perón seemed to be leaning heavily on
the support of militant organized labor. In June, he locked
up the headquarters of the meat-packing workers' union in
response to a strike threat. By July 2, he had backed down,
fearing talk of a general strike to follow the meat-packers'
strike which was already in progress. He was talking threat-
eningly about "profit-sharing" schemes; and when 862 of
937 local Argentine business, industrial, and banking associ-
ations signed a manifesto against the military government
and against Perón in particular, Perón retorted that he now
had enough forces in the regular army and "in that other
Army of labor" to put down any insurrection.[19] Sir David
Kelly, the British Ambassador in Buenos Aires, wanted to
take a conciliatory approach to Perón, hoping thereby to
extract an Argentine commitment to protect British investments. Braden did not trust Perón; he did not feel the risk
was a good one.

Sir David [Braden told reporters] keeps coming back to the point
that British investments are so much more important than American. My reply has been No matter—[sic] if this guy keeps on
your investments will be worth nothing either through him or
by a reaction to communism.[20]

Braden was taking the inverse approach from that of the
New York Times. Perón was a gangster, no doubt, and in the
simplified political rhetoric of the time he was therefore in
some sense a "fascist." But Perón's revolutionary national-

ism was the real threat; it could lead to communism "by a reaction" set off through its unleashing the political power of labor. Moreover, Argentina had been a fascist gateway to the hemisphere during the war; there was no reason to rule out the possibility that she might as easily become a communist gateway after the war.

The main point was that Peronism might lead to an internal upheaval which would undercut the security of all external capital investments in Argentina. The Argentine example might also prove uncommonly dangerous as a precedent for other Latin American countries. The *New York Times* worried about the external forces of communism which would be strengthened by United States support for Perón; Braden feared that support for Perón would lead to internal revolution, followed by communism. Between them, they covered most of the spectrum of anti-Peronism.

Somewhere in the middle of this spectrum stood Nelson Rockefeller, the man who had so largely influenced actual formation of United States policy toward Argentina until the newspapers had undercut him. Rockefeller fundamentally agreed with both positions; he wanted to avoid strengthening Soviet communism as an external threat to the Americas, and he wanted to avoid a buildup of Argentine revolutionary nationalism which might lead to an internal communist threat. But he differed from both positions, too, in that his tactical assumptions were different. He felt that the best hope of undercutting both these communist threats was by working through Perón, rather than against him.

It is not entirely clear just when Rockefeller first decided that the United States could work with the Peronist regime. As early as January 1945, Rockefeller had received word through Under Secretary of State Grew that the Argentine government might be ready to talk about a rapprochement, "owing to the pressure to which they were being subjected."[21] At the opening of the Chapultepec Conference in late February, Rockefeller began moving to bring about such a rapprochement. In the meantime, he worked to consolidate his control over aspects of Latin American policy formulation in the State Department. He attempted to institute a rather strict and unprecedented arrangement by which all United States diplomatic chiefs of mission coming from Latin America to report in person to President Roosevelt had to report to the State Department first. Chiefs of mission were to visit the President only if accompanied either by Rockefeller or by Secretary Stettinius himself. The rule was abandoned after Ambassador George Messersmith told Stettinius that any attempt to enforce it would "make him and Nelson look ridiculous."[22] Nevertheless, Rockefeller continued his efforts to centralize Latin American policy formulation under his own control.

Rockefeller took great pains to see that there were no State Department Argentine experts present at the Chapultepec Conference to challenge his authority. At the conference, Secretary Stettinius, who spoke no Spanish, was, according to Ambassador Messersmith, "completely beyond his depth" and was "depending very largely for counsel on Nelson Rockefeller." Stettinius sincerely thought he was taking a firm position at the conference in regard to Argentina's pro-fascist foreign policy. He very probably did not realize, as Messersmith noted privately, that the "real decisions" at Chapultepec in respect to policy questions were being made by Senators Connally and Austin, Will Clayton, and a few others, including, of course, Rockefeller.[23] Stettinius told his Cabinet colleagues in the wartime Committee of Three, Secretaries Stimson and Forrestal, of the "very excellent result he had achieved in Mexico on the Argentina question." He told of how he had "met with a block [sic] of recalcitrant young good neighbors in South America consisting of Colombia and Venezuela, Peru, Chile, and one or two others who were siding up with Argentina and forgiving her without any assurances that she would reform and join the United Nations."

Stettinius had "stood them off . . . told them flatly that if they tried that sort of thing, why the United States would leave the conference"; he noted that he "finally got a united front, reading the lesson to Argentina that, if she would declare war and come in and be good and adopt the program of the other nations, she could come in and be welcome but until then no." Stettinius also expressed concern to his colleagues that the British "were not quite playing a good game in regard to Argentina."[24]

Stettinius' version of the conference outcome was more optimistic than accurate. Article 59 of the Final Act of the conference stated the conditions under which Argentina could be invited to sign the Final Act. She was required to declare war on the Axis powers and to eliminate all Axis

influences within her borders. The net result of the conference action was that Argentina was given a diplomatic opening the size of which depended upon who would judge
Argentina's anti-Axis performance. Rockefeller took every
opportunity to assure as liberal an assessment of Argentina's
performance as possible. The State Department evidently
realized that by the end of March, Argentina had actually
taken "no serious action" against local Axis business interests. The Department was deeply divided as to whether or
not Argentina's strangely worded declaration of war on
March 27 (she declared war on Germany "in its capacity as
an ally of Japan") plus her unguaranteed promises of action
against Axis influences at home justified an invitation to
sign the Final Act of the Chapultepec Conference. The leni-
ent approach prevailed; Argentina was invited to sign the
Act, in accordance with a Pan American Union resolution
which was sponsored by the United States because the other
American republics were still so divided in their opinions on
the subject.[25]

Stettinius now felt the weight of Rockefeller's influence
in the matter. Shortly after the resumption of normal diplomatic relations between Argentina and the United States on
April 4, 1945, the Secretary of State decided not to include
Rockefeller among the official State Department advisers to
the United States delegation at the San Francisco Conference.[26] Rockefeller, for his part, decided to go to San Francisco anyway, in an unofficial capacity. Despite his lack of
official position there, he managed to make himself the chief
contact man between the United States and Latin American
delegations. In particular, he was the person upon whom
Senator Vandenberg, the key figure in the United States
delegation, relied almost completely for his information on
Latin American views and reactions. Rockefeller was also in
constant touch with Acting Secretary of State Grew in
Washington, again despite his wholly unofficial presence at
the San Francisco Conference.[27]

After Argentine admission had been secured, Rockefeller returned to Washington for hearings on the budget
for the Office of Inter-American Affairs. While in Washington, he met with Grew and President Truman at the White
House to explain the Argentine situation. After the meeting
Grew in turn told Cordell Hull that "there was nothing to
do but to go along with the wishes of the Latin American
Republics which wanted Argentina in, and that if we had

not done so there was the risk of their withdrawing and ruining the conference."[28] Rockefeller also prepared a public statement on the Argentine situation for Grew to release.

When Grew called Stettinius in San Francisco the next day, the Secretary of State refused authorization to release Rockefeller's statement. Stettinius told Grew only that he could say that "neither he [Stettinius] nor [Grew] liked the situation any better than anyone else but that it was a practical matter that had to be done. . . . The Argentines had abided by the Act of Chapultepec," the Secretary added, "and . . . the Soviets would have broken up the conference if their two republics had not been taken care of. . . . The Latin Americans would not have voted for the two republics unless Argentina was included."

Therefore [Stettinius concluded] this was not our fight but was one between the Soviet Union and South America. . . . The Conference decided to let the Argentines in on that basis. If that action had not been taken the Conference would not have continued.[29]

Although Stettinius would not let Grew release Rockefeller's statement as an official State Department view, Stettinius' own version of the events corresponded in virtually every particular to Rockefeller's interpretation. Stettinius, however, had missed the most important point. Until Rockefeller had stepped in, the problem had indeed been "our fight," as Stettinius put it. Rockefeller had moved into the middle of two United States fights, one with the Latin Americans over Argentina and one with the Russians over the Russian republics (and Poland), and had very neatly extricated the United States from both of them, leaving one big fight between the Russians and the Latin Americans. Senator Vandenberg's analysis notwithstanding, it was Nelson Rockefeller and not Foreign Minister Molotov who had "done more in four days to solidify Pan America against Russia than anything that ever happened."

Vandenberg himself provided an interesting footnote to this part of the San Francisco Conference. At an off-the-record luncheon during the conference, Vandenberg told Rockefeller that he had "always been a little dubious of his Pan-American activities, and questioned some of the appropriations that had been made, but . . . after he saw the solid bloc of votes come in, he could be counted on to back the program to practically any extent." At one point in the conference proceedings, just after Argentine admission had been secured, the question had come up as to whether the United States delegation should insist that a committee chairmanship or rapporteurship be left vacant for Argentina. The delegation decided not to insist, so as not to antagonize the Russians further on an unimportant matter. Senator Vandenberg, according to the official minutes of the delegation meeting, "stated that he thought the decision was a 'lousy' one, but that, if Mr. Rockefeller was agreeable, he would accept it. Anything, he said, that pleased Mr. Rockefeller on this question would satisfy him." When the conference ended, Vandenberg summed up his feelings about the work of the Assistant Secretary of State in regard to promoting a solid inter-American front:

I want to add a word about the work of Assistant Secretary Nelson Rockefeller [Vandenberg wrote in his diary]. He has been responsible for our Pan-American contacts. I never realized before how important the work of his department is in keeping our "good neighbors" united with us.
  Now that we are going into an international organization where, as a practical matter, we shall NEED VOTES *from time to time in the General Assembly, as well as for other reasons, I think Rockefeller's work is indispensable.* I do not see how anyone could be more efficient.[30]

3. . . . And after

By the time the San Francisco Conference ended in June 1945, the basic American policy decision regarding Argentina had been worked out to its logical regional conclusion. Argentina had been started on the path to reintegration into the hemispheric system, while the system itself had achieved the sought-for juridical and political autonomy as well as a strong dose of built-in anti-communism.

Rockefeller's views on the internal political and economic situation in Argentina were perfectly consistent with his views on the larger hemispheric and world-wide significance of the Argentine problem. While liberal-labor groups in the United States such as the CIO were actively supporting Ambassador Braden and attacking the "fascist" regime in Buenos Aires, Rockefeller had already discounted the seriousness of Peronism as a threat from the extreme right. He sponsored Argentine admission to the United Nations Conference knowing of her actual performance in regard to her Chapultepec commitments. He was ready to go along with State Department aide Avra Warren's recommendation to give military supplies to Perón, and was dissuaded only by

the pressure exerted from Buenos Aires by Ambassador
Braden.[31]

Rockefeller could afford to take this indulgent view of Peronism. All through 1944, it had been clear from Ambassador Norman Armour's reports that Perón himself was not in fact a representative of the most nationalistic elements in the Argentine military. In January 1945, Rockefeller had had indications that the Argentine government was ready to seek a rapprochement with the United States. After the Chapultepec Conference, Perón had acted unusually fast, if somewhat halfheartedly, in declaring war on the Axis. Argentina had also made an ostentatious gift of five million bushels of wheat to UNRRA. Most important, in the course of Avra Warren's visit to Buenos Aires with General Brett in early April, Warren had had encouraging discussions with Argentine business leaders about the reopening of Argentine markets to United States industrial exports. The Argentines were as anxious as were American businessmen to unclog trade and investment channels and normalize Argentine-American business relations. Close business relations, as Rockefeller well knew, were the surest way to undercut a dangerously anti-American nationalism in Argentina. Rockefeller therefore moved to eliminate the remaining diplomatic obstacles to an Argentine-American rapprochement.[32]

By the end of the San Francisco Conference, the foundation of the rapprochement was secure. Rockefeller had unwittingly undercut his own position, but his policy had been accepted by the State Department. In an interview years later, a former ranking State Department official stated categorically that Rockefeller's dismissal from the Department in August 1945 was a gesture to public opinion in the United States and nothing more; in no way did it denote a substantive change in United States policy toward Argentina. By August 1945, Rockefeller, who was a Republican anyway, was becoming a political liability to the State Department; it was easy enough to dispense with his services without having to dispense with his policy approach. The selection of Ambassador Braden to replace Rockefeller as Assistant Secretary of State for Latin American Affairs was merely the other side of the coin in this public relations move. Braden was considered by the influential newspapers to be a firm anti-Peronist; putting him in to replace Rockefeller was the obvious gesture to satisfy the anti-Peronists in the United States. Again, this move indicated no change in policy.[33]

Braden's fundamental strategic position on Argentina was not really different from Rockefeller's anyway. Both men accepted the strategic premise that Argentine political and economic nationalism must be undercut. They differed only with respect to tactics. Rockefeller was convinced by late April 1945 that Perón could be used as the means to an Argentine-American rapprochement. He decided to work through Perón. Braden, more frightened by Perón's labor support and by his political flirtation with the Argentine communists in the late summer of 1945, decided it was necessary to work *against* Perón. Years later, Braden recalled that many American businessmen had disagreed with his analysis. A close friend told him that during his ambassadorship in Argentina, Braden had been "the most unpopular man on Wall Street." Braden's reply was swift and to the point: "You can't do business with Hitler," he said.[34] But Rockefeller and the Wall Streeters had already figured out that Perón *wasn't* Hitler, and that Americans probably *could* do business with him. Rockefeller's policy, moreover, had been consolidated before Braden even returned to Washington. Braden's personal anti-Peronism was therefore, in the end, quixotic.

Some observers believed it might not have been had Braden been allowed to stay on in Buenos Aires through the election campaign of the fall of 1945. *New York Times* correspondent Arnaldo Cortesi wrote from Buenos Aires that at the time Braden left, he was looked to by the anti-Peronists in the capital city as a "visible symbol of sympathy for their cause." Sir David Kelly, the British Ambassador in Argentina, later stated that had Braden stayed on "he might just possibly have brought it off," that is, an anti-Peronist victory.[35]

Once away from the center of events, however, Braden was deprived of his only effective point of leverage, while the anti-Peronists were deprived of his day-to-day assistance. Braden's anti-Peronism-from-a-distance quickly degenerated into a simple propaganda offensive, which Perón cleverly turned against Braden by campaigning on the theme of defense of Argentine national sovereignty. "Braden or Perón" was the astute Colonel's victory slogan. Months later, after Perón had been elected President of Argentina by a substantial majority, he summed up his feelings on the election campaign for the new American Ambassador to Argentina, George Messersmith:

As an Argentine [Perón told Messersmith], I must resent Mr.

Braden's intervention in our internal affairs and in the election;
as Juan Perón, I am deeply grateful to him.[36]

In the end, Braden's tenure as Assistant Secretary of State was a total anachronism. By putting tremendous pressure upon his State Department colleagues, Braden did succeed in having the proposed Rio Conference on hemispheric military security postponed for a time, because of anticipated Peronist obstructionism. This Braden did much to the consternation of Senators Vandenberg and Connally, who by October 1945 were in the vanguard of the conciliationist wing among United States policy-makers. In a letter to newspaper publisher Roy Howard in October 1945, Vandenberg summed up his feelings about the conciliationist policy which Braden's elevation to the Assistant Secretaryship threatened to disrupt:

I certainly do not want to have any part of even an indirect encouragement to the military regime [in Argentina]. . . . The difficulty is that there are many considerations (other than the internal Argentine affairs) involved in the present showdown between the country and the State Department. . . . They seriously involve the maintenance of completely friendly relations with the *other* Latin-American Republics. They involve a potential Communist menace throughout Central and South America which *could* be far more dangerous than the Fascist problem in the Argentine. . . .

So far as I am concerned, the dreadfully important fundamental point is that the State Department has been dealing not only with the Argentine problem but also with the Rio Conference on a purely unilateral basis whereas we have seven specific treaty obligations with the other twenty American Republics to *"consult"* about such matters and to act on a *multilateral* basis. If our Pan American neighbors get it into their heads that the "colossus of the North" has again "gone imperialistic" on a big stick basis our Inter-American system will blow up higher than a kite.[37]

All through 1946, however, Braden, with public opinion in the United States still largely favorable to his anti-"fascist" position, continued to take his "promotion" seriously and issued numerous broadsides aimed at the "neurotic nationalism" of the Perón regime in Argentina. Meanwhile, his replacement in Buenos Aires, George Messersmith, was by order of Secretary Byrnes and President Truman quietly working at cross-purposes with Braden, trying desperately to re-establish friendly relations between the United States and Argentina so that the Rio Conference could proceed.[38] Braden and Messersmith kept a lively debate going through the diplomatic mails all during the last half of 1946. When Messersmith sent long dispatches to Washington warning of dire consequences for "our whole collaboration program in this hemisphere" and for "our considerable interests in the Argentine" if the defense pact was not speedily concluded, Braden raised a number of telling arguments against hasty procedures. He even questioned at one point whether, in view of Argentina's voluminous professions of "good faith," the pact was so urgently necessary or perhaps necessary at all, considering the existence of the Declaration of Havana, the Act of Chapultepec, the United Nations Charter, and the Monroe Doctrine. The proposed Rio Treaty, Braden noted, was primarily aimed at preventing direct military aggression from sources outside the Western Hemisphere. "Insofar as aggression from within the hemisphere is concerned," Braden wrote to Messersmith, "the fact is that the [Rio] treaty would not offer any protection against the newer and more dangerous method of expansion by political and economic penetration with the aim of reducing small states to vassalage."[39]

When it came to actual policy execution, Braden's tenure in Washington ultimately was no more than a delaying action. By January 1947, Senator Vandenberg was calling publicly for convening of the Rio Conference, in a speech which included a virtual demand for Braden's resignation. At first the new Secretary of State, General of the Army George C. Marshall, was preoccupied with European problems. But by the late spring of that year, the Secretary, along with President Truman, had decided that the conference had been postponed long enough. Braden was quietly informed that his services would no longer be needed. He agreed to resign voluntarily on condition that Messersmith also be recalled. Accordingly, the "resignations" of both officials were announced early in June 1947, and the State Department moved ahead with preparations for the long-postponed conference to implement the military provisions of the Act of Chapultepec.[40] Braden's tactical disagreement with his "conciliationist" colleagues had resulted in an impressively long policy delay, but the tactical approach which had been worked out in the spring of 1945 by Nelson Rockefeller, Senator Vandenberg, and other like-minded policy-makers ultimately carried the day. Perón was to be wooed—and won. The fly-swatter approach had not worked; there was nothing left but to try the flypaper.[41]

XI. Formalizing the system: A closed hemisphere in an open world

Spruille Braden's stubborn anti-Peronism delayed the completion of a formal inter-American military system. But while Braden's tactics were postponing the conference which had been called to ratify the system, other United States officials continued to move ahead with plans and policies designed to insure that once the system had been formalized, it would function properly in a properly organized world, a world responsive to the larger national interests of the United States.

By the summer of 1945, the overall strategy of the new Truman administration was becoming clear. The administration's Latin American policy centered on the idea of a closed hemisphere in an Open World. At the San Francisco Conference, President Truman had approved a strong American position on regionalism, figuring that while this would give the United States leverage for the creation of a tightly knit, well-controlled system in the Western Hemisphere, the United States could still use its superior economic and political strength to pressure the Russians into forgoing parallel action in Eastern Europe.

At the Potsdam Conference in July 1945, Truman pursued the Open World aspect of the strategy with vigor. He began pressing for more Western influence in the lately pro-Axis states of Bulgaria and Rumania on the Russian border. He triumphantly informed Stalin of the success of the atomic bomb tests, and almost immediately began to depart sharply from the principle of great-power unity on the all-important German question.

On the crucial issue of reparations, Truman and Secretary of State James F. Byrnes moved to abandon the principle of multilateral allocation of reparations material from all sectors, and proposed instead that each power take reparations from its own sector, knowing full well that the Western powers, not the Russians, were in control of the industrial supplies which the Russians so badly needed. The Western powers finally agreed to provide limited industrial reparations to the Russians, but these shipments were unilaterally canceled before another year was out.[1] In the Far East, on August 6, 1945, the United States dropped the first atomic bomb on Japan in an effort to end the war there before the Russians could get in. The Truman administration wanted to be able to organize and control the Far Eastern peace settlement alone and without Russian interference. All the while, State Department negotiators went ahead with plans to open up British Empire markets and other market areas to American capital and industry, simultaneously attempting to move forward with plans to close off the Western Hemisphere to penetration from any other great power.[2] This was the general pattern of the Truman administration's program for a closed Western Hemisphere in an otherwise Open World for United States influence.

1. Nature of the closed hemisphere: military policy

It soon became clear just what kind of a closed hemisphere Truman and his leading policy advisers were planning. The fight at San Francisco over Argentine admission to the conference had signaled a first, not particularly subtle step in the "solidifying of Pan America against Russia," as Senator Vandenberg had put it. Former Secretary of State Cordell Hull pointed out the significance of the move in a conversation with Secretary of War Stimson early in June 1945. "Two underlings in the State Department," Hull explained with some bitterness, "had been responsible for the row over Argentina and . . . had gotten the United States entangled into support of a perfectly Fascist party in that country," all in the name of anti-Soviet "solidarity." The two "underlings" were presumably Nelson Rockefeller and American Republics Division chief Avra Warren. Hull was particularly upset, Stimson noted in his memo of the conversation, that the Argentine-Soviet debacle should have interfered with great-power unity, which had been built on Hull's own strenuous efforts at the wartime Moscow conference of 1943.[3]

By early August 1945, Senator Vandenberg was himself hard at work drafting the details of the closed-hemisphere approach. He explained in a letter to Secretary of State Byrnes his position on the question of providing peacekeep-

ing forces for United Nations operations in the Western
Hemisphere:

We might well accept, in connection with our inter-American
Allies and pursuant to the Treaty which will soon implement the
Act of Chapultepec, the exclusive responsibility for any armed
forces required to maintain peace and security in the Western
Hemisphere. I doubt whether we shall ever want *any other* armed
forces to enter this area.[4]

Vandenberg's position, which he proceeded to make public,
brought sharp protests from a concerned citizens' group
called Americans United for World Organization. The
group's president telegraphed to Vandenberg, warning that
"if the United States [took] the position that the forces of
no other nation may help to carry out the mandates of the
security council in the Western Hemisphere, Britain and
Russia [might] do likewise as regards the Eastern Hemisphere. This could mean only a further retreat to the spheres
of influence principle and a dismal outlook not only for the
smaller nations . . . but for the millions throughout the
world who today shudder, even though they may be the
victors, over the vistas opened by the use of the atomic
bomb." Vandenberg's reply, a further clarification of his
position, was a classic mixture of deliberate naiveté and
coolheaded sophistication.

I never have and I never shall suggest that we assume "exclusive
responsibility for peace in the Western Hemisphere." On the contrary, as the American member of the Regional Committee of the
San Francisco Conference, I made it my prime duty to see to it
that all *"regional* arrangements" should always be subordinate
to the final paramount authority of the *Security Council* of the
United *Nations.* I want *world security.* I shall not compromise
for less.

Vandenberg noted, however, that the United Nations Charter
provided for the use of regional peacekeeping forces in certain circumstances, and this he also endorsed. "It is the
clear purpose" of the charter, Vandenberg wrote, "to *start*
with *regional* forces, wherever possible, in the event military
sanctions are imposed."

I submit that this is elementary common sense. I have simply
taken the obvious and logical correlary [sic] step when I suggest
that the Pan-American Union *permanently* volunteer to co-operate
in this area in the exercise of this secondary responsibility. It
would not occur to me that this "destroys world unity." . . . On
the contrary, I would expect it to be accepted as one more

forward step in implementing the explicit and obvious program envisioned at San Francisco. By accepting this *total* responsibility, under the supreme authority of the Security Council, I would think that we *increased*, rather than *diminished*, the arsenal of the United Nations.

Vandenberg blandly ignored the most obvious point: those countries whose troops were given the important strategic advantage of *starting* the peacekeeping machinery working would in all probability dominate the military phase of any crisis, and it was precisely this crucial initial military involvement which Vandenberg wished to reserve in the Western Hemisphere for the United States and its inter-American "allies." Vandenberg mentioned President Truman's commitment to hold an early conference to put the Act of Chapultepec into "permanent treaty form."

Was the President thus undermining "world unity"? Was he thus moving back toward "isolationism"? I do not think so. Indeed, we all *know* better. The result will simply be to build one more steel girder into the international, co-operative structure for world peace and security.

That the United States would *strengthen* "world unity" by pre-empting military control of Western Hemisphere disputes was a proposition of dubious certainty, particularly in light of Vandenberg's proposal to prevent parallel Soviet Russian action in Eastern Europe. "The sound mutuality of *legitimate* 'regional arrangements,'" he wrote, "is quite a different thing from super-imposed 'spheres of influence' of the sort I am sure you have in mind. (*Much* could be said on *that* subject!)," the Senator added knowingly.[5]

Yet it all made perfect sense to Vandenberg, because behind it was one unifying principle: maximization of United States influence and minimization of Soviet influence. The twin assumptions of American benevolence and Soviet malevolence gave this unique logical structure a firm theological underpinning. By April 1946, Vandenberg would be writing to his friend John Foster Dulles, stating his readiness to get on with the business of Soviet-American confrontation. "The difference between us," Vandenberg wrote, "is only one of temperament. You are a philosopher in your ivory tower. I am a sadist who thirsts for a practical showdown." Dulles, for his own part, was now publicly describing Latin America as one of the "outer zones" of Soviet communist penetration of the free world.[6]

Early in May 1946, President Truman sent to Congress a draft bill for an Inter-American Military Cooperation Act. It authorized the administration to take certain actions to build up Latin American military establishments, pursuant to the anticipated inter-American treaty of reciprocal military aid. The bill had a number of important purposes. Admiral Chester Nimitz, Chief of Naval Operations, told the House Foreign Affairs Committee that the Act would establish a military supply system which would free the Latin Americans entirely from dependence on European suppliers. General of the Army Dwight D. Eisenhower, then Army Chief of Staff, added that the Act would "tend to improve the security of the United States by securing within the vital areas of South America a structure that is oriented toward us militarily." Significantly, when Secretary of State Byrnes was questioned by interested congressmen as to whether or not the proposed program might also give certain Latin American governments the military leverage to "stay in power over the desires of any other faction or group within" their countries, he replied that such a result "would be entirely in conflict with our policy"—but did not indicate how the program could be designed to prevent it.[7]

The second session of the 79th Congress adjourned before taking action on the proposed Inter-American Military Cooperation Act. President Truman reintroduced the Act into the new 80th Congress when it convened in January 1947. At the next round of House Foreign Affairs Committee hearings, Secretary of War Robert Patterson stressed the importance of excluding all non-American military participation from the Western Hemisphere.

We learned from World War II that the introduction of foreign equipment, foreign training methods, are a hazard, a definite hazard to the security of the United States, a definite hazard to the security of the Panama Canal. If we do not furnish them, someone else will, and I think that it is wise policy to remove the existing impediments.[8]

General Eisenhower added that the Act would include an arrangement whereby the Latin American governments would "agree that they would procure arms from no one else" other than the United States government. Congressman Sol Bloom of New York pressed this point. Bloom thought a United States arms supply monopoly in the Western Hemisphere was a good idea, but he saw nothing in the language of the bill to guarantee such a monopoly. "Perhaps not as far as law is concerned," Eisenhower responded, "but practically it would." The General noted that the State Department was expected to establish a gentlemen's agreement confirming the monopoly arrangement with the Latin American governments.[9]

The aim of the Truman administration was now clear. It was not only to abolish Latin American military dependence on non-American producers, but in the same process to *establish* Latin American dependence upon the United States. Such military supply monopoly arrangements perfectly complemented Senator Vandenberg's thesis on the necessity for maintaining effective monopoly control of military personnel movements.

The program for a militarily closed hemisphere under United States domination had other potential benefits for the United States as well. In November 1944, Secretary of War Stimson had commented upon the economic benefits to be derived by the United States from cultivating "good relations" with the South American military, who might become increasingly interested in buying United States aircraft after the war. By May 1945, General Arnold had reported to Stimson that the Army Air Corps was already engaged in a program of using surplus war material "to help Brazil to cultivate her air force." Stimson noted in his diary that Arnold had "made a very persuasive argument for doing it [and] I told him to go ahead so far as we were concerned."[10] At the 1947 hearings on the Inter-American Military Cooperation Act, Air Force General Hoyt S. Vandenberg brought the Arnold-Stimson approach up to date:

In the first place, it would aid us in keeping the aircraft industry healthy by allowing the South American and Central American and all the other countries of the hemisphere to purchase aircraft at the tail end of our contract and thereby get them cheaper for themselves, and also cheaper for the United States.

It would also give enough added impetus to the aircraft industry to aid in that objective of a healthy industry in which we are so interested.[11]

A June 1947 memo from Secretary of State Marshall to President Truman underlined the immediate practical importance of both the political and economic aspects of the military buildup. The Peronist government in Argentina was requesting construction of a number of naval vessels in

the United States for purchase by the Argentine navy. Since
the Argentine regime was now officially "rehabilitated"
politically in the eyes of the United States government,
Marshall stated, the Secretaries of State, War, and Navy
were now recommending that the President approve this
construction and purchase request.

As a basis for this recommendation [Marshall informed the
President], the following points are paramount:
  1. The shipbuilding industry in this country is badly in
need of work in order to maintain its existence.
  2. Should the United States refuse the Argentine request,
the Argentines will undoubtedly contract for the ships elsewhere.

Truman approved the Argentine request on June 26, and the
program proceeded.[12]

A report issued the following month by the Civil Aeronautics Administration showed how the United States was
already moving ahead vigorously with a program to implement civilian as well as military aviation expansion projects
in Latin America. All of this was distinctly in line with the
political and economic closed-hemisphere approach espoused by leading policy-makers in both major American
political parties. "Through its program," the report stated,
"the Civil Aeronautics Administration aims to promote U.S.
aviation standards, encourage the provision of suitable facilities for U.S. flag air carriers, provide markets for U.S.
aviation products, and develop data applicable to hemisphere defense." The report discussed flight-training programs, aviation code discussions, airport engineering
studies, and other projects which the CAA was already
sponsoring in such countries as Mexico, Peru, and Colombia, and which it was planning for in Bolivia, Ecuador,
Panama, Venezuela, Argentina, and Brazil.

The effects of the Civil Aeronautics Administration program upon
U.S. foreign trade [the report noted] are not easily segregated
from other influences. The attached charts, however, would seem
to indicate a rather direct and sizeable effect on U.S. exports of
aviation products to Latin America. Export licenses issued for
civil aircraft and components during the last quarters of 1946 ex-
ceeded $18,000,000 compared with a little less than $1,000,000 for
the corresponding period of 1945.[13]

2. Nature of the closed hemisphere: economic policy

The entire program, civilian and military, fit together
perfectly with the larger strategy of the Truman adminis-

tration's Latin American policy. The larger strategy was to organize the hemisphere in such a way as to insure both minimal challenge to the United States' political leadership and maximal advantage for the operations of North American private enterprise in Latin America. The broad outlines of the strategy were enunciated publicly and bluntly by various policy-makers. Just as General Eisenhower had told a congressional committee of the point of the military "cooperation" program, so did Assistant Secretary of State Spruille Braden publicly set forth the administration's position on economic issues. Braden summed up the postwar approach in a speech to the Chicago Executives' Club in September 1946:

I wish to emphasize that private enterprise is the best and in most circumstances the only really sound means to develop the known or unknown resources of a new country, because there has appeared a school of thought which, when considering United States cooperation in the development of Latin America, overlooks or even in a few cases condemns the use of private capital. Instead it advocates that the requisite financing be done by our government, either in the form of loans at low rates of interest or of what is tantamount to outright grants, in the case of certain public health, nutrition, and educational projects. . . .

The institution of private property ranks with those of religion and the family as a bulwark of civilization. To tamper with private enterprise, except to apply well-conceived, legal, and essential controls, will precipitate a disintegration of life and liberty as we conceive and treasure them.

"The time has come," Braden added, "to realize that the United States Treasury is not an inexhaustible reservoir."[14]

Braden's speech was not only a defense of the private enterprise approach in developing Latin American resources in a manner consonant with United States interests. It was also a particularly strong attack on the statist-oriented economic nationalism still popular in many Latin American countries. "Private enterprise" was once again the key watchword, for reasons both ideological and practical. Braden did list certain types of "legitimate channels" for the use of United States government money in international economic life. They included (1) procurement of strategic materials in wartime; (2) long-term government loans, such as the British loan, and investments, such as those made by the IBRD and the IMF, to "prevent world-wide economic chaos"; (3) donations in war-ravaged areas; (4) some health and cultural endeavors; and, finally, (5) short-term credits

to finance United States exports and/or imports. "Self-evi-
dently," Braden stated, "our Government should undertake
no financial operation when the effect will be to harm American investments or foreign trade." Of course, he added, government "should not compete with commercial banks or
private investors and it will be unnecessary for it to do so,
if these latter will demonstrate . . . progressiveness and
imagination."[15]

Applied to postwar policy formulation, Braden's meaning was clear. Legitimate governmental activities included
precisely those large-scale endeavors then being undertaken
in the name of European reconstruction, and which would
soon be enlarged even further in the creation of the Marshall
Plan. But such legitimate activities did not include those activities most urgently needed in Latin America, particularly
efforts to help build the needed infrastructure upon which
a thriving, diversified economy could then be constructed.

Nevertheless, the policy was conceived of as benevolent.
Early in 1947, political theologian John Foster Dulles blessed
the vigorous private-enterprise approach in Latin America
as one designed to rescue the Latin Americans from the
ever-ambitious, grasping clutches of the Soviet Union. In a
speech to the Inland Daily Press Association in Chicago,
Dulles described the nature of the Soviet challenge in Latin
America and his prescription for an American response to it.

Soviet policy in South America subjects the Monroe Doctrine to
its severest test. There is a highly organized effort to extend to
the South American countries the Soviet system of proletariat
dictatorship. It ignores the declaration of President Monroe,
made to Russia and others in 1823, that "to extend their system to
any portions of this Hemisphere is dangerous to our peace and
security.". . .
We should develop hemispheric solidarity along the lines of
the Declaration of Chapultepec which, in turn, is sanctioned by
the United Nations Charter. It is not enough, however, to rely on
inter-governmental compacts and their protestations of unity
and friendship. We must help the countries of South America to
get more vigorous and healthy economies which will end the
masses of discontent which too widely prevail. *That will not require any vast outpouring of our money. Rather, it requires an
intelligent comprehension of the possibilities of these naturally
rich lands* [emphasis added].[16]

While Dulles stressed the benevolence of the postwar approach, other observers concentrated upon the practical
realities of the Latin American situation and of the Truman

administration's policy proposals. During the discussions on the proposed Inter-American Military Cooperation Act in 1947, House Foreign Affairs Committee Chairman Charles Eaton of New Jersey put the question bluntly to Secretary of State Marshall:

Can we be sure that thought will be given under this legislation, and arrangements made, to protect the national interests of the United States by putting into the bargain, "secure access to and protection of United States property, rights, or its citizens' rights, in strategic minerals or materials in Latin America"?

"My answer to that," Marshall replied, "is in the affirmative."[17]

The Truman administration's approach to Latin American military and economic development had at least one curious feature. Braden (and Dulles) had strongly emphasized the need for private enterprise in all development programs, yet the United States government was taking a strong hand in promoting a Latin American military buildup for admittedly *economic* as well as political reasons. Actually, this was no paradox. It was simply a continuation of the old New Deal tactic of using government's power to protect and promote American private enterprise at home and abroad. If government action along these lines could serve to prevent or eliminate troublesome threats of other, "foreign" interference in Latin American affairs, so much the better.

Braden himself did object, up to the time of his departure from the State Department, to a policy of arming the Perón regime in Argentina with American-manufactured military equipment. But such an objection did not really signify a basic dissent on Braden's part from the larger strategy of the Truman administration. The larger strategy included the use of the Latin American military buildup to combat and undercut dangerous nationalist, statist doctrines and policies in Latin America. As Secretary Marshall had told Congressman Eaton, the military buildup could even be used as a lever to *guarantee* the security of American private property and private enterprise in Latin America. Braden had heartily endorsed the private-enterprise approach in his Executives' Club speech, and had in a number of other public statements delivered some of the most scathing attacks on Latin American economic nationalism made by any United States government official. He simply did not think Perón

was a reliable ally in the fight *against* such nationalism. Once
Perón had demonstrated his reliability to the satisfaction of
Braden's superiors in the State Department, however, Perón
could quickly be brought into the general "partnership,"
though it also required Braden's resignation to smooth the
way.

With or without Braden's personal participation as a
policy-maker, however, there was a consensus on basic
strategy. United States economic policy in Latin America
was to be vigorously and carefully directed toward the promotion of American private enterprise there; policy was
also to be directed toward discouraging economic statism.
Occasionally the policy precipitated loud complaints from
some Latin Americans. In December 1945, some Brazilian
newspapers complained bitterly about the export subsidies
which the United States was paying to domestic cotton producers. The subsidization policy, according to São Paulo's
Folha da Manha, made it appear "as if there were the deliberate intention to deprive São Paulo, and Brazil, of resources." Late in 1947, Chilean writer Salvador Ocampo
strongly criticized the conditions set forth by the Export-
Import Bank as prerequisite for a loan to the Chilean government. Ocampo's article, published in the American *New
Republic,* was entitled "You Have Invaded My Country."[18]
Such challenges, however, did not substantively affect American policy.

Indeed, it would have been strange if United States
policy-makers had heeded such complaints from the Latin
Americans any more than they heeded similar complaints
from other nations. The anti-statist, anti-nationalist approach adopted in regard to Latin America was, after all,
only one regional application of a policy which was simultaneously being applied elsewhere as well. If a powerful nation such as Great Britain could actually be forced by such
an aggressive policy to loosen the bonds of its nationalistic
Imperial Preference System, why should the objections of
weaker nations such as Brazil and Chile be cause for alarm?
On the contrary, some United States observers were much
more worried about what would happen if the United States
backed down from its anti-nationalist economic policies in
dealing with other countries. Elder statesman Bernard
Baruch set the tone in a ringing statement to the Senate
Military Affairs Committee in the summer of 1945. "Please

read my cross-examination," Baruch proudly wrote to a friend, "about American free enterprise having to meet the nationalized and totalized industry of the world."[19]

In August 1945, French Provisional President Charles de Gaulle visited the United States in order to conduct negotiations for a loan to the French government. Baruch took the opportunity to read de Gaulle a lecture on the effects of nationalization of industry in European countries upon American attitudes. Describing his conversation with de Gaulle and the French Ambassador in Washington, Baruch noted:

I called to their attention what I have said publicly, that the nationalization of French industries like the nationalization of English industries was now a part of a system which whether they desired it or not was vis-à-vis the American system of free enterprise; that I, as a private citizen, felt that that had to be considered.

Baruch tried to persuade de Gaulle that nationalized economies were not in the interest of either the United States or the nationalizing nation.

I told him that the vast French empire opened untold possibilities for enormous development; that if they would open them up instead of keeping them closed as they have for centuries, they would develop French initiative with the assistance of others. I told him I thought it would be advisable to induce American capital and enterprise to go into France and the French colonies. I told him what the Mormons had done for Utah which was practically wilderness when they reached there.

In November 1945, Baruch wrote a letter to Representative Albert Gore of Tennessee, which the latter immediately read to the House of Representatives and then inserted into the *Congressional Record*. Generalizing from the British and French experiences in regard to nationalization, Baruch warned that further nationalization in *any* country could force retaliatory nationalization upon the United States. "The totalization or nationalization of industry," Baruch wrote, "keeps moving towards Statism and towards the destruction of the system which has made this country great." The United States "must be careful," he admonished, "when we give aid to other countries, that this aid is not used to nationalize their industries against us, to destroy our own competitive system which, I think should be preserved."[20]

Government officials in Washington quickly picked up

the thread of Baruch's thought. In January 1946, Treasury
Department economists prepared a list of questions and
answers on the current negotiations for a large loan to
Great Britain. "Will England use the credit," ran one question, "to nationalize her industries?" The answer was
instructive:

This credit is to help England meet her foreign exchange problem which would be precisely the same under a Labor Government or a Conservative Government. The money will be used
only to buy goods and services from abroad. It will be used to
help *eliminate* wartime trade and exchange restrictions which
are entirely unrelated to the nationalization of British industries.

The real gain to the United States from the British loan,
stated the memo, would be precisely in loosening British
control of the international sterling trade area, or in undercutting the international effects of British economic nationalism. As the memo euphemistically put it: "All danger
of a division of the world into conflicting British and American economic blocs will be averted." Or, as Will Clayton
had put it earlier in discussing the effects of the British loan
with a friend: "I can assure you that their chances of excluding American businessmen from world trade are extremely slim." To Baruch, Clayton later wrote: "We loaded
the British loan negotiations with all the conditions that the
traffic would bear."[21]

The application of and extension of these policies to
Latin America was no coincidence. The general strategy
was to get United States businesses into as much of the
world economy as possible and to oust competitors where
that was also possible. The tactic was to structure other
national economies, and United States relations with them,
in such a way as to promote these ends. At the Havana Conference on international trade in November 1947, Will Clayton attempted to do for the Latin American markets what
the British loan negotiations had already done for the
British Empire markets: eliminate restrictions on the entry
of American goods. In the case of Latin America, this specifically meant stumping for low tariffs. The Latin Americans,
however, in many cases took a strong protectionist stand.
"The underdeveloped countries," as one American business
analyst noted indignantly, "were primarily interested in
the right to use import quotas as a means of protecting their
'infant industries.' Somehow they seemed to attach more

attach more importance to that than to . . . securing an adequate influx of investment capital from abroad."

While the Havana Conference was in progress, Secretary of the Treasury John W. Snyder went down to Clayton's old stamping grounds in Texas to make a speech to the Houston Chamber of Commerce. The conference, Snyder told his audience, was "designed to encourage international trade and sound economic development" among all participating nations. "Your city and your state," he noted, "with their far-flung trading activities, have a real stake in these efforts to substitute a rule of reason and common interest for cut-throat competitive economic nationalism in the trade relations between countries."[22]

Sometimes, triangular United States–European–Latin American relationships directly influenced United States postwar negotiations. Early in 1946, Senator Robert A. Taft invited Bernard Baruch to testify before the Senate Banking and Currency Committee in regard to the British loan. Baruch wrote to Taft asking for certain information which would be helpful in preparing his remarks. "How much in dollar balances, and securities," Baruch asked, "have the other countries of Europe here and in other countries, particularly in South America? . . . If your committee has that information, it will shorten the work I will have to do in order to make my appearance."[23] Baruch's intention was obvious. Ultimately, the British were not forced to liquidate all their foreign dollar balances in order to receive the American loan; but they were forced to make old sterling debts owed them by other countries more freely convertible into dollars, so as to facilitate the incursion of dollar-based trade activities into formerly all-sterling areas.

Later, after the British loan negotiations had been concluded, the subject of triangular financial relationships came up again in connection with the new Anglo-Argentine trade agreement concluded at the end of 1946. The agreement appeared to make it possible for the British to demand that whenever Argentina incurred a balance-of-payments deficit in respect to sterling, she be required to give her sterling debts priority treatment and convert her other foreign exchange reserves (including dollars) into sterling so as to liquidate these debts ahead of all others. Secretary of the Treasury Snyder made immediate representations to the British on this point. On February 4, 1947, Chancellor of

the Exchequer Hugh Dalton assured Snyder in writing that
the British had no intention of making any such demands.
Such demands, Dalton agreed, would be contrary to relevant
provisions of the Anglo-American Financial Agreement under
which the British loan had been made.[24]

The net result of these maneuvers was to increase
United States influence in Latin American economies just as
European influence was declining. After the war, a great deal
of private United States investment capital began moving
into key Latin American industrial and mineral enterprises,
which the Americans wanted not only to profit from but
also if possible to control. Among the key areas were petroleum, rubber, rayon, and, to a lesser degree, iron and steel.
At Perón's inauguration in June 1946, New Orleans ship-
builder Andrew Jackson Higgins sat at the new President's
side, symbolizing the growing alliance between "respectable" Juan Perón and certain United States businessmen.
In Venezuela, where the provisional government of Romulo
Betancourt wanted to maximize production and government
profits in the oil industry before Middle Eastern competition got into full swing, there was a rapid influx of American
capital. Early in January 1946, the government enacted a
temporary excess profits tax in order to make sure of its
share of the increased wealth. But the top rate established
was only 20 per cent, and that was on profits above an annual level of 2 million bolivares; shortly thereafter the government pledged not to increase taxes beyond this level. The
result was soon apparent. The Standard Oil affiliate in Venezuela, Creole Petroleum, almost immediately announced
plans for a 20 per cent production increase. Caribbean
Petroleum announced a $4.5 million expansion program. The
Sinclair affiliate, Venezuelan Petroleum Corporation, announced the expenditure of over $10 million for capital as-
set additions, while the Phillips corporation announced the
establishment of a new Venezuelan subsidiary. All told, between 1946 and 1949, net foreign investments (including
reinvestments) in Venezuelan oil increased by $957 million,
while net income after taxes averaged over 19 per cent of
capital employed in the six years 1943–1949. Almost half of
this income was repatriated to the United States as dividends; the rest was reinvested.[25]

With the help of an influx of American capital, rayon,
rubber, and steel experienced lesser booms. Soon after the

war ended, Brazil, Chile, Peru, Cuba, and Mexico announced the completion of new rayon production facilities, while Argentina, Colombia, and Venezuela announced they would soon follow suit. The United States Rubber Company increased its Latin American investments from $1.5 million to $3.6 million early in 1946, while Goodyear moved to set up new tire manufacturing plants in Colombia, Venezuela, and Cuba. Republic Steel acquired new iron ore properties in Mexico.[26]

While private capital was moving into some key areas of Latin American industry, however, there was actually very little United States government money going into the Latin American economy. One reason was given by Spruille Braden when he reminded the Executives' Club in Chicago that the United States Treasury was "not an inexhaustible reservoir." State Department personnel had had enough trouble at first convincing congressmen even of the necessity for the British loan. It was much more difficult to justify large-scale appropriations to Latin America as a good business deal for the United States.

Assistant Treasury Secretary Harry Dexter White could go on the radio with Senator Kilgore of West Virginia to boost the British loan by showing how it would lead immediately to increased purchases by industrialized Britain of iron and steel goods, coal, lumber, and chemicals—all of which were produced in Kilgore's home state. "That means," White remarked, "more jobs in your state and more profits for business in your state." Senator Kilgore agreed: "That's what we are after—more jobs and business for our people." In the case of the French loan negotiations, also taking place in 1946, it could likewise be argued that the loan "would in no way be intended to prolong a deficit situation futilely but, on the contrary, would furnish France the productive help which is essential to permit it to achieve the reconstruction and modernization of its economy rapidly by its own efforts. In other words, it would operate to give to the total efforts of France the maximum effectiveness in the minimum time."[27]

Such arguments could not easily be made in regard to loans to Latin America. What the Latin Americans needed most was not capital for short-term, "instant-acting" reconstruction projects for existing industrial structures, but long-term, slow-acting capital loans to build up nonexistent infra-

structures. Quick and tangible returns on such loans could
not be claimed for the good and simple reason that they
would not in fact be forthcoming. In their public dialogue on
the British loan, Harry Dexter White and Senator Kilgore
had agreed very explicitly that this loan was *not* to be considered a precedent for credits to other countries. Such credits,
White noted, would be more properly sought from the Export-Import Bank and the new World Bank, or International
Bank for Reconstruction and Development.[28] But while the
British loan of more than $3 billion finally went sailing
through Congress (mainly because of all the strings which
Will Clayton and the others had been able to attach to it,
especially in regard to opening up the sterling bloc), in the
nine years from fiscal 1946 through fiscal 1954 the Eximbank
extended to Latin America less than $600 million in author-
ized "development" project credits.[29] The IBRD advanced
less than that in total loans through the end of 1954. A second
major reason why more United States public funds were not
forthcoming for Latin American development projects was
precisely that the development of transport, communications, and hydroelectric power were those projects most
likely to involve long-term state control. United States
policy-makers did not care to promote the growth of state-
controlled enterprises in this highly nationalistic era by
sponsoring such enterprises with United States government
funds.

Ironically, despite this disinclination on the part of
United States policy-makers to commit funds for Latin
American development, American officials continued to
press the Latin Americans for contributions to European
reconstruction. Sometimes Latin American reactions were
those of sardonic amusement. One Chilean journal printed
a cartoon showing a skinny and ragged Juan Pueblo (John
Q. Public) approaching a sleek and well-tailored UNRRA
Director Herbert Hoover with Latin America's contribution
to UNRRA—bags of produce labeled *desnutrición, miseria,
inflación, hambre* (malnutrition, poverty, inflation, hunger),
and so forth. But some reactions were quite serious, particularly in respect to Latin American politicians returning
empty-handed from negotiations with American authorities.
In 1946, the Brazilian Minister of Communications came to
Washington to request a $50 million loan for port recon-
struction and transport building. American officials hesi-

tated, noting pressing needs for United States government capital in Europe and Asia, and suggesting that these Brazilian jobs were probably best done by private capital anyway. The Minister finally returned to Rio de Janeiro empty-handed, and promptly lost his job.[30]

As late as 1947, Harry Dexter White still adhered to the view (and not without reason) that what was lacking in Latin America was mainly capital goods, and not liquid capital wealth. White told an International Monetary Fund meeting in March 1947:

Some countries, particularly in Latin America, find themselves handicapped in production because they can't get imports. For the most part they have the money to pay for imports but are stopped because we won't let them buy—we want the things ourselves. We've got a terrific backlog of domestic demand. But in another year or two things will change and Latin America will be able to get the supplies she needs and so be able to increase her own production.[31]

White soon realized that financial capital was again becoming even more necessary than just capital goods, especially with wartime dollar balances steadily shrinking in Latin America through purchases of less-needed consumer goods, repatriation of outstanding dollar bonds, and services on old commercial arrears. By January 1948, White was writing to the director general of the Bank of Mexico, suggesting a plan for a long-term $2.5 billion developmental loan to Mexico alone. White enclosed a sixty-six-page outline summary of a program for long-range Mexican-American economic cooperation, including a breakdown of proposed credit allotments and a tentative scheme of fund-raising possibilities. This large outlay of capital, White admitted, could not get under way until some time after the recently proposed Marshall Plan for Europe had been set up and allowed to run its course of interaction with the American economy. The Mexican loan, he noted, would in fact be timed to dovetail with the Marshall Plan so as to help keep American export sales high as the effects of the Marshall Plan began to recede. White stressed, however, the basic difference between Marshall Plan aid to Europe and the proposed loan to Mexico.

Aid to Europe under the Marshall Plan is motivated chiefly by political reasons and is for reconstruction. Aid to Mexico would be chiefly for economic reasons and would be for development.

Aid under the Marshall Plan can at best do little more than return Europe to her pre-war economic status; the program for
Mexico would enable her to break through a centuries-long
vicious circle of unjustifiably low productivity and standard of
living.[32]

In the meantime, however, Mexico (and the rest of Latin
America) would have to wait for such lavish aid until the
more "pressing" tasks were accomplished. The prevailing
United States approach to Mexico was well summed up by
the American economist who noted that the United States
government bought up "virtually the entire output of Mexico's meat-packing industry" for shipment to Europe under
the Marshall Plan aid program, thus clearly orienting the
Mexican industry "toward export markets rather than toward domestic consumption." Building up the domestic
market was the developmental task; it could wait. Supplying food to the external market was a security problem; it
needed immediate attention, especially with Argentina turning the screws on Western Europe in order to insure maximal concessions and payments for Argentine food supplies.[33]

The European situation affected United States economic
policies in Latin America in more ways than one. Such commodity purchase programs as the Mexican meat-purchase
program showed clearly the political influence at work in
the economic arena. This political influence also came out
clearly in the case of Cuban sugar. "Buy the Cuban sugar
crop," Bernard Baruch wrote to Secretary of Commerce
Averell Harriman in July 1947. "Cuba is disturbed. Why not
relieve her disturbance by buying her sugar?" In a letter to
Secretary of State Marshall, Baruch added another cogent
reason for purchasing as much Cuban sugar as possible: "If
there is going to be a shortage of food," he wrote, "this
should be done as sugar is a most important part. Europe
will want much of it. For the time we purchase the crop, our
action will be as effective as having exclusive ownership of
the atom bomb."[34]

3. The situation in Latin America

Within Latin America, the chief postwar concern continued to be national economic development rather than
American political and economic security. In many countries, wartime inflation continued well into the postwar period, aggravated by widespread food shortages. July 1945

saw food riots in El Salvador, with the army taking over distribution of locally stored grain at prices well below current market quotations. The President of El Salvador also requisitioned local bakery facilities in the capital city of San Salvador in order to keep riots from spreading from outlying areas into the capital. The next year brought food riots to the Brazilian capital of Rio de Janeiro.[35]

In Cuba, Ramón Grau San Martín began his second year as President amid continuing food shortages, rising inflation, and serious labor problems in the all-important sugar industry. One journal called Cuba's inflation the worst since the fabled "Dance of the Millions" of the 1920's. In Peru, the entire cabinet resigned over economic reorganization problems just before a general strike on October 5; in the meantime, the country continued to depend on large-scale imports of meats, fats, and oils. Venezuela also needed large-scale food imports, while the Lescot government in Haiti was ousted in a revolution springing largely from widespread economic dislocation and distress.[36]

On January 30, 1946, Chilean miners clashed with police during a combination riot-strike which underlined the continuing low standard of living of workers in that country. A shirt still cost the average worker one and a half days' pay, it was reported, while a pair of shoes cost two and a half days' earnings. In the Dominican Republic, the repressive Trujillo dictatorship kept the lid on popular manifestations of economic discontent. Nevertheless, basic food costs continued to rise, and the discontent, though unheralded, was present. Rice had jumped in a few years from 1¢ per pound to 16¢ per pound; salt, sold through a Trujillo government monopoly, had gone from 1¢ to 4¢ per pound; while sugar, which Trujillo left carefully alone because it was a United States preserve, cost more in Ciudad Trujillo than in New York City (as did coffee).[37]

Occasionally, there were signs that a government was actually encouraging inflation for devious purposes of its own. One American observer accused the Perón regime in Argentina of deliberately sponsoring price increases, of which the government always took a substantial slice in tax revenues, in order to pay for the growing Argentine military budget. Perón, this commentator noted, was also using import controls and other devices to siphon off funds from civilian into military sectors, while systematically ignoring the civilian economic problems created by shortages of machinery imports and consumer and producer goods.[38] But in a sense Perón was, again, in this as in so many other activities, the exception which proved the rule. The Argentine government, its economy still solidly based on Argentina's indispensable role as food supplier to hungry Europe, could afford to experiment with such arbitrary and otherwise dangerous inflationary tactics; the other Latin American governments could not.

In general, the machinery situation was little better than the food situation. Before the war ended, a United States National Planning Association study had recommended advance planning and placing of orders for capital equipment in Latin America, with estimates of expected demand and production schedules for capital goods producers in the United States and Great Britain. But the end of the war had instead brought an early end to United States allocation procedures, leaving the Latin Americans to compete with both domestic United States buyers and European purchasing agents. As a result, Laurence Duggan later noted, Latin America "received a smaller proportion of goods in short supply since than during the war."[39] There were two ways of looking at this situation. One American analyst noted that "in some cases, perhaps, the failure to obtain machinery may prove to be a blessing in disguise, since it hinders establishment of industries which might prosper in wartime but prove uneconomical in the peace to come." Another observer, however, stressed the impact of machinery shortages on already-existing Latin American industries. In some cases, such as that of Chilean textiles, he noted, existing mills might even be undercut by cheap competition from the more advanced countries before machinery replacements arrived to help lower production costs from the high levels dictated by the use of obsolete machinery in Chile.[40]

The impact of equipment shortages on transportation systems, in Brazil and elsewhere, was also serious. Broad sectors of entire national economies depended upon the availability of efficient, cheap transport. The Europeans were making the most of their political channels to secure virtually all machinery and merchandise from the United States, and in some cases seemed to be planning for "not merely rehabilitation, but enough machinery and equipment to create an industrial set-up far beyond anything they have ever known, and more than they could probably ever pay for." Their degree of success, one commentator noted, was "all the more astonishing when one considers that they are planning to buy a large part of their material on long-term credits (established by the U.S. Government), while the Latin-American nations are aching to pay spot cash in good Yankee dollars."

Significantly, this observer drew an important comparison between United States policies in Latin America and those of another so-called "Bad Neighbor." He stated:

> We hear a great deal these days about how the Argentine government is ignoring the agreements it signed at the Chapultepec Conference in Mexico City. Without trying to excuse the Argentines, it might be pointed out that the United States also has failed to fulfill certain of her Chapultepec commitments.
>
> True, we are not imprisoning people and breaking their bones because they differ with our political beliefs. But as this is written, we are embarked on a course of indifference to Latin America's economic necessities which might result in greater and more permanent damage to hemisphere relations and economy than all the Buenos Aires Government's totalitarian flounderings.[41]

4. Toward the Rio pact

Hemisphere economic relationships were simply not developing within a framework of strong multilateral cooperation. Nonetheless, America's comparative economic strength, coupled with the weakness of the Latin Americans, gave the United States needed leverage to move forcefully ahead with efforts toward political stabilization under United States leadership. More and more, the arguments of leading Washington policy-makers were being couched in terms of hemispheric defense against the encroachments of international communism.

Some policy-makers seemed appalled by the communist "menace" in Latin America. In the spring of 1946, Senator Vandenberg wrote to John Foster Dulles warning that Latin America could not be considered to be a "vigorous, healthy society," and that it therefore had to be included on the list of potential trouble spots in the growing Russian-American struggle for power and influence. Writing from the Paris peace conference in May 1946, Vandenberg warned Dulles:

I am more than ever convinced that Communism is on the march

on a world-wide scale which only America can stop. I am
equally convinced that we can stop it *short of* WAR IF *we take* the
moral leadership which a dismayed and disorganized world
awaits (with waning expectancy) and *if we clear the track at
home.* But—*God give us* MEN!

Vandenberg seemed to see communist influence at work
everywhere, including in the United States Senate. He noted
in his diary during the Paris Conference:

[Senator Claude] Pepper [of Florida] accused me, in this week's
"Look," of heading up an "imperialistic, anti-Red bloc" in the
Senate. This is typical, Communistic, smear technique. The "fel-
low travellers" (in spirit if not in fact) are getting bolder.

To a Michigan constituent he wrote during the summer of
1946, just as his re-election campaign was getting under way:

I am flattered to find myself at the top of the Communist "purge"
list all around the world. I fully expect they will break loose with
plenty of subversive mud in the Michigan campaign before it is
over. But if the people understand that they are "dropping a
letter to Stalin in the mailbox" when they drop their votes in the
ballot box, I have no doubt of the outcome.[42]

Fear of communism as both a political and economic
force in the postwar world came easily to Vandenberg. Even
during the San Francisco Conference, he had noted with apprehension the possible uses which the Russians might make
of the proposed Economic and Social Council: "In the matter of economics (covered by the proposed 'Social & Economic Council')," he wrote, "Capitalism collides with Communism. Which one will the new Council promote?" Later,
he extended his fears to include the activities of other
countries. "The smaller powers," he noted, "are constantly
enlarging the powers of the new Social and Economic Council and setting up standards and demands which *could* be
used to influence the communizing of the world."[43]

Dulles did not seem to hold such strong private fears of
communist strength and aggressiveness as did Vandenberg.
Publicly, however, Dulles stated the problem just as
strongly, and in some cases, more strongly. In June 1946, he
told the graduating class of the College of the City of New
York that "Soviet leaders now seek world-wide acceptance
of their system" because of their "honest belief that individual human freedom is a basic cause of human unrest
and that if it is taken away it will promote world-wide peace
and security." The Russians were also acting, said Dulles,

out of fear that "world-wide extension of their system" was "the only way to prevent their labors at home from being undone." By January 1947, he was calling for early negotiation of the Rio defense pact in order to undercut "communist leaders" in Latin America, who were "effectively agitating against the so-called 'capitalism' and 'imperialism' of the United States" and giving the Monroe Doctrine its "sternest test."[44]

Diplomat George Messersmith had a somewhat different perspective on the basic challenge facing the United States in Latin America. Like many others, Messersmith believed that the exaggerated nationalism of the Perón regime in Argentina was the prime threat. At first, Messersmith felt it was impossible to work with Perón at all. As late as March 1946, he wrote to Assistant Secretary of State Spruille Braden from his post in Mexico City, telling Braden that he, Messersmith, had assured President Avila Camacho that "as far as the United States was concerned, we could take no attitude other than to refuse to enter into a defense agreement with the present Government of the Argentine or any growing out of it and containing the same elements which had such close connection with our common enemies." Messersmith told the President of Mexico that "for us to enter into such an agreement with the Argentine under these conditions would be a negation of everything we had fought for and of all our principles."[45] But when Messersmith went to Argentina at the end of May 1946 as the Truman administration's new Ambassador there, he did a political flip-flop almost overnight regarding Perón, Peronism, and the inter-American security problem. In his first conversation with Perón, Messersmith was fairly swept off his feet by the new President-elect. Immediately afterward, Messersmith sent off to Secretary of State Byrnes a six-page telegram, followed shortly thereafter by a twenty-seven-page (single-spaced) letter, reversing his previous position completely. Messersmith warned that the main task, namely getting Argentina to "turn her eyes away from Europe . . . and to turn them to this hemisphere," could not be done by imposing the United States' will on Argentina, but would have to be done by a true "process of consultation," which if followed wisely might show that American leadership in the hemisphere would be "fully accepted as inevitable and necessary and useful and constructive."

Perón realized, Messersmith stated, that "the orienta-
tion of the Argentine to Europe has been a mistake and that
the Argentine must look to the Americas while maintaining
her interest in all people of the world." Perón had also stated
"in the most categoric terms" that the Argentine government would "work fully in the American picture and in the
field of defense." Interestingly, Messersmith expressed his
own personal opinion that a rumored Colombian initiative,
aimed at holding the proposed Bogotá Conference on hemispheric political and economic organization before the Rio
Conference on military organization, should be opposed by
the United States; the Rio meeting, he noted, was "far more
important," and such a reversal of priorities "would seriously prejudice the whole American picture."[46]

Perón attempted to convince the new United States Ambassador that another world war was already on the way,
and could be avoided only by "formation of a united and
clear front against Soviet Russian moves by all the States in
this hemisphere and democratic states throughout the
world." Years later, in recalling this conversation, Messersmith insisted he had been given considerable pause by
Perón's assertion that the United States and Argentina
"were the only two states in the Americas that could really
do something effective about" communism. His dispatch to
Washington at the time of the conversation indicates that,
rather than taking exception to this statement, Messersmith
simply pointed out to the State Department the far more
important and serious threat posed by Perón's interest in
promoting a southern regional "bloc" in South America.
Writing to Secretary of State Byrnes, Messersmith stressed
the overriding importance of an early conclusion of the Rio
Pact (with Argentina included), to outflank "undoubted
Argentine activities toward the formation of a southern
bloc." Soviet communism as an isolated external threat was,
in Messersmith's view, perhaps a menace, but a secondary
one. Nationalist challenges to hemisphere unity under
United States leadership were what gave the Soviet challenge its immediacy.[47]

Political stabilization of Latin America was nevertheless
a good anti-communist prescription as well as an anti-
nationalist prescription. It was not long after the war that
policy-planners in Washington began making the rather obvious connection between external Soviet communist ad-

vances and internal Latin American instabilities "caused" by local communist elements in political and economic life. While still Ambassador to Mexico, Messersmith himself wrote to the State Department commenting on a series of local articles and broadcasts attacking the United States generally and him personally. These attacks, he noted, were "an indication of the definite Moscow and Communist interest in attacking us here in Mexico, and of course one of the most natural ways is to attack me." Messersmith wrote: "We can't escape the fact that Soviet Russia does not like inter-American collaboration and they want to break up this collaboration between Mexico and the United States, for they consider Mexico a key country in this whole American picture." By the fall of 1946, Assistant Secretary of State Braden and John Foster Dulles were exchanging correspondence agreeing that certain anti-American leaflets printed in Mexico by members of the Irrigation Workers' Union were clearly communist-inspired.[48] The long jump between anti-Americanism and communism was becoming shorter and shorter.

Occasionally a United States observer would perform the *reductio ad absurdum* of this kind of thinking, taking the view that anything Russia opposed in Latin America must be something the United States should support. From his new post in Buenos Aires, George Messersmith wrote to his colleague in Brazil, Ambassador William Pawley, enlarging upon the vital need for an inter-American defense pact. "I think one of the best proofs that it is so utterly important," Messersmith noted, "lies in the fact that Soviet Russia is almost ranting about it." Shortly after this, Messersmith wrote to Dean Acheson, stating in part:

There is no doubt that the inter-American system will remain under constant attack from Moscow, and there is increasing activity on the part of Moscow in the countries of the Americas. . . . The Argentine and Colombia are really the only two countries in the other Americas today which we can depend upon completely to combat Soviet influence and penetration, and in an effective way.

It was therefore doubly important, Messersmith added, to work closely with Perón.[49]

Soviet motives and Latin American problems were now spoken of with barely a comma in between them. The problem was hemispheric in scope. As John Foster Dulles put it:

"In South America, communists *and left-wingers* [emphasis added], with Soviet support, agitate against the United States and seek to promote there the Soviet system of pro-letariat dictatorship."[50] When one lumped communists "and left-wingers" together as agents of Moscow, and added to this the already popular assumption that communism bred on instability, only a minimal amount of verbal maneuvering was necessary to show that instability was itself at least potentially, if not actually, both a left-wing threat and a direct Russian threat to Latin America.

So the Rio pact finally went forward. The State Department announced itself satisfied with Argentina's performance in respect to her anti-Axis commitments under the Chapultepec agreements. The defense treaty was concluded in a special conference held at the end of the summer of 1947 at Quitandinha, near Rio de Janeiro in Brazil.[51] Faithfully transmitting the views of the Argentine government right up to his last days as Ambassador to Argentina, George Messersmith continued to insist that Perón had in fact fulfilled these commitments satisfactorily; he also gave Perón special credit for being so alert and effective in his policies toward the communist menace in Latin America. But the indications seem clear in retrospect that with or without Messersmith's protestations, the State Department had decided that the Rio pact could not safely be put off any longer, and therefore Perón was going to be "reintegrated," ready or not. The military organization of the hemisphere was too important for further delay.[52]

The Truman administration was not able to go quite as far as it wanted at this point in harnessing congressional power to promote military integration of the Western Hemisphere under United States leadership. When the Inter-American Military Cooperation Act was reintroduced in Congress in 1947 after failing to come to a vote in 1946, it ran into more opposition than had been anticipated. Former House Foreign Affairs Committee chairman Sol Bloom, still the ranking Democrat on the committee, expressed fear that United States military aid "might give assistance to some of the other countries to the south, to enable them to embark into internal revolutionary affairs, civil wars and the like." Republican Congressman Jacob Javits of New York noted that the bill might promote a dangerous imbalance in armaments between rich nations and poor nations in Latin America. "Is it not a fact," Javits asked Secretary of War Patterson, "that if this program is just left to take its own lead, the rich country will be able to get the most modern equipment, and its poor neighbors will get only the surplus equipment which may be almost obsolete, because they cannot pay for it?" "That is possible," Patterson admitted. "That will depend upon the administration of the act."

Liberal Democrat Helen Gahagan Douglas of California expressed apprehension that peoples of Latin American nations where the governments were oppressive would hate the United States for adding to the military strength of those governments. "I can also see," Mrs. Douglas added, "in the future, where hysteria and fear can lead certain of our people here in this country to begin to back forces in opposition to communism in South American countries which will only promote communism." Former Pan American Union official Ernesto Galarza told the Foreign Affairs Committee that in a number of Latin American countries, parades and peaceful demonstrations were already being broken up by government troops using weapons obtained from the United States under the Lend-Lease program. The proposed armaments program contained in the Military Cooperation Act would only intensify such developments, Galarza warned. In general, the members of the House Foreign Affairs Committee remained too dissatisfied with the vague authority and loose controls provided by the bill to take a chance on endorsing it. So the Inter-American Military Cooperation Act languished in committee and never came to a vote.[53]

The Rio defense pact, however, did go forward. To counter the loss of the Inter-American Military Cooperation Act, Washington policy-makers moved to make the Rio treaty as strong as possible. At the Rio Conference, once again Senator Vandenberg proved to be the key figure in the United States delegation. Vandenberg, who was by now chairman of the Senate Foreign Relations Committee and also President *pro tempore* of the Republican-controlled Senate, fought down an Argentine proposal to limit the inter-American defense treaty to aggression from outside the hemisphere. The whole point of the United States' position at Chapultepec two years earlier had been to reserve maximal freedom and leverage for the United States to intervene, *if it so chose*, in intra-hemispheric disputes or crises as well as crises which originated because of the actions of some

outside power. In a dramatic showdown on August 30, 1947,
Vandenberg won his point, and the treaty was approved in
a form which covered internal problems as well as those
stemming from the actions of "outsiders." The United Press
reported from Brazil on the August 30 showdown: "It was
a dramatic end to the fire which had been smoldering
throughout the conference—Argentina's determination to
limit the treaty to minimum obligations, and the U.S. efforts
to obtain maximum obligations."[54]

By the end of 1947, the Rio treaty had been ratified by
the United States Senate and was in the process of being
ratified by the governments of the Latin American republics as well. All that now remained of immediate concern to
United States officials was formal Latin American ratification of the political and economic aspects of the postwar
inter-American "system." This was to be accomplished at
the Bogotá Conference, which had been called for the purpose of completing the institutional framework that had
been developing since 1945.

5. The conference at Bogotá

There seems little reason to doubt that, at least in the
short run, the Bogotá Conference was a distinct political
triumph for the United States. Secretary of State Marshall
led a delegation determined to secure maximum concessions
to political stability while making only minimal commitments to economic development. Basically, the United States
succeeded in obtaining both these objectives. The conference produced both an organic charter for a new political
Organization of American States and a comprehensive
Treaty on Pacific Settlement (known as the Pact of Bogotá).
It also produced a comprehensive Economic Agreement of
Bogotá. The Economic Agreement, however, "did little
more," according to Laurence Duggan, "than repeat the arguments and statements of principle already made at Mexico City"; the agreement was eventually ratified by only
three American states, of which the United States was not
one.[55]

At the conference, the Latin Americans once again attempted to bind the United States to acceptance of a *Latin*
American concept of hemispheric political security. They
secured the insertion into the OAS Charter of a prohibition
on political, military, or economic intervention in the affairs

of any state by any other state or group of states. But the United States actually carried the day by securing the inclusion of a special resolution condemning "international communism or any other totalitarian doctrine" as being "incompatible with the concept of American freedom."[56] Years later, the United States was to demonstrate forcefully (and forcibly) through its actions in Cuba and in the Dominican Republic just how strongly this resolution on "Preservation and Defense of Democracy in America" took precedence over the Latin American prohibitions, one of which denied even temporary military occupation of another state "on any grounds whatever." But even in 1948, the potential divergence in American versus Latin American approaches to the problem of political stabilization of the hemisphere could be seen clearly in the outcome at Bogotá.

Events at the conference also showed continuing Latin American discontent with the United States' approach to Latin American economic development. As far as the Latin Americans were concerned, their old fears concerning the inadequacy of the World Bank as an agency for promoting Latin American development had been borne out in the three years since the Chapultepec Conference. They therefore continued to press for the creation of a separate Inter-American Bank. The United States delegation openly admitted in its report of the conference proceedings that it "was not in a position" to offer the Latin Americans "the amounts of financial and other economic assistance" which they were seeking through inter-governmental arrangements. As a public relations gesture, President Truman did announce, during the course of the conference, that he would ask Congress to increase the lending authority of the Export-Import Bank by $500 million, the increased funds to be devoted primarily to Latin American development.[57] But this was a comparatively small sum considering the long-term magnitude of the job to be done in Latin America, and, as the Latin Americans already knew from their prewar experience, the approach of the Export-Import Bank was sharply different from the approach which they hoped would be institutionalized in a truly multilateral Inter-American Bank.

The American delegation at Bogotá continued to adhere to the position that "private capital, whether domestic or foreign, would have to be counted upon and should be

allowed to do the main part of the job." The United States
maintained this stand despite the fact that the Latin Americans strongly favored giving their own economic development its "principal" impetus "not by private initiative as it is known in the United States, but through governmental development corporations financed by foreign and local government capital, or, at the most, mixed governmental and private financing, *with a considerable degree of government influence and control* in planning and operations" (emphasis added).[58]

In his address to the second plenary meeting of the delegates on April 1, Secretary of State Marshall had cited the European Recovery Program as an excuse for the inability of the United States to make immediate large-scale commitments to Latin America. Nonetheless, the implication was clear in the American delegation's later report that such large-scale governmental aid probably would not have been forthcoming even if there were no European Recovery Program. The delegation stressed its primary concern with the security of United States private enterprise in Latin America. "There had been considerable interest among business leaders in the United States," the delegation report noted, "in obtaining satisfactory provisions regarding the treatment of private investments, which would encourage the flow of private United States capital to the other American republics"; Secretary Marshall's opening address likewise emphasized as a "dominant theme" the "role which private capital might play in the economic development of Latin America." The United States position at the Bogotá Conference was only a formalization of the approach outlined by Assistant Secretary of State Spruille Braden in his Chicago Executives' Club speech of September 1946.[59]

After the conference was over, the new OAS Secretary-General, Alberto Lleras Camargo of Colombia, attempted to reassure the Americans that the type of "political administration predominating south of the Rio Grande" was not really "socialist or collectivist." This was not the case, he noted, "if it is examined *as a tendency*," though it was true "with respect to some particular cases." Dr. Lleras also noted that it had not been the intention of the participating Latin American nations to demand a "Marshall Plan for the Americas," whatever the feelings of some persons present. Their intention, he stated, had simply been to set up "an agreement upon economic cooperation that would establish the basic`principles on which that cooperation could be achieved as a permanent activity intended to solve, with no time limitation, the general problem of the economic relations of the American States"; in this effort they had been successful.[60]

If one looked at the record of the conference itself, however, it was striking to see how many Latin American delegations stood firm in support of their contention that economic activities, including the disposition of private investments and private property, were to be considered subject to certain government controls in the name of national economic interest. When the United States forced the inclusion in the Economic Agreement of a sentence stating that "any expropriation shall be accompanied by payment of fair compensation in a prompt, adequate and effective manner," seven of the Latin American delegations appended to their ratification agreements specific reservations noting the primacy of their respective constitutional requirements over the language of the Economic Agreement. The Latin Americans also threw out entirely a United States–sponsored draft proposal which would have included in this statement a clause limiting such expropriations to "clearly defined public purposes." With respect to Dr. Lleras' second point, the United States delegation itself commented in its report concerning the widespread discontent among the Latin American delegates in regard to the type of aid commitments which the United States was unprepared to make. Back in the United States, no less an authority on inter-American affairs than former Under Secretary of State Sumner Welles was calling in precisely these terms for a "Marshall Plan for the Americas." The clash was real, and it was widely noted. It was between security for the United States and for its enterprising nationals on the one hand, and local control of Latin American economic development on the other.[61]

By the end of 1948, certain basic trends were clear. The United States was, if anything, even further away than it had been in 1940 from establishing the institutional means necessary for giving the Latin Americans the "share" to which they felt entitled under their own definition of the inter-American economic situation. As for yielding to the Latin Americans the basic decision-making authority over their own economy—so that it would be the United States

which might *receive* the share and the Latin Americans who
would *give* it—such had never been the goal of United
States policy anyway. In the prewar period, President Roosevelt and his major advisers had tried to work out a program to give the Latin Americans enough of a minority
participation in the decision-making process so as to undercut nationalist resentment against the United States, and
thus avoid anti-American economic action. But the Roosevelt approach had provoked skepticism on both sides, while
the war interrupted such multilateral work as had been
put in progress. Moreover, the war starkly underlined, and
reinforced, Latin America's traditional dependence upon
commodity exports to the United States as well as manufactured imports from the United States. Occasional industrial
development commitments, such as the Volta Redonda steel
project in Brazil, continued to receive American attention
during the war because of their political importance. In the
main, however, Latin America emerged from the war years
disorganized, dislocated, undersupplied, undernourished,
and underprotected in the face of the vastly strengthened
United States economic system.

Only prosperous, independent, defiantly nationalistic
Argentina stood at the end of the war as a challenging coun-
ter-example to the accepted wartime thesis of inter-American economic "cooperation." As the Perón regime continued
to extract increasingly large financial and political concessions from the victorious Western allies, while the rest of
Latin America languished under a postwar United States
policy of reduced governmental aid and continuously inadequate industrial goods deliveries, the idea of nationalism,
even nationalism with revolutionary implications, began to
seem more attractive to a number of other Latin American
countries, particularly those with large segments of their
economic resources still under foreign control. The notion
of economic independence began to seem increasingly necessary in Latin America.

The United States' response to such nationalism was distinctly negative. The accepted postwar thesis in Washington
centered on the idea that in an increasingly polarized world
situation, nationalism quickly shaded over into anti-Americanism, while anti-Americanism in turn quickly shaded over
into something close to communism. In some countries,
Washington was able to handle the situation by combining

an anti-governmental political stance with aggressive economic pressure. In the more complex and more dangerous Argentine situation, where a truly revolutionary alliance between militant sections of organized labor and the army was threatening to set a whole new pattern for Latin American nationalist development, the reaction had to be more subtle. What was called for was a quiet wooing of the nationalist regime away from its left-wing base of labor support, while anachronistic public opinion and official policy pronouncements in the United States were permitted to run their course of anti-rightist fury. By early 1947, the Argentine situation was so far under control as to permit work to proceed on a more ambitious and far-reaching political-military stabilization of the entire hemisphere under United States supervision.

In the meantime, the growth of economic nationalism within certain governmental circles in Latin America had further invalidated the concept of inter-governmental cooperative action as a primary means for effecting hemispheric economic development. A return to the ethic and policy of private initiative could be justified at least temporarily in the name of the higher-priority European Recovery Program and its demands upon United States economic resources. But private enterprise was now also seen as justifiable in a more permanent sense, precisely because of the increasingly unacceptable risk of giving official United States sanction to Latin American governmental agencies taking more than Latin America's allotted "share" of its own resources. With men like Spruille Braden influencing the making of American *economic* policy toward Latin America in the Truman administration, and political and military figures such as James F. Byrnes, Senator Vandenberg, John Foster Dulles, and George C. Marshall taking command of *political* relations with the Good Neighbors to the south, stability became *both the economic and political watchword* of the postwar approach. Stability provided not only a form of political security against fancied external invasion, but also a form of insurance against meaningful internal social upheaval, however necessary such upheaval might be to advance the cause of popularly based national economic development.

The dangers inherent in these postwar policies were not entirely unnoticed at the time. Shortly before his death, former State Department Political Adviser Laurence Duggan warned of the "grave danger should United States policy makers try to fortify the inter-American system by capitalizing on the fear of Soviet influence which possesses the Latin American oligarchies." Such a course, Duggan noted, "would further poison our relations with the Soviet Union at a time when a satisfactory working arrangement between the two strongest powers is the most important prerequisite of world peace." They would also, Duggan might have added, further poison United States relations with those portions of the Latin American populations that could not be included among the ranks of the "oligarchies." In a later passage, Duggan remarked:

At the risk of becoming tiresome, I repeat that United States aid in developing the resources of Latin America and thereby raising the standard of living will be much more potent in creating an environment in which democracy can flourish than anything we can do directly to encourage political democracy while present economic conditions continue.[62]

Duggan's argument was by no means only theoretical. A particularly poignant demonstration of the essential irrelevance of the stability-oriented approach to economic development and social change had already been provided by the outbreak of serious and widespread rioting in Bogotá during the inter-American conference proceedings. The *Bogotazo*, as the rioting was called, was touched off by the assassination on April 9, 1948, of Jorge Eliezer Gaitan, demagogic leader of the left wing of the Colombian Liberal party and popular symbol of the rising power of Colombia's urban masses. But the *Bogotazo* was more than simply a series of street riots. It was the surface manifestation of a tremendous undercurrent of economic and social unrest which had been building up ever since the end of the war; the riots only exposed to plain view the social and economic bankruptcy that had descended upon Colombia's political system years before.[63]

The *Bogotazo* was a direct reminder that political stability without economic development could never insure security. Characteristically, however, United States policymakers and many oligarchic Latin American governmental officials joined in seizing upon the presence of some Colombian communists in the demonstrations as "proof" that the entire affair was "communist-inspired," and could therefore be dismissed as such. The social implications of the rioting could thus be ignored, while the rioting itself was turned into an excuse for anti-communist propaganda. Some informed Americans did realize that there was more to the *Bogotazo* than simply "communist-inspired" rioting. World Bank president John J. McCloy wrote to his old War Department boss, Henry L. Stimson, offering his opinion that "general social conditions not only in Colombia but in other countries are such as to make possible, even without communist inspiration, flash powder explosions such as the Bogotá affair."[64]

It was much easier, and politically safer for that matter, however, to write off the *Bogotazo* as a "communist-inspired" aberration. Certainly the Colombian government itself could not, and did not, admit of the serious problems which underlay the outburst.[65] United States officials evidently thought it equally disastrous to admit, particularly in view of the Colombian government's need to gloss over the problem, that the United States had been caught trying to paper over the problems of social revolution with a flimsy tissue of political stability. Thus it turned out that, years later, the ingenuous official American explanation of the *Bogotazo* would be passed on to students of inter-American relations by respectable academic historians, who could explain the *Bogotazo* simply by stating, as one did: "International Communism had resorted to direct action in Bogotá to break up and discredit the great conference of American states."[66]

The primary point was not the official United States explanation of the *Bogotazo*, however. The point was the behavior of the United States at the Bogotá Conference itself. United States policy-makers had exactly reversed Laurence Duggan's suggested order of priorities regarding political stability and healthy economic development. They had reversed the order for obvious reasons. The United States was now unquestionably in a position to implement the historic Good Neighbor Policy assumption that *hemispheric political stability under United States leadership must both precede and ultimately govern the nature of Latin American economic development*. United States policy-makers were not about to abandon that position.

The containment of Latin America

Over the long run, the Good Neighbor Policy was a failure. Taking up where the Roosevelt administration had left off, the Truman administration completed the building of an inter-American system which was intended to ratify United States supervision and control of Latin American economic development. Subsequent administrations were able in many cases to promote or maintain in power, through the use of military, political, or economic leverage, those kinds of political regimes in Latin America most willing to acquiesce in United States dominance. But in the long run, United States policy-makers failed to win general Latin American acquiescence in the arrangement. They failed to convince Latin Americans that the Good Neighbor Policy was really a policy of institutionalized benevolence. Most important, they failed to overcome or to obviate the need for Latin American revolutionary nationalism.

On the contrary, after an initial setback in the Rio and Bogotá conferences, Latin American revolutionary nationalism became increasingly widespread in the decade and a half that followed. Its influence was dramatically illustrated by events in Bolivia in 1952, in Guatemala in 1953, in Cuba in 1959, in Brazil in 1961, in the Dominican Republic in 1965, and in Peru in 1968. Its influence also ebbed and flowed throughout this period in such countries as Argentina, Venezuela, Chile, and Panama. As United States involvement in anti-nationalist military and political maneuvers in Latin America increased, whether through the direct use of American military and civilian (including Central Intelligence Agency) personnel or indirectly through the use of military weaponry and technology supplied by the United States for "counter-insurgency" and "stabilization" purposes, it became clear that the Good Neighbor Policy approach, stressing a closed hemisphere in an Open World, had led to a policy of containment of Latin America.

This was an ironic development indeed. The containment strategy was enunciated by the State Department early in the Cold War era as a tactic for dealing with potentially expansionist *enemies* of the United States, particularly Soviet Russia. By 1954, when the Department and the Central Intelligence Agency joined in sponsoring an anti-nationalist military *coup* in Guatemala in order to contain revolutionary nationalism there, it was evident that revolutionary nationalism in Latin America had likewise achieved the rank of enemy. Thus United States policy-makers were led by their own policy assumptions to move toward containment of their presumed allies as well as their presumed adversaries.*

There were signs of a developing antagonism between the United States and Latin America even in the late 1940's. Publicly, American commentators continued to stress the "cooperative" nature of the inter-American system. "The unilateral Monroe Doctrine," John Foster Dulles told the graduating class of the University of Pennsylvania in February 1949, "has been merged into the multilateral Pact of Rio."[2] But privately, even before the convening of the Bogotá Conference, American officials were becoming wary of Latin American skepticism of United States "leadership." In going over the draft of a report on inter-American technical and cultural cooperation, which was to be published just prior to the Bogotá Conference, a State Department official noted:

---

* While not acknowledging American involvement in the Guatemalan *coup*, the State Department expressed strong approval on the grounds that it had undercut a "communist subversive" threat to hemispheric peace. The Department pointed to the presence of known communists in the regime of President Jacobo Arbenz, and to Guatemalan purchases of Soviet-bloc arms, as evidence that the country was being taken over by forces inimical to its own well-being and to the well-being of the hemisphere. The Department also objected to Guatemala's refusal to provide "fair" compensation for lands expropriated from the American-owned United Fruit Company.[1]

Two points are especially important regarding the *coup*. First, the United States, in sponsoring it, overrode Guatemala's sovereignty in deciding whom the elected President of Guatemala might legitimately choose as his advisers and his country's trading partners. Second, Arbenz's policies suggested that in the 1950's, as is the thirties and forties, revolutionary nationalism in Latin America (with or without the catalyst of communist organizers) led naturally to actions—such as expropriation—which American officials had always denounced as "socialistic," "extreme radical," or "communistic." If so, this might explain why the United States branded the Guatemalan government as "communist." In the mid-1940's, because of the war, American spokesmen could still attack nationalism directly as being contrary to the requirements of hemispheric cooperation. By the mid-1950's, Latin Americans were becoming more disenchanted with the results of such "cooperation." An American campaign against nationalism might have backfired. Therefore it was politically safer to attack Guatemalan "communism"—a much more appealing target in the heyday of McCarthyism.

It should be borne in mind that the primary audience is intended to be Latin Americans; the Congress and the American public are secondary audiences. Hence, a toning different from our usual budget justification is needed. This means particularly that we omit such references as U.S. leadership, superiority of U.S. technique and selling American equipment.[3]

Soon after the end of the Bogotá Conference, the Latin Americans went to the United Nations and insisted upon the establishment of an official Economic Commission for Latin America (ECLA) to aid in drawing plans for Latin American economic development. ECLA was set up despite the protests of the United States, which felt that some ECLA recommendations on Latin American development might conflict with recommendations and principles laid down by the United States at the Chapultepec and Bogotá meetings. Such American fears were soon justified, as ECLA economists led by Raul Prebisch of Argentina began calling for a Latin American development policy based on soundly planned export diversification and import substitution— both of which would tend to decrease Latin American dependency on the United States. United States officials began once again to fear the growth of anti-American economic doctrines in Latin America. A former OCIAA economist wrote in connection with the ECLA approach that it tended "to be closely associated with the effort to reduce vulnerability to changes in world markets. . . . This objective," he added, "immediately defines the character and restricts the potential of development activity in this area."[4]

Under the heading "obstacles to the investment of private [American] capital abroad," Truman's Treasury Secretary John W. Snyder included such things as "the growth of ideologies favoring state ownership and control of industry" and "the existence of political instability and extreme nationalism." Snyder told members of the Senate Banking and Currency Committee in August 1949:

As to the question of what can be done to increase the volume of investments and to distribute them more broadly, we must address ourselves primarily to the problems of eliminating the obstacles which stand in the way of the investment of American capital abroad. It is essential that the task of removing such obstacles should be attacked both by foreign countries and by the United States. Foreign countries must, however, accept the major responsibility for clearing the existing obstruction to a broad and beneficial flow of private capital.

An official of the Standard Oil Company of New Jersey wrote to a member of the Banking and Currency Committee, summing up his company's position on investment in Latin America: "All we ask or hope for is that Americans in Brazil have the same opportunity to participate in Brazil's industrial development as Brazilians now have in the United States."[5]

Appropriately, investment statistics regarding United States participation in postwar Latin American industrial development told the story more strikingly than did the ECLA policy pronouncements, as embarrassing as those pronouncements might have been to United States officials. A policy memo sent by Treasury Secretary Fred M. Vinson to President Truman in March 1946 predicted a long period of healthy and productive American investment in foreign countries:

As long as new American investment exceeds interest and amortization on outstanding foreign investment, the question of net repayment on our total foreign investment will not arise, although as individual investments are paid off the composition of our foreign investment may shift. It is impossible to prophesy when receipts on foreign investment will exceed new investment, as American investment abroad will depend on many future developments. In a world of peace, prosperity, and a liberal trade policy, there may well be a revival and continuation of American private investment on a large scale, including a reinvestment of the profits of industry, that will put the period of net repayment far in the future.[6]

But this optimistic forecast was not borne out by events. The "period of net repayment" began almost immediately.[7]

In later years, such respected historians as the Brazilian Caio Prado, Jr., came to view United States investment statistics as an indication of the ultimate tendency of foreign capital always to "decapitalize" developing nations through remittance abroad of excessive profits. Whatever the initial stimulus to development provided by such investment, he noted, "in time it is transformed into an obstruction." ECLA economist Aníbal Quijano Obregon analyzed the nature of Peruvian economic development in the post-1948 period and concluded that Peru's growing financial, commercial, and industrial bourgeoisie was more dependent on foreign, and particularly American, capital than were the traditionally foreign-dominated agricultural, mining, and cattle-raising sectors. "The country's economic growth," he noted, "has

served only to accentuate our dependence on foreign investment, our internal colonialism and metropolitan domination, and the increasing tendency toward the pauperization
of the largest part of the population." Former State Department and OCIAA economist George Wythe summed up development trends in Latin America as of the early 1960's:

In practice, rapid economic development has widened the gap
between the rich and the poor, and has created flagrant examples
of vulgarity and luxury. Unfortunately, it has been precisely such
types of development with which the United States has been most
closely associated.[8]

The Good Neighbor Policy affected not only the nature
of Latin America's postwar economic development. It also
had a sharp, and fundamentally ironic, impact on Latin
American political development. The Good Neighbor Policy
had assumed that political stability in Latin America was a
prerequisite for "healthy" economic development under
United States supervision. But by the mid-1950's, it was
clear that the economic dependency which the United States
had fostered in Latin America was seriously *undermining*
political stability. American political scientist Merle Kling
listed thirty-one occasions between 1945 and 1955 on which
"occupance of key governmental positions" in Latin America had been secured "in disregard of formal procedures."
The list, Kling noted, did not include "the numerous 'unsuccessful' plots, suppressed uprisings, arrests, deportations,
declarations of state of siege, boycotts, riots, and fraudulent
'elections' that have punctuated Latin American politics in
the last decade." Kling traced in detail the striking relationship between foreign control of economic resources and the
behavior of those Latin Americans who controlled political
power in their respective countries. "The discrepancy between the political independence and the economic colonialism of the Latin American states," Kling wrote, "permits
government, in the power system of Latin America, to occupy an unusual position as a shifting base of political
power." While economic control remained "static" in the
hands of foreigners, political control of local government
machinery in Latin America passed swiftly from hand to
hand among various local groups, all competing for the
wealth and power which could be theirs through "cooperation" with the United States on an inter-governmental basis.
Therefore, Kling concluded, *"chronic political instability"*

—one of the most important targets of the Good Neighbor Policy—was in fact *"a function of the contradiction between the realities of a colonial economy and the political requirements of legal sovereignty among the Latin American states."*

Interestingly, Kling saw a dilemma in United States policy which had promoted this state of affairs in Latin America:

Economic colonialism promotes political instability, which detracts from the power of reliable diplomatic allies of the United States; but, while the achievement of political stability would augment the power of the Latin American states, the elimination of a status of economic colonialism may diminish the diplomatic reliability of their governments! And the dilemma . . . has never been publicly acknowledged by the United States Department of State.[9]

The dilemma, however, was no dilemma at all. Kling assumed that the State Department preferred to deal with allies who were both dependable *and* strong. But in the Western Hemisphere, there was no real need for strong allies, because there was no real external threat against which the United States needed strong allies for defense purposes. In the unlikely event of an attack by a major non-American power, hemisphere security would essentially rest upon United States military strength anyway. The whole point of the political approach of the Good Neighbor Policy was that the United States preferred allies in the Western Hemisphere who were dependable *and weak.*

In the early 1960's, the Alliance for Progress emerged as a modernized version of the Good Neighbor Policy. John F. Kennedy's Good Neighbor Policy, like that of Franklin D. Roosevelt, was initially a response to a powerful and dangerous outburst of revolutionary nationalism in Latin America. In Roosevelt's time, the key event had been the Mexican oil expropriations of 1938. In Kennedy's time, it was the Cuban revolution led by Fidel Castro. Both events had prompted an effort by United States policy-makers to head off the spread of such revolutionary nationalism in Latin America. Both efforts seemed to center on the use of public and private United States funds to increase rather than diminish American leverage over the direction of Latin America's economic development. In particular, the Kennedy administration's emphasis on preventing the use of United States government

funds for such nationalistic purposes as the purchase and redistribution of foreign-owned land[10] seemed to indicate that
in the early 1960's, United States policy-makers still operated
on the old assumption that had been articulated by President Roosevelt in 1940.

The idea was still to insure that the Latin Americans did
nothing to interfere substantially with United States holdings or influence in Latin America. The United States would
retain the decision-making power, and would continue to
"give" the "share" rather than receive it. "Give them a
share," John Kennedy might have said in 1961, had not
Franklin Roosevelt already said it in 1940. ("They think
they're just as good as we are, and many of them are.") This
approach was, in the 1960's, still the essence of United States
policy toward Latin America. It was also the reason why the
Good Neighbor Policy, as historically defined and implemented by two generations of United States policy-makers,
had led naturally to a policy of containment of Latin
America.

Notes

NOTES

Preface: The politics of benevolence

1. *Public Papers and Addresses of Franklin D. Roosevelt* (New York, 1938), II (1933), 14. For representative Latin American reactions to Roosevelt's death, see the *New York Times*, April 13, 1945, p. 10; April 14, 1945, p. 6.
2. See, for example, Edward O. Guerrant, *Roosevelt's Good Neighbor Policy* (Albuquerque, N. M., 1950), p. 212. "The United States," Guerrant writes, "has never had a foreign policy toward any area that was more successful than the Good Neighbor Policy was from 1933 to 1945." Also see J. Lloyd Mecham, *A Survey of United States–Latin American Relations* (Boston, 1965), p. 465. "We do not say that the distrust of American hegemony was entirely removed," Mecham notes, "but Latin-American reverence for Franklin Roosevelt was responsible for the most extraordinary *entente cordiale* ever achieved between the peoples of the hemisphere." All italics are in original unless otherwise noted.

   For other comments on the success of Roosevelt's policy, see Samuel Flagg Bemis, *The Latin American Policy of the United States* (New York, 1943), pp. 392–393; Hubert Herring, *A History of Latin America* (3rd ed., New York, 1968), p. 920; and Bryce Wood, *The Making of the Good Neighbor Policy* (New York, 1961), p. 360. Wood devotes an entire chapter to Latin American reactions to Senator Hugh Butler's attack on the Good Neighbor Policy in late 1943. "The principal outcome of the affair," Wood writes, "was that it provided the occasion for the firmest and most spontaneous expression of Latin American confidence in the policy of the United States in the recent history of inter-American relations." *Ibid.*, p. 326.
3. See Alexander DeConde, *Herbert Hoover's Latin-American Policy* (Stanford, 1951), p. 125. DeConde argues that "in its main essentials, the good-neighbor policy had its roots in the Hoover administration; Roosevelt only adopted and expanded it." Mecham, *Survey*, p. 114, agrees that the Hoover approach "contained all of the components of the Roosevelt Good Neighbor Policy with one exception: the *formal* renunciation of intervention" in the internal affairs of Latin American nations. Guerrant, *Good Neighbor Policy*, p. 2, argues that the Roosevelt policies were "decidedly different" from those of previous administrations, though he ignores the Hoover record entirely in this regard. Wood, *Making*, pp. 133–135, takes the view that Roosevelt did not simply "adopt and enlarge upon" Hoover's policies. Hoover could not and did not develop any "positive policies of cooperation," Wood notes, and only Roosevelt really "created confidence among Latin Americans that pre-1928 policies would not be revived."
4. See on this point DeConde, *Latin-American Policy*, p. 127; Guerrant, *Good Neighbor Policy*, p. 211; and Wood, *Making*, p. 10. On Washington's wartime troubles with the stubbornly neutralist and sometimes pro-Axis Argentine government, see

Arthur P. Whitaker, *The United States and Argentina* (Cambridge, Mass., 1954); Harold F. Peterson, *Argentina and the United States, 1810–1960* (New York, 1964); an account by Roosevelt's Secretary of State, Cordell Hull, in *The Memoirs of Cordell Hull* (New York, 1948), vol. II; and two books critical of the Hull approach to Argentina—both by former Under Secretary of State Sumner Welles—entitled *The Time for Decision* (New York, 1944), and *Where Are We Heading?* (New York, 1946). Also see chapters VI, X, *infra.*

5. Guerrant, *Good Neighbor Policy*, p. 212, writing in 1950, criticized the "abrupt *volte face* of the Department of State from that of assiduously cultivating the good will of Latin America for a period of twelve years to that of neglecting them during the last four years." Arthur Schlesinger, Jr., remarks that "the United States government, preoccupied first with the recovery of Europe and then with the Korean War, forgot Latin America—a bipartisan error pursued with equal fidelity by the Truman and Eisenhower administrations." See *A Thousand Days: John F. Kennedy in the White House* (New York, 1965), pp. 163–164, For comment on the "bankers' criteria that apparently determined economic policy toward Latin America in 1945–1960," see Edwin Lieuwen, *United States Policy in Latin America* (New York, 1965), p. 133. On U.S. military policy in the postwar period, see Lieuwen, *Arms and Politics in Latin America* (New York, 1961), pp. 203ff., and John Gerassi, *The Great Fear in Latin America* (New York, 1965), pp. 305ff.

6. See Lincoln Gordon, *A New Deal for Latin America: The Alliance for Progress* (Cambridge, Mass., 1963). Gordon is a former U.S. Ambassador to Brazil and former Assistant Secretary of State for Inter-American Affairs.

7. The terms "revolution" and "nationalism," particularly when used in conjunction, are among the most controversial in the social scientist's vocabulary. Like many potentially "value-laden" terms, they are difficult to define in a precise and "value-free" way. A substantial and diverse literature deals with the phenomenon of revolutionary nationalism in Latin America and other areas of the underdeveloped world. See, for example, Arthur P. Whitaker, *Nationalism in Latin America* (Gainesville, Fla., 1962); Kalman H. Silvert, ed., *Expectant Peoples: Nationalism and Development* (New York, 1963); Kalman H. Silvert, *The Conflict Society: Reaction and Revolution in Latin America* (New York, 1966); John D. Martz, ed., *The Dynamics of Change in Latin America* (Englewood Cliffs, N. J., 1965); and James Petras and Maurice Zeitlin, eds., *Latin America: Reform or Revolution?* (New York, 1968).

In his book *Political Change in Underdeveloped Countries: Nationalism and Communism* (New York, 1967), John Kautsky writes: "Unless they are virtually inaccessible, underdeveloped countries almost by necessity stand economically in a colonial relationship to industrial countries, in which the former serve as suppliers of raw materials (often made available by cheap native labor) and sometimes as markets for the industries of the latter. Anti-colonialism, then, must here be understood as opposition not merely to colonialism narrowly defined but also to a colonial economic status.

"It is opposition to colonialism so defined and to those natives who benefit from the colonial relationship that constitutes nationalism in underdeveloped countries" (pp. 38–39).

In the present discussion I shall use the term "nationalism" in much the same sense as does Kautsky. The term "revolutionary" is added to suggest the social consequences of the economic changes desired by Latin American nationalists. Cultural nationalism is omitted except insofar as it bears directly upon socio-economic problems.

8. See chapter IV, *infra*. The Mexican-American conflict over oil properties during the period 1938–1941, a special case which functioned as an important learning experience for New Deal policy-makers, receives special attention in chapters I and II. Note in particular the comments by Bernard Baruch on the connection between U.S. national security, the American standard of living, and U.S. control of the resources of underdeveloped countries. For an excellent discussion of the global context of wartime American strategy in this regard, see Lloyd Gardner, *Economic Aspects of New Deal Diplomacy* (Madison, Wisc., 1964). See also Wood, *Making*, chapter X, for an application of the lessons learned during the Mexican oil crisis.

As E. David Cronon points out, Roosevelt's Good Neighbor Policy may not have been merely a "clever and sophisticated attempt to tighten up and extend United States dominance in the Western Hemisphere," but neither was it simply an "idealistic yet realistic effort by a powerful nation to treat its weaker neighbors with understanding, tolerance, and restraint." See *Josephus Daniels in Mexico* (Madison, Wisc., 1960), pp. viii–ix.

9. A crucial point here is the relationship between Latin American nationalism, the U.S. government, and private American businessmen. Bryce Wood notes that Roosevelt's State Department "established as a fundamental principle of the Good Neighbor policy that there was a national interest of the United States in its relations with Latin America, different from and superior to the private interests of any sector of business enterprise or of business enterprise as a whole. That interest, it became clear in 1939, was nothing less than the security of the United States." Wood, *Making*, p. 167. The question remains, however, whether or not the Roosevelt administration ultimately defined U.S. national security in such a way that it *was* in conflict with the interests of "business enterprise as a whole."

Moreover, when considering this point in the context of Latin American economic development, one should bear in mind the difference between balanced development and the mere increase in production of natural resources or even manufactured goods in an underdeveloped society. When production increases occur under the supervision of foreign business interests, and when most of the wealth generated by such increases is siphoned off by the foreigners, the result

may be perpetuation of, rather than escape from, underde-
velopment. See Andre Gunder Frank, *Capitalism and Under-development in Latin America* (New York, 1968). This is not to say that U.S. government officials *desired* the perpetuation of Latin American underdevelopment. But in some cases their relationship to private interests may have promoted it.
10. See chapters VII, VIII, *infra.*
11. Wood, *Making,* pp. 296–297.

I: United States policy and the challenge of nationalism

1. Remarks by Clay in House of Representatives, March 24, 1818, in *Annals of Congress,* 15th Cong., 1st sess., II, 1476, 1485, 1482.
2. C. F. Adams, ed., *Memoirs of John Quincy Adams, Comprising Portions of His Diary from 1795 to 1848* (Philadelphia, 1875), V, 176. All emphases are as in the original unless otherwise noted.
3. W. C. Ford, ed., *The Writings of John Quincy Adams* (New York, 1917), VII, 466, 474; also *Memoirs,* VI, 192. Note the similarity between Adams' formulation of this commercial principle of equality and the later "fair field, no favor" dictum of the Open Door policy. The consistency of assumptions is notable.
4. Annual Message to Congress, December 2, 1823, in *Annals of Congress,* 18th Cong., 1st sess., I, 22. For an excellent discussion of the broad international background of the Monroe Doctrine, see R. W. Van Alstyne, *The Rising American Empire* (New York, 1960), pp. 98–99.
5. Edwin Lieuwen, *United States Policy in Latin America* (New York, 1965), pp. 52–54.
6. See A. T. Volwiler, "Harrison, Blaine, and American Foreign Policy, 1889–1893," in *Proceedings of the American Philosophical Society,* LXXIX, No. 4 (November 1938).
7. See Olney's statement in Donald Dozer, ed., *The Monroe Doctrine: Its Modern Significance* (New York, 1965), p. 14.
8. Annual Message to Congress, December 6, 1904, in *Congressional Record,* 58th Cong., 3rd sess., XXXIX, 19.
9. *Ibid.,* p. 19. On administration of the Dominican customs houses, see Edward O. Guerrant, *Roosevelt's Good Neighbor Policy* (Albuquerque, N.M., 1950), p. 15.
10. For an influential historian's appraisal of U.S. policy during this era, see Samuel Flagg Bemis, *The Latin American Policy of the United States* (New York, 1943), pp. 385–386. Bemis writes: "A careful and conscientious appraisal of United States imperialism shows, I am convinced, that it was never deep-rooted in the character of the people, that it was essentially a protective imperialism, designed to protect, first the security of the Continental Republic, next the security of the entire New World, against intervention by the imperialistic powers of the Old World. It was, if you will, an imperialism against imperialism. It did not last long and it was not really bad."
11. José Enrique Rodó, *Ariel* (Montevideo, 1941), and Hubert Herring, *A History of Latin America* (3rd ed., New York, 1968), p. 798.
12. See Bemis, *Latin American Policy,* pp. 237–238.

13. Bemis considers Roosevelt's behavior in the Panama Canal crisis "the one really black mark in the Latin American policy of the United States, and a great big black mark, too." It was only "rubbed off," he notes, "after much grief, by the reparations treaty of 1921." *Ibid.*, p. 151.

14. In discussing such United States economic moves, Dana G. Munro, in *Intervention and Dollar Diplomacy in the Caribbean, 1900–1921* (Princeton, 1964), takes the view (p. 531) that the motives which inspired U.S. policy in this era, at least in regard to the Caribbean area, were "basically political rather than economic." Munro stresses the United States' attempt to "put an end to conditions that threatened the independence of some of the Caribbean states and were consequently a potential danger to the security of the United States." Dollar diplomacy, he notes (p. 537), "might have brought profits to American bankers if it had been more successful, but its purpose, under Taft as well as under Wilson, was purely political." Also see Bemis, *Latin American Policy*, p. 166. This argument misses the forest for the trees. Initially, the State Department had to take the lead in order to develop political alternatives to European action in the area. But in the long run, as both Taft and his Secretary of State, Philander C. Knox, knew and stated, the policy would also tend to make Latin America safe for U.S. investments. For statements by Taft and Knox, see H. F. Pringle, *The Life and Times of William Howard Taft* (New York, 1939), II, 678–679.

15. For a discussion of the amount of Mexican natural resource wealth dispensed to foreigners "with a bountiful and profligate hand" by dictator Porfirio Díaz, see E. David Cronon, *Josephus Daniels in Mexico* (Madison, Wisc., 1960), pp. 32–36.

16. On Lansing's efforts, see his dispatches to United States representatives in Mexico, in Department of State, *Foreign Relations of the United States, 1917* (Washington, D.C., 1926), pp. 946–983, esp. 947–949. (This series cited hereafter as *FR*.) For some recent material on the Mexican oil controversy during the Harding era, see Eugene P. Trani, "Harding Administration and Recognition of Mexico," in *Ohio History*, LXXV (Spring–Summer 1966), 137–148.

17. For statistics, see Raymond F. Mikesell, *Foreign Investments in Latin America* (Washington, D.C., 1955), p. 11.

18. The most recent work on the Nicaraguan intervention is Neill Macaulay's *The Sandino Affair* (Chicago, 1967). For Kellogg's remarks concerning the Mexican position, see T. A. Bailey, *A Diplomatic History of the American People* (7th ed., New York, 1964), p. 679.

19. It is the judgment of a number of American historians that the Hawley-Smoot tariff caused more anger than economic damage in Latin America. See, for example, Alexander DeConde, *Herbert Hoover's Latin-American Policy* (Stanford, 1951), p. 75; also Bryce Wood, *The Making of the Good Neighbor Policy* (New York, 1961), p. 128. The anger was still politically important, however. Also see Lieuwen, *United States Policy*, pp. 58–59.

20. For statistics concerning "decapitalization" of Latin America in the 1920's, see United Nations, Department of Economic and Social Affairs, "The Growth of Foreign Investments in Latin America," in Marvin Bernstein, ed., *Foreign Investment in Latin America* (New York, 1968), p. 64.

21. Memo by James H. Drumm to Joseph Rovensky, March 9, 1942, in Records of the Office of Inter-American Affairs: Entry No. 25: File entitled "Investment of Capital in Other American Republics," housed in Department of State Archives, National Archives, Washington, D.C. (Hereafter cited as OIAA: 25: Investment of Capital in Other American Republics.)

22. For an excellent discussion of Hoover's position on foreign loans in the 1920's, see Herbert Feis, *The Diplomacy of the Dollar* (New York, 1966), pp. 18ff.

23. See text of the Clark Memorandum in Dozer, ed., *Monroe Doctrine*, pp. 116–122.

24. The Cuban situation had been building up for years. For an analysis of both Hoover's and Roosevelt's problems in Cuba, see Wood, *Making*, chapters II, III. For background material on U.S. economic interests in Cuba as of 1933, see Robert F. Smith, *The United States and Cuba: Business and Diplomacy, 1917–1960* (New York, 1961).

25. Wood, *Making*, p. 70.

26. *FR*, 1933, V, 381–383, 385–386, 384.

27. Quoted in Wood, *Making*, p. 76.

28. *FR*, 1933, V, 424.

29. *Ibid.*, pp. 469–472.

30. Wood, *Making*, p. 91; also *FR*, 1933, V, 487–491.

31. The suggestion is made by Wood, *Making*, pp. 82–83.

32. *New York Times*, January 17, 1934. In his book *The Americas: The Search for Hemisphere Security* (New York, 1949), former State Department Political Adviser Laurence Duggan wrote that Batista gave up on Grau when he "saw that it was hopeless for Cuba, whose life depended on a restored sugar market in the United States" (p. 62).

33. See discussion of these arrangements in Arthur R. Upgren, "The Postwar Trade Role of the United States," in Council on Foreign Relations, *Studies of American Interests in the War and the Peace* (New York, various dates), Economic and Financial Series, No. E-B 10, May 11, 1940, pp. 8–10, "Note on Sugar." (This series cited hereafter as Council on Foreign Relations, *War and Peace Studies*.)

34. Statement by Mr. Benjamin Wallace, United States Tariff Commission, in "The Political and Economic Implications of Inter-American Solidarity," *Proceedings of the 17th Institute Under the Auspices of the Norman Wait Harris Memorial Foundation* (Chicago, 1941), pp. 141–142 (hereafter cited as *Chicago Round Table*).

35. Upgren, "Trade Role," p. 9.

36. See statement by Wood, *Making*, p. 109. Lester D. Langley points out that "the end of Machado and the Platt Amendment had not destroyed American economic influence, which in 1940 rested on a $1400 million investment in Cuba." See his

The Cuban Policy of the United States (New York, 1968), p. 163. Meanwhile, ironically, it took the U.S.-backed Mendieta regime two years to consolidate its control over the still disgruntled pro-Grau faction. See Wood, *Making*, p. 106.

37. Welles's comment, see *FR*, 1933, V, 406. For Berle's, see the *New York Times*, September 22, 1933.

38. Caffery quoted in Wood, *Making*, p. 86.

39. *FR*, 1933, V, 469. Roosevelt's press conference remark is quoted in Wood, *Making*, p. 86.

40. For a discussion of unsuccessful efforts by Josephus Daniels, U.S. Ambassador to Mexico, to convince Roosevelt to handle the Cuban situation through multilateral channels, see Cronon, *Josephus Daniels*, pp. 69–73.

41. For an excellent discussion of Roosevelt's monetary policies at this time, see Arthur M. Schlesinger, Jr., *The Coming of the New Deal* (Cambridge, Mass., 1959), chapters 12–14. Schlesinger sums up the internationalist basis of Roosevelt's monetary policy as follows: "It seemed nationalistic insofar as it sought to replace the international gold standard by national monetary management. But it was by no means nationalistic in the sense that it required movement toward economic self-sufficiency. A managed monetary system could promote either trade or self-containment, depending on the objectives of the managers. Indeed, while the Roosevelt administration was gaining freedom of national action in the monetary sphere, it was steadily moving away from isolation in the world of commerce" (p. 253).

42. *Ibid.*, pp. 254–259. See also Lloyd Gardner, *Economic Aspects of New Deal Diplomacy* (Madison, Wisc., 1964), for a discussion of the relationship between the trade agreements act and the New Deal recovery program.

43. Hull to Roosevelt, November 9, 1933, in Official File No. 567, 1933–1935, Franklin D. Roosevelt Manuscripts, Franklin D. Roosevelt Library, Hyde Park, New York (hereafter cited as OF 567, FDR MS).

44. Memo by Hull of conversation with Brazilian counselor of Embassy, Washington, August 27, 1935, in Folder 192, Cordell Hull Manuscripts, Library of Congress, Washington, D.C. (hereafter Folder 192, Hull MS).

45. Brazilian trade statistics are in Brazil. Ministerio da Fazenda. Diretoria de Estatistica Commercial. *Commercio Exterior do Brasil, 1933–1937* (Rio de Janeiro, 1940), pp. 30–36. It was only when President Getulio Vargas felt that the political danger from fascist sources was becoming too great in Brazil that, in November 1937, he moved against the local Brazilian fascist party, the *Integralistas*, and thereafter also moved away from Germany and closer to the United States economically. See N. P. McDonald, *Hitler over Latin America* (London, 1941), pp. 96–100; also *FR*, 1938, IV, 326.

46. Thomas W. Palmer, counsel for Standard Oil Company, to Laurence Duggan, Political Adviser to the Department of State, March 23, 1937, in File No. 824.6363 St2, Document No. 84, Decimal File, Department of State Archives, National Archives (hereafter cited as 824.6363 St2/84, DSA, NA).

47. Editorial in *La Calle,* La Paz, Bolivia, March 16, 1937.
48. Norweb to Hull, La Paz, March 18, 1937, in 824.6363 St2/81, DSA, NA. Also Norweb to Hull, La Paz, March 22, 1937, in ˋ824.6363 St2/87, DSA, NA.
49. Palmer to Duggan, April 21, 1937, in 824.6363 St2/113, DSA, NA.
50. James D. Mooney to Hull, April 28, 1937, in 824.6363 St2/117, DSA, NA. See also a similar statement in a letter from National Foreign Trade Council president Eugene Thomas to Hull, May 3, 1937, in 824.6363 St2/122, DSA, NA.
51. Memo by Duggan, April 28, 1937, in 824.6363 St2/129, DSA, NA. See also memo by Legal Adviser, Department of State, March 29, 1937, in 824.6363 St2/105, and memo by Legal Adviser's Office, April 9, 1937, in 824.6363 St2/106, DSA, NA.
52. Norweb to Hull, La Paz, May 5, 1937, in 824.6363 St2/133, DSA, NA. Finot also linked the expropriation to the Chaco negotiations. See Norweb to Hull, La Paz, May 8, 1937, in 824.6363 St2/127, DSA, NA.
53. Hull to Norweb, May 8, 1937, in 824.6363 St2/126A, DSA, NA; Norweb to Hull, La Paz, May 16, 1937, in 824.6363 St2/134, DSA, NA; and Norweb to Hull, La Paz, May 17, 1937, in 824.6363 St2/137, DSA, NA.
54. Welles to Palmer, June 10, 1937, and Memo by Division of American Republics, Department of State, June 7, 1937, both in 824.6363 St2/147, DSA, NA.
55. Palmer to Welles, February 1, 1938, in 824.6363 St2/221, DSA, NA; memo by Flournoy, Legal Adviser's Office, Department of State, February 7, 1938, in 824.6363 St2/230, DSA, NA; memo by Flournoy, February 9, 1938, in 824.6363 St2/232, DSA, NA; and Eugene Holman to Welles, March 31, 1938, in 824.6363 St2/249, DSA, NA.
56. After March 1939, when the company lost its appeal to the Bolivian Supreme Court, the State Department began to apply economic pressure on Bolivia in favor of the company. For discussion of this later phase of the conflict and its international context, see chapter II, *infra.*
57. A brief note sent to the State Department's Legal Adviser by one of his staff attorneys stated: "The confiscation of the Standard Oil properties in Bolivia may have had a relationship to the confiscation in Mexico." See Flournoy to Hackworth, March 31, 1938, in 824.6363 St2/240, DSA, NA. For a dramatic account of the events in Mexico surrounding the oil expropriations, see Howard Cline, *The United States and Mexico* (Cambridge, Mass., 1953), pp. 236ff.
58. For an excellent discussion of the developing conflict between Mexico and the foreign interests, see Cronon, *Josephus Daniels* chapters, V, VI. Also see Joe C. Ashby, *Organized Labor and the Mexican Revolution Under Lázaro Cárdenas* (Chapel Hill, 1967).
59. Cronon, *Josephus Daniels,* pp. 154–155.
60. See *ibid.,* pp. 159–163, for a detailed narrative of these events.
61. Daniels' letters to Roosevelt and Hull are quoted in *ibid.,* pp. 171, 173, respectively. As an illustration of the companies' intransigence, Daniels reported that they had turned down an

offer by the Mexican Finance Minister to prove to them from their own tax records that they could afford the wage increases recommended by the Arbitration Board. *Ibid.*, p. 179.

62. *Ibid.*, pp. 165, 173.
63. Quoted in Allan S. Everest, *Morgenthau, the New Deal, and Silver* (New York, 1950), p. 87.
64. See Cronon, *Josephus Daniels*, pp. 186–189; also Wood, *Making*, p. 208.
65. *FR*, 1938, V, 729–733. See also Cronon, *Josephus Daniels*, pp. 189–192.
66. *Ibid.*, pp. 192–197; also Wood, *Making*, 209–213. Years later, former Mexican Under Secretary for Foreign Affairs Ramón Beteta told Cronon that Mexico would have broken diplomatic relations if Daniels had presented the March 26 note formally. Cronon points out that Mexico did break relations with Britain when the British government formally presented such a note. *Josephus Daniels*, p. 198. The episode certainly stands as a tribute to Daniels' personal sagacity. Whether it thereby also reflects positively on the State Department can perhaps be gauged from the very negative nature of Hull's reaction when he later found out what Daniels had done. See *ibid.*, p. 196; also Wood, *Making*, pp. 214–217.
67. See discussion of the larger inter-American context of the Mexican oil expropriations in Gardner, *New Deal Diplomacy*, pp. 112–123.
68. Memo by Baruch, March 29, 1938, in Special Memoranda File (1938–1939), Bernard Baruch Manuscripts, Princeton University Library, Princeton, New Jersey (hereafter Baruch MS). This memo was sent to Secretary Hull, who acknowledged receipt on March 30, 1938, terming it "of exceptional interest and timeliness." See Hull to Baruch, March 30, 1938, in Correspondence File, Baruch MS.
69. Memo by Baruch, March 29, 1938, Special Memoranda, 1938–1939, Baruch MS. See also Baruch to Daniels, April 11, 1938, Correspondence File, Baruch MS.
70. Baruch to Daniels, June 28, 1938, Correspondence File, Baruch MS.
71. Baruch to President Roosevelt, October 11, 1938, Special Memoranda, 1938–1939; Baruch to Byrnes, October 18, 1938, Correspondence File; LaGuardia to Baruch, October 17, 1938, Correspondence File; and Baruch to LaGuardia, October 18, 1938, Correspondence File, Baruch MS.

II: The new technique

1. Laurence Duggan, *The Americas: The Search for Hemisphere Security* (New York, 1949), p. 160.
2. Quoted in E. David Cronon, *Josephus Daniels in Mexico* (Madison, Wisc., 1960), p. 235.
3. Press Conference of January 12, 1940, No. 614-A, President's Personal File No. 1P (hereafter PPF-1P), FDR MS.
4. The Portuguese text of the 1937 constitution can be found in Antonio Figueira de Almeida, *A Constituicao de Dez de Novembro Explicada ao Povo* (Rio de Janeiro, 1940). See also

the analysis of this constitution in George Wythe, *Industry*
in Latin America (New York, 1945), pp. 46, 181–190.

5. Baruch to Davies, May 23, 1938; Baruch to Sloan, May 25, 1938, in Correspondence File, Baruch MS.

6. See Jones to President Roosevelt, March 4, 1939, in Box 29, Presidential Correspondence (Roosevelt, Franklin D., 1939), Jesse Jones Manuscripts, Library of Congress, Washington, D.C. (hereafter cited as Box 29, Jones MS). On Hull's position in respect to the 1939 Brazilian agreement, see W. Feuerlein and E. Hannan, *Dollars in Latin America* (New York, 1941), p. 39.

7. Memo by Klein, enclosed in McClintock to Rockefeller, September 16, 1940, in Box 1891, File 400 U.S.-L.A. (Trade Promotion 1939–1940), Records of the Bureau of Foreign and Domestic Commerce (Record Group No. 151), National Archives (hereafter cited as BFDC, NA). Also McClintock to Klein, September 21, 1940, in Box 861, File 97634/5, General Records of The Department of Commerce (Record Group No. 40), National Archives (hereafter cited as GRDC, NA).

8. For a proposal that the Department of Commerce lobby for export subsidies for machinery, see Robert Patchin, vice-president of W. R. Grace and Co., to Richard C. Patterson, Assistant Secretary of Commerce, March 18, 1939, in Box 1889, File G, BFDC, NA. The report of the Business Advisory Council, dated January 1940, is in Box 948, File 102500/6 (No. 7), GRDC, NA. President Vargas' speech is quoted on p. 40 of the report.

9. Messersmith to Welles, Havana, January 31, 1941, George S. Messersmith Manuscripts, University of Delaware Library, Newark, Delaware (hereafter Messersmith MS). All citations from these manuscripts are from the Correspondence File unless otherwise noted.

The Roosevelt Administration ran into such serious political trouble at home over this Cuban sugar purchase agreement that Secretary of State Hull tried at the last minute to hold up the agreement; Messersmith had to threaten to resign in order to get it through. See vol. II, No. 2, of Messersmith's unpublished memoir manuscript (hereafter Memoirs, II, No. 2), Messersmith MS. Messersmith took the view that the agreement was important not only in itself but as "an act of faith for all Latin America."

10. See, for example, Robert Triffin, "Central Banking and Monetary Management in Latin America," in Seymour Harris, ed., *Economic Problems of Latin America* (New York, 1944), pp. 104–105. Triffin was an associate economist for the Federal Reserve System. See also George Soule, David Efron, and Norman T. Ness, *Latin America in the Future World* (New York, 1945), pp. 106–108.

11. Statement of Dr. Daniel Samper Ortega, Bogotá, Colombia, in *Chicago Round Table*, pp. 103–104.

12. Memo of conference with the President and Under Secretary of State Welles, April 10, 1940, in Box 29, Presidential Correspondence (Correspondence—Photostats, 1940), Jones MS.

13. Forrestal to Baruch, July 26, 1940; Baruch to Forrestal, August 1, 1940, in Correspondence File, Baruch MS.
14. Baruch to Jones, September 30, 1940; Jones to Baruch, October 2, 1940, in Correspondence File, Baruch MS. On the refusal of the United States Steel Corporation to help finance the Brazilian steel project, see memo of a conversation with E. R. Stettinius, Jr., of U.S. Steel, September 16, 1940, in OIAA: 17: Steel. Stettinius gave several reasons why U.S. Steel had turned down the request, one of which was that "no American investment that has been made in Brazil is worth anything at the present time and the Brazilian Government has defaulted on all of its debts to the United States." Stettinius himself was ultimately to move into the State Department, where, as Under Secretary and then as Secretary of State, he was to become a pillar of the late wartime government-business coalition.
15. Baruch to President Roosevelt, October 11, 1938, Special Memoranda, 1938–1939, Baruch MS.
16. White to President Roosevelt, October 17, 1938, in File No. 14, Harry Dexter White Manuscripts, Princeton University Library, Princeton, New Jersey (hereafter White MS).
17. White to Secretary of the Treasury Morgenthau, March 30, 1939, File 15; also White to Morgenthau, March 31, 1939, File 14, White MS.
18. Welles to President Roosevelt, June 16, 1939, enclosing letter from the Argentine Popular Union, in Presidential Secretary's File, Argentina 1933–1939, FDR MS (hereafter cited as PSF, FDR MS).
19. See Department of State, Conference Series, No. 44. *Report of the Delegate of the United States of America to the Meeting of the Foreign Ministers of the American Republics. Panama. September 23–October 3, 1939* (Washington, D.C., 1940), p. 6. Hereafter *Panama Conference Report*.
20. A copy of the joint letter of the Secretaries can be found in Folder 134, Hull MS.
21. See Joe Alex Morris, *Nelson Rockefeller: A Biography* (New York, 1960), pp. 112, 126, 128–130.
22. Memo by Nelson Rockefeller and Associates, New York City, June 1940 (no exact date), in OIAA: 30: Plans for Trade and Economic Defense.
23. Jones to Wyckoff, January 7, 1939, in Box 1891, File 400 U.S.-L.A. (Trade Promotion 1939–1940), BFDC, NA.
24. Memo by Hull of conversation with Bolivian Minister in Washington, April 11, 1939, in Folder 191, Hull MS.
25. *FR*, 1939, V, 313. A number of State Department officials thought the decision of the Bolivian Supreme Court was tainted by the extreme political pressure of Bolivian public opinion. Bryce Wood, *The Making of the Good Neighbor Policy* (New York, 1961), p. 181, shows that one Supreme Court justice did resign just before the decision was handed down, and expressed fear that the intense political pressure would compromise the Court's reputation for "probity." In all fairness, it should be pointed out that proof of the existence of

such pressure, even accompanied by proof of the Court's awareness of it, does not thereby constitute proof that the Court would have rendered a different decision in the absence of such pressure, or even that the pressure was responsible for the decision the Court made.

26. See Laurence Duggan, "Background for Revolution," in *Inter-American*, September 1946, pp. 16–17.
27. Wood, *Making*, pp. 191–192.
28. *Ibid.*, pp. 195–200.
29. See chapter VI, *infra*.
30. Cronon, *Josephus Daniels*, p. 247.
31. *Ibid.*, pp. 245, 248–249.
32. *Ibid.*, p. 250; also see Wood, *Making*, pp. 242–243. Wood interprets Hull's note of April 3 as an attempt to outflank the oil companies by proving to them the impossibility of obtaining arbitration. Such an interpretation, while certainly plausible, is nonetheless speculative, and seems to underrate the importance of the Sinclair negotiations as a background to the note.
33. Cronon, *Josephus Daniels*, pp. 251, 253–254.
34. *Ibid.*, pp. 260, 267–268.
35. *Ibid.*, pp. 260–261.
36. *Ibid.*, pp. 269–270. The commission also flatly rejected the companies' contention that they be compensated for lost potential profits on oil still in the ground.
37. See Wood, *Making*, chapter X.
38. A wealth of detail concerning the airlines story is in William A. M. Burden, *The Struggle for Airways in Latin America* (New York, 1943). Burden was Special Assistant for Aviation in the Department of Commerce. The statement by Berle can be found in Lloyd Gardner, *Economic Aspects of New Deal Diplomacy* (Madison, Wisc., 1964), p. 123.
39. See statement by Commander Carlos Fallon of Colombia, in *Chicago Round Table*, p. 221. Fallon's statement was corroborated by Edgar Dean of the Council on Foreign Relations, *ibid.*, p. 221.
40. Braden to Taussig, Bogotá, November 30, 1939, in Caribbean File, Charles W. Taussig Manuscripts, Franklin D. Roosevelt Library, Hyde Park, N.Y. (hereafter Taussig MS). A copy of Rockefeller's press statement of January 8, 1941, announcing the anti-Axis campaign, is in Box 861, File 97634/5, GRDC, NA. On wartime inter-American efforts to replace remaining Axis personnel, see Pan American Union, *Recent Trends in Inter-American Economic Cooperation* (Washington, D.C., 1943).

III: Skeptics south and north

1. See Under Secretary of States Welles's report on American draft proposals for the Panama Conference, in *Panama Conference Report*, p. 16. For Pierson's general views on international loans, see his statement on Eximbank operations, dated July 15, 1940, in OIAA:25:Loans Misc. In considering a loan, Pierson noted, "Among the questions the responsible officers of the Bank must ask themselves are the following: . . . Will

the accommodation result in stimulating desirable export business in a 'natural' sphere? How will the interests of private United States creditors of the foreign country be affected?"

2. See text of Welles's address in telegram, Welles to Hull, Panama, September 20, 1939, in 740.00111A.R./304, DSA, NA. The italicized portion of the quoted extract is an addendum suggested by Assistant Secretary of State Adolf Berle. See Department to Welles (from Berle), September 21, 1939, in 740.00111A.R./304, DSA, NA; also Welles's return telegram indicating that suggested change has been made, Welles to Hull, Panama, September 24, 1939, in 740.00111A.R./341, DSA, NA.

3. Welles to Hull, Panama, September 25, 1939, and Department to Welles, September 27, 1939, in 740.00111A.R./357, DSA, NA.

4. Welles to Hull, Ancon, Canal Zone, October 1, 1939, in 740.00111-A.R./457, DSA, NA. See also *Panama Conference Report*, pp. 73–74, 50.

5. A copy of the questionnaire can be found in 710.FEAC/143, DSA, NA.

6. Most of the responses to the questionnaire—including all those referred to here—can be found, in their original language, in the document group 710.FEAC/143, DSA, NA. The others can be found under a different document number in the same file group, e.g., the Uruguayan response is in 710.FEAC/155v, DSA, NA.

7. Memo No. 10, by Peru, dated November 29, 1939, to Subcommittee I of IAFEAC, in 710.FEAC/143, DSA, NA. See also the letter from Dr. Larranaga to Welles, January 20, 1940, in 710.Bank/29a, DSA, NA. Also Memo No. 16, by Peru, dated December 20, 1939, to Subcommittee I of IAFEAC, in 710.FEAC/143, DSA, NA.

8. See draft of the convention enclosed in Welles to Hull, February 16, 1940, in 710.Bank/36, DSA, NA.

9. For representative Latin American reactions, see Wilson to Hull, Montevideo, February 16, 1940, in 710.Bank/25, DSA, NA; Corrigan to Hull, Caracas, March 7, 1940, in 710.Bank/41, DSA, NA; Chargé in San Jose to Hull, March 7, 1940, in 710.Bank/47, DSA, NA; and DesPortes to Hull, Guatemala City, March 18, 1940, in 710.Bank/67, DSA, NA. See also memo by Collado of State Department of conversation with the Nicaraguan Minister in Washington, March 20, 1940, in 710.Bank/65, DSA, NA; memo by Finley of State Department of conversation with Haitian Minister and Pierson, March 21, 1940, in 710.Bank/84, DSA, NA; Caffery to Hull, Rio de Janeiro, April 2, 1940, in 710.Bank/79, DSA, NA; and Bowers to Hull, Santiago, March 14, 1940, in 710.Bank/58, DSA, NA.

10. Berle to Welles, May 4, 1940, in 710.Bank/161, DSA, NA. Appended note from Bonsal gives Welles's reply. On Nicaraguan position, see Nicholson to Hull, Managua, March 27, 1940, in 710.Bank/74, DSA, NA.

11. Memo by Rovensky, September 4, 1940, to which is appended minutes of OCIAA executive committee meeting of September 11, 1940, in OIAA:5: Executive.

12. See Collado to Duggan, Berle, and Welles, November 7, 1940,
and Duggan to Berle and Welles, November 8, 1940, both in
710.Bank/219, DSA, NA.
13. Baruch to President Roosevelt, June 26, 1940, and Baruch to
Richard Hooker, September 25, 1940, both in Correspondence
File, Baruch MS.
14. Vandenberg to Mrs. L. B. Winton, February 2, 1940, Correspondence File, Arthur H. Vandenberg Manuscripts, William
L. Clements Library, Ann Arbor, Michigan (hereafter Vandenberg MS). To a Michigan constituent: "Fundamentally, the
Hull Treaties are un-Constitutional and I have no doubt that
the Supreme Court (even as it is presently constituted) will
say so. It is an un-Constitutional delegation of discretionary
legislative power to the Executive Department of the Government." See Vandenberg to Paul O. Strawhecker, January 19,
1940, Correspondence File, Vandenberg MS.
15. Taft to President of Armco International Corporation, September 13, 1940, in OIAA: 17: Steel.
16. See Lancaster to Welles, May 29, 1940, enclosing letter from
Burgess to Morgenthau, in 710.Bank/193, DSA, NA. Burgess,
one might add, knew what he was talking about; see memo
from Collado to Berle, April 8, 1940, in which Collado notes
that it may sometimes be "deemed desirable to force down
interest rates by competing with existing institutions," in
710.Bank/99, DSA, NA.
17. Welles to Lancaster, June 11, 1940, in 710.Bank/193, DSA, NA.
Also Lancaster to Welles, June 16, 1940, in 710.Bank/194, DSA,
NA.
18. For summaries of these meetings, see Excerpts from Executive Committee meetings of January 10, 15, 1941, and February 5, 12, 1941, in OIAA: 25: Banks. See also memo by Collado,
February 24, 1941, listing participants in these meetings, and
indicating solution found, in 710.Bank/229, DSA, NA. For text
of letter from Secretary Hull to Senator George of the
Foreign Relations Committee, stating the intention of the
United States government to have the Bank's charter so
amended, see U.S. Congress. Senate. Committee on Foreign
Relations. *Hearings on the Inter-American Bank. May 5, 6,
1941.* 77th Cong., 1st sess. (Washington, D.C., 1941), pp. 15–16.
19. Statement of Hon. Adolf Berle, *ibid.*, pp. 18, 19; statement of
Hon. Joseph Rovensky, *ibid.*, p. 26; statement of Hon. William
L. Clayton, *ibid.*, p. 28. For Pierson's position, see his article
in *Proceedings of the Academy of Political Science,* XIX, No.
1 (May 1940), 92–93. For a specific example of Pierson's influence on behalf of the private banks, see Rockefeller to Pierson, September 26, 1941, in OIAA: 17: Brazil—Investments, in
which Rockefeller informs Pierson that as a result of Pierson's
visit to Brazil (during which Pierson told Brazilian officials
that the United States was "willing to continue financial and
economic aid but naturally this could not be done unless
Brazil was willing to cooperate"), President Vargas had just
signed a bill exempting banks owned by citizens of American
nations from a decree-law of April 9, 1941. The effect of this

exemption was specifically to permit National City Bank of New York to continue its operations there.

20. A copy of the subcommittee report is available in File No. Executive K, 76th Cong., 3rd sess., Records of the Senate, in the Legislative Records Branch, National Archives (Record Group No. 46) (hereafter cited as Senate, LRB, NA).

21. Glass to Harrison, May 27, 1941, and Glass to Harrison, June 17, 1941, both in Correspondence File, George Leslie Harrison Manuscripts, Columbia University Library, New York City (hereafter Harrison MS).

22. Harrison to Glass, July 3, 1941, in Box 412, Carter Glass Manuscripts, University of Virginia Library, Charlottesville, Virginia (hereafter Glass MS).

23. Burgess to Glass, July 22, 1941, in Box 412, Glass MS.

24. On the January 1942 effort in the Senate Foreign Relations Committee, see Sen. Pepper to Bernard Baruch, January 20, 1942, Correspondence File, Baruch MS; also State Department memo of March 25, 1942, in Box 412, Glass MS. On Welles's efforts to have President Roosevelt intervene, see Welles to Roosevelt, March 25, 1942, and Welles to Glass, April 24, 1942, both in Correspondence File, Baruch MS. See also Eccles to Glass, June 6, 1942, and Glass to Eccles, June 17, 1942, Correspondence File, Baruch MS. See also Projects Director of the Inter-American Development Commission to Vice-Chairman of the IADC, February 25, 1942, in OIAA:25:Banks.

25. Years later, Adolf Berle told the present writer that it was his impression that Burgess had simply backed out of the agreement which he and the other New York bankers had made with the State Department to support a modified Bank convention, and had told Glass to "kill" the bill. "Treachery on the face of it," was how Berle described Burgess' alleged action. Interview with Adolf Berle, New York City, March 28, 1967.

Whether or not one reads Burgess' letter to Glass as a request to kill the bill outright, it is clear that Burgess was deeply concerned over the effect the Bank might have on commercial banking operations in Latin America. On the other hand, Glass himself seems to have needed little prodding in the direction of destroying the bill entirely, and may not have been above engaging in a bit of political maneuvering in order to achieve that purpose. In a letter to Under Secretary of State Welles in April 1942, Glass stated that he was holding the Bank bill in abeyance because RFC administrator Jesse Jones had told him that the RFC was making all necessary loans to Latin America. See Glass to Welles, April 22, 1942, in 710.Bank/255, DSA, NA. A separate memo from Berle to Welles, attached to this letter, states that Jones never confirmed this assertion by Senator Glass.

26. Unsigned, unaddressed memo, August 15, 1940, in OIAA:25: Investments Miscellaneous.

27. The text of the original resolution is in 710.Dev.Com./1, DSA, NA. It was ironic, considering the later history of the Inter-American Bank fight, that at the time of the founding of the

IAB and the IADC, Sumner Welles wrote to President Roosevelt proposing that private American banking interests be
given direct representation on the IADC and mentioning the
name of W. Randolph Burgess as a suitable candidate. See
memo, Welles to Duggan, January 30, 1940, in 710.Dev.Com./5,
DSA, NA. The President, however, vetoed this idea. In a letter
to Welles, dated April 5, 1940, he specifically ruled out New
York bankers, and advised Welles to talk to Harry Hopkins,
who might come up with a more "suitable" idea. See 710.Dev.-
Com./21, DSA, NA.
28. Emphasis added. The Dávila Report is included in Report No.
4 of Subcommittee II of IAFEAC, of which a copy is available
in 710.Dev.Com./2, DSA, NA.
29. For a list of IADC projects to July 25, 1941, see Projects Director of IADC to Collado of State Department, July 25, 1941,
enclosing an IADC interim report, in 710.Dev.Com./113½, DSA,
NA. The projects included a retail goods merchandising advisory service; a mandioca starch processing plant in Brazil,
later abandoned in favor of a technical assistance program; a
pencil factory in Argentina; a dairy industries program; and a
program for rubber development to make the hemisphere free
from dependence upon outside sources of rubber.
30. See memo by S. G. Hanson, October 21, 1940, in OIAA:17:
Brazil—Steel. See also Jamison to Eichel, March 1, 1941, in
OIAA:17:Brazil—Steel, in which the writer points out that
"the countries who will lose most of the Brazil business which
will ultimately be handled by this plant are England and
Germany."
31. White to Vice-President Wallace, December 1, 1941, File 19a,
White MS.
32. See, respectively, Armour to Hull, Buenos Aires, March 28,
1941, in 710.Dev.Com./84, DSA, NA; Norweb to Hull, Lima,
April 17, 1941, in 710.Dev.Com./86, DSA, NA; and Chargé ad
interim to Hull, Bogotá, May 12, 1941, in 710.Dev.Com./90,
DSA, NA.
33. McClintock to Duggan, July 13, 1940, in 710.Dev.Com./34, DSA,
NA; and Commercial Attaché to Hull, Rio de Janeiro, August
17, 1940, in 710.Dev.Com./44, DSA, NA.
34. The Eximbank view is in McClintock to Duggan, September
23, 1940, in 710.Dev.Com./53, DSA, NA; the Brazilian reply is in
Chargé a.i. to Hull, Rio de Janeiro, October 25, 1940, in 710.Dev.-
Com./57, DSA, NA.
35. See 710.Dev.Com./113½, DSA, NA.
36. Memo by S. G. Hanson, January 27, 1941, in OIAA:17:Colombia
—Country Study, January 1–31, 1941. Also see Hanson and
Winks to Rovensky, June 21, 1941, in OIAA:24:Creation of
Inter-American Development Corp.
37. See draft bill, dated June 9, 1941, in OIAA:24:Creation of
Inter-American Development Corp.
38. On "striking oil," owning utilities, and other dangers, see
memo, Hanson to Rovensky, June 11, 1941, in OIAA:24:Crea-
tion of Inter-American Development Corp. For supporting
views, see memo, McQueen and Chrysler to Friele, June 12,

1941, in the same file. Also minutes of OCIAA Commercial meeting, June 6, 1941, in the same file.

39. Memo, Hanson to Spaeth, June 19, 1941, in OIAA:18:Plans.

40. For a divergence of views between the State Department and the Foreign Bondholders' Protective Council in regard to debt settlements, see memo, Rovensky to Rockefeller, January 18, 1940, in OIAA:25:Defaulted Debts, on the Council's rejection of a proposed debt adjustment plan in Colombia which the State Department had tacitly approved. On a more general level, see Hanson memo, March 12, 1941, and letter, Rovensky to Clayton, April 17, 1941, both in OIAA:25:Defaulted Debts, remarking on the inability of the Bondholders' Council to fit its area of activity into the "broader inter-American economic program of the United States Government," and recommending a full-scale revamping of the Council, including immediate changes in key personnel, plus moving the headquarters of the Council from New York City to Washington, in order to bring the Council closer to the government's influence and outlook.

41. See Hanson-Winks memo to Rovensky, June 21, 1941, in OIAA:24:Creation of Inter-American Development Corp. Also Rovensky memo, July 2, 1941, in OIAA:25:Investments-Loans, August–December 1941; and memo to Rovensky, July 11, 1941, in OIAA:29:Financing of Developmental Programs, defending unguaranteed loans as an emergency measure.

42. For the vigorously activist view, see Hanson and Winks to Rovensky, June 26, 1941, in OIAA:25:Investments-Loans, August–December 1941. For views opposed to any U.S. initiative in regard to large-scale planning, see memo by Rovensky, July 2, 1941, in OIAA:29:Financing of Developmental Programs, and memo, Chrysler to Rovensky, July 11, 1941, in OIAA:25:Investment-Loans, August–December 1941, expressing the opinion that any program of large-scale blueprinting of developmental plans by United States officials "would be viewed with suspicion and doubt and should not be considered, except at specific request of a Latin-American Government."

43. This speech was released as State Department Press Release No. 318, on June 23, 1941. A copy is also available in 610.1131/478, DSA, NA.

IV: The impact of war

1. Rockefeller to Secretary of Commerce, January 22, 1941, in OIAA:30:Trade and Economic Defense Problems.

2. Memo, Machold to Rovensky, May 10, 1941, in OIAA:18:Plans. The writer recommended, in essence, the recognition of the existence of two separate programs—emergency and long-range —and suggested establishing an OCIAA Research Unit to study data useful in planning postwar projects.

3. Rockefeller to Welles, June 4, 1941, in 710.Dev.Com./110, DSA, NA (drafts enclosed). Welles's notation of approval is attached.

4. Unsigned memo, dated March 23, 1941, on "Economic Defense: Latin America," in OIAA:30:Plans for Trade and Economic

Defense. For material on one such program, see memo by [317
Simon G. Hanson, December 16, 1940, in OIAA:26: Surveys—
Country Studies, 1940–1942, and the entire file OIAA:17: Colombia, Country Study. Rockefeller to Wallace, August 13, 1941, in
OIAA:30: Plans for Trade and Economic Defense.
5. An information circular put out by the Bureau of Mines of the
United States Department of the Interior in December 1939, a
copy of which will be found in OIAA:25: Strategic and Critical
Materials Reports, gave the following definitions of these
items:
"Strategic materials are those essential to national defense,
for the supply of which in war dependence must be placed in
whole, or in substantial part, on sources outside the continental limits of the United States; and for which strict
conservation and distribution control measures will be
necessary."
"Critical materials are those essential to national defense,
the procurement problems of which in war would be less difficult than those of strategic materials either because they
have a lesser degree of essentiality or are obtainable in more
adequate quantities from domestic sources; and for which
some degree of conservation and distribution control measures will be necessary."
The circular listed fourteen strategic materials, including:
antimony, chromium, coconut shell char, manganese (fer-
rograde), manila fiber, mercury, mica, nickel, quartz crystal,
quinine, rubber, silk, tin, and tungsten. It listed fifteen critical
materials, including: aluminum, asbestos, cork, graphite,
hides, iodine, kapok, opium, optical glass, phenol, platinum,
tanning materials, toluol, vanadium, and wool. Note in this
connection Laurence Duggan's statement that during the war,
the United States depended on Latin America for the following percentages of her "new supply" of various raw materials,
including some strategic and critical ones: balsa 100 per cent,
kapok 100 per cent, quinine bark 100 per cent, quartz crystal
99.8 per cent, manila fiber 77.8 per cent, tin 56.4 per cent, sugar
63 per cent, henequen 56 per cent, crude natural rubber 42.8
per cent, and copper 32 per cent. See Laurence Duggan, *The
Americas: The Search for Hemisphere Security* (New York,
1949), p. 99.
6. Bulletin No. 4, IADC, December 1, 1941, in OIAA:24: IADC
1942 Misc.
7. See minutes of Inter-agency Policy Committee meeting of
March 13, 1942, regarding favorable action on a project to
build shiploading facilities in Brazil, in OIAA:19: Interagency
Foreign Research Committee.
8. McClintock, OCIAA, to Collado, State Department, January 7,
1942 (proposals dated January 5, 1942), in 710.Dev.Com./133½,
DSA, NA.
9. See Project Evaluation by M. D. Carrel, Projects Director,
IADC, November 2, 1944, in OIAA:24: Merchandising Advisory
Service, IADC. See also Report of Activities of IADC from
Founding Through February 18, 1942, enclosed in Rockefeller

(as chairman of IADC) to Welles, March 3, 1942, in 710.Dev.-Com./129, DSA, NA, esp. p. 4.

10. Memo, Hanson to Spaeth, August 10, 1941, in OIAA:17: Investments.

11. See Summary Report of IADC activities, July 1 to September 30, 1942, enclosed in Rockefeller to Welles, October 14, 1942, in 710.Dev.Com./176, DSA, NA. The fourth quarter summary report is enclosed in Rockefeller to Welles, January 20, 1943, in 710.Dev.Com./189, DSA, NA.

12. See Duggan to Zimmer, May 9, 1942, in 710.Dev.Com./144, also Zimmer to Duggan, May 19, 1942, in 710.Dev.Com./149, DSA, NA. Also memo, Carrel to Nitze, February 6, 1942, in OIAA:17: Argentina—Country Studies 1942.

13. Memo, Rovensky to William Clark, April 29, 1943, in OIAA:17: Brazil—Industrial Development. For more on the Cooke Mission, see *infra*, chapter VIII, n. 42.

14. James H. Drumm, OCIAA, to B. J. McKenna, BEW, July 28, 1942, in OIAA:17: Argentina—Export Licenses.

15. See minutes of Inter-agency Policy Committee meetings, April 2, 7, 1942, in OIAA:19: Interagency Foreign Research Committee.

16. Unsigned, undated memo on results of Rio Conference (identified as Draft X of this statement) and objectives of hemisphere policy, in OIAA:18: Policy.

17. Memo entitled "Report to President," dated October 16, 1940, in Box 29, Presidential Correspondence 1940, Jones MS.

18. See, for example, supporting letters from W. R. Grace & Co. to Duggan, June 7, 1940, in 610.1131/302, and to Welles, June 13, 1940, in 610.1131/313, DSA, NA; also Anglo-American Trading Corporation to President Roosevelt, June 18, 1940, in 610.1131/359, DSA, NA.

19. Inter-Continental Trade Co., Portland, Oregon, to Grady, State Department, June 26, 1940, in 610.1131/329, DSA, NA. See also Anglo-American Trading Corp. to Hull, June 27, 1940, in 610.1131/321, DSA, NA.

20. Eugene Thomas to Senator Wagner, September 10, 1940, enclosing copy of Thomas' speech to National Foreign Trade Convention, July 31, 1940, in File No. S4204, 76th Cong., 3rd sess., LRB, NA. Quotations are from the speech.

21. See the speech cited above.

22. Editorial in *La Hora*, Santiago, August 21, 1940. News article in *A Noticia*, Rio de Janeiro, July 3, 1940.

23. Agricultural attaché to Hull, Buenos Aires, August 13, 1940, in 610.1131/400, DSA, NA, includes a résumé of a conversation with the representative of the Argentine Congress of Rural Societies. Also see Daniels to Hull, Mexico City, July 5, 1940, in 610.1131/344, DSA, NA; and article by Sr. Guillermo Montt in *El Diario Ilustrado*, Santiago, August 15, 1940.

24. Memo by Stanley K. Hornbeck, June 19, 1940, in Folder 134, Hull MS.

25. Memos by Clayton and Rovensky, presented to executive committee meeting of September 4, 1940. See minutes of meeting, and these memos, in OIAA:30: Trade Miscellaneous.

26. See Hawkins, State Department Trade Agreements Division, to Hull, March 12, 1941, in 610.1131/470, DSA, NA. For chart summary of bilateral negotiations through February 15, 1941, see 60.1131/465, DSA, NA.

27. See "A Pan-American Trade Bloc: A Study of Bloc Combinations Varying According to Importance of Economic and Defense Problems," in Council on Foreign Relations, *War and Peace Studies*, Economic and Financial Series, No. E-B 12, Supplement I, July 26, 1940, pp. 1, 4.

28. Arthur R. Upgren, "A Pan-American Trade Bloc," in Council on Foreign Relations, *War and Peace Studies*, Economic and Financial Series, No. E-B 12, June 7, 1940, p. 2.

29. For the September 1940 circular on buying from Latin America, see President Roosevelt to All Departments and Defense Agencies, September 27, 1940, in OF 87, FDR MS. For the April 1941 circular on deliveries of goods to Latin America, see President Roosevelt to William S. Knudsen, director general of OPM (Office of Production Management), April 5, 1941, copy in OIAA:21:Miscellaneous Correspondence re Priorities.

30. Memo, Rockefeller to President Roosevelt, May 28, 1941, in OIAA:29:Shipping Quotas and Allocations. See also supplementary memo by Rockefeller, June 5, 1941, in OIAA:29:Shipping Relief Measures, noting that 59 per cent of total requisitioned tonnage was being taken from Latin America–bound shipping. For Clayton's warning, see W. L. Clayton and W. Y. Elliott to Admiral Land, January 15, 1942, in Box 8, Alphabetical File—Confidential Papers (1940–1942), William L. Clayton Manuscripts, Harry S. Truman Library, Independence, Missouri (hereafter Clayton MS).

31. Memo to Rockefeller, July 21, 1941, in OIAA:30:Inter-American Trade—Economic Department. See also Assistant Director, BEW, to Duggan, February 19, 1942, in OIAA:26:Surveys, and Vice-Chairman of IADC to Rockefeller, July 22, 1942, in OIAA:17:Argentina—Exports Miscellaneous.

32. Memo, F. T. Cole to Kelso Peck, January 5, 1941, in OIAA:29: Exports—Price Ceilings. See also memo, Kelso Peck, OCIAA, to J. Peurifoy, State Department Division of Controls, August 25, 1941, in OIAA:29:Miscellaneous Price Control.

33. McClintock to Rockefeller, Santiago, October 6, 1941, and Fishburn to Spaeth and Rovensky, November 7, 1941, in OIAA: 29:Exports—Ceiling Prices. The writer of the latter memo pointed out that current OPA policies of pegging export price ceilings at the same level as domestic ceilings, plus only extra cost allowance, had stopped many exports entirely.

34. A memo from T. Munson to Rovensky, November 12, 1941, in OIAA:29:Exports—Ceiling Prices, stressed the growth of "fly-by-night" firms in the United States. A memo from M. Carrel to Rovensky, January 26, 1942, in OIAA:25:Investments-Loans, August–December 1941, cited profiteering at the Latin American end of the line. See minutes of the IADC meeting of February 10, 1942, in OIAA:24:Report of Activities of Inter-American Development Corp., for Rockefeller's announcement of the switch from priorities to allocations. See Micou to Harrison,

OCIAA, June 8, 1942, in OIAA:17:Brazil—Country Study, for reports of Brazilian complaints that the United States was "appeasing" pro-Axis Argentina, and was filling Argentine orders more quickly than Brazilian orders.

35. At first, some OCIAA observers looked at dwindling British supply statistics for 1940 and wondered if the main question was not simply how fast the United States could move to take up the supply slack. See memo, Hanson to Spaeth, March 10, 1941, in OIAA:17:Argentina—Trade, especially the section entitled, "Can the British Deliver?" Within four months, this assessment had changed markedly. On British deliveries to Colombia in the first half of 1941, see K. Olsen to McClintock, July 12, 1941, in OIAA:17:Colombia—Economic Development. This later memo also includes remarks on Colombian barter trade with Germany, which continued despite strong Colombian fears of the consequences of a German victory in the war.

36. Memo, Col. F. R. Kerr, BEW, to Col. R. B. Lord, BEW, May 25, 1942, in OIAA:29:Shipping Relief Measures. See also in this connection the minutes of the June 3, 1941, meeting of the Inter-departmental Committee on Inter-American Affairs, in OIAA:6:Inter-departmental Committee on Inter-American Affairs, for a statement by Collado of the State Department warning of certain considerations which might arise in the event of a *British* victory. "There had been indications of thinking among the British," he noted, "which indicated an inclination to practices not far from those of the totalitarian powers. The distinction was more of motivation than of technique."

37. Onyx Chemical Corporation, Jersey City, to Rovensky, December 1, 1942, in OIAA:17:Argentina—Exports Miscellaneous.

38. Memo by Frank W. Fetter to Rovensky, Ruml, Welsh, Hart, and Drumm, April 10, 1942, in OIAA:25:Investments-Loans 1942. The writer noted the necessity for coordinating credit policies and prioritiy policies, and stated that, in view of existing conditions, the prevailing approach must be primarily in terms of priorities.

39. Note Baruch to President Roosevelt, June 27, 1938, Special Memoranda, 1938–1939, Baruch MS. See Rockefeller to Director, Office of Foreign Agricultural Relations, Department of Agriculture, December 2, 1941, in OIAA:17:Brazil—Castor Oil, regarding a program for preclusive buying of castor beans and oil from Brazil. On buying Chilean copper, see Harding to McClintock, December 11, 1940, in OIAA:17:Chile—Copper; Corry to Rockefeller, December 11, 1940, in OIAA:25:Strategic and Critical Materials Reports; and minutes of Inter-departmental Committee on Inter-American Affairs, meeting of October 8, 1940, in OIAA:5:Inter-departmental Committee on Inter-American Affairs. See also discussions regarding purchases of Chilean nitrates in these same minutes, and in memo from Emerson, BEW, to Spaeth, OCIAA, November 25, 1941, in OIAA:17:Chile—Nitrates, on the need to keep this commodity out of pro-Axis, particularly Japanese, hands.

By January 1941, Jesse Jones was writing to President Roosevelt warning that a copper shortage was expected in the United States after all. See Jones to President Roosevelt, January 16, 23, 1941, in Box 30, Presidential Correspondence —Photostats 1941, Jones MS. For information on the Brazilian and Bolivian purchase contracts, see Jones to President Roosevelt, June 26, 1941, also Box 30, Jones MS. In regard to the Brazilian contract, Jones noted: "We have made a commitment to the Brazilian Government to purchase the production of such materials at stated prices slightly below the current market." This price reduction became a feature of a number of preclusive buying contracts.

40. Editorial, *El Mercurio*, Santiago, February 16, 1941.

41. See discussion of this program in Assistant Director, BEW, to Duggan, February 19, 1942, in OIAA: 26: Surveys.

42. See discussion of both the Chilean and Cuban laws in George Wythe, *Industry in Latin America* (New York, 1945), pp. 216–217, 329. The statement by the Mexican educator Alejandro Carrillo of Mexico City is in *Chicago Round Table*, p. 44.

43. Memo from M. L. Bohan, Rio de Janeiro, to Spaeth, Collado, January 21, 1942, in OIAA: 17: Brazil—Rio Conference, Editorial Reaction, January 21 to February 17, 1942. Bohan headed the United States Economic Mission to Bolivia. Also see memo by Frank W. Fetter, April 3, 1942, in OIAA: 17: Bolivia—Commodities; and report by J. L. Apodaca, BEW, to Nitze, April 13, 1942, on tin and tungsten, enclosed in A. Lee, OCIAA, to C. Micou, BEW-OCIAA liaison, April 23, 1942, in OIAA: 17: Bolivia—Inter-American Development Corp.

44. Memo to Frank W. Fetter, April 3, 1942, in OIAA: 17: Bolivia—Commodities.

45. Memo by McClintock, July 20, 1944, of conversation with Laurence Duggan, in OIAA: 17: Bolivia—Commodities.

46. See comments on the Bolivian tin situation in Horace Graham to Rockefeller, Santiago, January 18, 1944, in OIAA: 17: Chile—Economic Development. For a more detailed treatment of the Bolivian revolution of 1943–1944, see *infra*, chapter VI.

47. See President Roosevelt to Vice-President Wallace, November 10, 1942, in OF 510, FDR MS. Cancellation request is in memo from Leo Crowley to President Roosevelt, May 10, 1944, OF 510, FDR MS (memo initialed "OK FDR").

48. D. Humphrey, "Haiti," in Seymour Harris, ed., *Economic Problems of Latin America* (New York, 1944), pp. 367–368, 371, 361. This did not mean, to be sure, that SHADA was a total wartime failure. On the contrary, it built up a flourishing pine lumber industry in the Haitian forests, turning Haiti into a net exporter of lumber by the end of the war. See Eugene Swan, Jr., "Haiti Builds an Industry," in *Inter-American*, March 1946, pp. 28–30. But the failure of the cryptostegia project was still serious.

49. For the story on the Rubber Reserve Corporation and the Brazilian contract, and on comparative prices of bids and contracts, see memo by I. B. White, January 17, 1942, in OIAA:

17: Brazil—Rubber. In the case of Bolivia, see Robbins to McClintock, August 3, 1942, in OIAA: 17: Bolivia—Rubber. The latter memo notes that Bolivia accepted the lower American bid partly because of the "superior position of the United States as a customer of Bolivia and as a purveyor of goods which cannot be obtained from Argentina."

50. Ickes to Baruch, July 29, 1942, in Correspondence File, Baruch MS.

51. See discussion of the program in Jones to William Jeffers, Rubber Director for the War Production Board, December 16, 1942, in Box 31, Presidential Correspondence 1942, Jones MS.

52. On Henderson's visit to Brazil and his statement on rubber prices, see minutes of meeting of Brazilian national subcommission of IADC, March 25, 1942, Rio de Janeiro, in OIAA: 17: Brazil—IADC. On Crowley's later action contradicting Henderson's statement on the irrelevance of prices to production, see memo from Crowley to President Roosevelt, February 7, 1944, in OF 510, FDR MS.

For Rockefeller's statement, see U.S. Congress. House of Representatives. Ways and Means Committee. *Hearings on Extension of the Reciprocal Trade Act. May 4, 1945.* 79th Cong., 1st sess. (Washington, D.C., 1945), p. 377. For BEW's position on the Brazilian purchasing agency, see Spaeth, BEW (American Hemisphere Division) to Will Clayton (as Deputy Administrator, Federal Loan Administration), March 1, 1942, in OIAA: 17: Brazil—Rubber.

53. On the Mexican problem, see Ambassador Messersmith to Duggan, Mexico City, June 12, 1944, in Messersmith MS. On the food problem in Peru, see Director, Office of Inter-American Relations, Stanford University, to Chief of State Department Division of Inter-American Cultural Affairs, April 6, 1943, enclosing report of Peruvian Chief of Bureau of Census, in 710.-Dev.Com./213, DSA, NA. See also Duggan, *Americas*, p. 100.

54. A basic policy memo by Harris dated August 12, 1942, and entitled, "The Need for Inter-American Price Control," is in OIAA: 29: Rationing. On problems of maintaining controls, see various articles in Harris, ed., *Economic Problems of Latin America*, especially Harris' articles on "Price Stabilization Programs in Latin America" and "Exchanges and Prices," and the article by Lewis and Beitscher entitled "Colombia: With Particular Reference to Price Control," pp. 143, 187, and pp. 322, 333–334, respectively.

55. For material on the OCIAA Food Supply Division, see Annual Reports of OCIAA Institute of Inter-American Affairs, for fiscal years ending June 30, 1943, and June 30, 1944, in OF 4512, FDR MS. The exchanges between the State Department and OCIAA can be found in 823.5018/38–56, inclusive, DSA, NA. See in particular, Collado, State Department, to Ambassador Norweb, January 11, 1943, in 823.5018/41; Hull to American Embassy, Lima, March 24, 1943, in 823.5018/54; and especially the exchange between Rockefeller and Welles, in Welles to Rockefeller, March 3, 1943, 823.5018/55, and Rockefeller to Welles, March 10, 1943, 823.5018/56, DSA, NA. The agreement

was finally signed on May 19, 1943. See Norweb to Hull, Lima,
May 29, 1943, in 823.5018/68, DSA, NA.

56. See Department of State Circular to all American Embassies in Latin America, May 27, 1942, in OIAA:17:Argentina—Shipments.

57. Memos, President Roosevelt to Secretary of the Treasury Morgenthau, November 6, 1942, and May 10, 1943, in OF 4512, FDR MS. See also letters from Ambassador Messersmith to Duggan, August 14, 1942, and to Welles, September 27, 1942, stressing the importance of this work, in Messersmith MS. To Duggan, Messersmith wrote that this job was so important to the war effort, in respect to moving goods to the Panama Canal, that the United States should if necessary take the initiative in respect to railroad rehabilitation in Mexico. To Welles, he wrote: "This railway rehabilitation program is at the basis [sic] of our whole program of political, economic, and military cooperation with Mexico. If the railways are not put in shape to carry the traffic we are demanding and which we need for our war effort, our whole program will break down."

58. See memo by Micou, May 9, 1942, in OIAA:17:Brazil—Ore: Itabira Report.

59. Counselor of Embassy to Hull, Lima, August 17, 1943, in 823.5018/78; also Norweb to Hull, Lima, September 9, 1943, in 823.5018/144, DSA, NA. For an analysis of the Brazilian transport situation, see minutes of meeting of Brazilian subcommission of IADC, May 8, 1942, Rio de Janeiro, in OIAA:17:Brazil—IADC; also FEA report by J. F. Winchester, "Review of Motor Equipment Situation in Brazil," July 10 to October 10, 1944, in OIAA:17:Brazil—Landways. On auto parts situation, see memo from W. A. Anderson to Francisco and McClintock, June 2, 1944, in OIAA:29:Miscellaneous Price Control.

60. See Department of State Circular to American Diplomatic Officers in the Other American Republics except Argentina and Chile, September 12, 1942, in OIAA:29:Transfer of Idle Plant Machinery to O.A.R.; and Rockefeller to Paul Hoffman, February 8, 1943, in OIAA:30:Trade Fairs. For summary statement on Brazil and Colombia, see memo, McQueen to Rovensky, January 5, 1943, in OIAA:17:Brazil—Trade-Export Licenses.

61. Harris, *Economic Problems of Latin America*, p. 37. Also see Duggan, *Americas*, p. 126.

62. Luis Alberto Sanchez, "What's Left of Inter-Americanism?", in *Inter-American*, January 1945, pp. 13–14.

63. See, for example, memos of conversations between Hull and the British Ambassador, December 22, 27, 1943, in Folder 216, Hull MS. Also see E. Louise Peffer, "Cordell Hull's Argentine Policy and Britain's Meat Supply," in *Inter-American Economic Affairs*, X (Autumn 1956), 3–21; and on Hull's attempts to get the American Secretaries of War and Navy to pressure the British through the Combined Chiefs of Staff in London, see Lloyd Gardner, *Economic Aspects of New Deal Diplomacy* (Madison, Wisc., 1964), p. 203.

A more detailed analysis of later wartime and postwar United States policy toward Argentina will be found in chapters VI, X, *infra*.

V: Planning for peace

1. Henry R. Luce, *The American Century* (New York, 1941), p. 27.
2. *Ibid.*, pp. 33, 23, 35–39, 40.
3. *Ibid.*, pp. 26–27.
4. For Luce on Roosevelt and the Democratic party, see *ibid.*, p. 14.
5. "For example," wrote Luce, "we think of Asia as being worth only a few hundred millions a year to us. Actually, in the decades to come Asia will be worth to us exactly zero—or else it will be worth to us four, five, ten billions of dollars a year. And the latter are the terms we must think in, or else confess a pitiful impotence." *Ibid.*, pp. 36–37. For Clayton's testimony on world prosperity see U.S. Congress. Senate Committee on Foreign Relations. *Hearings on the Nominations of Joseph C. Grew, Nelson A. Rockefeller, W. L. Clayton, et al.* (Washington, D.C., 1944), pp. 40, 41, 67.
6. *Congressional Record*, 78th Cong., 1st sess., LXXXIX, Part 7, November 18, 1943, 9678, 9679.
7. The text of the Atlantic Charter is available in William A. Williams, ed., *The Shaping of American Diplomacy* (Chicago, 1956), pp. 914–915. "It would be regrettable," wrote Republican party foreign policy strategist John Foster Dulles, "if this [British Empire exception] or some undisclosed arrangements should nullify the opportunity of peoples generally to have effective access to the trade and raw materials of the world." See "Long Range Peace Objectives: Including An Analysis of the Roosevelt-Churchill Eight Point Declaration," a statement submitted to the Commission to Study the Bases of a Just and Durable Peace, by Its Chairman, John Foster Dulles, September 18, 1941 (p. 5). In Group I, Area C, John Foster Dulles Manuscripts, Princeton University Library, Princeton, New Jersey (hereafter cited as Dulles MS). This commission was created by the Federal Council of Churches of Christ.
8. See Sumner Welles, *Seven Decisions That Shaped History* (New York, 1951), pp. 138–139.
9. Hamilton Fish Armstrong to Hull, April 21, 1943, in Folder 155, Hull MS. See also Armaments Group, Council on Foreign Relations, "Problems Involved in Regional vs. World-wide Security Organization," in Council on Foreign Relations, *War and Peace Studies*, Armaments Series, No. A-B 90, June 21, 1943, p. 8.
10. See President Roosevelt to George W. Norris, September 21, 1943, in PPF 880, FDR MS.
11. Morgenthau to President Roosevelt, May 16, 1942, in OF 229, FDR MS.
12. Wallace to Jones, October 30, 1941, Box 26, Wallace Correspondence, Jones MS. See also copy of Jones's speech to Committee for Economic Development, New York City, April 14, 1943, in Box 226, Speech File, Jones MS.
13. See "Questions and Answers on the Bank for Reconstruction

and Development," February 1944, in File 24, Box 9, White MS.
Also note in this connection Assistant Secretary of State Dean
Acheson's speech to the Commonwealth Club of San Francisco, March 23, 1945, in *Department of State Bulletin*, March
25, 1945, p. 473. "The Bank," Acheson told his audience, "is not
created to supersede private banks; it has been created in
order to help private banks."

14. Statement of Henry Wallace before the Senate Committee on
Commerce, January 25, 1945, copy available in File 19a, White
MS (p. 13). See also statement by Emilio Collado, Marshall
Plan Collection, Oral History Project, Columbia University
Library, New York City (hereafter Marshall Plan Oral History
MS), pp. 6-7.

15. Statement by Professor Quincy Wright, University of Chicago,
in *Chicago Round Table*, p. 276.

16. On the exchange between Hull and the Colombian government, see Ruth B. Russell, *A History of the United Nations
Charter* (Washington, D.C., 1958), p. 473. On the Latin American view of the Dumbarton Oaks conversations, see chapters
VI, IX, *infra*.

17. Grayson Kirk, "Problems of Regional Security Organization,"
in Council on Foreign Relations, *War and Peace Studies*, Armaments Series, No. A-B 119, November 28, 1944, p. 6.

18. President Roosevelt to Hull, April 9, 1943, in OF 5300, FDR MS.

19. All this material is available in OF 5300, FDR MS. The OCIAA
report will be cited hereafter as *Resources Division Report*.

20. Inter-departmental committee summary statement, p. 2, in
OF 5300, FDR MS.

21. *Resources Division Report*, p. 43. See also White to Vice-
President Wallace, December 1, 1941, File 19a, White MS; and
Resources Division Report, p. 46. Note also in this connection
the Anglo-American Caribbean Commission's *Report of the
West Indian Conference Held in Barbados, 21-30 March 1944*
(Washington, D.C., 1944), for the following statement on
tariffs and industry in the Caribbean area (pp. 35-36):
"It may be desirable to grant special assistance, by tariff
protection or otherwise, for a limited period in order to enable
a new industry to establish itself. . . . Industries which could
survive if they were not exposed to predatory dumping should
be safeguarded against this form of unfair competition. The
governments of the leading industrial countries such as
Great Britain and the United States should be asked by the
Conference for an assurance that their post-war plans will include the prevention of predatory dumping in the Caribbean
area."
A copy of this report is available in the Caribbean File,
Taussig MS.

22. See *Resources Division Report*, pp. 2, 4.

23. Emphasis added. Interdepartmental committee summary
statement, pp. 2-3, in OF 5300, FDR MS.

24. *Ibid.*, pp. 3-4.

25. *Resources Division Report*, pp. 7-8.

26. *Ibid.*, pp. 25-37; quote is from p. 38.

27. *Ibid.*, pp. 45–46.
28. On the President's original request for a report on ten-cent stores in Latin America, see memo, McClintock, OCIAA, to Wilson, Bureau of Foreign and Domestic Commerce, January 31, 1941, in Box 1892, File 400 U.S.-L.A. (Trade Promotion 1941–1945), BFDC, NA; also memo, Rockefeller to President Roosevelt, March 7, 1941, in OF 813-B, FDR MS. On the President's request in June 1943 for a public relations campaign, see President Roosevelt to Rockefeller, June 11, 1943, in OF 4512, FDR MS. The President's assumption was that North America's keeping its share (in Terre Haute) depended on Latin America's having a share (in Brazil). The President's letter acknowledging receipt of the interdepartmental committee report is in OF 5300, FDR MS.
29. Copy of text of American Forum of the Air radio program, May 9, 1944, in OIAA:24:Conference, National Commissions, IADC. The other participants in this forum included Nelson Rockefeller, Gen. H. H. Arnold of the Army Air Corps, Dr. Eduardo Villasenor of the Bank of Mexico, and Dr. Valentim Boucas of the Brazilian IADC national subcommission.
30. Speech by Joseph C. Rovensky to Boston Conference on Distribution, October 17, 1944, in Caribbean File, Taussig MS.
31. George Soule, David Efron, and Norman T. Ness, *Latin America in the Future World* (New York, 1945), p. 59. This book was prepared under the supervision of Alvin Hansen of the National Planning Association, and was the outcome of a project sponsored jointly by the Association and the OCIAA.
32. W. Feuerlein and E. Hannan, *Dollars in Latin America* (New York, 1941), p. 95. Also see statement of Duncan Aikman of *PM*, New York City, in *Chicago Round Table*, p. 140, and Jacob Viner, Outline for Round Table No. 4, *ibid.*, p. 90.
33. Soule, *et al.*, *Latin America*, pp. 306–310. See also Seymour Harris, ed., *Economic Problems of Latin America* (New York, 1944), p. 21.
34. Soule, *et al.*, *Latin America*, pp. 311, 324–333.
35. National Foreign Trade Council, *Final Declaration of the Thirtieth National Foreign Trade Convention, New York City, October 25–27, 1943* (New York, 1943).
36. National Foreign Trade Council, *Final Declaration of the Thirty-First National Foreign Trade Convention, New York City, October 9–11, 1944* (New York, 1944).
37. Speech by Joseph C. Rovensky to Boston Conference on Distribution, October 17, 1944, in Caribbean File, Taussig MS.
38. Inter-American Development Commission, *Proceedings of the Conference of Commissions of Inter-American Development, New York, May 9–18, 1944* (Washington, D.C., 1944). The statements by Roosevelt, Hull, and Rockefeller are on pp. v, vi, and 34, respectively.
39. See circular from Acting Coordinator, OCIAA, to Chairmen of Coordinating Committees in Latin America, August 15, 1944, in OIAA:24:Conference, National Commissions, IADC. See also Acting Coordinator, OCIAA, to Vice-President, National Foreign Trade Council, November 3, 1944, in OIAA:29:Declarations of National Foreign Trade Council.

40. Memo, Duggan to Welles, December 29, 1942, and Welles to Rockefeller, February 17, 1943, in 710.Dev.Com./202, DSA, NA.

VI: Hedging the bets

1. Henry R. Luce, *The American Century* (New York, 1941), p. 31.
2. Interview with Adolf Berle, New York City, June 18, 1968.
3. Note in this connection the June 1941 remark by State Department official Emilio Collado, cited *supra*, chapter IV, n. 36, to the effect that certain British trade practices in Latin America were "not far from those of the totalitarian powers."
4. *Aide-memoire*, July 9, 1943, enclosed in memo by Hull of conversation with the British Ambassador (who called "at his [own] request"), July 10, 1943, Folder 216, Hull MS.
5. See report on wartime British trade promotion in Latin America in memo, Frank Waring to Director, Bureau of Foreign and Domestic Commerce, January 24, 1945, in Box 1882, File 400 U.K.-L.A. (Trade Promotion 1945), BFDC, NA.
6. *South American Journal*, February 5, 1944, p. 89; *ibid.*, March 11, 1944, pp. 149–150.
7. *Ibid.*, March 25, 1944, p. 180; *ibid.*, April 1, 1944, p. 185.
8. Memo by Rovensky, October 23, 1940, in OIAA: 17: Argentina—Investments.
9. Memo, Hanson to Will Clayton, November 2, 1940, in OIAA: 30: Foreign Trade in Other American Republics. See also in this connection a memo from the Chase National Bank to Rovensky, November 13, 1940, in OIAA: 17: Argentina—Loans, on the possibility of the United States buying up Argentine gold held in England, then making a loan to Argentina with which the Argentines could repatriate some of their securities in London. The proposal for the billion-dollar Argentine securities purchase is in an unsigned memo entitled, "An Argentine Trade," dated April 3, 1944, in OF 366, FDR MS. Note in addition an OCIAA memo of March 5, 1942, on having the Interdepartmental Committee on Inter-American Affairs prepare a memo on the advisability of acquiring British investments in Argentina as partial settlement of Lend-Lease obligations, in OIAA: 25: Balance of Payments. A notation on this memo says it has already been cleared with H. D. White of the Treasury Department.
10. Memo, McClintock to Rockefeller, January 1, 1944, in OIAA: 17: Argentina—Investments, citing cable from Winant, London, December 28, 1943. See also memo, McClintock to Rockefeller, July 31, 1944, in OIAA: 17: Brazil—Publications, enclosing excerpts from *Correio da Manha, Rio de Janeiro*, July 8, 1944.
11. It is important to see this U.S. fear of social revolutionary ideology in Latin America in its wider context. In his book *The Politics of War: United States Foreign Policy and the World, 1943–1945* (New York, 1968), Gabriel Kolko shows that U.S. policy planners in the late wartime era suffered from a general "fear of the left" in Europe. "Left" ideology, both in Europe and in the underdeveloped world, often sprang from local conditions and developed local adherents quite independently of Moscow-controlled communist organizers. Indeed, Kolko shows that the Soviet Union was a restraining

force upon the independent European left, a fact to which the Americans were indifferent since they opposed social revolutionary ideology regardless of its source. In Latin America, the independent strength of social revolutionary ideology and the weakness of Russian influence was more obvious than in Europe. Nonetheless, as we shall see, this did not predispose Americans to be any less hostile either to the Russians or to indigenous Latin American social revolutionaries.

12. State Department circular enclosed in S. F. Bonsal to Arthur Bliss Lane, December 9, 1943, Lane MS, Yale University Library, New Haven, Connecticut. See also Messersmith to Bonsal, Mexico City, December 13, 1943, Messersmith MS. Messersmith noted that the total demand for goods in Latin America would probably go way up after the war, and that, in any case, Russia would probably compete more with England, and displace former German activities, than she would displace the United States, because of the nature of the goods she would be marketing. See in addition Messersmith to Hull, Mexico City, December 13, 1943, Messersmith MS.

13. Messersmith to Stettinius, Mexico City, January 25, 1945, Messersmith MS, pp. 2, 4. On Stettinius' rejection of diplomatic immunity in Latin America, see Lloyd Gardner, *Economic Aspects of New Deal Diplomacy* (Madison, Wisc., 1964), p. 215.

14. Text of the December 13 decree is quoted in Woodward to Hull, La Paz, December 14, 1943, in 824.00/1386, DSA, NA. Information on arrests of protesters is in Woodward to Hull, La Paz, December 14, 1943, in 824.00/1385, DSA, NA. See also Boal to Hull, La Paz, December 17, 1943, in 824.00/1347, DSA, NA.

15. Boal to Hull, La Paz, December 20, 1943, in 824.00/1277 and 1281, both in DSA, NA. The latter communication includes portions of Paz Estenssoro's interview with the *Baltimore Sun*, as well as information on the decree of the Minister of Labor.

16. Boal to Hull, La Paz, December 20, 1943, in 824.00/1282; Armour to Hull, Buenos Aires, December 21, 1943, in 824.00/1284; Bowers to Hull, Santiago, December 20, 1943, in 824.00/1287; and Bowers to Hull, Santiago, December 20, 1943, in 824.00/1288, all in DSA, NA.

17. Long to Hull, Guatemala City, December 21, 1943, in 824.00/1285; Warren to Hull, Ciudad Trujillo, December 21, 1943, in 824.00/1286; Patterson to Hull, Lima, December 21, 1943, in 824.00/1295; and Dawson to Hull, Montevideo, December 22, 1943, in 824.00/1307, all in DSA, NA.

18. Boal to Hull, La Paz, December 23, 1943, in 824.00/1311; Boal to Hull, La Paz, December 23, 1943, in 824.01/102; Boal to Hull, La Paz, December 23, 1943, in 824.00/1311, all in DSA, NA. See also Lane to Hull, Bogotá, December 23, 1943, in 824.00/1329, DSA, NA.

19. Memo by Duggan of conversation with Bolivian Ambassador in Washington, December 21, 1943, in 824.00/1401, DSA, NA.

20. Boal to Hull, La Paz, December 25, 1943, enclosing report of

interview with Paz Estenssoro, in 824.00/1354, all in DSA, NA.

21. Boal to Hull, La Paz, December 30, 1943, including translation of interview with Baldivieso, in 824.00/1407, DSA, NA.

22. Memo by Hull of conversation with Mexican Ambassador in Washington, December 23, 1943, in 824.00/1412, DSA, NA.

23. For Warren's comments, see memo by W. Tapley Bennett, Jr., cited *infra*, n. 28.

24. Division of American Republics, "Fascist Connections of the New Bolivian Regime," dated January 1, 1944, in 824.00/1-144, DSA, NA. All quotations are from pp. 1–4.

25. Memo by Division of American Republics, "Attitude of Mining Interests Toward Present Bolivian Junta," dated March 16, 1944, in 824.01/759, DSA, NA.

26. Paraphrase of message from Boal to Berle, La Paz, December 22, 1943, in 824.00/1404b, DSA, NA.

27. Woodward to Hull, La Paz, March 16, 1944, in 824.00/1914. On Otazo "resignation," see Woodward to Hull, La Paz, April 7, 1944, in 824.00/2078; Woodward to Hull, La Paz, April 27, 1944, in 824.00/3026; and for report of Paz Estenssoro's remarks, see Woodward to Hull, La Paz, April 25, 1944, in 824.00/3048, all in DSA, NA.

28. Memo by W. Tapley Bennett, Jr., of conversations held by Ambassador Avra Warren in La Paz, May 7–20, 1944, in 824.00/3298, DSA, NA, pp. 2, 3.

29. Report by Ambassador Warren of his mission to Bolivia, May 1944, in 824.00/3194B, DSA, NA, pp. 9, 10, 20.

30. An excellent background discussion of the Argentine revolution of 1943 can be found in Ysabel Rennie, *The Argentine Republic* (New York, 1945).

31. See Welles to Messersmith, June 12, 1943, in 835.01/104, DSA, NA. For Argentine assurances that a break in relations with the Axis would soon be forthcoming, see Armour to Hull, Buenos Aires, June 5, 1943, in Department of State, *Foreign Relations of the United States, 1943* (Washington, D.C., 1963), V, 366. This assurance came indirectly through a Paraguayan liaison with the new Argentine government, during the period in which Ambassador Armour was refraining from direct communication with the government on orders from the State Department.

32. Memo by Hull of conversation with the British Ambassador, Washington, January 5, 1944, in Folder 216, Hull MS.

33. Memo by Hull of conversation with Sir Ronald Campbell, January 10, 1944, in 835.00/2285, DSA, NA. See also memos by Hull of conversations with the British Ambassador, January 19, 23, 1944, both in Folder 216, Hull MS.

34. Memo by Hull of conversation with Argentine chargé d'affaires, Washington, January 27, 1944, in Folder 187, Hull MS. Also Hull to Armour, January 31, 1944, in 835.00/2338A, DSA, NA, and memo by Hull of conversation with Argentine Ambassador, Washington, February 3, 1944, in Folder 187, Hull MS. Regarding Hull's pressure upon Buenos Aires, recently declassified material suggests that the Americans were ready to offer naval and even air support to a pro-American

faction within the Argentine government should a showdown become inevitable. See Armour to Hull, Buenos Aires, June 5, 1944, in 835.00/2868, DSA, NA.

35. Armour to Hull, Buenos Aires, February 16, 1944, in 835.00/2354, DSA, NA. See also Armour to Hull, Buenos Aires, February 25, 1944, in 835.00/2388, DSA, NA.

36. Armour to Hull, Buenos Aires, March 2, 1944, in 835.00/2489, DSA, NA.

37. Bowers to Hull, Santiago, March 3, 1944, in 835.00/2509, DSA, NA; see also memo by Hull of conversation with the Chilean Ambassador, Washington, March 22, 1944, in Folder 195, Hull MS.

38. Woodward to Hull, La Paz, March 6, 1944, in 835.01/210; memo from Stettinius to Hull, March 9, 1944, in 835.01/271, both in DSA, NA.

39. Armour to Hull, Buenos, Aires, March 8, 1944, in 835.01/203, DSA, NA.

40. Armour to Hull, Buenos Aires, March 15, 1944, in 835.00/2652; Armour to Hull, Buenos Aires, March 17, 1944, in 835.00/2667, includes Armour's summation of the situation; and Armour to Hull, Buenos Aires, March 17, 1944, in 835.00/2710, gives Armour's impression of Perón's personal position. All in DSA, NA.

41. Armour to Hull, Buenos Aires, April 26, 1944, in 835.00/2799, DSA, NA.

42. Armour to Hull, Buenos Aires, June 6, 1944, in 835.00/2872, DSA, NA.

43. Memo by Hull of conversation with Brazilian and Mexican Ambassadors, Washington, June 23, 1944, in Folder 192, Hull MS. Memo of conversation with Ambassadors of Costa Rica, El Salvador, Guatemala, Honduras, Nicaragua, and Panama, June 26, 1944, in Folder 198, Hull MS. Memo of conversation with Ambassadors of Dominican Republic and Haiti, and Cuban chargé d'affaires, June 27, 1944, in Folder 202, Hull MS. Memo of conversation with the Ambassador of Uruguay, June 26, 1944, in 835.01/535A, DSA, NA.

44. Memo by Hull of conversation with British Ambassador, Washington, June 26, 1944, in 835.01/535A, DSA, NA (copy also available in Folder 216, Hull MS). Memo of conversation with British Ambassador, Washington, June 29, 1944, in Folder 216, Hull MS.

45. McLaughlin to Hull, La Paz, July 7, 1944, in 835.01/7–744, DSA, NA. Memo by Hull of conversation with Bolivian chargé d'affaires, Washington, July 12, 1944, in 835.01/7–1244, DSA, NA (copy also available in Folder 191, Hull MS).

46. Sumner Welles, *The Time for Decision* (New York, 1944), p. 237. For Hull's comments on "snipers" and "pure trouble-makers," see memo by Hull of conversation with Chilean chargé d'affaires, Washington, July 1, 1944, in Folder 195, Hull MS., and memo by Hull of conversation with Brazilian Ambassador, July 1, 1944, in Folder 192, Hull MS. For example of a reprint of a Welles article in a South American newspaper, see First Secretary of Embassy to Hull, Rio de Janeiro,

August 12, 1944, in 835.01/8–1244, DSA, NA, which includes a
translation of a large portion of an article in the *Diario
Carioca* of Rio de Janeiro.

47. See, for example, memo by Hull of conversation with the
Venezuelan Ambassador in Washington, July 3, 1944, in Folder
258, Hull MS; in this conversation, Hull expressed regret that
Venezuela "had abandoned its position of joint leadership" in
regard to the Argentine issue by failing to recall its Ambassador from Buenos Aires (the Venezuelan Ambassador in Argentina was recalled on July 10). See also the text of the State
Department's circular of July 25, 1944, stressing the "multilateral" nature of the controversy, in 835.01/7–2544, DSA, NA.
48. For reference to the *New Statesman* article, see Reed to Hull,
Buenos Aires, July 26, 1944, in 835.01/7–2644; for reference to
the *Daily Mail* article, see Reed to Hull, Buenos Aires, August
3, 1944, in 835.01/8–344, DSA, NA. See also Reed to Hull, Buenos
Aires, July 29, 1944, in 835.01/7–2944, and Reed to Hull, Buenos
Aires, August 2, 1944, in 835.01/8–244, both in DSA, NA.
49. See memo by Gray for Stettinius, August 7, 1944, in 835.01/8–
744; DSA, NA.
50. Memo by Hull of conversation with British Ambassador,
Washington, September 16, 1944, and memo by Stettinius of
conversation with British Ambassador, October 18, 1944, in
Folder 216, Hull MS.
51. Messersmith to Bonsal, Mexico City, December 13, 1943, in
Messersmith MS.
52. See congratulatory letter from President Roosevelt to President Vargas of Brazil, November 8, 1944, referring to Brazil's
"very generous contribution," which would be converted into
"badly needed supplies for the relief of the war-torn areas of
Europe and Asia." OF 4725, FDR MS.
53. Stettinius to President Roosevelt, October 18, 1944, in OF 313,
FDR MS. At first, in this message, Stettinius tried to put down
Santos' feelings to the fact that "through fortuitous circumstances, he received less attention during his recent visit here
than he is accustomed to receiving." But then see Stettinius to
President Roosevelt, January 9, 1945, in OF 313, FDR MS, for
Stettinius' later, more apprehensive evaluation of the situation.
54. See Ruth B. Russell, *A History of the United Nations Charter*
(Washington, D.C., 1958), pp. 551–552, 554.
55. See record of conversation with Padilla, in Messersmith to
Hull, Mexico City, June 8, 1944, Messersmith MS.
56. See Diary of Breckinridge Long, July 5, 1944, in Breckinridge
Long Manuscripts, Library of Congress, Washington, D.C.
(hereafter Long MS). When the policy subcommittee took up
the Argentine question in November, Long stressed the need
to avoid direct talks with the Argentines on the situation. It
was a situation, he noted, "which only Argentina [could]
change and that by her own actions. It needs no conference
and we can't deal with her until she does." Long Diary,
November 1, 1944, Long MS.
57. On Padilla's position in Mexico, see Messersmith to Armour,

Mexico City, November 9, 1944, and Messersmith to Hull, Mexico City, November 12, 1944, Messersmith MS. On the Department's decision, see Long Diary, November 13, 15, 1944, Long MS.

VII: The postwar role of Latin America: View from the north

1. See *supra*, chapter VI, n. 56.
2. See *Department of State Bulletin*, October 15, 1944, p. 398.
3. Stettinius' telegram is in Department of State, *Foreign Relations of the United States: The Conferences at Malta and Yalta* (Washington, D.C., 1955), pp. 794–797. President Roosevelt's remark on the Argentine–Latin American solution is in Alger Hiss's notes on the plenary meeting of February 8, 1945, *ibid.*, p. 783.
4. See Ruth B. Russell, *A History of the United Nations Charter* (Washington, D.C., 1958), p. 561.
5. The text of the declaration is in *Department of State Bulletin*, March 4, 1945, pp. 339–340.
6. See Department of State, Conference Series No. 85. *Report of the Delegation of the United States of America to the Inter-American Conference on Problems of War and Peace. Mexico City, Mexico. February 21–March 8, 1945* (Washington, D.C., 1946), p. 104. See Ambassador Martins' suggestion in Department of State, *Foreign Relations of the United States, 1945* (Washington, D.C., 1967), I, 42.
7. See Stettinius' statement in Russell, *United Nations Charter*, p. 557.
8. Text of Clayton's speech is in *Department of State Bulletin*, March 4, 1945, pp. 334–338.
9. *Report . . . Inter-American Conference*, pp. 275–276. For full citation, see n. 6, *supra*.
10. *Ibid.*, pp. 277–280.
11. For details of the Inter-American Bank controversy, see *supra*, chapter III.
12. For Clayton's and Viner's remarks at the Committee for Economic Development meeting, see discussion notes of meeting, November 11, 12, 1944, Chicago, in Box 16, Alphabetical File (1943–1944 Committee for Economic Development), Folder 1, Clayton MS. See testimony of Clayton, Rockefeller, *et al.*, in U.S. Congress. House of Representatives. Ways and Means Committee. *Hearings on Extension of the Reciprocal Trade Act. May 4, 1945*. 79th Cong., 1st sess. (Washington, D.C., 1945).
13. Memo, Howe to Hull (copy to President Roosevelt), November 9, 1933, in OF 567 (1933–1935), FDR MS.
14. Unsigned copy of Revised Draft of Recommendations for Conference of Commissions of Inter-American Development Commission, to be Held in May 1944 (draft prepared April 1944), in File 97634/1, GRDC, NA, pp. 19, 15.
15. Memo by August Maffry, Chief of International Economics and Statistics Unit, Bureau of Foreign and Domestic Commerce, to Under Secretary of Commerce, May 23, 1944, in Box 860, File 97634/1, GRDC, NA.
16. This appropriation was also used for coastal defenses in

Brazil. The total Lend-Lease figures were released shortly after the end of the war. See *Inter-American*, October 1945, p. 41. For expenditures in connection with the Brazilian role in the North African landing, and in connection with defense of the Panama Canal, see *Thirteenth Report to Congress on Lend-Lease Operations, for the Period Ended November 30, 1943*, p. 36. Copy in OIAA:30:Lend-Lease.

17. Unsigned, undated memo, in OIAA:30:Lend-Lease.

18. Memo, Hanson to Clayton, January 15, 1941, in OIAA:17:Colombian Investments.

19. The Chileans, for example, expressed strong concern over Lend-Lease shipments to Peru. The Chilean Ambassador in Washington told Secretary of State Hull that the Chilean government was the proper agency for defending the Pacific Coast of South America. He noted Chilean fears of Peruvian military superiority. See memo by Hull of conversation with Chilean Ambassador, December 27, 1943, in Folder 195, Hull MS.

20. On jurisdictional disputes, see Stimson Diary, November 28, 1944, in Henry L. Stimson Manuscripts, Yale University Library (hereafter Stimson MS). On later report on inter-American military planning, see account of conversation with General Embick in Stimson Diary, March 18, 1945, Stimson MS.

21. See Stimson Diary, November 1, 1944, Stimson MS.

22. See, for example, a memo of a conversation between Under Secretary of State Grew and the dean of the Columbia University School of Journalism, December 29, 1944, in Joseph C. Grew Manuscripts, Harvard University Library, Cambridge, Massachusetts (hereafter Grew MS). The Dean warned Grew that "the Mexicans and Russians, under the supervision of Mr. Oumansky, the Soviet representative in Mexico, are steadily outmaneuvering us."

See also an account in the unpublished manuscript memoirs of Ambassador Messersmith (Memoirs, III, No. 11, Messersmith MS), in which the Ambassador describes how one day Oumansky insisted on giving him a guided tour of the Russian Embassy in Mexico City, in order to "prove" to him that there were no elaborate "spy facilities" there. Messersmith wrote of this occurrence: "I had the very definite impression that he was carrying through this performance because he had been told to do it and make the effort. He himself was far too intelligent to think that any purpose would be served by it." Oumansky evidently asked Messersmith to make an official statement to the effect that no "spy facilities" existed, and of course Messersmith declined to do so. Oumansky said he understood, hence Messersmith's later comment on Oumansky's probable motive in making the attempt in the first place.

In his recollection of the event, Messersmith also noted: "There is little doubt that the Soviet Government had intended to use Mexico City as the basis for its Communist activity through Latin America." Interestingly, Messersmith stated in addition that there was good reason to believe that Ouman-

sky actually did try to do so, and equally good reason to believe that he accomplished practically nothing. But Messersmith's dispatches at the time did not include this last sanguine evaluation of the situation. See *infra*, n. 23.
23. Messersmith to Rockefeller, Mexico City, February 12, 1945, Messersmith MS.
24. Stimson Diary, June 26–30, 1945, Stimson MS.
25. See *Report . . . Inter-American Conference*, Article 59 of the Final Act of the Conference, for the complete terms of the Argentine "rehabilitation" formula.
26. For Senator Austin's comments, see *Congressional Record*, XCI, Pt. 2, 2026. For General Embick's comment, see Stimson Diary, March 18, 1945, Stimson MS. On the atmosphere of "sweetness and light" at the Chapultepec Conference, see J. Lloyd Mecham, *The United States and Inter-American Security, 1889–1960* (Austin, Tex., 1961), p. 267.

VIII: The postwar role of Latin America: View from the south
1. Messersmith to President Roosevelt, Mexico City, March 12, 1945, Messersmith MS. Copy also in OF 5690, FDR MS.
2. See report in Messersmith to President Roosevelt, Mexico City, October 2, 1943, in Messersmith MS.
3. See Grew to Mrs. Grew, March 14, 1945, in Grew MS. On Vargas' alliance with Prestes and the Brazilian communists, see Federico del Villar, "What Happened in Brazil," in *Inter-American*, February 1946, p. 37. After the anti-Vargas *coup* of October 1945, the communists quickly dropped Vargas, thus indicating the essentially reciprocal nature of this temporary marriage of convenience. An interesting sidelight on the American view of communist activity in Latin America is indicated by the fact that the establishment of Brazilian-Russian diplomatic relations was evidently a response to an initiative of President Roosevelt himself. Interview with Sra. Alzira Vargas do Amaral Peixoto, Rio de Janeiro, August 3, 1967.
4. See Perón's news conference of February 26, 1945, as reported in *Inter-American*, March 1945, p. 7.
5. Braden to Hull, Havana, December 27, 1943, enclosing Embassy Dispatch No. 5530 of December 27 and including a memo of a conversation with the Coalition (Batista-backed) candidate for President, December 24. See Folder 164, Hull MS. Ironically, the coalition candidate lost to that old 1933 "radical," Ramón Grau San Martín.
6. Ruth B. Russell, *A History of the United Nations Charter* (Washington, D.C., 1958), p. 561. United States motivation for rejecting the resolution was also largely based on fear of giving Russia an excuse for parallel action in Eastern Europe. Nevertheless, the motivation of the Latin Americans in supporting the resolution was clear enough.
7. Laurence Duggan, *The Americas: The Search for Hemisphere Security* (New York, 1949), p. 147; also George Wythe, *Industry in Latin America* (New York, 1945), p. 61.
8. See Chairman, São Paulo Office, OCIAA, to Rockefeller, December 22, 1943, in OIAA:17:Brazil—Economic Development.

9. Chairman, Coordinating Committee for Argentina, Buenos
   Aires, to Rockefeller, June 7, 1944, in OIAA: 17: Argentina—
   Research Miscellaneous. See reply in McClintock to Chairman,
   Coordinating Committee for Argentina, June 22, 1944, in
   OIAA: 17: Argentina—Advertising. Also see Clayton to Senator
   Walter George, April 13, 1945, in Box 29, Alphabetical File
   (1945—Cotton), Clayton MS. The cotton subsidy was main-
   tained, however.
10. For a record of a conversation with Pinedo, see Armour to
    Hull, Buenos Aires, June 21, 1940, in 610.1131/322, DSA, NA.
    On the Davila Plan and a customs union, see memo from
    Guthrie to Assistant Secretary of Commerce Noble (who was
    then chairman of the IADC), June 3, 1940, in OIAA: 25: Invest-
    ment of Capital in Other American Republics. On the 1941
    South American meeting, see *Chicago Round Table*, p. 151.
       Late in 1943, Hull warned the Paraguayan Ambassador in
    Washington against a customs union with Argentina, given
    the current Argentine "situation." See memo of conversation,
    November 20, 1943, in Folder 243, Hull MS.
11. Ambassador Caffery to Hull, Rio de Janeiro, April 20, 1943, en-
    closing a letter from Aranha, in Folder 155, Hull MS. Also see
    Wythe, *Industry in Latin America*, p. 330. The Cuban action
    was not a new departure in Latin America. Brazil had enacted
    a similar decree for plant equipment for a cement industry
    in 1932. Mexico had also enacted similar legislation in 1940 and
    1941. See *ibid.*, pp. 67–69.
12. *Report . . . Inter-American Conference*, pp. 216–217. On both
    the Chilean and Brazilian policies, see *Inter-American*, Sep-
    tember 1945, pp. 35–36. The Chileans had been negotiating a
    reduction on copper duties since 1943. See memo of conver-
    sation between Secretary Hull and the Chilean Ambassador in
    Washington, December 1, 1943, in Folder 195, Hull MS.
13. On Colombian policy, see Wythe, *Industry in Latin America*,
    pp. 267–268. On Brazilian policy, see Corwin D. Edwards,
    "Brazil," in Seymour Harris, ed., *Economic Problems of Latin
    America* (New York, 1944), pp. 296–297. Edwards had been a
    member of the U.S. Industrial Mission to Brazil in 1942.
14. See Collado, State Department, to Cooke, December 16, 1942,
    enclosing a plan for a Brazilian development bank, sent as
    Enclosure No. 2 in Dispatch No. 9367, U.S. Embassy in Rio
    de Janeiro to the State Department, December 8, 1942, in
    Brazil File, Morris L. Cooke Manuscripts, Franklin D. Roose-
    velt Library (hereafter Cooke MS). See also James H. Causey
    to Cooke, September 17, 1942, Cooke MS.
15. Memo, Drumm to Rovensky, March 9, 1942, in OIAA: 25: Invest-
    ment of Capital in Other American Republics. Note also in
    connection with foreign ownership in Latin America a memo
    sent from OCIAA economist Simon Hanson to Assistant Co-
    ordinator Carl Spaeth, December 16, 1940, in OIAA: 18: Policy.
    Hanson warned that in taking steps to oust Axis-controlled
    firms from the hemisphere, the United States should be very
    careful not to become sole owner or holder of such foreign
    investments, lest it become exposed to anti-foreign feelings

and European-inspired expropriation propaganda. A National
Planning Association study also recommended that new developmental investments be arranged "on a gradually increasing basis, with amortization of the foreign investments, until
the enterprise becomes completely a domestic one." George
Soule, David Efron, and Norman T. Ness, *Latin America in
the Future World* (New York, 1945), p. 313.

16. William A. M. Burden, *The Struggle for Airways in Latin
America* (New York, 1943), p. 153.

17. United States direct investments in Latin America remained
at about the same level throughout the war; they totaled
$2,771,000,000 in 1940 and $2,721,000,000 at the end of 1943. See
Raymond F. Mikesell, *Foreign Investments in Latin America*
(Washington, D.C., 1955), pp. 12, 17. This was in marked contrast to British investments, however; British investments
dropped from a value of 754 million pounds in 1938 to 536 million pounds at the end of 1945. See United Nations. Department of Economic and Social Affairs. *Foreign Capital in Latin
America* (New York, 1955), p. 156, and Mikesell, *Foreign Investments*, p. 10.

18. The episode is recounted in Messersmith's unpublished manuscript of his Memoirs, II, No. 17, 29–39, in Messersmith MS.

19. See Jones's memo to the President, April 27, 1942, in Box 30
(Photostats, March–April 1942), Jones MS. Also see notation at
bottom of memo to Clay Johnson, May 4, 1942, in Box 30
(Photostats, May–June 1942), Jones MS.

20. See *supra*, n. 18.

21. See summary discussion of status of the Fomento corporations in Soule, *et al.*, *Latin America in the Future World*, pp.
273ff.

22. On the State Department's attitude in the oil expropriation
and loan issues, see Ambassador Jenkins to Hull, La Paz,
March 18, 1940, in 710.Bank/68, DSA, NA. For data on the troubles the Bolivian government went through in trying to negotiate an international loan for construction of a tin smelter
after the British smelting interests (which were controlled
by the Patino interests) refused to process government-owned
Bolivian tin, see Laurence Duggan, "Background for Revolution," in *Inter-American*, September 1946, pp. 16–17.

23. See Paz Estenssoro's statement in Boal to Hull, La Paz, October 27, 1942, in OIAA: 17: Bolivia—Investments. On the State
Department response to the Bolivian revolution of December
1943, see *supra*, chapter VI. On the Haitian rubber development program, see *supra*, chapter IV.

24. Scott Seagers, "The World's Best Business Set-Up," in *Inter-
American*, August 1946, pp. 12–13.

25. See Sanford Mosk, *Industrial Revolution in Mexico* (Berkeley,
1954), pp. 33–34. Note the New Group alliance with the Mexican
CTM (Mexican Labor Confederation) after Chapultepec, *ibid.*,
p. 104. On Cárdenas' call for Latin American collaboration, see
Messersmith to Secretary of State Stettinius, Mexico City,
January 8, 1945, and Messersmith to Assistant Secretary of

State Nelson Rockefeller, March 15, 1945, both in Messersmith
MS.
26. W. Feuerlein and E. Hannan, *Dollars in Latin America* (New York, 1941), p. 66. See also statement by Dr. Eduardo Villasenor in *Chicago Round Table*, pp. 193–194. An interesting exchange took place at this meeting when a Foreign Policy Association spokesman took the view that there was a shortage of available labor for the Amazon Valley rubber development project in Brazil. He was challenged on this point by a Cuban economist who insisted that Brazil did have a large enough potential labor supply, but that it was "necessary to treat those Brazilian laborers as human beings, not as they are treated in the Far East and Malaya," in order to get them to do the work. The American replied: "I said cheap and plentiful labor. I agree, if you are willing to pay the price you may get the necessary labor. We must bear in mind that the United States consumer must be willing to pay the price. If the United States consumer is willing to pay the price, all right." *Ibid.*, p. 136.
27. Memo, David J. Saposs to John M. Clark, January 30, 1942, in OIAA: 18: Policy.
28. Memo of "conversations on the activities of the BEW and other Agencies of our Government in Mexico," dated January 31, 1943, p. 6, in Messersmith MS. See also Messersmith to Duggan, Mexico City, February 26, 1944, Messersmith MS.
29. See *Inter-American*, March 1946, "News Survey of the Month."
30. Quotations are from account in Counselor of Embassy to Hull, Lima, August 16, 1943, in 823.504/141, DSA, NA.
31. First Secretary of Embassy to Hull, Lima, August 20, 1943, in 823.504/142, DSA, NA.
32. *New York Times*, May 20, 1945, p. 18, gives Lombardo Toledano's position. Also see Messersmith to Assistant Secretary of State Braden, Mexico City, January 16, 1946, in Messersmith MS, and Robert Alexander, *Communism in Latin America* (New Brunswick, N.J., 1957), pp. 33–34. On the rise of noncommunist "populism" in Latin America during this period, see Arthur P. Whitaker, *Nationalism in Latin America* (Gainesville, Fla., 1962), pp. 59, 69.
33. M. A. Saignes, *Latifundio* (Mexico, 1938), p. 222, quoted by Soule, *et al.*, *Latin America in the Future World*, p. 82.
34. *Ibid.*, p. 62.
35. *Ibid.*, p. 63. Also pp. 78, 83–84.
36. Speech by Taussig to Yale Institute of International Relations, July 28, 1944, p. 15, in Caribbean File, Taussig MS.
37. Duggan, *Americas*, p. 134.
38. *Report . . . Inter-American Conference*, pp. 321, 326.
39. *Ibid.*, pp. 208–210. See *ibid.*, p. 78, for the text for Resolution No. 9 creating the Inter-American Economic and Social Council. An editorial in the March 3, 1945, issue of *El Mercurio* of Santiago, Chile, supported the government's proposal as a means of avoiding "a ruinous competition through the repetition of the same industrial activities in the various countries."

40. *Report . . . Inter-American Conference*, p. 114. On the Coffee agreement, see George Wythe, *The United States and Inter-American Relations* (New York, 1962), p. 107. Note also that on March 8, 1945, the last day of the Chapultepec Conference, fourteen coffee-producing nations had asked the United States to raise the ceiling price on coffee in the United States. The State Department refused, on the grounds that such a price increase would promote the danger of inflation both in the United States and in Latin America. See *Department of State Bulletin*, March 25, 1945, p. 512.

41. During his term as Ambassador to Cuba, George Messersmith had negotiated the first Cuban sugar purchase agreement in 1941. After his transfer to Mexico, he continued to take a lively interest in the question of Cuban sugar. On August 15, 1945, he wrote to Secretary of State Byrnes from Mexico City (see Messersmith MS) pointing out that wartime United States purchases of Cuban sugar had indeed stabilized the Cuban economy, but had also created a corner on Cuban sugar supplies. Moreover, Messersmith added, United States plans for the 1946 contract were not leaving enough free sugar allocated to Cuban sellers to assure equitable supplies for civilian consumers in sugar-deficient countries of Latin America, including Mexico. Later in the year, Cuban producers attempted to get a three-year contract with the United States which included a much larger retained quota of free sugar. See *Inter-American*, December 1945, p. 36. Such agreements clearly involved problems on both sides.

42. Note, for example, the OCIAA pilot "Country Study" of Colombia begun in late 1940 and referred to, *supra*, chapter II. See also discussion of the Caribbean Fishery Survey in OIAA: 32: Caribbean Fishery Survey.

   The most ambitious survey done during the war in terms of breadth of coverage was that of the United States Technical Mission to Brazil in 1942, headed by industrial engineer Morris L. Cooke. The Cooke Mission compiled a two-volume report on the industrial potential of Brazil, and recommended a development program based on a trilogy of electricity, air transport, and light metals such as aluminum. The Cooke Mission report was favorably reviewed by OCIAA Economic Analysis Section personnel. See review enclosed in Waring to Rockefeller, November 19, 1943, in OIAA: 17: Brazil—Industrial Development. Nothing concrete ever came of the mission, however, except some wartime improvements in the organization of the Brazilian Office of Economic Mobilization. For Cooke's reaction to the apparent indifference of the State Department to the work of the mission, see Cooke to State Department, June 1, 1943, in Brazil File, Cooke MS.

   At the end of the war, OCIAA sponsored a technical cooperation mission to Guatemala. The price-control expert on this mission was no less a person than former OPA chief Leon Henderson. See Oreamuno to Rockefeller, July 13, 1945, in OIAA: 24: Technical Experts for IADC.

43. On government recommendations for cooperative action, see

Resources Division Report of May 1943, cited *supra*, chapter
V. On nongovernment recommendations, see suggestion of
Soule, *et al., Latin America in the Future World*, p. 312,
that power, sanitation, agriculture, and basic manufacturing
projects be "integrated" with each other on a regional basis,
somewhat on the model of the Tennessee Valley Authority,
wherever possible. See also unsigned, undated OCIAA memo
on postwar "integration" of Latin America's economic organization, in OIAA:30:Plans for Trade and Economic Defense;
also a memo from Leonard Weiss to Joseph Rovensky, October 21, 1942, on integrating the economy of the Caribbean
area more closely with that of the United States, in OIAA:30:
Trade Miscellaneous.
44. *Report . . . Inter-American Conference*, p. 120.
45. *Ibid.*, p. 123.
46. The Bank's statement is quoted in Harris, ed., *Economic
Problems of Latin America*, p. 387. The comment by Norman
T. Ness is taken from his article "Mexico: With Special Reference to Its International Economic Relations," *ibid.*, p. 387.
47. See Harris article, *ibid.*, p. 7. Also Wallich article, *ibid.*, p. 134.
48. Carlos Lleras Restrepo, "La Política Economica Continental,"
in *Revista de America*, II (April 1945), 9.
49. See *Report . . . Inter-American Conference*, p. 27.
50. Statement by Hon. Wayne C. Taylor, in U.S. House of Representatives. Committee on Banking and Currency. *Hearings on
the Bretton Woods Proposals*. 79th Cong., 1st sess. (Washington, D.C., 1945), p. 326.
51. Corrigan to Hull, Caracas, March 31, 1944, in 831.504/132,
DSA, NA.
52. Berle's comment on the Brazilian communists is in Berle to
President Truman, Rio de Janeiro, August 13, 1945, in OF 606,
Harry S. Truman Manuscripts, Harry S. Truman Library, Independence, Missouri (hereafter HST MS). Berle's later comment on the Chapultepec Conference was made in an interview with the present writer, June 18, 1968.

IX: Building one world

1. Stimson Diary, April 23, 1945, Stimson MS.
2. Stimson to President Truman, May 16, 1945, enclosed in Diary,
May 16, 1945, Stimson MS.
3. For a pro-Churchill account of the wartime Roosevelt-
Churchill confrontations on the question of Indo-China, see
Bernard Fall, *The Two Vietnams* (New York, 1967), pp. 51ff.,
especially the discussion of the Tehran Conference, p. 52. See
also Ellen J. Hammer, *The Struggle for Indochina* (Stanford,
1966), p. 44, n. 11.
4. For these and other statistics, taken from an official statement
of the Extraordinary State Committee of the USSR, see David
Horowitz, *The Free World Colossus* (London, 1965), p. 51n.
5. See Baruch to President Truman, April 20, 1945 (Baruch did
not get back from London until after President Roosevelt
died), in Correspondence File, Baruch MS, p. 2. Hereafter
cited as *Baruch Report, 1945*.

6. *Baruch Report, 1945*, pp. 3, 4. See also Lloyd Gardner, *Economic Aspects of New Deal Diplomacy* (Madison, Wisc., 1964), pp. 314, 315.

7. *New York Times*, June 24, 1941, p. 7.

8. See Harry S. Truman, *Year of Decisions* (New York, 1965), p. 99. In Truman's own published version of his meeting with his advisers, he states that he said that "if the Russians did not wish to join us, that would be too bad." *Ibid.*, p. 93. Ambassador Charles E. Bohlen, who was present at the meeting, reported the President's remark as quoted in the body of the present text. See William A. Williams, *The Tragedy of American Diplomacy* (New York, 1962), p. 203.

9. See *Baruch Report, 1945*, p. 22. It was also at about this time that James F. Byrnes, soon to become Secretary of State, first told Truman that "in his belief the [atomic] bomb might well put us in a position to dictate our own terms at the end of the war." Truman, *Year of Decisions*, p. 104. Truman himself told Averell Harriman on April 20, three days before Truman's meeting with Molotov, that he intended to be "firm" with the Russians. "The Russians," the President remarked, "needed us more than we needed them." *Ibid.*, p. 86.

10. Arthur H. Vandenberg, Jr., ed., *The Private Papers of Senator Vandenberg* (Boston, 1952), pp. 175–176. All italics are in the original unless otherwise noted.

11. On the subject of World Court jurisdiction, see *FR*, 1945, I, 271, 491. On the Mexican suggestion, see *ibid.*, p. 357. For Vandenberg's remark on keeping the Latin Americans "in line," see *infra*, n. 27.

12. For Truman's instructions, see Ruth B. Russell, *A History of the United Nations Charter* (Washington, D.C., 1958), p. 632.

13. This is the account later given of the episode by Ambassador Harriman to Marshal Stalin. See Robert E. Sherwood, *Roosevelt and Hopkins: An Intimate History* (New York, 1948), p. 898.

14. See Vandenberg's account of this meeting in Vandenberg, Jr., *Private Papers of Senator Vandenberg*, pp. 177–178.

15. See Minutes of the Sixteenth Meeting of the U.S. Delegation, San Francisco, April 25, 1945, 9:30 A.M., in *FR*, 1945, I, 389, 394–395, 396–397, 398, 401.

16. See Minutes of the Seventeenth Meeting of the U.S. Delegation, San Francisco, April 25, 1945, 8:40 P.M., *ibid.*, pp. 411–413. See also Minutes of Eighteenth Meeting, April 26, 1945, 9:30 A.M., *ibid.*, p. 416.

17. See Minutes of the Fourth Four-Power Preliminary Meeting on Questions of Organization and Admission, San Francisco, April 28, 1945, 6:45 P.M., *ibid.*, pp. 486–488.

18. *New York Times*, May 1, 1945; *Washington Post*, May 1, 1945.

19. See Vandenberg's San Francisco Diary, April 25, 1945 (afternoon), and April 25, 1945 (evening), in Vandenberg MS. Both of these extracts are omitted from the version published in Vandenberg, Jr., *Private Papers of Senator Vandenberg*.

20. San Francisco Diary, April 30, 1945, Vandenberg MS. This extract is also omitted from the published *Private Papers*.

21. San Francisco Diary, April 30, 1945.
22. San Francisco Diary, May 1, 1945. This entire entry is omitted from the *Private Papers*. See Vandenberg's telegram to President Truman, May 1, 1945, in OF 85-B, HST MS.
23. See, for example, Vandenberg's and Stassen's remarks in Minutes of the Twenty-Fourth Meeting of the U.S. Delegation, San Francisco, April 30, 1945, 6:20 P.M., in *FR*, 1945, I, 503.
24. See Minutes of the Twenty-Ninth Meeting of the U.S. Delegation, San Francisco, May 4, 1945, 9:05 A.M., *ibid.*, pp. 591, 594.
25. See Minutes of the Sixth Four-Power Preliminary Meeting on Questions of Organization and Admission, San Francisco, May 1, 1945, 7:15 P.M., *ibid.*, p. 510.
26. See Minutes of the Fifth Four-Power Consultative Meeting on Charter Proposals (Part II), San Francisco, May 4, 1945, 10 P.M., *ibid.*, pp. 610, 611.
27. On Rockefeller's efforts to see Stettinius, and his subsequent decision to work through Vandenberg, see Joe Alex Morris, *Nelson Rockefeller: A Biography* (New York, 1960), p. 216. Morris does not mention Stettinius' annoyance at Rockefeller's activities. That information was supplied to the present writer by Adolf Berle in an interview in New York City, March 28, 1967. Also see San Francisco Diary, May 5, 1945, Vandenberg MS. The phrase "and cannot much longer be held in line" is omitted from the published *Private Papers*.
28. Vandenberg to Stettinius, May 5, 1945, in Correspondence File, Vandenberg MS.
29. See San Francisco Diary, May 5, 7, 1945, in Vandenberg MS.
30. See Minutes of the Thirty-First Meeting of the U.S. Delegation, San Francisco, May 7, 1945, 9 A.M., in *FR*, 1945, I, 620, 621, 623, 624.
31. Stimson Diary, April 16, 26, 1945, Stimson MS.
32. Stimson Diary, April 27–29, May 2, 1945, Stimson MS.
33. Transcript of telephone conversation between McCloy, San Francisco, and Stimson, Washington, May 8, 1945, Stimson MS, pp. 3, 5, 6, 9, 12–13.
34. See McCloy's statement in Minutes of the Thirty-Third Meeting of the U.S. Delegation, San Francisco, May 8, 1945, 5 P.M., in *FR*, 1945, I, 643.
35. See Minutes of the Thirty-Fifth Meeting of the U.S. Delegation, San Francisco, May 10, 1945, 6:30 P.M., *ibid.*, p. 659.
36. See Minutes of the Third Five-Power Informal Consultative Meeting on Proposed Amendments (Part I), San Francisco, May 12, 1945, 2:30 P.M., *ibid.*, p. 692. See also San Francisco Diary, May 13, 1945, Vandenberg MS. This entire extract is omitted from the published *Private Papers*.
37. San Francisco Diary, May 15, 1945, Vandenberg MS. See also Stettinius' statement assuring the Latin Americans of United States intentions to go through with the hemispheric defense treaty, in Notes on Second Informal Consultative Meeting with Chairmen of Delegations of Certain American Republics, San Francisco, May 15, 1945, 2:45 P.M., *FR*, 1945, I, 731.

38. Vandenberg, Jr., *Private Papers of Senator Vandenberg*, pp. 177–178.
39. San Francisco Diary, May 19, 1945, Vandenberg MS. Both of these extracts are omitted from the published *Private Papers*.
40. See Gar Alperovitz, *Atomic Diplomacy* (New York, 1965), for Truman's political views and strategy regarding the bomb as a factor in Russian-American relations.
41. See Minutes of the Thirty-Ninth Meeting of the U.S. Delegation, San Francisco, May 15, 1945, 9 A.M., in *FR*, 1945, I, 722.
42. See *Inter-American*, August 1945, p. 41; February 1946, p. 18; and April 1946, p. 41.
43. Hull to Roosevelt, October 11, 1944, in OF 11, FDR MS, and Memo of conversation between Berle and Joseph Grew, June 13, 1945, in Grew MS. Also see unsigned memo to President Roosevelt, undated (1944), OF 396, FDR MS.
44. Interviews with Sra. Alzira Vargas do Amaral Peixoto, Rio de Janeiro, August 3, 1967, and Marshal Eurico Gaspar Dutra, Rio de Janeiro, August 4, 1967.
45. Interview with Adolf Berle, New York City, June 18, 1968, and *South American Journal*, December 8, 1945, p. 269.

X: Champion and challenger
1. Memo of telephone conversation between Stettinius and Grew, May 26, 1945, Grew MS.
2. See text of Stettinius' own published statement in *New York Times*, May 29, 1945, p. 8.
3. Laurence Duggan, *The Americas: The Search for Hemisphere Security* (New York, 1949), pp. 91–92.
4. See statistics published in *Inter-American*, December 1945, "Trade and Finance" section. Also see J. Fred Rippy, *Globe and Hemisphere* (Chicago, 1958), p. 64. For quote on Panama, see Magalhaes to Rockefeller, December 12, 1941, in OIAA: 24: Oreamuno-Magalhaes Trip.
5. George Soule, David Efron, and Norman T. Ness, *Latin America in the Future World* (New York, 1945), p. 14.
6. Seymour Harris, ed., *Economic Problems of Latin America* (New York, 1944), p. 176, gives data on wartime inflation. See *Inter-American*, March 1945, p. 41, for information on foreign exchange holdings of the various Latin American countries.
7. See statements of Argentine fears for postwar trade conditions, made by Argentine spokesmen at the Inter-American business conference in Rye, New York, in November 1944, as reported in *Inter-American*, January 1945, p. 40. For Harry Dexter White's views on the Argentine economy, see text of White's address to an IMF meeting, undated (early 1947), in File 27 (Monetary Fund), White MS.
8. See Ysabel Rennie, *The Argentine Republic* (New York, 1945), p. 322. Also Miron Burgin, "Argentina," in Harris, *Economic Problems in Latin America*, pp. 232–244. Burgin himself leaned to the view that the Pinedo Plan was not really necessary. This judgment, however, is independent of the motives of the government in scuttling it.

9. See industry rankings in Rennie, *Argentine Republic*, p. 329.
10. *Ibid.*, p. 284.
11. Harold F. Peterson, *Argentina and the United States, 1810–1960* (New York, 1964), p. 448. See also *New York Times*, July 20, 21, 23, August 3, 1945.
12. Burgin, "Argentina," p. 242.
13. Quoted in George Wythe, *The United States and Inter-American Relations* (New York, 1962), p. 81.
14. See the excellent discussion of the political vacuum which existed in respect to party representation of these groups in Rennie, *Argentine Republic*, pp. 341–342. In this respect the discrediting and decline of the Radical party is particularly worth noting.
15. See memo of a conversation, in Washington, between Carl Spaeth and Charles Burrows of the Buenos Aires Embassy staff, June 24, 1946, in Messersmith MS. Adolf Berle also gave this explanation of Rockefeller's dismissal in an interview in New York City, March 28, 1967. See also *New York Times*, May 20, 1945, p. 18; and *ibid.*, July 1, 1945, Section 4, p. 2. *Washington Post*, June 15, 1945.
16. *New York Times*, May 1, 1945, pp. 1, 14.
17. On nationalization of Argentine banks, see George Wythe, *Industry in Latin America* (New York, 1945), p. 92. Also *Inter-American*, May 1946, p. 8; June 1946, p. 40. In an interview in New York City, March 28, 1967, Braden recalled that he had sent two long dispatches to the State Department warning that Perón was working with the Argentine communists. These dispatches, he noted, never reached Secretary of State Byrnes, however; Braden noted that they had probably been intercepted by communists in the State Department.
18. *Inter-American*, April 1945, p. 40, and September 1945, p. 34.
19. *Ibid.*, August 1945, p. 7. On "profit-sharing," see *New York Times*, July 1, 1945, Section 4, p. 2. For Perón's reference to the "other Army of labor," see *Inter-American*, August 1945, p. 5.
20. Notes by Collins of UP, of Braden's press conference of September 18, 1945, Buenos Aires, in Messersmith MS.
21. Memo of conversation between Under Secretary of State Grew and Robert Woods Bliss, January 12, 1945, in Grew MS. Grew sent this memo on to Rockefeller.
22. Messersmith's unpublished Memoirs, III, No. 14, 5, Messersmith MS.
23. See *Inter-American*, May 1945, p. 7. For a report that Rockefeller also kept all dispatches regarding diplomatic recognition of Argentina away from the American Republics desk in the State Department, see *ibid.*, October 1945, p. 7. See also Messersmith Memoirs, III, No. 14, 2, Messersmith MS.
24. Stimson Diary, March 13, 1945, Stimson MS.
25. Ruth B. Russell, *A History of the United Nations Charter* (Washington, D.C., 1958), p. 571.
26. Interview with Adolf Berle, New York City, March 28, 1967.
27. For Rockefeller's role in securing Argentine admission to the conference, see *supra*, chapter IX. Also see memo of telephone

conversation between Rockefeller, San Francisco, and Grew, Washington, April 23, 1945, in Grew MS.

28. On Rockefeller's meeting with Grew and President Truman, see *New York Times*, May 4, 1945, p. 14. For Grew's subsequent statement to Hull, see memo of telephone conversation between Grew and Hull, May 3, 1945, Grew MS.

29. Memo of telephone conversation between Stettinius, San Francisco, and Grew, Washington, May 4, 1945, Grew MS.

30. For a report of the off-the-record luncheon, see Thomas McGee to Matthew Connally, Kansas City, May 25, 1945, in OF 87 (1945–1948), HST MS. On committee appointment for Argentina, see Minutes of the Twenty-Fourth Meeting of the U.S. Delegation, San Francisco, April 30, 1945, 6:20 P.M., in *FR*, 1945, I, 504. See Vandenberg's summary statement on Rockefeller's work in San Francisco Diary, June 23, 1945, Vandenberg MS. The italicized portion (not italicized in the original) is omitted from the published *Private Papers*. The capitalizations are as in the original.

31. See George Michanowsky, Executive Secretary, CIO Committee on Latin-American Affairs, to President Truman, August 6, 1945, in OF 366, HST MS. See also Rockefeller's speech of August 24, 1945, citing Argentine noncompliance with the Chapultepec accords, in *New York Times*, August 25, 1945, p. 1. On Braden's influence in reversing the decision to give military supplies to Perón, see *Inter-American*, July 1945, p. 6.

32. Rockefeller may also have noticed Perón's careful avoidance of any nationalistic pronouncements or actions in regard to the *frigoríficos* (meat-packing plants), Argentina's main source of export earnings, and the electric power industry, a key foundation of Argentina's internal economic activity. Both of these industries had considerable American capital invested in them. For this insight I am indebted to Prof. Darío Cantón of the Instituto Di Tella, Buenos Aires.

The *Inter-American* referred to the Rockefeller-Warren-Perón interchange in March and April of 1945 as a "farce in three acts." The acts were, in order: (1) Perón's meaningless declaration of war; (2) the State Department's approval and diplomatic recognition of the Argentine regime; and (3) Warren's visit to Buenos Aires. See *Inter-American*, May 1945, "News Survey of the Month." An editor of *Inter-American* reported that on his recent visit to Buenos Aires, he found foreign businessmen, including Americans, very complacent about the political situation. "Oh, don't pay too much attention to all these wild promises to labor," he quoted them as saying. "That's just campaign talk. Wait till he [Perón] gets in. We'll be able to do business with him on just as reasonable a basis as before." See Scott Seagers, "What If Perón Wins?", in *Inter-American*, February 1946, p. 13.

33. Berle interview, March 28, 1967. Superficially, the Braden promotion did look like an indication of a policy reversal. Both Under Secretary of State Grew and Assistant Secretary for Economic Affairs Will Clayton sent congratulatory messages to Braden, implying strong State Department approval

of his course of action in Argentina. Braden himself stated
in his last press conference before leaving Buenos Aires that
he would use the wider authority of his new post for a
stronger and more effective campaign against "fascism" in
Argentina. Privately, however, he tried to get Secretary of
State Byrnes and President Truman to let him delay his departure as long as possible, knowing that his leaving Buenos
Aires would weaken the anti-Peronists there. See Grew MS;
Box 1, Chronological File, Clayton MS. Also Braden interview.

34. Braden interview, March 28, 1967.
35. See commentary by Arnaldo Cortesi in *New York Times*,
    August 26, 1945, p. 16. Sir David Kelly's statement is quoted in
    T. F. McGann, "The Ambassador and the Dictator: The Braden
    Mission to Argentina and Its Significance for United States
    Relations with Latin America," in *Centennial Review*, VI
    (Summer 1962), 353.
36. Quoted by Messersmith in Messersmith to William Pawley,
    February 26, 1947, Messersmith MS. It is not at all clear, to
    be sure, that the anti-Peronists would have won if Braden had
    stayed on in Argentina. But an anti-Peronist victory which
    could have been achieved only with the help of the United
    States Ambassador in Argentina would have been a victory
    for the Rockefeller approach anyway, since the main goal
    was the same for Rockefeller and Braden, namely, an under-
    cutting of the basis of *independent* Argentine nationalism.
37. Vandenberg to Roy Howard, October 12, 1945, in Correspon-
    dence File, Vandenberg MS. Also see *Congressional Record*,
    XCI, Part 8, 9899–9908, and Harold F. Peterson, *Argentina and
    the United States, 1810–1960* (New York, 1964), p. 451.
38. See, for example, Braden's article entitled "Latin American
    Industrialization and Foreign Trade," in Lloyd J. Hughlett,
    ed., *Industrialization of Latin America* (New York, 1946), pp.
    486–493. "Either the exaggerated nationalisms now so preva-
    lent everywhere, must be completely extirpated from rela-
    tions between peoples," Braden wrote, "or those nationalisms
    will prevent reconstruction, destroy trade and investment,
    lower living standards, and again imperil civilization." For
    Messersmith's approach to Perón, see *infra*, chapter XI.
39. Messersmith to Byrnes, Buenos Aires, June 15, 1946, p. 17,
    Messersmith MS. See also Braden to Messersmith, July 22,
    1946, Messersmith MS.
40. See account of Vandenberg's January 11 speech in *New York
    World Telegram*, January 12, 1947. "Senator Vandenberg,"
    stated the *World Telegram* editorial, "has given General
    Marshall a blueprint for his guidance as Secretary of State.
    We think an overwhelming majority of Americans can sup-
    port the sort of program it contemplates." The information
    on Braden's resignation was supplied by Mr. Braden in an
    interview, March 28, 1967. On June 4, 1947, Secretary of State
    Marshall sent to Ambassador Messersmith a "personal" tele-
    gram, which read in part: "The President instructs me to
    inform you that your mission having been completed as
    announced in the press yesterday, your resignation is ac-

cepted, and it is desired that you return to the United States. In reaching this decision the President has been moved by the overriding interests of the country. . . ." Correspondence File, Messersmith MS.

41. Perhaps the most ironic comment was given by a Peronist newspaper in Buenos Aires, which claimed that it was Messersmith, rather than Braden, who understood "that our revolution was not of rightist but rather of leftist tendency." See *Democracia*, Buenos Aires, August 5, 1946, quoted in memo by Messersmith, August 5, 1946, Messersmith MS.

For a stimulating discussion attacking the entire analytic relevance of the traditional left-right spectrum to the Argentine situation in the 1940's, see "Party Alignment in Argentina Between 1912 and 1955," a paper presented to the Seventh World Congress of the International Political Science Association, Brussels, September 1967, by Prof. Darío Cantón of the Instituto Di Tella, Buenos Aires (graciously made available to me in manuscript form by the author).

XI: Formalizing the system

1. On Truman at Potsdam, see Gar Alperovitz, *Atomic Diplomacy* (New York, 1965), pp. 145ff.
2. See *ibid.*, pp. 191ff. The British loan negotiations of 1945, as Will Clayton noted, were specifically designed to open up Empire markets to U.S. commercial interests. "If we make the loan," Clayton wrote, "one of the principal purposes will be to enable the British people to open up their commerce to the United States and all other countries instead of confining it to the British Empire as they would largely be compelled to do if they were not able to obtain the necessary assistance to get their trade back on a multilateral basis." Clayton to Gen. R. D. Wood, November 17, 1945, in Box 1, Chronological File (November–December 1945), Clayton MS.
3. Stimson Diary, June 4, 1945, Stimson MS.
4. Vandenberg to Secretary of State Byrnes, August 3, 1945, Correspondence File, Vandenberg MS.
5. Telegram, Mrs. J. Borden Harriman to Vandenberg, August 7, 1945, and Vandenberg to Mrs. Harriman, August 13, 1945, Vandenberg MS.
6. Vandenberg to Dulles, April 7, 1946, Entry II (Communist Party folder), Dulles MS. This letter contained comments by Vandenberg on a manuscript prepared by Dulles for publication in Henry Luce's *Life* magazine (see issues of June 3 and 10, 1946). Dulles referred in this manuscript to "inner" and "outer" zones of Soviet penetration, Moscow being the center of such operations, and Latin America being part of the "outer zone" area, subject to agitation by communists and "fellow-travelers." Vandenberg called it a "magnificent analysis."
7. See testimony of Admiral Nimitz, General Eisenhower, and Secretary Byrnes in U.S. Congress. House of Representatives. Committee on Foreign Affairs. *Hearings on Inter-American*

Military Cooperation Act, 1946 (Washington, D.C., 1946), pp. 3, 17, and 34, respectively.

8. U.S. Congress. House of Representatives. Committee on Foreign Affairs. *Hearings on Inter-American Military Cooperation Act, 1947* (Washington, D.C., 1947), p. 26.

9. *Ibid.*, pp. 43–44.

10. For Stimson's comment on cultivating "good relations" with South American military, see *supra*, chapter VII, n. 21. On General Arnold's report, see Stimson Diary, May 16, 1945, Stimson MS.

11. *Hearings on Inter-American Military Cooperation Act, 1947*, p. 81. Testimony such as Vandenberg's was scored by former Pan American Union official Ernesto Galarza, who testified against the Act, stating: "One of the pressures upon the Latin-American governments to buy arms will be not so much their needs to buy, as our needs to sell." *Ibid.*, p. 111.

12. Memo from Secretary Marshall to the President, June 26, 1947, in OF 366, HST MS. The memo bears the notation, "approved, HST, June 26, 1947."

13. Coordinator of International Cooperation Programs, Department of Commerce. "Cooperation with the American Republics," in *Annual Report for Fiscal Year 1947 of Department of Commerce.* See section entitled "Report of Civil Aeronautics Administration." In File No. 97634/1, GRDC, NA.

14. U.S. Department of State. Inter-American Series No. 32. *Private Enterprise in the Development of the Americas.* An Address by Assistant Secretary Braden Before the Executives' Club of Chicago, September 13, 1946 (Washington, D.C., 1946), pp. 2–3, 5.

15. *Ibid.*, pp. 7, 8, 9.

16. See text of speech, enclosed in Dulles to Vandenberg, January 29, 1947, in Correspondence File, Vandenberg MS. Quotes are from pp. 12, 15 of text.

17. *Hearings on Inter-American Military Cooperation Act, 1947*, p. 6.

18. See extracts from *Folha da Manha* and the *Diario de São Paulo*, reprinted in the *South American Journal*, December 29, 1945, p. 304. The Ocampo article is in the December 1, 1947 issue of *New Republic*.

19. Baruch to Brendan Bracken, August 24, 1945; see also Baruch to Henry Wallace, July 9, 1945, both in Correspondence File, Baruch MS.

20. For Baruch's comments on his talk with de Gaulle, see memo by Baruch for Secretary of State Byrnes, August 27, 1945, Correspondence File, Baruch MS. See also Baruch to Gore, November 9, 1945, Correspondence File, Baruch MS. This last letter is reprinted in the *Congressional Record* for November 14, 1945, in Appendix, p. A5239.
    Shortly afterward, Baruch wrote to his old friend, former Prime Minister Winston Churchill, noting that "nationalization of one country will finally end up by the whole world being nationalized and the greatest economic warfare will then

be upon us." Baruch to Churchill, November 30, 1945, Correspondence File, Baruch MS.

21. See "Questions and Answers on the British Loan," in File on S.J. Res. 138, 79th Cong., 2nd sess. (1946), Senate LRB, NA. See also Clayton to David Scholtz, October 4, 1945, in Box 1, Chronological File (October–November 15, 1945), Clayton MS; and Clayton to Baruch, April 26, 1946, Correspondence File, Baruch MS.

22. Michael A. Heilperin, "How the U.S. Lost the ITO Conference," *Fortune*, September 1949, p. 82. See also copy of speech by Snyder to Houston Chamber of Commerce, December 6, 1947, in Box 24 (Snyder Correspondence), Jones MS.

23. Baruch to Senator Taft, March 8, 1946, in Correspondence File, Baruch MS.

24. See Dalton to Snyder, February 4, 1947, in Alphabetical File, Argentina—General (1946–1947), John W. Snyder Manuscripts, Harry S. Truman Library, Independence, Missouri. See also President Truman to Sen. Henry Dworshak of Idaho, February 13, 1947, apprising Dworshak of the Dalton-Snyder agreement, in OF 212-A, HST MS.

25. See *Inter-American*, February 1946, p. 43, on the original Venezuelan tax decree. See *ibid.*, April 1946, p. 42, on the pledge not to increase the tax level. See *ibid.*, pp. 42–43, and May 1946, p. 41, for immediate effects; and for statistics on overall expansion in Venezuelan oil investment, see United Nations. Department of Economic and Social Affairs. *Foreign Capital in Latin America*, pp. 145–146.

26. On rayon, see *Inter-American*, November 1946, p. 43. On the rubber companies, see *ibid.*, April 1946, p. 42. On steel company expansion, see *ibid.*, July 1946, p. 34.

27. Transcript of radio broadcast by White and Kilgore, recorded April 10, 1946, in File 26 (Britain), White MS. Also see "Information Submitted by the French in the Loan Negotiations," with statement of French delegation, March 25, 1946, p. 11, in File 25 (France), White MS.

28. White-Kilgore transcript, p. 12.

29. For statistics, see Raymond F. Mikesell, *Foreign Investments in Latin America* (Washington, D.C., 1955), pp. 21, 22. See also remark on the "bankers' criteria that apparently determined economic policy toward Latin America in 1945–1960," in Edwin Lieuwen, *United States Policy in Latin America* (New York, 1965), p. 133. A crucial point here is that whereas direct investments were extensions of foreign control for increased foreign profit on a more or less permanent basis (since in general the rush of U.S. capital to Latin American oilfields, etc., was not for "self-liquidating" investments), foreign government loans would usually be used under local auspices to increase production and development under local control. Such loans would also be self-liquidating. Hence the Latin Americans' desire for a higher ratio of loans to investments.

30. See cartoon from *Topaze*, of Santiago, reprinted in *Inter-American*, September 1946, p. 35. See also George Wythe,

The United States and Inter-American Relations (New York,
1962), p. 18.

31. See text of White's address in File 27, White MS.
32. White to Carlos Nevea, January 12, 1948, outline summary enclosed, in File 28 (Mexico), White MS. This plan was never followed up after White died in August 1948.
33. See Sanford Mosk, *Industrial Revolution in Mexico* (Berkeley, 1954), p. 169. Also note report by congressional staff economists on Latin America and the European Recovery Program in *Preliminary Report of the House Select Committee on Foreign Aid*, House Miscellaneous Reports, 80th Cong., 2nd sess.
34. Baruch to Harriman, July 1, 1947, and Baruch to Secretary of State Marshall, July 1, 1947, in Correspondence File, Baruch MS.
35. See *Inter-American*, September 1945, p. 11. A later article on inflation in El Salvador is Hester Scott's "The Sky Is the Limit," *ibid.*, November 1946, pp. 26–29, in which it is also pointed out that Americans were often to blame for rent increases in the capital city, since they had more money and bid up rent prices. Also see T. Lynn Smith, *Brazil* (Baton Rouge, La., 1963), p. 215.
36. On Cuba, see *Inter-American*, November 1945, p. 10, and *ibid.*, February 1946, p. 8. On Peru, see *ibid.*, November 1945, p. 11. See same issue on food imports. On the Haitian revolution, see *ibid.*, February 1946, p. 7.
37. See Moises Poblete Troncoso, "Which Way Chilean Labor?", *ibid.*, April 1946, pp. 30–31, 46. Also George Kent, "God and Trujillo," *ibid.*, March 1946, pp. 14–16, 38.
38. Robert Rennie, "Where Does Perón Get the Money?", *ibid.*, March 1946, pp. 17–19, 46–47.
39. George Soule, David Efron, and Norman T. Ness, *Latin America in the Future World* (New York, 1945), pp. 308–309. Laurence Duggan, *The Americas: The Search for Hemisphere Security* (New York, 1949), p. 124.
40. George Wythe, *Industry in Latin America* (New York, 1945), p. 352. See also John Brown Payson, "Are We Welching on Latin America?", in *Inter-American*, December 1945, pp. 12–13, 41–43.
41. *Ibid.*, p. 41. The long extract comparing Argentine and American nonfulfillment of obligations is from p. 12. Toward the end of this comprehensive and informative article, the writer warned: "If we expect our neighboring nations to believe in capitalism and free enterprise, we must give them the means of reaping some of the benefits of this system we believe in so fiercely." See p. 43.

For a detailed account of one aspect of the postwar supply problem, relating to the delivery of equipment for port installations, see Alice L. Raine, "Harbor Headaches," *ibid.*, September 1946.
42. See Vandenberg to Dulles, May 13, 1946, Entry II (Communist Party folder), Dulles MS. All emphases are reproduced as in the original. Also see Vandenberg Paris Conference Diary

(Correspondence File), April 28, 1946, in Vandenberg MS. In this extract the word "Communistic" and the sentence about "fellow-travellers" were omitted from the published *Private Papers*. And see Vandenberg to J. W. Blodgett, August 23, 1946, Correspondence File, Vandenberg MS.

43. San Francisco Diary, May 19, 31, 1945, Vandenberg MS.

44. Copy of Dulles' commencement address at City College of New York, June 19, 1946, is in Entry I, File E, Dulles MS. See also text of address to the National Publishers' Association, January 17, 1947, Dulles MS.

45. Messersmith to Braden, March 14, 1946, Mexico City, Messersmith MS. Also see Messersmith to Braden, February 28 and March 16, 1946, Messersmith MS.

46. The quoted extracts are all from Messersmith's letter to Byrnes, dated June 15, 1946, pp. 2, 5, 9, and, on the Bogotá Conference, p. 27. The telegram is dated May 29, 1946. See Messersmith MS. Extremely interesting in the letter is Messersmith's idea that U.S. "leadership" could become acceptable to the Latin Americans if only it was done without forceful imposition. The tactic was a more sophisticated version of Hull's old blunt unilateral interpretation of multilateralism. Messersmith also assured Byrnes that Perón had expressed his intention to "safeguard the rights of property of foreign interest though he does intend to proceed with a program of nationalization of certain public services," such as the railways. "He has made it clear, however," Messersmith added, "that he intends to proceed in this field with caution, and there is reason to believe that he has already learned that he must proceed with caution." See p. 9 of the letter.

47. Messersmith's later recollection of this first conversation with Perón is in the Memoirs, II, No. 21. His comment on communism is on p. 8 of this manuscript. Messersmith MS. Perón's statement on the possibility of another world war is in the May 29 telegram, p. 2.

48. Messersmith to Carrigan, Mexico City, January 12, 1946, Messersmith MS. See also Messersmith to Braden, Mexico City, January 16, 1946, in which Messersmith comments upon Vicente Lombardo Toledano's hopes of becoming the leader of all of Latin America's labor movement "in order to collaborate with Russia." Messersmith MS.

See also Braden to Dulles, October 3, 1946, acknowledging Dulles's letter of September 23, and enclosing a clipping from *Ultimas Noticias* of Mexico City. See Entry II, Dulles MS.

49. Messersmith to Pawley, Buenos Aires, August 6, 1946, Messersmith MS. See also Messersmith to Acheson, Buenos Aires, October 2, 1946, Messersmith MS. And see Messersmith's forty-three-page, single-spaced letter to Arthur Sulzberger of the *New York Times*, dated September 25, 1946, in which Messersmith enlarges upon the communist danger to Latin America, and Perón's role in combating such a danger. See especially p. 26 of this letter, in which Messersmith states that "we will find the Argentine one of the most helpful countries in the other Americas in combatting communist penetration and,

in my opinion, the time has come when the American republics will have to think very seriously of what steps they can
take to prevent further communist penetration."
50. Copy of Dulles' address, entitled "Foreign Policy—Ideals, Not
    Deals," delivered to Inland Daily Press Association, Chicago,
    February 10, 1947, p. 5, in Entry I, File E, Dulles MS.
51. See U.S. Department of State, *Report of the Delegation of
    the United States of America to the Inter-American Confer-
    ence for the Maintenance of Continental Peace and Security,
    Quitandinha, Brazil, August 15–September 2, 1947* (Washington,
    D.C., 1947). For the Department's explicit statement on Argen-
    tine compliance with her Chapultepec agreements, see the ex-
    change between Rep. Javits of New York and Secretary of
    State Marshall in *Hearings on the Inter-American ~Military
    Cooperation Act, 1947*, p. 17.
52. See Messersmith to Secretary of State Marshall, Buenos Aires,
    May 8, 1947, Messersmith MS. Messersmith also wrote during
    this time to a friend on the Joint Mexican–United States De-
    fense Commission in the Pentagon, expressing his amazement
    that Mrs. Eleanor Roosevelt, Leon Henderson, and certain
    other people were organizing a new group to fight "Peronism
    and communism." Said Messersmith: "The essence of Peron-
    ism is to fight Communism, and the very things in the social
    field and in the way of social justice that these people are
    standing for are the things which the present Government of
    the Argentine is trying to carry through." See Messersmith to
    Col. Charles H. Deerwester, Buenos Aires, April 2, 1947, Mes-
    sersmith MS. "The world," Messersmith added, "is screwy
    and cock-eyed these days."
        During this time, Messersmith also bombarded the State
    Department with a series of communications noting that the
    Argentine government was not really going nearly so far
    toward economic nationalism as was popularly rumored. In
    particular, he noted, Perón was coming around to the view
    that participation of foreign oil companies was necessary for
    the sound development of Argentine oil properties. See Mes-
    sersmith to Byrnes, October 30, November 12, 1946, and also a
    forty-one-page memo of a conversation with Perón on Novem-
    ber 28, 1946. See, in addition, Messersmith to Marshall, March
    12, 1947, on Argentine banking procedures, in which Messer-
    smith notes that U.S. concerns, such as National City of New
    York, were really having no trouble operating in Buenos
    Aires despite certain Argentine government restrictions, and
    that National City's Buenos Aires branch "was showing the
    best profit last year and so far this year in the history of the
    branch." Messersmith MS.
53. *Hearings on Inter-American Military Cooperation Act, 1947*,
    pp. 7–8, 33, 49–50, 113. The committee members may also have
    been impressed by Galarza's reminder that even Dr. Eduardo
    Santos, former President of Colombia and a chief "architect
    of Chapultepec," did not include such an act as being neces-
    sary or proper to the defense of the inter-American system.
    Ibid., p. 109. Veteran socialist Norman Thomas took an ironic

swipe at the bill, pointing out the obvious intention of the Truman administration to use the authority of the Act to supply military aid to Perón. "Parenthetically, it must be observed," Thomas remarked dryly, "that he won't buy the junk we can fob off on the little countries." *Ibid.*, p. 102.

54. UP report from Petropolis, August 30, 1947, in Scrapbook, Vol. 19 (1947), Vandenberg MS.

55. Duggan, *Americas*, p. 199.

56. See U.S. Department of State. *Ninth International Conference of American States. Report of the Delegation of the United States of America.* (Washington, D.C., 1948), pp. 169–170, 266–267, respectively (hereafter cited as *Bogotá Conference Report*).

57. Note suggestion for this increase in Eximbank lending authority in Ambassador William Pawley to President Truman, Rio de Janeiro, February 17, 1948, in OF 27-B, Export-Import Bank (1945–1949), HST MS. "It would go a long way," Pawley noted, "in creating a much more favorable climate for the negotiations at Bogotá."

58. For the Latin American position on the Inter-American Bank, see Resolution XV of the Final Act, authorizing the Inter-American Economic and Social Council to "study the possibility and advisability of creating" such an institution, in *Bogotá Conference Report*, p. 239. For the U.S. position, see the summary report of the U.S. delegation, *ibid.*, p. 64.

59. See text of Marshall's address in *ibid.*, pp. 309–317. See delegation summary report, *ibid.*, pp. 64, 312–314.

60. See Dr. Lleras' statement in Organization of American States, *Annals*, I, No. 1 (1949), 58, 55.

61. *Bogotá Conference Report*, pp. 209, 215–216, 66. See Sumner Welles's comments in the *New York Herald-Tribune*, October 19, 23, 1948.

62. Duggan, *Americas*, pp. 122, 214.

63. See Vernon Lee Fluharty, *Dance of the Millions: Military Rule and the Social Revolution in Colombia, 1930–1956* (Pittsburgh, 1957), pp. 91ff.

64. See McCloy to Stimson, May 14, 1948, Stimson MS.

65. John Martz, *Colombia: A Contemporary Political Survey* (Chapel Hill, 1962), p. 68.

66. J. Lloyd Mecham, *The United States and Inter-American Security* (Austin, Tex., 1961), p. 301. For a contemporary reaction, see Assistant Secretary of State Norman Armour's speech in *Department of State Bulletin*, XVIII (May 30, 1948), 715.

Epilogue: The containment of Latin America

1. For an account of U.S. involvement in the *coup*, see David Wise and Thomas Ross, *The Invisible Government* (New York, 1964). For an account favorable to the Eisenhower administration, see Ronald Schneider, *Communism in Guatemala, 1944–1954* (New York, 1959).

2. Copy of "Evolution or Revolution," address by John Foster Dulles to the graduating class of the University of Pennsylvania, February 12, 1949, in Entry I, File E, Dulles MS.

3. R. Rommel, State Department, to J. Miller, Commerce Department, February 19, 1948, in Box 2229, File 430 General—Latin
   America (1945-1950), BFDC, NA.
4. On U.S. objection to ECLA, see Marvin Bernstein, ed., *Foreign
   Investment in Latin America* (New York, 1968), p. 29. The
   former OCIAA economist is Simon Hanson. See his *Economic
   Development in Latin America* (Washington, 1951), p. 104.
5. Statement of Hon. John W. Snyder, in stenographic transcript
   of hearings before the Senate Banking and Currency Committee, August 9, 1949, p. 6, in File on S. 2197, 81st Cong., 1st
   sess. (1949), Senate, LRB, NA. Also see letter from R. T. Has-
   lam, Standard Oil Company of New Jersey, to Senator May-
   bank, July 18, 1949, in the same file.
6. "Statement of the Foreign Loan Policy of the United States
   Government by the National Advisory Council on International Monetary and Financial Problems," enclosed in memo
   from Secretary Vinson to President Truman, March 1, 1946, in
   OF 212-A, HST MS. This statement was signed by Vinson,
   Secretary of State Byrnes, Secretary of Commerce Wallace,
   Federal Reserve Board chairman Marriner Eccles, and Export-Import Bank board chairman William McChesney Martin.
7. For statistics on U.S. investments and capital movements in
   Latin America in the 1946-1953 period, see my article, "The
   Cold War Comes to Latin America," in Barton J. Bernstein, ed.,
   Politics and Policies of the Truman Administration (Chicago,
   1970), p. 181.
8. The statement by Caio Prado, Jr., is quoted in Maurice Hal-
   perin, "Growth and Crisis in the Latin American Economy,"
   in James Petras and Maurice Zeitlin, eds., *Latin America: Reform or Revolution?* (New York, 1968), p. 68. See also Aníbal
   Quijano Obregon, "Tendencies in Peruvian Development and
   in the Class Structure," *ibid.*, pp. 315, 326. And see George
   Wythe, *The United States and Inter-American Relations* (New
   York, 1962), p. 153.
9. Merle Kling, "Toward a Theory of Power and Political Instability in Latin America," in Petras and Zeitlin, *Reform or
   Revolution?*, pp. 80, 91, 91–92, 92–93.
10. Section 1.04a of the Social Progress Trust Fund statute states
    that "resources of the Fund shall not be used for the purchase
    of agricultural land." For an analysis of the fund and its re-
    lationship to the Alliance for Progress, see John Gerassi, *The
    Great Fear in Latin America* (New York, 1965), p. 266f.

A NOTE ON SOURCES

1. Unpublished materials

In the main, the manuscripts upon which this book is based are available in four United States government depositories: the National Archives, Washington, D.C.; the Library of Congress, Washington, D.C.; the Franklin D. Roosevelt Library, Hyde Park, New York; and the Harry S. Truman Library, Independence, Missouri. I do not by any means claim to have exhausted the relevant resources of these institutions. Such an effort could well consume a lifetime of research. The records which have been of most value to me are as follows:

National Archives: Records of the Department of State (Record Group 59); Records of the Office of Inter-American Affairs (RG 229); General Records of the Department of Commerce (RG 40); Records of the Bureau of Foreign and Domestic Commerce (RG 151); Records of the Senate and House of Representatives, in Legislative Records Branch (RG 46).

Library of Congress: Papers of Cordell Hull, Jesse Jones, Breckinridge Long. The Library also has an excellent collection of journals, newspapers, and other periodicals of United States, Latin American, and European origin.

Franklin D. Roosevelt Library: Most important are the papers of President Roosevelt, which are catalogued into three main files—the Official File, the Presidential Secretary's File, and the President's Personal File. Also useful are the papers of Charles Taussig (former co-chairman, Anglo-American Caribbean Commission), and Morris L. Cooke (United States member, Mexican-American mixed commission on oil properties, 1941, and chairman, United States Industrial Mission to Brazil, 1942). Recently opened are the papers of former Treasury Secretary Morgenthau.

Harry S. Truman Library: The papers of President Truman, like those of Roosevelt, are divided into an Official File, Presidential Secretary's File, and President's Personal File. The papers of William L. Clayton are important to a study of Latin American policy, as are those of former Treasury Secretary John W. Snyder. For the period of the early 1950's, the papers of former Ambassador to Brazil Herschel Johnson are available.

In addition to the above depositories, a number of university libraries contain important manuscript collections. The Houghton Library at Harvard contains the papers of former Under Secretary of State Joseph C. Grew. The Sterling Memorial Library at Yale houses the papers of Henry L. Stimson, including the extremely important Stimson Diary; Yale also has the papers of Arthur Bliss Lane, former Ambassador to Colombia. Princeton has the papers of Bernard Baruch, Harry Dexter White, John Foster Dulles, and James V. Forrestal. Special permission is needed to use the Dulles and Forrestal collections. Columbia University has the papers of George Leslie Harrison, former governor of the Federal Reserve Bank of New York. There is also an extensive Oral History collection at Columbia, including material on the San Francisco Conference and the Marshall Plan, and interviews with several key American officials involved in Latin American policy. The William L. Clayton interview is available, and may be quoted with special permission of the Clayton family. The interview with Spruille Braden can be seen with Mr. Braden's permission. At the time of this writing, the Adolf Berle and Nelson Rockefeller interviews are still generally unavailable. Those wishing further information should contact the Oral History Center at the Butler Library, Columbia University.

The papers of George S. Messersmith, formerly Ambassador to Cuba, Mexico, and Argentina, successively, are available at the University of Delaware Library, Newark, Delaware. The papers of former Senator Carter Glass of Virginia are at the Library of the University of Virginia. Also at Virginia, though not yet available for scholarly research, are the papers of former Secretary of State Edward R. Stettinius, Jr. The papers of former Senator Arthur H. Vandenberg of Michigan can be seen at the William L. Clements Library at the University of Michigan, Ann Arbor, Michigan. Vandenberg's San Francisco Conference Diary is especially worth reading. The library of the Council on Foreign Relations in New York City has a complete file of the informative and provocative *Studies of the American Interest in the War and the Peace*, written between 1940 and 1945 by a wide variety of politically active academics. Also at this library are the summary transcripts of the Study Group discussions on postwar foreign policy planning held at the Council headquarters in late 1944 and early 1945. These *Study Group Reports*, which contain the views of leading government officials, businessmen, and scholars, are available for reading but not for quotation. They are, nevertheless, a worthwhile source for the contemporary thinking of some influential members of the American policy-making community.

Interviews can also be a fruitful source of new information and ideas. In New York City, I had very helpful conversations with Messrs. Adolf Berle and Spruille Braden. In Buenos Aires, I interviewed Sr. Mauricio Birabent, former director of the Banco Industrial of Argentina; in Rio de Janeiro, I had informative discussions with Sra. Alzira Vargas do Amaral Peixoto (daughter of the late President Getulio Vargas); former President Eurico Gaspar Dutra; Dr. Henrique Mindlin, formerly assistant director of the Brazilian Section of the Brazilian-American Joint Industrial Commission, 1942; and General Nelson Werneck Sodré. To all of the above interviewees I would like to express my deepest gratitude for their graciousness and helpfulness.

2. Published materials

Published government documents are an extremely important source of information. Particularly useful among United States government publications are the following: the *Congressional Record*; hearings and reports of various congressional committees (see the *Cumulative Index of Congressional Hearings*, plus the indices in the various published congressional reports—arranged chronologically by number of Congress and session—for complete listings); the annual *Public Papers and Addresses* of the Presidents; the *Foreign Commerce Weekly*, published by the Department of Commerce; the *Department of State Bulletin*; the *Inter-American Series* and *Conference Series*, both published by the Department of State; various miscellaneous reports of the Department of State, such as the famous Blue Book on Argentina of 1946; and, finally, the Department's multi-volume series, *Foreign Relations of the United States*. The *Foreign Relations* series is extremely important to American historians; however, because of the high degree of selectivity necessarily used in choosing documents for publication, this series, when used for serious research purposes, should always be used to supplement, and not to substitute for, research in the Department of State Archives in Washington, D.C.

The United Nations has also published a number of useful documents and studies relating to inter-American affairs. Chief among these are the studies and surveys of the Economic Council for Latin America (ECLA). The five-volume summary proceedings of the San Francisco Conference are also helpful.

Many Latin American governments have published the debates and minutes of their respective national legislatures, which contain much information on foreign policy attitudes. Also available are various *Boletims Estatisticos* and *Memorías de Relaciones Exteriores*. The American reader will find a number of these in the Library of Congress. In addition, the Columbus Library of the Pan American Union in Washington, D.C., has a great many useful documents, particularly the complete minutes of many inter-American conferences and congresses.

In regard to secondary works, including books and articles, the publishing explosion has not excluded the field of inter-American relations. Rather than offer a separate selective bibliography here, I would refer the reader to the notes of this book and to the articles, indices, and book reviews contained in such journals as the *American Historical Review*, the *Journal of American History*, the *Inter-American Economic Review*, the (unfortunately now defunct) *Hispanic American Report*, the *Journal of Inter-American Studies*, and many others listed in the annual *Handbook of Latin American Studies*. For the beginning reader, a useful secondary bibliography is available in the late Hubert Herring's *A History of Latin America* (3rd ed., New York, 1968).

Acheson, Dean, 280; chairman, interdepartmental committee on postwar development in Latin America, 124; explains World Bank, 325n.

Act of Chapultepec (see also Mexico City Conference), 172, 226, 229, 232, 254; views of Senator Vandenberg, 257, 258

Adams, John Quincy, 3, 4

Aid, economic (see also Military aid, U.S.): to Bolivia, 51–52; Braden speech on postwar grants, 262; postwar, 173; wartime, 91

Aikman, Duncan, 130–131

Air transport, Latin American: Axis penetration of, 56; postwar plans for, 180–181; U.S. policy on, 56–57, 192

Alliance for Progress: and Good Neighbor Policy, viii, 296–297

Aluminum: Brazilian development of, recommended by Cooke Mission, 90; as strategic material, 317n.

American Century (see also Luce, Henry R.), 113–116, 136, 137; and Open World, 117, 210, 213

APRA (see also Peru), 9, 199; and election of 1931, 11

Aranha, Oswaldo, 189

Arbenz, Jacobo, 292

Arbitration: and Mexican oil dispute, 53–54

Argentina (see also Perón, Juan Domingo), 179; agricultural policy in, 94, 95, 242; Anglo-American rivalry in, 241–242, 247, 327n.; Anglo-Argentine trade agreement of 1946, 268–269; anti-Americanism in, 238; anti-communism in, 280; and Bolivian revolution of 1943, 143–144; Britain, wartime exports to, 139–140, 239, 241–242; declares war on Germany, Japan, 216, 248; election campaign of 1945–1946, 252–253; Farrell regime in, 156–163, 238; landed vs. industrial groups in, 240–243; meat, U.S. embargo on, 10; and Mexico City Conference, 166–167, 169, 182; nationalism in, U.S. response to, 46, 234–235, 288; participation in IADC, 77; postwar price increases in, 274–275; revolution of 1930, 11; revolution of 1943, 153–163, 240–243; and Rio Pact, 282–283; sale of naval vessels to, by U.S., 260–261; and San Francisco Conference, 215, 217–222, 237–238; and Soviet-American conflict, 222, 238; supports nonintervention, 6; tariff policy in, 188–189; U.S. export licenses for, wartime, 90; U.S. military aid to, opposed by Braden, 264; wartime machinery shortages, effect of, 97; wartime prosperity in, 112, 153, 239–240, 287

Armour, Norman: U.S. Ambassador to Argentina, 154–160; declines to meet with Perón, 156–158; recalled, 160

Armstrong, Hamilton Fish, 118, 233

Arnold, General H. H., 180–181, 260

Atlantic Charter, 115, 116, 137; and Bolivian revolution of 1943, 143; British attitude toward, 117, 324n.

Austin, Senator Warren, 182, 201, 247

Automobiles: wartime shortages of, in Latin America, 109–110

Avila Camacho, Manuel, 185–186, 192–193, 278

Axis (see also Germany; Italy; Japan), 33–35, 37–38, 46, 49, 51; Argentina, wartime relations with, 153, 216; fear of postwar resurgence, 224–226

Balance of payments (see also Tariffs; Trade), 11, 40

Baldivieso, Enrique, 146–147, 152

Bananas, 43, 127

Banks (see also Inter-American Bank; International Bank for Reconstruction and Development): in Argentina, 351n.; in Brazil, 190–191, 313n.–314n.; European, export of Latin American capital to, 10; U.S., in Latin America, 68–73, 80

Baruch, Bernard M., 39–40, 67, 273; Axis threat in Latin America, views on, 33–35, 45, 100; and British loan, 266, 269; Mexican oil crisis and, 33–34; mission to London, 211, 213; opposes nationalization, statism, 265–266, 347n.–348n.; see Russia as postwar trading partner, 212; Volta Redonda, views on, 44–45, 80

Batista, Fulgencio: and Cuban revolution of 1933, 14–18, 305n.

Beef: Argentine, wartime sales of, 112, 153, 242; and U.S. policy toward Argentine revolution of 1943, 155, 160–163

Berle, Adolf, 56, 137, 163; Grau regime in Cuba, reaction to, 17; and Inter-American Bank, 62, 65, 69–70; Kingston, Ontario speech, 81–83; Mexico City Conference, views on, 208, 214; Petropolis speech in Brazil, 235

Betancourt, Romulo, 269

Beveridge, Senator Albert J., 6

Black market: wartime, in Latin America, 97

Blaine, James G., 4–5

Bloom, Sol, 281

Boal, Pierre, 143–146, 150

Board of Economic Warfare (BEW), 90, 98, 196–197; efforts to increase strategic materials production in Latin America, 100–102; preclusive buying contracts, 100–101

Bogotá Conference (see also Bogotazo; Organization of American States), 279, 292–293; proceedings, 283–286

Bogotazo: causes, 289; U.S. reaction to, 289–290

Bolivia (*see also* Movimiento Nacional Revolucionario; Tin; Tungsten), viii, 8, 63; expropriation of Standard Oil properties in, 23–27, 49–52, 310n.; revolution of 1943, 142–152, 181; wartime dependence on Argentina, 153, 157, 160–161

Bonds, defaulted (*see also* Foreign Bondholders' Protective Council), 10, 21–22, 40–41

Bowers, Claude, 144

Braden, Spruille, 57, 186, 235, 280; Ambassador to Argentina, 237–238, 242, 244–246, 252; Assistant Secretary of State, 251; defends private enterprise in Latin American development, 262–263, 270, 285, 288; opposes nationalism in Argentina, 250–251, 252–255, 264–265; resigns, 254

Brazil (*see also* Vargas, Getulio; Volta Redonda), 9, 40–41, 46, 100, 153, 239; agricultural exports, 93–95; British capital in, 140–141; communists in, 208; Constitution of 1937, 38–39; economic policies at Mexico City Conference, 201–202; first IADC project in, 77–78; food riots of 1946 in, 274; foreign trade in 1930's, 21–23; industrialization and tariffs in, 20, 188–190; Itabira mining properties, 109; Lend-Lease aid to, 179; relations with Russia, 186; revolution of 1930, 11; rubber development in, 104–106; transportation shortages in, 109–110; Vitoria-Minas railway, 109

Brett, General George: military mission to Latin America, 180–182

Bretton Woods Conference (*see also* International Bank for Reconstruction and Development; International Monetary Fund), 121, 176, 206

Brown, Irving, 197–198

Burgess, W. Randolph (*see also* Inter-American Bank), 68–69, 71–72, 314n., 315n.

Busch, Germán, 50–51

Byrnes, James F. (*see also* State, U.S. Department of), 256, 278, 288; Argentine policies of, 253–254; at Potsdam Conference, 255–256; supports Inter-American Military Cooperation Act, 259

Caffery, Jefferson, 17–18

Calder, Curtis, 41

Calvo Clause, 25–27

Cantilo, José, 242

Cárdenas, Lázaro (*see also* Mexico), 195; expropriates American and British oil properties, 27–29, 31–32, 53; role in Mexican Revolution, 28–29

Caribbean (*see also* individual countries): wartime economic integration with U.S., 95

Carranza, Venustiano, 8

Castillo, Ramón S. (*see also* Argentina):

alliance with Argentine landowners, 241–242; overthrown, 240

Castro, Fidel, 296

"Catavi massacres," 103, 143

Cattle (*see also* Beef; Meat), 242; in postwar Peru, 294

Central America (*see also* individual countries): wartime economic integration with U.S., 95

Céspedes, Carlos Manuel de, 14

Chaco War, 23, 27

Chapultepec Conference (*see* Mexico City Conference)

Chile, 9, 11, 62–63, 144–145, 157, 265; agricultural exports, 93, 95; American purchases of strategic raw materials in, 100; continental industrialization plan presented at Mexico City Conference, 202; diversification of industry in, 101; land usage in, 200; mining, U.S. investments in, 8; Popular Front in, viii; postwar riots in, 274; tariff policy in, 190

Churchill, Winston S., 155, 210; British Empire and One World concept, views on, 117, 210; co-sponsors Atlantic Charter, 115; supports regionalist approach to world security, 118

Civil Aeronautics Administration, 261

Clark, J. Reuben, 21

Clark Memorandum, 13

Clay, Henry, 3, 4

Clayton, William L., 96, 124, 247; and British loan negotiations, 267; cotton export subsidies, views on, 189; and Inter-American Bank, 68–70; Mexico City Conference, speech at, 173–175, 182; opposes hemispheric agricultural cartels, 94; postwar prosperity, views on, 116, 177

Coffee: marketing of, 94–95, 203

Cold War (*see also* Soviet Union; United States), 209–210, 291–292

Collado, Emilio, 66, 69, 121, 124

Colombia (*see also* Bogotá Conference; Bogotazo), 6, 62–63, 77, 122, 145; draft resolution on hemispheric defense, Mexico City Conference, 187; Industrial Development Institute in, 190; OCIAA study on economic development of, 49; tariff policy, 189–190

Commerce, U.S. Department of (*see also* Private enterprise, U.S. government), 41–42, 49

Committee for Economic Development, 120

Commodities, agricultural and mineral (*see also* individual items): OCIAA survey of postwar markets for, 127–128; wartime buying of, by U.S., 94–95

Communism: and Bogotazo, 290; and instability in Latin America, 279–280; Latin American views of, 185–187; relationship to Peronism, 243–246; U.S. government fears of, in Latin America, 14–15, 37, 207, 276–277, 292; views of U.S. labor leaders on, 198

Communists: in Brazil, 186, 334n.; in Colombia, 289; in Cuba, 186; in Guatemala, 292; in Peru, 198

Confederación de Trabajadores Mexicanos (CTM), 29

Congress, U.S.: and Export-Import Bank funding, 42; fears of "giveaway" programs, 80

Congress of Industrial Organizations (CIO), 197; opposes Perón, 250

Connally, Senator Tom, 247, 253

Cooke, Morris L.: heads BEW Industrial Mission to Brazil, 90, 190, 338n.

Coolidge, Calvin, 6, 12

Copper, 127, 190, 335n.; American preclusive buying of, in Chile, 100; U.S. dependence on Latin America for, 317n.

Cordoba reforms, 9

Corn, 127; wartime production of, in Mexico, 107

Corrigan, Frank, 207–208

Cotton: American export subsidies for, 189, 205, 265, 335n.; Brazilian reaction, 265

Council on Foreign Relations, 95–96, 118, 130

Credits (*see also* Banks; Export-Import Bank; Loans): postwar, 271; wartime, 92, 99

Crowley, Leo (*see also* Foreign Economic Administration), 106, 212

Cuba, 95, 201; communists, and election of 1944, 186; "dance of the millions," 9, 274; diversification of agriculture in, 101; land usage, 200; postwar inflation in, 274; reciprocal trade agreement with U.S., 20, revolution of 1933, 13–18, 20–21, 148; sugar purchase agreement with U.S., 43, 203, 309n., 338n.; tariff policy, 189

Customs union, 189

Daniels, Josephus: Ambassador to Mexico, 29–33, 38, 53–56; role in Mexican oil crisis, 30–33, 53–56; views on Mexican Revolution, 30

Davies, Joseph, 39

Dávila, Carlos, 75, 189

Debts, Latin American, 21, 48, 63–64; and development loans, U.S. policy on, 80

Decapitalization, 10, 294

Defense (*see also* Inter-American Military Cooperation Act; Regionalism; United Nations): and Bogotá Conference, 283–284; and economic development, wartime, 85–92; postwar planning for, 180; and Rio Pact, 281–283

DeGaulle, General Charles, 209, 266

Depression: and Good Neighbor Policy, 18–19; impact of, in Latin America, 11–12

Development, economic (*see also* Economic Agreement of Bogotá; Economic Charter of the Americas; Export-Import Bank; Inter-American

Bank; Inter-American Development Commission), 43–48; OCIAA report on, 124–129

Díaz, Porfirio, 304n.

Dictatorship, military: and depression, 11–12; and U.S. aid, viii, 259, 282

Diversification (*see also* individual countries), 43, 101

Dominican Republic (*see also* Trujillo, Rafael): depression in, 11; postwar cost of living in, 274; U.S. intervention in, 5, 7–8

Douglas, Helen Gahagan, 282

Drumm, James H., 191–192

Duggan, Laurence, 25, 89–90, 103, 107, 146, 201, 238, 275; Economic Agreement of Bogotá, views on, 283; government-business relationship, analyzes, 134–135; nationalism in Latin America, views on, 188; sums up Latin American contribution to war effort, 111; supports Inter-American Bank, 66; views on U.S. policy toward Latin American economic development, 37, 289, 290

Dulles, John Foster, 214, 228, 233, 276–277, 280, 288, 292; calls for Rio Pact, 278; City College speech of 1946, 277–278; defends private enterprise in development of Latin America, 263; and Foreign Bondholders' Council, 21; Russian penetration of Latin America, views on, 258, 263, 281, 346n.

Dumbarton Oaks Conference, 166, 169, 172; Bretton Woods Conference, relationship to, 121; and San Francisco Conference, 222–223, 229; U.S. position on regionalism at, 122; and Yalta Conference, 170–171

Dunn, James Clement, 218, 228

Dutra, Marshal Eurico Gaspar, 235

Eaton, Charles, 264

Economic Agreement of Bogotá, 283, 286

Economic Charter of the Americas, 178, 182; U.S. draft of, 175–176; version adopted, 204–205

Economic Council for Latin America (ECLA), 293

Ecuador, 194

Eden, Anthony, 155, 231

Education, 9, 197

Eisenhower, General Dwight D., 259–260

Electricity: in Argentina, 241; and Cooke Mission to Brazil, 338n.

El Salvador, 62–63, 274

Embick, General Stanley, 182, 223

Europe (*see also* individual countries): Eastern, U.S.-Russian clash in, 211; market for Latin American exports, 8, 94, 95; postwar Latin American contributions to, 271; U.S. aid to, 170, 173–174, 176

Exchange controls, 40, 191, 205–206

Export-Import Bank, 42, 74, 78–79, 173, 284; Brazil, loans to, 40, 44–45, 77–78,

Export-Import Bank—*Cont.*
109; and development corporations in Latin America, 194; Latin American indebtedness to, 1945, 239; postwar loans to Latin America, 265, 271
Exports (*see also* Tariffs; Trade): British, and American Century, 138; Latin American, 10, 42–43, 92–94; U.S., 10, 75, 97–99, 261, 275–276
Expropriation: and Bogotá Conference, 286; in Bolivia, 23–27, 49–52, 310n.; in Mexico, 8, 27–28, 31–35, 45, 52–56, 307n.

Farrell, General Edelmiro (*see also* Argentina; Perón, Juan Domingo), 156
Fascism (*see also* Nazism), 34, 37; and Argentine revolution of 1943, 154; and Bolivian revolution of 1943, 148–149; relationship to Peronism, 243–246, 250
Finot, Enrique, 24–26
Fomentos, 194
Food (*see also* specific foods): and American Century, 114; in Europe, postwar shortages of, 273; in Latin America, wartime shortages of, 107, 108, 153
Foreign Bondholders' Protective Council, 21, 316n.
Foreign Economic Administration, 103, 110
Foreign exchange (*see also* Exchange controls): in Argentina, 239; and depression, 191; and development, 43, 205–206; postwar conservation of, 206
Forrestal, James V., 44, 247
France: U.S. postwar loan to, 266, 270; and Western unity, 209
Friele, Berent, 41

Gaitán, Jorge Eliécer (*see also* Bogotazo), 289
Galarza, Ernesto, 282
General Motors Corporation, 25, 39
Germany, 33–38, 163–164, 209, 255–256; barter trade with Latin America, 37; and Bolivian revolution of 1943, 144, 147, 149; expansion into Latin American airlines, 56; outsells U.S. in Brazil, 22; wartime trade with Latin America, 98, 320n.
Glass, Senator Carter, 71–73, 176
Gold, 111, 239
Good Neighbor Policy, 26–27, 147, 290, 295–296; Axis threat, relationship to, 37, 58; and containment policy, 297; and depression, 18–19; effect of war economy upon, 96, 112; evaluated by scholars, vii, 300n.; and loans to Latin America, 46; U.S. private enterprise and, 193–194
Grau San Martín, Ramón, 274, 334n.; and Cuban revolution of 1933, 14–18
Great Britain, 123, 153, 185; and American Century, 137–138; and Argentine revolution of 1943, policy toward, 112, 154–155, 160–163; Baruch mission to, 211;

and Caribbean agriculture, 200–201; and Imperial Preference System, 211, 265; investments in Argentina, 139–140, 241–242; postwar U.S. loan to, 267, 268–269, 270–271; wartime exports, 98–99, 320n.
Grew, Joseph C., 186; and U.S. policy toward Argentina, 225, 237–238, 246, 248–249
Guatemala, 62–63; and depression, 11; 1954 military coup in, 292; nationalists in, viii–ix
Guevara, Ernesto "Che," 10

Haiti, 62–63; development corporation (SHADA) in, 104, 194–195; rubber development program, 104; U.S. intervention in, 7, 8
Halifax, Viscount: and British policy toward Argentina, 154–155, 160, 162–163
Hannon, Sir Patrick, 139
Hanson, Simon G., 76, 78, 89, 353n.
Harding, Warren G., 8
Harriman, W. Averell, 273
Harris, Seymour, 111, 131; price controls in Latin America, aids in establishing, 108; views on exchange controls and investment, 205–206
Harrison, Benjamin, 5
Harrison, George Leslie, 71
Havana Conference of 1928, 7
Havana Conference of 1940, 74
Havana Trade Conference of 1947, 267–268
Henderson, Leon, 106
Honduras, 11, 185
Hoover, Herbert: Latin American policies of, 12–13, 300n.; as UNRRA director, 271
Hopkins, Harry, 48
Hornbeck, Stanley, 94
Howe, Louis Henry, 177
Hughes, Charles Evans, 7
Hull, Cordell (*see also* State, U.S. Department of), 40–41, 124, 133, 138, 177, 235; Argentina, policy toward, 112, 153–163, 238–239, 329n.–330n.; Argentine admission to San Francisco Conference, views on, 237–238, 248–249, 256; asks Anglo-American solid front against Argentina, 154–155, 162–163; and Bolivian revolution of 1943, 147–152; and Cuban revolution of 1933, 14–15; introduces Reciprocal Trade Agreements program, 19; Latin American debts to U.S. investors, views on, 21–22; negotiates reciprocal trade agreement with Brazil, 21–22; Open World concept and spheres of influence, views on, 116–117, 119, 122; opposes inter-American conference during war, 165–166, 169; opposes Pauley contract in Mexico, 192; policy in Bolivian oil crisis, 26, 49–50; policy in Mexican oil crisis, 30–32, 53–55; resigns as Secretary of State, 163; seeks

Hull, Cordell—*Cont.*
united inter-American stand against Argentina, 157, 159–161
Hurley, Patrick, 53–54

Ibáñez, Carlos, 9
Ickes, Harold L., , 105, 192, 193
Import controls: and exchange controls, 206
Import substitution, 189–190; ECLA policy on, 293
Industry (*see also* Development, economic), 141, 173–174, 202, 211; and Argentine revolution of 1943, 240–243; aviation, postwar planning for, 180–181; IADC and, 75–76; Inter-American Bank and, 63; postwar development of, plans for, 125, 204; and tariffs, 188–190; wartime growth of, in Latin America, 99
Inflation: in Latin America, wartime, 107–111, 239; postwar, 273–276; price control and, 107–108
Integralistas, 306n.
Inter-American Bank (IAB), 60–74; charter, 64; Latin American views on, 64–65, 206–207, 284; and private banks, 69; Roosevelt administration and, 65–74; Senate Banking and Currency Committee and, 73, 176; withdrawn by Truman, 73
Inter-American Development Commission (IADC): continental industrialization and, 202; early projects, 75, 315n.; effects of war on projects, 85–89; May 1944 meeting of subcommissions, 133–134, 178–179; organized, 74, 77; purpose, 74–75, 83; wartime project reports, surveys, 89, 203
Inter-American Development Corporation, 79–80
Inter-American Financial and Economic Advisory Committee (IAFEAC): and continental industrialization, 202; created, 61–62; and Inter-American Bank, 62–64
Inter-American Military Cooperation Act, 259–260, 281–282
Interior, U.S. Department of, 55
International Bank for Reconstruction and Development (IBRD): Latin American views of, 207, 284; origins, 119; and postwar loans, 174, 201, 262, 271; and private investment, 120, 325n.; as replacement for IAB, 176; role of U.S. in, 119
International Labor Organization (ILO), 176
International Monetary Fund (IMF), 262; Harry Dexter White speech to, 1947, 272; and IAB, 176; origins, 119; role in international trade, 121; role of U.S. in, 119
Intervention, ix, 18, 300n.; and Bogotá Conference, 283–284; in Caribbean, 304n.; and Havana Conference of 1928, 7

Investments (in Latin America), 8, 10; British, in Argentina, 139–140, 241–242, 327n.; and decapitalization, 10–11, 294; and depression, 12; exchange controls and, 205–206; local and foreign ownership of, in Brazil, 190–191; postwar, OCIAA views on, 127; prewar problems concerning, 124–125; self-liquidating, 191–192; wartime, British and American, 336n.
Italy: and Bolivian revolution of 1943, 144, 149; and Mexican oil crisis, 31, 33–34, 38

Japan: atomic bomb and, 256; and Bolivian revolution of 1943, 149; and Mexican oil crisis, 31, 33–34, 38
Javits, Jacob, 281–282
Johnson Act, 21
Johnston, Eric: suggests American Century in Latin America, 139, 179; supports Brazilian steel development, 129–130; talks with Stalin on U.S.-Russian trade, 212
Jones, Grosvenor, 49
Jones, Jesse, 40; Committee for Economic Development, 1943 speech to, 120; and Inter-American Bank, 66; opposes Pauley contract in Mexico, 193; and rubber development program, 105; Volta Redonda, views on, 44–45
Jones-Costigan Act, 16

Kellogg, Frank B., 9
Kelly, Sir David, 160, 252; attitude toward Perón, 245
Kennedy, John F., viii, 296–297
Kilgore, Senator Harley M., 270–271
Kirk, Grayson, 122
Klein, Dr. Julius, 41
Knox, Philander C., 304n.

Labor: AFL-CIO tour of Peru, 1943, 197–198; in Bolivia, and mining interests, 143; and Brazilian rubber development, 337n.; and foreign enterprises, 195–197; organized, growth of, 9; and strategic materials production, 196–197
LaGuardia, Fiorello, 34–35
Land: Alliance for Progress and, 296–297; in Argentina, and revolution of 1943, 240; tenure, and power, 199–200; usage, production, and profit, 200
Lane, Arthur Bliss, 145
Lansing, Robert, 7–8, 30
Latin America (*see also* individual countries), 157, 159–161, 167–168, 170; and American Century, 142, 234; automotive transport, wartime, 110; Bolivian revolution of 1943, reactions to, 144–145; cold war, economic effect upon, 164, 170; communist influence in, 186–187; contributions to European reconstruction, 164; and defensive autonomy, 215, 230–232; depres-

Latin America—*Cont.*
sion and, 11–13, 19; dollar balances in, postwar, 176; economic dependence on U.S., wartime, 101–104, 287; and First World War, 8; Hull's fear of revolution in, 147; inflation in, 107–111; Lend-Lease aid to, 179–180; machinery shortages, postwar, 275; and Open World, 121–122, 234; profiteering, wartime, 98; and Rio Pact, 283; sales of industrial goods to, postwar, 173–174; Second World War, effect on, 85–86, 95–96, 101; solidarity at San Francisco Conference, 222; tariff policy and industrialization in, 190; Truman policies toward nationalism in, 262, 264–265, 267–268; U.S. investment in, postwar, 269–270

Lend-Lease: and British investments in Argentina, 327n.; effect on British exports to Latin America, 139; and military aid to Latin America, 179–180

Lescot, Elie, 274

Lins de Barros, João Alberto, 106

Lleras Camargo, Alberto, 285–286

Lleras Restrepo, Carlos, 206

Loans (*see also* Banks; Export-Import Bank; International Bank for Research and Development; International Monetary Fund; etc.): to France, 1946, 270; to Great Britain, 267, 270, 346n.; versus investments, 348n.; as substitute for internal taxation, 10

Lombardo Toledano, Vicente, 198–199

Long, Breckinridge: opposes Mexico City Conference, 167, 169; opposes talks with Argentina, 331n.

Lopez, Alfonso, 165

Lothian, Lord, 138

Luce, Henry R. (*see also* American Century): attacks isolationism, 113; views on Roosevelt, New Deal, 115–116

Machado, Gerardo (*see also* Cuba), 13–14

Machinery: OCIAA "idle machinery" export program, 110; shortages, postwar, 275–276; shortages, wartime, 97–98, 100; U.S. restrictions on exports of, 109; and Volta Redonda, 45

Manganese, 87, 127, 317n.

Marshall, General George C., 254, 264, 288; speech to Bogotá Conference, 285; supports U.S. naval sales to Argentina, 260–261

Marshall Plan, 263, 272–273; and Bogotá Conference, 285

Martins, Carlos, 172

Marxism (*see also* Communism; Socialism): in Latin American education, 9

McClintock, John, 41, 134, 140

McCloy, John J., 230; *Bogotazo*, views on, 290; position on regionalism at San Francisco Conference, 223, 227–230, 232

McDonald, David J., 197–198

Meat, 127; and international companies, 199–200; Mexican, postwar sales of, 273; packinghouse workers in Argentina, and revolution of 1943, 241

Mendieta, Carlos (*see also* Cuba): becomes President of Cuba, 15; problems in maintaining stability, 17–18

Messersmith, George S., 42–43, 154, 167, 195, 247, 252; appointed Ambassador to Argentina, 253; BEW mining contract in Mexico, intervenes in, 196–197; Cuban sugar purchase agreement, supports, 43; inter-American defense pact, views on, 280; Lombardo Toledano and, 199; Mexico City Conference, analysis of, 185–186; opposes Pauley contract in Mexico, 192–193; and Perón, 253–254, 278, 281, 350n.–351n.; postwar economic neglect of Latin America, warns against, 164; "resigns," 345n.–346n.; Russian activities in Latin America, views on, 141–142, 181, 280, 333n.; U.S. leadership in hemisphere, notes need for, 278–279, 350n.

Mexican Revolution (*see also* Mexico): and Constitution of 1917, 7; Robert Lansing and, 7–8; and nationalism, viii, 7, 28

Mexico, 7; anticlericalism in, 9; Axis, sales of oil to, 38; Bank of Mexico, report on exchange controls, 205; BEW mining contract in, 196–197; contract labor in U.S. and, 197; evaluation of U.S. oil properties in, 54–55; Export-Import Bank, indebtedness to, 239; and Inter-American Bank, 61–62; meat industry, and European reconstruction, 273; "Mexicanization" of industry, and New Group, 195; nationalization of U.S. and British oil properties in, 27–35, 52–56; oilseed production in, wartime, 106–107; Pauley contract in, 192–193; Pemex, establishment of, 28; postwar development loan to, proposed by H. D. White, 272–273; rehabilitation of railroads in, wartime, 109; Russia, relations with, 186; Sinclair interests, negotiations with, 53; and United Nations organization, 215; U.S. fear of communism in, 280

Mexico City Conference (*see also* Act of Chapultepec; Economic Charter of the Americas), 208, 215; and American policy, ix, 167, 175–176, 182–183, 214; conference proceedings, 171–177, 187, 189–190, 201–207; Latin American economic position at, 195, 201–207; regional security, Latin American views on, 171–172; speech by Clayton, 173–175, 182

Military aid, U.S.: to Argentina, recommended by Avra Warren, 250–251; to Bolivia, and U.S. military mission, 51; and Inter-American Military Cooperation Act, 259–260; political uses of,

Military aid, U.S.—*Cont.*
181, 264; postwar, 179–181, 259; wartime, Lend-Lease, 179–180
Molotov, V. M., 223; meeting with Truman, 212–214; opposes Argentine admission to San Francisco Conference, 219–220; regional defense arrangements, views on, 224; Vandenberg's views of, 221, 249
Monroe, James, 4
Monroe Doctrine, 4, 254, 278; Lombardo Toledano, views on, 199; and Rio Pact, 292; and San Francisco Conference, 222–223, 225, 227–228
Morgenthau, Henry, Jr.: and Mexican nationalism, 31; proposes reconstruction credit to Russia, 212; silver policy of, during Mexican oil crisis, 31–32; White Plan, views on, 119
Moscow Conference of 1943, 117, 256
Movimiento Nacional Revolucionario (MNR), Bolivia: American hopes for disintegration of, 151; and Bolivian revolution of 1943, 103, 143, 148–152; eliminated from revolutionary government, 150–151; 1942 manifesto, 148–149; Paz Estenssoro, criticizes U.S. control of Bolivian Development Corporation, 194; U.S. committed to overthrow of, 149–150, 152, 194
Multilateralism: effect of war upon, 87, 111–112, 287; and IADC, 75; and Inter-American Bank, 83; Latin American views on, 59–60; and Mexico City Conference, 168; in postwar planning, 128, 165

National Foreign Trade Council, 132, 307n.
National Planning Association, 131, 199–200
Nationalism, 291; and Alliance for Progress, 296; and American Century, 137, 142; in Argentina, 158, 241–242, 287; and Axis influences in Latin America, 57; in Bolivia, 24, 147, 152; and communism, 186–187, 207; and foreign investment, 12, 22, 191, 195–196; and IADC conference of 1944, 178; and labor, 195; and land, 201; in Mexican oil crisis, 28, 30, 34, 56, 195; and Mexico City Conference, 167–168, 170, 175, 187–188, 204–205; and military aid, U.S., 181–182; and political stabilization, 279; postwar threat to U.S., 142, 207, 264, 287; and revolution, viii, 37, 242, 287, 291, 301n.; and "southern bloc," 279; Truman policies and, 264–265, 267–268, 271, 287–288, 291; Volta Redonda, relationship to, 45
Nazism: and Argentine revolution of 1943, 154; and Bolivian revolution of 1943, 147–149; Mexican oil crisis and, 33–34; U.S. fears of, in Latin America, 33–35, 154
Nelson, Donald, 87, 212
New Deal: and American Century, 116;

and Good Neighbor Policy, 18–19, 21–23, 58; private enterprise and, 20, 22–23, 39–40, 264; and White Plan, 119
New York Times, 220, 244–246; role in Rockefeller dismissal, 244
Nicaragua: U.S. intervention in, 7–9
Nimitz, Admiral Chester, 259
Nitrates: American preclusive buying of, in Chile, 100
Nixon, Richard M., viii
Nonintervention (*see also* Intervention), vii, 6, 13
Norweb, Henry, 24–26, 109

Obregón, Alvaro, 28
Office of the Coordinator of Inter-American Affairs (OCIAA), 97, 125; asks export price differentials to stimulate wartime exports, 97; and Bolivian tin, wartime development of, 102; Coordinating Committees of, 133–134; created, 49; disagreements with State Department, 59; Food Supply Missions, 107–108; government participation in economic development, views on, 133; idle machinery export program, attempts, 110; and IADC, 74–77; and Inter-American Bank, 65–66; and labor, in strategic materials programs, 196; memo on Lend-Lease military aid, 179–180; Resources Division Report on Latin American development, 124–129; Nelson Rockefeller appointed coordinator, 49; wartime objectives, 88; wartime surveys, 203
Office of Price Administration (OPA), 97, 108, 319n.
Oil: in Argentina, refineries, 241; in Bolivia, expropriation of Standard Oil properties, 23–27, 49–52, 310n.; in Mexico, expropriation of British and U.S. properties, 27–35, 52–56; Pauley contract, in Mexico, 192–193; U.S. import quotas, 52; U.S. investments in, 8, 43, 269
Olney, Richard, 5
Open World, 137, 213; and Eastern Europe, 211–212; and Inter-American Bank, 176; and inter-American "system," 121, 255; in OCIAA plans for postwar development, 128; and One World concept, 116; and San Francisco Conference, 233–234; and tariffs, 177; Truman's views on, 213, 255
Organization of American States (OAS): charter, 283; and communism, 284; and nonintervention, 283–284
Oumansky, Constantine, 181, 333n.

Padilla, Ezequiel, 166–167, 218
Panama, 63; effect of Canal Zone upon local economy, 195; wartime defense of, 179
Panama Canal: Axis threat to, 56–57; and Panamanian revolution of 1903, 6; security of, 259; Theodore Roosevelt and, 6, 304n.

Panama Conference of 1939, 47, 92
Pan American Airways, Inc., 41, 57
Pan American Union, 4, 248, 257
Paraguay, 95, 153, 157
Patterson, Robert, 282
Pauley, Edwin W.: attempts to gain oil contract in Mexico, 192–193
Pawley, William, 280, 352n.
Paz Estenssoro, Victor (*see also* Bolivia; MNR), 143–144; attacked by U.S. State Department, 149, 152, 194; attacks economic oligarchies in Bolivia, 151; becomes Minister of Finance, 143; Bolivian Development Corporation, views on, 194; denies Axis influences in revolution of 1943, 146
Pearl Harbor, 51, 105
Peñaranda, Enrique (*see also* Bolivia): Axis plot to overthrow, 51; domestic policies, 142–143; MNR, attacked by, 149; overthrown, 52, 143; Standard Oil dispute, negotiates resolution of, 51–52; wartime tin production, policy on, 103, 142
Pepper, Senator Claude, 70, 277
Perón, Juan Domingo (*see also* Argentina), 156–158, 245; becomes Secretary of Labor, Vice-President, 241; becomes Secretary of War, 156; "Braden or Perón," campaign slogan, 252; inauguration, 269; industrialists and, 243; and Messersmith, 278–280; Perlinger, struggle with, 158–159; policy on *frigoríficos*, electric power, 344n.; popular support, development of, 199, 240–241, 243–245, 344n.; Soviet Union, views on, 186; threat to U.S. power, 234
Peronism: emerges as independent political phenomenon, 243; relationship to fascism and communism, 243–246
Peru (*see also* APRA), 63–64, 145; Amazon Development Corporation in, 194; election of 1931 in, 11; foreign capital in, effects of, 294–295; nationalists in, viii–ix; postwar economic problems of, 274, 294; strategic materials programs, effect on food production, 107, 109; visit of U.S. labor leaders to, 197–198; wartime dependence on Argentina, 153
Pfeiffer, Curt, 41
Pierson, Warren Lee (*see also* Export-Import Bank), 60, 70, 311n.–312n.; visit to Brazil, 313n.–314n.
Pinedo, Federico, 189, 240
Platt Amendment (*see also* Cuba), 13, 305n.
Poland, 209, 219
Potsdam Conference, 234
Prestes, Luis Carlos, 186
Price control: wartime, in Latin America, 107–108
Priorities, export, 98, 99, 211
Private enterprise: and American Century, 114; American, refusal to partic-
ipate in Volta Redonda, 44; and Axis threat to Latin American airlines, 56–57; at Bogotá Conference, U.S. position on, 284–285; and Bolivian revolution of 1943, 147–150, 152; Braden speech on, 262; foreign, and Latin American nationalism, 38–39, 191, 195, 302n.; and Inter-American Bank, 66–74; and labor, in Latin America, 195; and Mexican oil dispute, 55; at Mexico City Conference, U.S. position on, 175; New York businessmen's memo on, 48; OCIAA views on, 127–128; in postwar Latin America, and U.S. government, 20–21, 26, 30–31, 38, 40–42, 48, 55, 59, 67, 175, 262, 284–285, 288, 302n.

Quinine, 317n.
Quintanilla, Carlos, 51

Railroads: foreign ownership of, in Latin America, 200; U.S. investment in, 6; wartime rehabilitation of, in Latin America, 109, 323n.
Ramirez, General Pedro P., 156
Raw materials (*see also* individual commodities): production of, effect of war upon, 91
Rayon, 269–270
Reciprocal Trade Agreements Act (*see also* Tariffs; Trade): introduced and passed, 19–20; Republican opposition to, 19
Reconstruction Finance Corporation (RFC), 82, 105
Regionalism: and anti-communism, in Western hemisphere, 250; and Articles 51 and 52, United Nations Charter, 232; danger to Open World, 121–122; economic, threat to U.S. industrial expansion, 123; and hemisphere defense, 256–258; Latin American position on, at Mexico City Conference, 171–172, 215; and Monroe Doctrine, 222–223, 225; and Russian policy in Eastern Europe, 223–224, 232; at San Francisco Conference, 218, 222–232; Stassen proposal on, 231; Stimson, views on, 228–230; U.S. position on, at Mexico City Conference, 172; Vandenberg letter on, 225–227
Richberg, Donald, 53
Rio Conference of 1942, 51, 159
Rio Conference of 1947: Argentina and, 281–283; and Chapultepec, 282–283; postponed from October 1945, 253
Rios, Juan Antonio, 157
Rockefeller, Nelson (*see also* OCIAA), 48, 57, 85–86, 124, 129, 181; appointed Coordinator of Inter-American Affairs, 49; Argentine policies of, adopted by State Department, 251, 254; asks wartime maintenance of shipping space for inter-American commerce, 96; becomes Assistant Secretary of State, 166; defends wartime

Rockefeller, Nelson—*Cont.*
development programs in Latin America, 86; dismissal as Assistant Secretary, significance of, 244, 251; and IADC subcommissions meeting of 1944, 133–134; notes low price paid for Latin American rubber during war, 106; and Perón, 246, 251–252; personal background in Latin America, 48; position on regional autonomy, 224–225, 227–228; at San Francisco Conference, 217–218, 224–225, 227–228, 234, 248–250; State Department policy on Latin America, attempts to centralize control of, 246–247; supports Argentine admission to San Francisco Conference, 218, 250, 256; supports renewal of Reciprocal Trade Agreements Act, 177; views on hemispheric solidarity and East-West conflict, 234, 249; wartime trade fair, rejects, 110; works with Vandenberg at San Francisco Conference, 248–250

Rodó, José Enrique, 6

Roosevelt, Mrs. Eleanor: opposes Perón, 351n.

Roosevelt, Franklin D. (*see also* Good Neighbor Policy; New Deal), 155, 165, 169; and American Century, 115–116; announces "four sheriffs" plan, 119; Blair House speech, October 1944, 169; "bombshell message" of 1933, 19; Cuban revolution of 1933, policy toward, 13–18; death, vii, 212; describes Grau regime in Cuba, 18; Executive Orders on wartime priorities for Latin America, 96; Export-Import Bank, requests additional funds for, 42; first inaugural address, viii; Great Power competition, views on, 210, 211; Haitian rubber development program, approves cancellation of, 104; Inter-American Bank and, 73; inter-American wartime economic relations, views on, 47–48; and Latin American nationalism, ix, 287; message to IADC conference of 1944, 133; Mexican railroads, allocates funds for rehabilitation of, 109; Mexico City Conference, economic approach to, 176; monetary policies of, 19, 306n.; naval bases in Mexico, requests, 54; and origins of Good Neighbor Policy, 18–19; Poland, correspondence with Stalin on, 210; postwar Latin American development, interdepartmental memo to, 123–124, 129; and Reciprocal Trade Agreements program, 19–20; Russian votes in U.N., views on, 216–217, 220; sends Baruch to London, 210–211; suggests development of ten-cent stores in Latin America, 129; underdeveloped areas, views on, 210; Yalta commitment on regionalism, 170–172

Roosevelt, Theodore, 7; and Panama Canal, 6, 304n.; and Roosevelt Corollary, 5

Roosevelt Corollary, 5; and Clark Memorandum, 13

Rovensky, Joseph C., 65–66, 110; asks government backing for U.S. investors, 132–133; favors unguaranteed Export-Import Bank loans, 81; opposes discriminatory trade practices, 94–95; proposes three-way deal to finance British war effort, 139–140; supports Inter-American Bank, 69–70; supports U.S. aid to heavy industry in Brazil, Mexico, 130

Rubber: postwar U.S. investments in, 269–270; as strategic material, 317n.; synthetic, 105; wartime development of, in Latin America, 104–106

Rubber Reserve Corporation, U.S., 104–105

Russia (*see* Soviet Union)

Saavedra Lamas, Carlos, 242

Salisbury, Lord, 5

Samper Ortega, Dr. Daniel, 43

Sanchez, Luis Alberto, 111–112

Sandino, Augusto, 9

San Francisco Conference (*see also* United Nations), 165, 169–170, 212, 215; anti-Axis defense treaties and, 224; Argentina, Russian republics admitted to, 218–220, 248–249; Great Power diplomacy prior to, 210; inter-American solidarity and, 208, 214, 217; proceedings, 218–233, 237, 248–250; regionalism, U.S. policy on, 222–232, 250; Russia sends three delegations to, 216; Stimson's fears for, 209; Vandenberg's views on, 233, 250, 256, 277

Santos, Eduardo, 164–165, 351n.

São Paulo: British Chamber of Commerce in, 140–141; effects of wartime machinery shortages on factories in, 97; OCIAA office in, 188

Senate Foreign Relations Committee: and Inter-American Bank, 69–71

Shipping: wartime shortages of, 87, 96, 319n.

Silver: U.S. policy on, and Mexican oil dispute, 31–32

Sinclair Oil Company: and Mexican oil crisis, 53–54

Sloan, Alfred P., Jr., 39–40

Snyder, John W., 268, 293

Socialism: and Bolivian oil crisis, 24; U.S. fears of, in Latin America, 37; views of U.S. labor leaders on, 198

South American Journal (London), 139

Soviet Union: and American Century, 137–138, 210; industry, effects of war upon, 123, 210; and Latin American students, 9; Latin American views of, 185–187; Mexico, relations with, 181–182; and Mexico City Conference, 208; and Open World, 121–122; postwar reconstruction in, 210–211, 255–256; at Potsdam Conference, 255–256; and regional security, 229; relations with

Soviet Union—*Cont.*
U.S., effect on Latin America, 163–164; and San Francisco Conference, 214, 216–224, 227, 230–231, 232–234; Truman's views on, 212–214; U.S. fears of, in Latin America, 141–142, 181–182, 263, 280–281; and Western Hemisphere solidarity, 222
Stabilization, monetary, 19
Stalin, Joseph V., 255; Poland, correspondence with Roosevelt on, 210; Vandenberg's views of, 214, 233; views on Russian security and Open World, 117–118
Standard Oil Company (New Jersey): Bolivian holdings expropriated, 23–27; opposes compromise settlement in Mexican oil dispute, 53; policy on investment in Brazil, 294; receives compensation, 50–52; tax records of, and Mexican oil dispute, 55
Stassen, Harold, 218; proposal on regional self-defense at San Francisco Conference, 231
State, U.S. Department of, 179, 209; accepts Rockefeller's Argentine policies, 251, 254; and anti-Americanism in Argentina, 239; and Bolivian oil crisis, 24–27, 49–52; and Bolivian revolution of 1943, 148–152; and containment policy, 291–292; and instability in Latin America, 296; and interdepartmental report on postwar Latin American development, 124–129; in Mexican oil crisis, 29–32, 52–56; opposes Axis influences in Latin American airlines, 56–57; policy toward Argentine revolution of 1943, 154, 158, 161, 165–169; policy toward Latin American nationalism, 22, 46, 238–239; policy at San Francisco Conference, 227–228; policy toward Vargas, 1945, 234–235; position on Inter-American Bank, 60–61; relationship to U.S. investors, 21–23; supports Volta Redonda, 44; tariff policies of, 177–178; views on Russian activity in Western Hemisphere, 141
Statism: and IADC conference of 1944, 178–179; relationship to nationalism, 178; Truman policies toward, 262–265, 271
Steel (*see also* Volta Redonda): postwar U.S. expansion into, in Latin America, 269–270
Stettinius, Edward R., 157, 162–163, 165, 171, 247; attitude toward Volta Redonda, 310n.; becomes Secretary of State, 166; at Mexico City Conference, 172, 247; position on regionalism, 225–227; reaction to Vandenberg letter, 227; rejects diplomatic immunity for U.S. personnel in Latin America, 142; supports Argentine admission to San Francisco Conference, 218, 220, 237, 249
Stimson, Henry L., 247, 290; approves aviation supplies for Latin America,

260; Brett mission, views on, 181–182; comments on regionalism and world security, 228–230; criticizes State Department planning of San Francisco Conference, 209; Monroe Doctrine, views on, 228–229; and postwar defense planning, 180–181; Russian position in Eastern Europe, views on, 230; warns of communism in Central Europe, 209
Strategic and critical materials (*see also* individual commodities), 54, 173; enumerated, 317n.; preclusive buying of, 100, 321n.; U.S. dependence on Latin America for, 317n.; U.S. efforts to increase production of, in Latin America, 86–87, 100–101, 104–106
Subsidies, 125, 325n.; on cotton exports, U.S., 189, 205, 265; and "dumping," 189; on sugar, in Caribbean, 200
Sugar: in Caribbean, 200–201; effect on Cuban economy, 10, 16, 43, 95; postwar demand for, 273, 338n.
Surpluses, agricultural (*see also* individual commodities): and Mexico City Conference, 203–205; wartime marketing of, 48, 93–95

Taft, Senator Robert A., 269; opposes Volta Redonda, 68
Taft, William Howard, 7
Tariffs: and "dumping," 125, 189, 205, 325n.; Fordney-McCumber, 10; and Havana Trade Conference of 1947, 267–268; Hawley-Smoot, 10, 304n.; and IADC projects, 76–77; interdepartmental report, views on, 125; Latin American views on, 188–190, 204–205; Mexico City Conference, U.S. position at, 175; OCIAA views on, 128; and Open World, 177; and priorities, relationship to, 211; Reciprocal Trade Agreements program and, 19; on sugar, and Cuban revolution of 1933, 16–17
Taussig, Charles, 200
Taxation: and investment, 10
Taylor, Wayne, 206–207
Technical assistance: and American Century, 114; defense against Axis influence, 56; suggested by New York businessmen, 48
Thomas, Eugene, 42, 92–93, 307n.
Tin, 127; in Bolivia, wartime development of, 102–103, 142; and Bolivian revolution of 1943, 148; and "Catavi massacres," 103; smelter, Bolivian efforts to build, 336n.
Trade (*see also* Exports; Tariffs): role of, in U.S. postwar policy planning, 175,177; views on, of Eugene Thomas, 93
Transportation (*see also* Air transport; Automobiles; Railroads): postwar shortages, 275; wartime shortages, 108–110

Treasury, U.S. Department of: British loan, policy on, 267; Inter-American Bank, position on, 61; evaluates U.S. properties in Mexican oil crisis, 55
Trippe, Juan, 41
Trujillo, General Rafael, 145, 274
Truman, Harry S., 209, 222, 225, 233, 248, 254, 258; and American Century, Open World, 213, 234, 255; announces increase in Export-Import Bank lending, 284, 352n.; becomes President, 212; economic policy toward Latin America, 261–262, 264; meeting with Molotov, 212–213; military policy toward Latin America, 259–260, 264, 351n.–352n.; policy on Argentine admission to San Francisco Conference, 216, 218; policy toward Perón, 253–254; at Potsdam Conference, 255–256; proposes Inter-American Military Cooperation Act, 259; receives Baruch report, 213–214; and Roosevelt's Latin American policy, ix; views on dealing with Russians, Germans, 212; withdraws Inter-American Bank convention from Senate, 73
Tungsten: American preclusive buying of, in Bolivia, 100; and revolution in Bolivia, 148; strategic material, 317n.; wartime development of, 102–103, 142

Ubico, Jorge, 144–145
United Fruit Company, 292
United Nations (see also San Francisco Conference): Articles 51, 52, origins of, 232; and Dumbarton Oaks Conference, 166; Economic and Social Council, Vandenberg's fears of, 277; inter-American system, projected role in, 169–170; Latin American views of, 187, 215; and regionalism, 166, 222–223, 225–227, 231–232; and Security Council veto, 187, 226; and Western Hemisphere defense, 257–258
United Nations Relief and Rehabilitation Administration (UNRRA), 164–165, 271
United States, 40, 216, 248; and American Century, 115; Argentina, rivalry with, 153, 238; Bogotá Conference, economic policy at, 284–285, 290; and Bolivian revolution of 1943, 147–148, 152; and British investments in South America, 139–141; credits to Latin America, wartime, 99; Dumbarton Oaks Conference, position on regionalism at, 122; economic planning, postwar, 177; and European reconstruction, 164, 170, 288; government-business relationship, and Latin American development, 57–58, 80, 200–201, 288; investment capital, principal postwar supplier of, 125–126; and Latin American nationalism, 287–288; Mexico City Conference, position on regional security at, 172, 187; Perón, policy toward, 243–254, 288; at San

Francisco Conference, 165, 216–222
Uruguay, 6, 62–63; agricultural exports, 95; and Argentine revolution of 1943, 159; reaction to Bolivian revolution, 145
Utilities, public, 192

Vandenberg, Senator Arthur H.: communism in Latin America and elsewhere, views on, 253, 276–277; inter-American system and East-West conflict, views on, 215, 221–222, 224–225, 230–232, 256, 258; Monroe Doctrine, views on, 223, 225; opposes admission of Russian Republics to San Francisco Conference, 218, 220; opposes Braden policy on Argentina, 253; opposes Inter-American Bank, 68; opposes New Deal, 67–68, 313n.; regional autonomy, letter to Stettinius on, 225–227; and Rio Conference of 1947, 254, 282–283; Rockefeller, evaluation of, 249–250; Russia, views on, 232–234; Truman's attitude toward Russia, views on, 214; and Western Hemisphere military organization, 256–258, 288
Vandenberg, General Hoyt S., 260
Vargas, Getulio, 158; banking and investment policies of, 190–191, 313n.; and Brazilian communists, 186, 334n.; and Brazilian nationalism, viii, 190–191, 234–235; foreign capital, November 1938 speech on, 42; overthrown, 235; proclaims Constitution of 1937, 39; U.S. response to, 1945, 234–235
Venezuela, 63; communists in, 207–208; nationalists in, viii–ix; oil, U.S. investments in, 8, 56, 269
Villaroel, Major Gualberto, 151, 157; becomes Provisional President of Bolivia, 143; meeting with Avra Warren, 152
Viner, Jacob, 131, 177
Vinson, Fred M., 294
Volta Redonda: Export-Import Bank loans for, 44–45; and private American steel interests, 44, 310n.; U.S. industrial exports, anticipated effect on, 76, 315n.; wartime continuation of, 90–91, 287

Wallace, Henry A.: notes postwar world need for private capital, 119–120; notes role of IBRD, IMF in economic reconstruction, 120–121
War, U.S. Department of: and postwar military defense plans, 180–181; regional defense, position on, 222–223, 230–231
War Production Board, 91
Warren, Avra, 256; discussions with Argentine business leaders, 251; mission to Argentina, 1945, 250–251; mission to Bolivia, 1944, 151–152; recommends military aid to Perón, 250; views on Bolivian revolution, 148

Washington Post, 220, 222; role in Rockefeller dismissal, 244

Welles, Sumner, 47, 86, 135; as Ambassador to Cuba, 13–17; and Argentine revolution of 1943, 154; and Bolivian oil dispute, 26; Hull, criticisms of, 161, 330n.–331n.; and Inter-American Bank, 65, 69; leaves State Department, 161; at Panama Conference, 60–61; reaction to Grau San Martín government in Cuba, 14–17; views on Mexican oil expropriations, 31–32, 52

Wheat, 127, 153

White, Harry Dexter (*see also* White Plan): anti-Axis economic policies of, 46–47; Argentine economy, evaluation of, 239–240; death, 348n.; defends tariffs for Latin American industries, 76, 125; postwar Latin American import requirements, evaluation of, 272; radio broadcast on British loan, 270–271; suggests $2.5 billion development loan to Mexico, 272–273; views on IBRD and private investment, 120

White Plan (*see also* IBRD; IMF), 137; as economic analog of Open World proposal, 121; and Inter-American Bank, 176; relationship to American Century, New Deal, 119

Wilson, Woodrow: and American Century, 115; and Mexican Revolution, 6–8

Wool: as critical material, 317n.

World Bank (*see* International Bank for Reconstruction and Development)

World War, First, 8, 115

World War, Second, 85; effect on inter-American economic relations, 42, 87–88, 91, 110–112; and hemispheric solidarity, vii; and Mexican oil crisis, 54

Yalta Conference: Polish issue and, 213, 219; and Russian representation in United Nations, 216; U.S. position on regionalism at, 170–172

Zinc, 90, 127

A NOTE ON THE AUTHOR

David Green was born in New York City in 1942. After graduating from Cornell University with honors in history, he studied at Stanford University on a Woodrow Wilson fellowship and later received a Herbert H. Lehman fellowship at Cornell, where he was awarded a Ph.D. Mr. Green's research for this book included investigations in several Latin American countries. He is now Assistant Professor of History at the University of Saskatchewan.